MANAGING
for
PRODUCTIVITY
in
NURSING

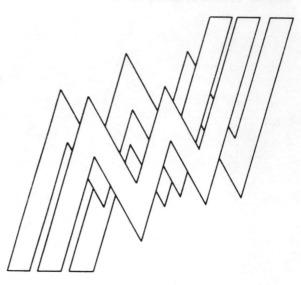

MANAGING
for
PRODUCTIVITY
in
NURSING

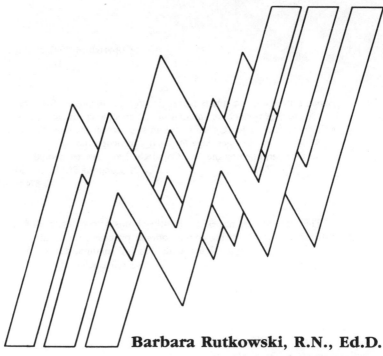

Barbara Rutkowski, R.N., Ed.D.
Nurse Consultation Services
Evansville, Indiana

AN ASPEN PUBLICATION®
Aspen Publishers, Inc.
Rockville, Maryland
Royal Tunbridge Wells
1987

Library of Congress Cataloging-in-Publication Data

Rutkowsi, Barbara Lang, 1945-
Managing for productivity in nursing.

"An Aspen publication."
Includes bibliographies and index.
1. Nursing services—Administration—Cost effectiveness.
I. Title. [DNLM: 1. Nursing Service, Hospital—economics.
2. Nursing Service, Hospital—organization & administra-
tion. WY 30 R977m]
RT89.R88   1987   362.1'73'0681   86-32224
ISBN: 0-87189-618-4

Editorial Services: Jane Coyle

Library of Congress Catalog Card Number: 86-32224
ISBN: 9-87189-618-4

Printed in the United States of America

1 2 3 4 5

In Loving Memory of

My Dad

Lieut. Col. Donald R. Lang

Table of Contents

Contributors

E. Marie Nelson, RN, BSN, CNA
Director of Nursing
St. Luke Hospital
Ft. Thomas, Kentucky

Joyce Rhoades, RN, MPA
Vice President
Welborn Baptist Hospital
Evansville, Indiana

Pacquine R. Fairless, RN, MSN
Director of Nursing
Welborn Baptist Hospital
Evansville, Indiana

Joyce M. Dungan, RN, EdD
Professor of Nursing
School of Nursing and Health Sciences
Evansville, Indiana

Preface

Productivity is the study of providing a defined level of nursing care in the most efficient, cost-effective manner. Simply expressed, productivity equals output divided by input $(P = O/I)$. If nursing had totally quantifiable products, this definition could be applied in the narrowest sense; however, it is not easily categorized, so this definition needs to be expanded. In this book, productivity in nursing is the process of dividing output by input and measuring the result against standards of effectiveness and efficiency in an open system of constant flux. True productivity is achieved when managers and staff integrate the productive process into all work efforts as an automatic necessity.

To be applicable to contemporary hospital nursing, the definition needs to go beyond obvious quantification through patient classification systems, staffing systems, and costing systems for nursing care.[1] The contemporary approach to improving productivity also must be integrated completely with every management function. Otherwise, the result is limited figures on paper that represent neither wise and calculated utilization of all resources nor the way services actually are delivered. Moreover, the programs and policies in place in the division actually may undo the economy gained by confining productivity measurement to narrow parameters.

OVERVIEW

This book is designed to allow nurse managers to view every part of their jobs in relation to how they impact on productivity. To be successful in this new era, this nontraditional approach of incorporating productivity into all nursing activities is a mandate. This necessarily includes where nursing is today, where it is trying to go, and how to escape expensive and avoidable problems that can have a negative effect on the best plans for being cost effective and productive in the rest of the operation.

Part I, Critical Aspects of Productivity, includes the typical topics that nurse managers look for in a book on productivity. While nursing has come a long way in viewing its services as a business, in integrating budgetary concepts even into the job of the front-line manager, in developing computerized staffing systems, and in trying to place a monetary value on its services, there still is a long way to go.

Important work has begun in putting an average price on each acuity level. However, such pricing is superficial, since there are not enough data on all the items and the requisite nursing labor that produces the figures. For example, the category termed "indirect costs" can include a wide range of sins under the cover of administrative expenses. Part I summarizes the existing situation in these areas. Many hospitals will put a great deal of continuing effort into developing a reliable patient classification system with an eye on pricing nursing care.

Part II, Results-Oriented Management, examines productivity in relation to the job of each level of manager. These chapters discuss issues that make a difference in effective and efficient managerial and staff performance as well as problems that must be confronted if productivity is to continue to improve.

For example, idea development and wise use of the professional staff members in relation to efficiency and effectiveness is dependent on how contemporary managers act to eliminate expensive red tape and streamline methods for enhancing work efforts by all nursing employees. Managerial effectiveness in developing and supporting staff members for their changing, more autonomous roles in creating, refining, and delivering services can affect directly the success or disaster of building a productive, satisfied nursing corps. Where these functions are separate intellectually from productivity planning and implementation, the managerial notion of how the division operates is far different from what staff nurses and consumers perceive.

This section also analyzes staff members' motives, since solving productivity problems involves understanding the context in which they operate. Where the nurses' psychological and physical framework is ignored, productivity suffers because of poor morale, absenteeism, expensive lawsuits, and Band-Aid management that rarely resolves the underlying problems. Once the needs and concerns of staff members are addressed, creativity can be encouraged. Such creative approaches constitute the primary area to explore when faced with the challenge of providing more quality care to sicker patients without increasing staff hours and supportive services.

Part III, Setting Standards of Performance, ties quantitative and qualitative standards into risk management and quality assurance efforts. To become more productive, nurse managers must work collaboratively with staff members to establish definite standards that are compatible with the philosophy of the division in relation to the desired quality of care within personnel constraints and that are measured regularly for compliance.

The risk management program and quality assurance efforts work together to guarantee that services are delivered in a manner that is safe, consistent, and effective both for providers and consumers. Where monitoring reveals problems in the environment or in the way services are provided, the quality of the work effort is compromised. Productivity is not successful where efficiency is achieved at the cost of effectiveness and safety in service delivery.

Part IV, Human Resources Management, is a major factor in achieving a high level of productivity, since nursing is a people-intensive industry. Resources and efforts directed toward fostering staff enthusiasm, team spirit, and initiative produce the most dramatic results in improving the quality of care and worker output within established budgetary constraints. Where enlightened techniques of human resources management are used, staff members thrive even when workloads are heavy.

Developing a positive, constructive attitude between managers and staff members is probably the single most important item in achieving a successful, productive division. In hospitals having difficulties in this area, the probability of poor work products, negative public relations, costly staff turnover, union problems, and expensive legal actions are increased greatly. All of these negative outcomes steal dollars away from positive efforts in productivity and the capital expenditures required to continue streamlining the operation.

This section demonstrates how work expectations are established as performance priorities are integrated throughout the employment cycle. An update on the legal aspects of employment law provides a national perspective on expensive, time-consuming problems that occur when hospitals neglect this important management area. Resources expended on remedial disciplinary activities are not available for hospital efforts to improve excellence.

Part V, Supportive Strategies, reports on how the staff development department and the marketing efforts in hospitals can be utilized to promote programs that enhance productivity.

When nurse managers have finished reading this text, they should have a more realistic, broad-based working definition of productivity that lends itself to a total, integrated approach to success.

NOTE

1. Leah Curtin, and Carolina Zurlage, *DRGs: The Reorganization of Health* (Chicago: S-N Publications, Inc., 1984).

Part I

Critical Aspects of Productivity

Chapter 1

Controlling the Business

To achieve improved productivity, managers must assess and control the direction in which the business is going. The approach needs to be systematic, logical, and consistent within the total system. Control of today is the first step and one that consumes most of those in the frenzied activity termed ''crisis management.'' Such crash programs are only temporary and usually do not result in lasting results. To meet productivity target goals, managers must allocate resources to opportunities, not problems. That means moving beyond the short-term goals of the immediate situation to view the big picture.

Being efficient is not enough. Managers must be effective in spotting opportunity and knowing what to do about it. They can achieve results when they are good at identifying a service for which people are willing to pay, then finding a cost-effective way of providing it. However, any business leadership position is transitory, at best. Once a service is publicized, others imitate it until it becomes an established practice.

For example, in birthing centers, fathers get a beeper to notify them when labor begins, and new parents get an ''It's a Boy!'' or ''It's a Girl!'' sign for the front yard after delivery. However, the success of these methods has caused many centers to use them, eliminating any uniqueness or market edge. Thus, such come-ons need to be updated continually to attract members of the public to the hospital, where they can then experience the effectiveness and thoroughness of the nursing care.[1]

Meeting new goals in cost containment and quality care also requires managers to adjust attitudes and expectations about how to do the job so that their efforts are in line with the realities. In the nursing revolution of the 1980s, managers should ask themselves where they can best spend their time to make themselves effective while helping make those efforts profitable. The question is not one of stretching efforts to the nth degree but of concentrating on what needs to be done.[2]

For example, one pediatric unit continued to offer daytime programs for children who would be admitted later for elective surgery. These programs were poorly attended and took efforts away from other parent education programs. To increase effectiveness, this program was replaced with a brief "touch and share" orientation on nights when a number of children were being prepared for next-day surgery.

IMPROVING PRODUCTIVITY

To begin to improve productivity, managers should concentrate on the goals of their units, division, and hospital, translating them into action by allocating resources to the productivity program. For example, absenteeism is a big drain on productive efforts. Instead of concentrating on correcting absenteeism after the fact, that time should be spent establishing a clear policy of expectations and outcomes for frequent abusers. Nurse administrators then should establish rewards, incentives, and reminders and build a positive climate so that staff members will look foward to coming to work.

Managers next should assess current services and projections for future ones. They must decide on what ones they will provide, their quality values, the market to be reached, and the market share that will be satisfactory. They should narrow their focus by looking back to their institutional mission, then asking: What should this department be in the future? How will it keep good programs going, discard dated ones, innovate services, make health care providers and consumers aware of what is offered, and develop the skills and techniques for implementing the quality programs that will achieve the desired results?

Goal achievement is contingent upon the setting of realistic objectives for these services, including adequate staff to implement them. In writing these objectives, nurse managers must include such factors as:

- What they must provide to give safe, effective care.
- What must be done to remain competitive with local services.
- What programs are needed to offset unprofitable but necessary services that must be continued.
- What changes in service delivery and equipment are needed to achieve the standard of care desired.
- What guidance, supplies, and education staff members require to update performance and improve productivity.
- What current methods/services require change to increase profitability, effectiveness, and consumer appeal.

These objectives then must be translated into dollars through the budgeting process, since allocation of resources will reflect priorities. In the implementation phase, objectives and allocated resources become a concrete work program of specific goals, individual assignments with accountability, and deadlines.[3]

For example, many hospitals mandate detailed discharge instructions refined to the special needs of each patient within a diagnostic group. However, the reality is that the discharge can be chaotic when there is inadequate time to explain everything and to document instructions. Some hospitals are solving this problem by asking each staff nurse to assume responsibility for writing a comprehensive plan for a major diagnosis seen on a unit. These master plans have space for individualizing discharge planning and a time frame that spans the entire length of stay. Such a format helps nurses be sure they do not omit necessary items and also standardizes the essentials given to all patients.

Documentation tends to be of the checklist and simple completion variety so that instructions can be made part of the permanent record and can be provided in writing to the patient and family. To develop this document, paid time and support from the nurse manager, librarian, and education department must be provided. Input from other nurses refines the form. When complete, this document saves valuable time for everyone while allowing nurses input into the process. Documenting care in this standardized manner also provides protection from legal liability while retaining quality and efficiency in complying with discharge standards.[4]

INTERFACING WITH STRATEGIC PLANNING

Managers have no choice but to attempt to predict the future, but many still feel that making five-year budget projections is among their hardest tasks. A frequent complaint is that health care is progressing so rapidly that what managers project now for the next five years is being implemented in as little as one year. Still, it is essential that nurse administrators commit even greater effort to this strategic planning process so they can be prepared for new challenges and trends in productivity. When plans remain vague and unspecific, programs fall short of goals since there is no definite way to determine whether or not they have been successful. Benchmarks can be reached when each development phase includes specific measurement criteria.

Systematic strategic planning is an entrepreneurial process of making risk-laden decisions about the future. To reduce adverse outcomes, this process must be implemented only after thorough research and in an organized manner in which results continuously are weighed against objectives, resource utilization, and changes in technology and the marketplace.[5]

Strategic planning is hard work because success in the future is dependent on the managers' ability to begin today in taking steps toward that future. Leaving future projects as an undefined whole is the fastest way to doom them. Breaking large projects into numerous ministeps is the best way to whittle away at a job.

Unfortunately, no crystal ball or bag of tricks is available to help in the difficult task of blending knowledge, analytic abilities, and creativity in strategic decision making. However, the nursing process can be utilized as a framework in problem analysis and in reaching solutions. The interesting point to note, though, is that effective plans need constant evaluation and modification in line with progress and changes.

Strategic planning should be thought of not in terms of what will be done in five years but of the implications of the effect present decisions and actions will have on the future. Current patterns then can be adjusted to point toward the desired destination.

For example, one hospital envisions broad diversification, profitability, and excellence in health care delivery in its five-year projection. However, today it is faced with employee morale problems and widespread inefficiency that it is ignoring. Public opinion as to its services falls far short of its visions. Yet it has done little to correct its people problems. As a matter of fact, its many management people are conspicuous by their absence from their jobs, constantly attending meetings.

Of course, there is a certain amount of risk in futuristic planning—but there also is a risk in failing to plan and instead flowing with whatever way the current is moving. For example, an area hospital provides specialty-based home health care. Nurses based on the orthopedic unit visit a patient in that specialty should home visitation be required. This system allows nurses to maintain their expertise and provide continuity of care. If administrators in other hospitals watch this system to assess whether their institutions should provide a similar program, that is prudent. However, if they merely observe the program passively without formulating some type of plan for their facilities, they may risk losing a significant market share in the future.

To remain competitive, nurse administrators must continually assess needs and responses of the patient population and initiate programs designed to keep competitive, effective, and efficient.[6]

COST-BENEFIT ANALYSIS

Managers begin a cost-benefit analysis by assessing their services, policies, and business directions. If they cannot identify their services, they certainly will not be able to list their priorities or know whether their resource expenditures are justified. Moreover, it will be difficult to assess the adequacy of what they are doing.

For example, in an admission assessment, do managers:

- Get all the facts needed and utilize the information already available?
- Include unneeded questions on the forms?

- Ascertain whether there is a better way to conduct this assessment to get more information in a shorter time?

- Use a process standardized enough so they can determine whether all patients have the opportunity to give at least the essential information required for the division to provide them with the hospital's defined minimum level of care, or more?

- Determine the cost-benefits of performing the admission the current way, versus the way other hospitals conduct theirs?

- Orient all nurses in the most productive way to use the forms and their time during this process?

This process must be continued until all of the nursing services have undergone careful scrutiny.

In short, productivity, marketing, service delivery, and finance must be married. If the nursing department has a valued service, it must be analyzed to determine whether or not resource allocations are adequate to deliver it in congruence with stated standards and philosophy. Such analyses also can help indicate when efforts and monies expended are disproportionate to the result.

For example, one hospital had a wellness center that persisted in offering individual programs in child rearing even when the turnout was poor and the tuition did not cover costs. In analyzing the problem, the hospital found that the costs did not even justify the secondary goal of promoting good will, because the public was critical of the poor attendance and lack of enthusiasm. Goals of the wellness effort needed to be revamped entirely to make the program achieve a better public image and an adequate financial return.

In its assessment, the hospital found that the wellness programs were aimed at the wrong target group, were not at convenient times, were poorly publicized, and were not easily located. By responding to these findings, the facility saved money and began providing a program whose outcome justified the input.

Along these same lines, productivity studies often reveal that a small number of a hospital's services is responsible for generating the bulk of its revenues. Thus, it is important to discard programs that cannot be conducted in a competitive manner. Merely revamping inadequate programs can mean throwing good money after bad. Hospitals find it difficult to eliminate programs since they have been accustomed to keeping all the old ones and merely adding on any new ones. Designing and marketing a good new program is no more expensive than trying to keep an outworn one working. Moreover, it is not always profitable to attempt to increase numbers of users beyond a certain point.

For example, the advent of diagnosis related groups (DRGs) taught many hospitals some surprising facts, such as that operating at full capacity in a large facility is not always as profitable as having a lower census. After a certain point, the costs of coordinating efforts with intermediaries can offset the income from greater numbers of patients. Some smaller hospitals with simpler bureaucracies can be much more effective and efficient.

Nurse managers should ask themselves:

- What is the optimal census in the unit?
- How does volume affect price per unit in all of the services offered?
- What does the number of empty beds per day cost in lost business at various census levels?

Hospitals have tightened their cost accounting procedures since Congress mandated cost containment. The truth, however, is that it is not possible, so far, to account for every penny spent because the costs of even the most common procedures are not known precisely.

For example, in one hospital, unit 5 West has 50 postoperative patients a year who have had their gallbladders removed. All of these had drains and absorbent dressings on their abdomens. Questions arise:

- What dressing is most cost effective and absorbent?
- Do all nurses use the same materials in performing the dressing change?
- Do all staff members understand the cost differences in using other than the dressing materials or frequency of dressing changes that the facility has tested and approved?

While this seems to be a minor example, the concept can be extended to all of the procedures done on the unit. Chances are the inconsistencies in practice would account for wide variances in the actual cost of patient care services.

Naturally, there are certain overhead costs in operating the unit, regardless of volume. One hospital that was not able to account for all nursing costs or to show indirect administrative expenditures simply allocated monies arbitrarily. In such a case, the problem is that even though administrators may know that costs are out of line, they find it difficult to identify the source of excessive spending when using an arbitrarily allocated costing system.

When a nursing unit had inpatients as the only product line, it could divide all costs by patient days. While this produced the cost per patient day, it was a gross estimation. Waste and excess expenditures for specified categories were not shown. It also meant that patients who performed total self-care had to pay the same for nursing services as those who required six linen changes and total assistance during the day.

Cost Accounting Era

In gearing up for this new cost accounting era, nurse administrators need to put a specific value on each transaction or activity. For example, all activity should be allocated to a specific goal. At a meeting, the time spent on each topic should be counted as a part of the budget for that activity. Such an allocation method can greatly increase awareness of time spent and might work to reduce the number and length of meetings.

Thus, it may be desirable to create forms on which the time spent by each person and the project number are entered in an upper corner. It then is possible to determine how much effort is required to get and service one customer, and how many meetings are required to get one program running smoothly.

In nursing, it may be advisable to develop a checklist of services provided, with a time figure for each to aid in costing out on a unit basis. Then managers can work to trim time off a procedure to optimize efficiency and effectiveness in relation to the standards established. Determining which transactions are appropriate for analysis is a big step in understanding nursing and its economics.

The challenge is greater for nursing than for many businesses since its practitioners work on a product, yet cannot control admission, medical orders, or discharges. Comparisons of costs in a profit center, therefore, can vary widely because of the differing measurement techniques and values assigned to time with the patient and desired outcomes. For too long, nursing has justified these differences as "quality" and continues in old habits in which it might be doing a marginal job for a very high cost.

Valuing Transactions

This era of cost containment is the perfect time to start all over again from the ground up. Nurse managers must evaluate all of their services in relation to the consumers' needs, the safety and adequacy of the procedure, and the most effective way to accomplish it. Then it must be priced. Consumers and third party payers will pay for quality, especially if nursing markets the elements offered in its various programs. Success is evident when the consumer has a choice of services yet continues to select one's own. Leadership in the marketplace is an economic term, validated by consumer use.

Staying competitive and relevant means constantly working on product/services definition, pricing, results, reliability, convenience, appearance, style, design, and maintenance. Those who design products as if they were static entities are missing the reality of human nature—that is, products appear, become popular, run their course, decline, and are replaced by others. If being objective on this services assessment seems difficult, it may be because politics also is interwoven in the process. Some managers have credited themselves with single-handedly building a program, and they do not want it altered in any way, even after time has eroded its effectiveness.

In valuing transactions, nurse administrators should cost out each product in a cost/profit center by adding up raw materials, labor, and all costs of getting it to the patient. They then can begin to determine which programs are cost effective. Each program and its costs are compared with the institutional mission, so that programs may be kept for reasons of productivity, qualitative decisions, or some combination of both.

When a product is not what nurse managers desire, they must barter in the bureaucracy to acquire the resources or power needed to change the situation. For example, they may be fortunate to have a clinical specialist on the unit and hope to utilize this expert in developing patient teaching programs and aids. However, this person is hostile and ineffective but happens to be the favorite cousin of the administrator. This situation must be changed before managers can move forward. In this case, money spent on an expensive expert is not worth the expenditure.

Finally, nurse administrators should consider how much they deviate from their budgets because of their crisis management orientation. For example, they may budget for new teaching aids but never get them. Instead, the money goes for continual repairs on equipment that has never been maintained properly. Managers should ask themselves: Is the budget working to (1) improve services or conceal problems, (2) correct incidents or prevent them, (3) solve staffing problems or chase them, (4) serve consumers better or justify programs that are not working? Using the answers as a basis, administrators can strive to put their resources to work more profitably for them.[7]

SUMMARY

Nurse managers have been frustrated in recent years over strategic and structural shifts as the impact of the health care revolution has made nursing adjust to a series of rapid changes. It is time to make sense of the mandate for improved productivity within the context of everything nurse managers do. A proactive, pragmatic, business-oriented approach, sensitive to human need, is necessary to achieve efficiency, effectiveness, and satisfaction in work efforts. Making the most of the resources available in nursing requires a thorough understanding of all factors involved in becoming more productive.[8]

NOTES

1. Thomas Peters, and Robert H. Waterman, *In Search of Excellence* (New York: Warner Books, Inc., 1982).

2. Val Olsen, *White Collar Waste* (Englewood Cliffs, N.J.: Prentice-Hall, Inc., 1983).

3. Barbara Lang Rutkowski, "DRGs: Now All Eyes Are on You," *Nursinglife* 15, no. 10 (March/April 1985): 30–32.

4. _____, "How DRGs Are Changing Your Charting," *Nursing* (October 1985): 49–51.

5. Peter F. Drucker, *Management: Tasks, Responsibilities, Practices* (New York: Harper & Row, Publishers, Inc., 1974).

6. Aaron Levenstein, "The Future of Nursing," *Nursing Management* (June 1985): 44–45.

7. Peter F. Drucker, *Managing in Turbulent Times* (New York: Harper & Row, Publishers, Inc., 1980).

8. Leah Curtin, "Editorial Opinion: A Nurse's Conscience," *Nursing Management* 14, no. 2 (February 1983): 7–8.

ACTION CHECKLIST

Nurse executives/managers should:

1. Think about expanding the definition of productivity to everything they do and every service that is provided in their department. Include managerial efforts as well as staff performance in this expanded definition.
2. Evaluate services/programs in the division or department, focusing on essential services it will provide, desirable services, and others that should be phased out. Place a value on each program and service delivered. Decide what the market is and what market share will constitute a satisfactory goal. Ask:

   - What should this division/department be like in the future?
   - How will good programs be kept going, dated ones discarded, and new services developed?
   - How can all of the potential publics be made aware of the programs and staff supportive of the efforts?
   - What skills, techniques, and educational programs are needed to be sure that the desired level of quality is achieved in all programs and services?

3. Write objectives for each service or program including:

   - what must be provided to give safe, effective care
   - what must be done to make the department's efforts competitive
   - what programs/services are needed to offset necessary but unprofitable operations
   - what changes in policies, equipment, staffing, and methods are required to achieve goals
   - what efforts are needed to improve performance and reduce costs
   - what current methods/services require a change to improve staff satisfaction, consumer appeal, profitability, and effectiveness.

4. Assign a dollar value to all service and programs, then view them in light of the overall mission.
5. Contrast the existing approach to all programs and services with alternative methods in a cost-benefit analysis to better justify management decisions. Utilize findings in light of nonquantitative factors to arrive at a course of action.
6. Review their own total job and that of their staff to see whether standards for quality and productivity are built into all work efforts.
7. Place qualitative and quantitative value on everything they do and every service/ program that their division or department offers as a way of deleting nonproductive efforts and setting priorities.
8. Begin to work on costing all basic components of work effort and product consumption to determine the true costs of programs and services.
9. Establish a goal of cutting waste, documenting savings, and applying found money to capital expenditures to ease the workload, improve the quality of care, and improve the satisfaction of the nursing staff.
10. View productivity efforts in a positive light; being negative does not help or remove the necessity for this accountability process. Carry out a systematic analysis one step at a time, setting deadlines for each step on a calendar to keep the process rolling. Rome was not built in a day!

Chapter 2

Budgetary Concepts

E. Marie Nelson

In an era of cost constraints, nurse managers have been compelled to function in a cost-effective manner, quantifying costs, improving productivity, and working toward operating units or centers at a profit. They thus must become comfortable with budgetary concepts. One familiar tool for getting a handle on a total program or group of services is the nursing process.

NURSING PROCESS APPLIED

The nursing process is the application of scientific problem solving to nursing care. This same process of data collection, assessment, diagnosis, planning, implementing, and evaluating can be applied to the management of cost-effective delivery of nursing services. Productivity improvement, like the nursing process, is a continuous cycle involving the same steps.

In an environment dominated by rapid change and competition among health care providers, nursing administrators must assume a leading role in the management and provision of quality health care with limited resources. This offers a great opportunity for nursing to assess what it does and justify what is important. It also is time for nurse managers to hone their business skills.

In this process, they analyze the environment, make strategic plans that are tied to the budget, implement actions to reach established goals, and evaluate the results. Continuous data collection and analysis is an important component of allocating resources where they are needed most in this volatile, changing scene.

The emphasis on productivity and cost accountability is not a passing fancy; it is a permanent change in the system of delivering nursing services. Pressures from government, private enterprise, and the health insurance industry demand a reduction in expenses without a decrease in quality.

For example, while the Utilization and Quality Control Peer Review Organization (PRO) in a state assesses compliance with the mandates of the Tax Equity and

Fiscal Responsibility Act (TEFRA) (P.L. 97–248), it also has other functions that are vital to hospitals' survival. It examines total care and costs at all hospitals to find those that do the best job in being productive, cost-effective, and quality conscious in their services. This information then becomes the basis for referring Medicaid patients to those preferred institutions. Corporations and health care insurers are using PRO research to help make decisions about where to send employees and what hospitals to include among their preferred provider organizations (PPOs). The PRO's indirect focus is evaluation of nursing, since that is a major reason people go to hospitals. The burden of providing excellent services at reasonable costs thus falls largely on the nursing division.

The advent of diagnosis related groups (DRGs) and the prospective payment system (PPS) is just the beginning of the cost-control measures that will be applied to the hospital industry. Stricter constraints can be expected. The federal government already has tightened the DRG program, and both insurance companies and health maintenance organizations are asking consumers to get special checkups and second opinions before submitting to care, particularly surgery. Outpatient services, which are less costly, are booming as wings of inpatient beds close or are utilized for other programs. Few persons can afford to pay directly for the costs of care in either an acute or long-term facility.

THE NURSING BUDGET

Since the budget of the nursing department involves up to two-thirds of the institution's budget, nurse managers are the key to controlling resource utilization while directing quality-of-service efforts. In the environment of the mid to late 1980s, therefore, they must be competent to make decisions based on quantifiable cost and quality-of-care data.

Nursing administrators must have the ability to analyze data and formulate short- and long-range plans for their department based on economic and clinical information. The same concern for cost containment must reach down to first-level managers because it is at that level that the action occurs. Good insight into costs versus benefits is necessary since it is the nurses who will know the condition of the patients and can collaborate with physicians in the use of resources to keep expenses at a reasonable level. Cost effectiveness must be considered in planning nursing care and in effective utilization of personnel to deliver and support direct services.

Nurse managers need not be accountants, but they must have financial management skills. Nurses must become familiar with accounting terminology and have a basic understanding of the financial workings of a hospital.

HISTORICAL PERSPECTIVE

The shift from a cost-based method to a PPS has moved the spotlight onto productivity issues in hospitals. Before the turn of the century, most hospitals charged patients a flat daily rate that covered all services, which were very limited. As care expanded, a system of special service charges was initiated. By 1920, the special service charge could equal or surpass the regular daily charge. Adverse public reaction caused the hospital industry to consider spreading costs among patients by using an all-inclusive rate system. In some hospitals the only variation in rate was length of stay and room accommodations. In that period, Ohio introduced a Workers' Compensation all-inclusive rate based on audited costs. This system of audited costs became a part of the foundation of the hospital financial structure.

Also in the early 1920s, Pennsylvania implemented a variation of the Ohio mechanism and paid hospitals based on estimated daily cost. In 1930 the federal government first became involved through the Children's Bureau, but paid only for direct patient care. Thus reimbursable costs became the other portion of the system.[1]

From that time on, except for the period when the Blue Cross system was forming, a flat rate system was used. Over the years a number of retrospective, prospective, incentive, and disincentive systems have been used to pay hospitals. Increased uniformity in cost accounting systems and charges among hospitals evolved. Audited reimbursable cost has been central to the development of the pricing system.

The most significant factor affecting hospital accounting has been the third party reimbursement system. Billings used to be on a retrospective basis, using historical costs, with a few on a negotiated rate basis. The costing system was the primary vehicle for pricing services, involving full costing with allocated general costs. To meet the DRG and PPS reimbursement requirements, the hospital industry developed accounting practices that affected the way financial records are kept and reports are presented. The Chart of Accounts published by the American Hospital Association provides a comprehensive organizational framework with a corresponding coding and cost assignment system.

BASIC ACCOUNTING TERMINOLOGY

If nurse managers are to be involved in financial planning and cost control, they need to be familiar with the following terms:

Entity: The hospital is viewed as an entity. Accounts are kept and reflect the events that affect the business. An assumption is made that the entity has an almost indefinite life.

Transaction: All transactions must be included in the accounting record.

Cost Valuation: The cost or price paid for an item is entered in the permanent accounting record.

Double Entry: This system reflects the two aspects of each transaction—the change in asset forms and in the source of financing, and the recording of assets and liabilities.

Accrual: This system of accounting requires revenues and losses to be recorded in the accounts when realized and expenses to be recorded in the period in which they affect operations.

Matching: This involves bringing together related income and expenses in the same accounting period. These rules may be modified in practice by materiality, consistency, conservatism, and industry practices.

Materiality: This involves not recording transactions that are insignificant and not relative to the total operation.

Consistency: Reports must be prepared on a consistent basis for comparison purposes.

Conservatism: This policy provides that an asset should be recorded in a manner least likely to overstate its value.

Industry Practice: The hospital industry has unique accounting practices that affect the way accounting records are kept and reports are presented.[2] For example, hospitals include nursing in the room rate and do not view it as revenue producing.

REVENUE CENTERS AND COST STRUCTURES

Hospital accounting systems over the years were based on identification of revenue centers—the organizational units producing the revenue. The systems determined how the cost centers would be established. The selection of appropriate revenue centers was the basis for pricing structures. Cost centers were set up for any activity in the hospital that generated a significant amount of costs. They existed for budgetary purposes, providing a logical method for planning and controlling expenditures. They also could be established to develop prices, providing for allocation of costs to revenue-producing centers.

Past methods of cost allocation may have created statistical information that is not helpful under the prospective payment system. When the costing system was the primary vehicle for pricing and reimbursement in hospitals, the accumulation and analysis of cost information was important; however, under cost-based reimbursement there was little or no incentive to develop cost management systems.

Traditionally, hospitals charged patients directly for many services, room, laboratory, drugs, physical therapy, etc. However, many other costs, such as plant operations, laundry, housekeeping, nursing service, etc., were not charged directly to patients. These services were identified as cost centers and their cost was allocated out to revenue-producing centers and charged to patients as part of their room rate or cost of procedure.

Factors used for allocating cost center totals to revenue-producing centers included:

Cost	Base
Plant operations	Square footage
Employee benefits	Salaries and wages
Housekeeping	Square footage
Laundry	Pounds per patient

Nursing departments usually include numerous cost centers based on their services and locations. Nursing care was included in the room rates of inpatient units and allocated on the basis of average hours of care/patient day for the type of service offered. In other types of nursing areas, the cost could be part of procedure costs or part of the per-visit fee. These charges were applied to nursing's cost centers, which thus were considered revenue producing. The reported revenue for the center reflected charges to its specific services rather than actual money received. Bad debts frequently were entered only in the hospital statement of revenue and expenses rather than in individual cost center reports.

Typical hospitals used this system of accounting for years. Under the old system of cost reimbursement, it worked to the institution's advantage, but in today's environment, with its unpredictable changes and ever-increasing outside regulations, planning, budgeting, and financial reporting systems are needed for the measurement and control of costs. Budgeting and financial reporting must respond to variations in workload and activity. Responsibility and authority for cost control should be at the lowest level possible.

Responsibility Accounting

Many hospitals have been using responsibility accounting systems. These are based on the assignment of responsibility within the hospital and link its accounting system to its organizational structure. In the process of identifying the responsibility center, its activities also are identified. Those with responsibilities for costs alone are identified as cost centers; those with responsibilities for both costs and revenue are called profit centers. A profit center usually has a fairly close relationship between cost and revenues. This enables management to emphasize its contribution (or lack thereof) to profits.

The concept of responsibility centers focuses on delegating to the lowest level possible the responsibility for specific goals, motivating managerial performance toward accomplishing goals, and measuring progress toward goal achievement. The accounting system should be integrated into the total management system and into any financial planning, productivity measurement, and reporting systems in use.

Responsibility accounting relates primarily to control. Revenues and costs must be classified and reported according to responsibility. Reported revenues and costs should be compared with budgets. Nursing managers must be able to focus on the elements necessary for the success of their departments. There are additional goals and related performance measures that cannot be tracked through the financial systems, such as empathy for terminal patients. Goals such as this are not quantifiable and tend to be less effectively monitored because their successes and failures are not measured easily. Nursing must incorporate its standards of practice into the overall planning and evaluating process and not compromise its responsibility to deliver safe, effective care. Quality standards must be part of the system of control and tied into the reporting system so it can be used as a measure of cost effectiveness.

Profit Centers

Profit centers recognize both cost and revenue that result from an operation. In a profit center, a manager is held responsible for both. Profit becomes the basis for evaluation of performance. Profit centers function best in a decentralized setting. Responsibility accounting is a tool and a guide to be used in establishing productivity goals and measuring results as part of an effective management control system. Under this system managers are responsible only for costs over which they have control. Common costs are not allocated.[3] To organize nursing as a profit center, its costs should be measured on the basis of the severity of illness. Costing out nursing care on an individual patient basis will provide data needed to analyze the cost of care on a case-mix basis. When nursing care is billed directly, a system will be in place to deal with it.

Establishing nursing as a profit center implies that its administrators have increased responsibility for decision making. It also means that those administrators must understand financial accounting techniques to collect the data needed and to analyze information to make sound financial decisions. It requires that nursing have access to current financial data and patient information. Managers of semiautonomous units are free to adjust to new opportunities and to take the initiative. But care must be taken to see that management directs that initiative to results that are congruent with professional standards as well as the goals of the hospital.

COST ACCOUNTING

Prospective pricing demands accurate accounting of costs. Cost-efficient allocation of resources depends on accurate cost data. Effective decision making requires the availability of current cost data. Strategic planning requires valid cost information and analysis. Budgeting and budgetary control must be based on sound financial information.

Because many hospitals still use outdated financial management systems and lack mechanisms for monitoring and controlling, the true costs of hospitalization are not available. Use of this per diem rate began more than a century ago when hospitals were for the care of the poor, the sick, and the dying. In the 1980s, the flat rate does not address the different levels of care patients require. Cost-setting techniques and routine daily charge calculations continue to be based on the traditional method of dividing total operating cost by total patient days. The cost-setting method does not reflect the actual hours of care. Nursing care has been accounted for on a per diem basis and the cost has been buried in the room rate.[4]

The need for cost control and increased productivity is forcing hospitals to come to grips with costs and pricing, and their managerial implications. There is a need to know the total costs for a service. Members of *Hospitals* magazine's Publishers Panel on Hospital Financial Management agreed in 1984 that in the past hospitals did not know what their costs were and that, even today, few hospitals know. However, they are beginning to use standard accounting systems to provide answers.[5] Information on managing operating costs through standard cost systems, flexible budgeting, and performance reporting is necessary. This system can determine the variable and fixed costs of procedures.

Purpose

The purpose of cost accounting is to associate costs with the activity for which they were incurred. It provides a structure for cost analysis and the means for breaking down proposed activities into segments of the total cost of the function. Communication of these data along with other pertinent information can serve as a basis for planning, budgeting, and cost control.

Principles

Cost accounting for managerial purposes is based on the principles of controllability and responsibility. Statements of purpose and strategy set the basic directions for the hospital. To succeed, the strategy must include specific measurable activities and desired results. This includes expressing the operating plan in financial terms. Specific activities must be defined and expressed in terms of dollars of expense, capital purchases, and revenues. Once a manager's responsibilities have been identified, the focus is on identifying the costs that individual is responsible for controlling.

A basic premise of cost accounting is that costs are a means to an end. Different costs are used for different purposes. Analysis of cost differences is needed to make specific, timely decisions. Planning requires estimates of future costs. Performance evaluations need a comparison of prior cost estimates and actual results. External reporting requires historical cost data. The users of cost accounting information need to understand its benefits and its limitations.

Management frequently must choose between two or more alternative courses of action, such as whether or not to add a new service, discontinue an existing one, purchase new technology, or choose between two services or technologies when only one is financially feasible. The information needed is how future costs and revenues will differ under each alternative.

Selecting the Right System

When planning, management is interested in future costs. It may be necessary to use analysis of past operations but those costs must be adjusted to reflect expectable changes in the future—not only in prices but also in the availability of resources, technology, and market. Once a budget is projected based on estimated costs, actual cost is compared with the standard for the unit of organization. Variances are noted and analyzed.

Hospitals need information for strategic planning and long-term and short-term goal setting. In the past there was little need to analyze the impact of change in case mix or volume on the cost of a service. With the constraints on financial resources of the 1980s, hospitals are looking for ways to better manage those resources and moving toward establishing cost accounting systems based on models used in industry.

Hospitals are in varying stages of developing their systems. The nurse administrators must know where the hospital stands in that process and be prepared to use patient acuity, quality monitoring, and variable staffing budget standards as part of the total management system, especially with regard to achieving a realistic level of productivity.

An appropriate cost accounting system will give first-line nursing managers the financial information needed to assess the cost of the activities at the unit level. It can provide the financial information necessary for efficient and effective use of available resources. A system that can identify nursing costs for the individual patient can provide accurate data for evaluating nursing service productivity. It also will supply the data base needed for flexible budgeting based on workload rather than inflexible budgeting based on average nursing hours per patient day.

An accounting system that costs out nursing service based on a sound patient classification system can give nursing management the ability to assess the delivery system and determine what levels of care can be provided at what cost. Regardless of how efficient the delivery of nursing care becomes, there is a point at which the lack of resources will cut into the quality of care. Levels of quality of care must be defined and measured and the costs of each level identified. With this type of information, the nursing department can pinpoint which activities can be eliminated and the level of quality that will exist when costs are reduced below this point.

COST/PROFIT ANALYSIS

Profit is the difference between cost and revenue. Even organizations identified as nonprofit have revenues that exceed their cost, if only by a small margin. Much of the revenue beyond expenses is put back into the organization to be used for growth and development; otherwise, the institution remains static and progress ceases. Even without a profit goal, an organization must have revenue to meet its costs.

Break-Even Analysis

Cost and revenue behaviors provide a useful tool for decision making, commonly referred to as break-even analysis. The term break-even refers to the volume at which the revenue equals the cost. In nursing, this could be the volume of admissions to a unit, the number of procedures performed, or the number of patient visits, depending on the services offered or the amount of usage of a piece of equipment.

Break-even analysis makes certain assumptions:

- that cost per unit of volume is fixed
- that fixed costs exist and are independent of volume
- that variable costs exist and change in proportion to volume.

An algebraic method can be used to determine the extent to which the break-even quantity changes in response to changes in costs. According to this method the break-even point (BEP) can be calculated using the following formula (graphed in Figure 2–1):

$BEQ = F/R-V$
where
BEQ = break-even quantity
F = fixed costs
R = revenue per unit
V = variable costs per unit[6]

An example would be the number of admissions necessary for revenue to meet the costs of a nursing unit. Cost and revenue per admission would have to be based

Figure 2–1 Determining the Break-Even Point

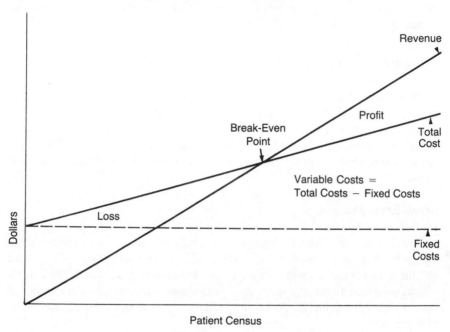

on averages. This is one of the limitations on accuracy in using the algebraic method. The use of regression analysis is a more accurate method but the algebraic method is much simpler and can be useful in decision making.

Break-even analysis is a technique that nursing can apply a number of ways in its financial planning:

- It can help project nursing costs and revenues associated with a changing volume of admissions.
- It can be used to identify the point at which nursing cost will need to be decreased, even though quality levels will decline, or identify the level of quality at which care can be delivered based on available revenue.
- It can be an indicator that consideration should be given to discontinuing certain services.

Further analysis is needed before decisions are made since other factors have to be considered. Hospital revenues from a number of departments are interrelated, so, for example, a loss in an inpatient nursing department might be compensated for by the revenue from inpatients in another department. This is one of the reasons that hospitals need a comprehensive accounting system as a basis for decision making.

The break-even point can be valuable when making decisions between alternative programs or courses of action. Goals and objectives of the nursing department obviously must be based on what is affordable. Careful consideration thus will have to be given to the use of financial and human resources in order to provide nursing care in the most effective and efficient manner.

COST CATEGORIES

To plan and control the level of productive effort commensurate with the desired quality, nurse managers need to understand the various categories of cost with which they must deal. For accounting purposes, costs are classified according to their relationship to departments, volume, and their controllability at the department level.

Direct and Indirect Costs

Based on their relationship to departments, costs are classified as direct or indirect:

- Direct costs are traceable to a given cost objective. This category includes supplies and direct labor costs. Direct labor costs consist of the salaries of employees providing direct services.
- Indirect costs cannot be traced to a given cost objective without resorting to some arbitrary method of allocation. Examples are costs of utilities, plant operations, housekeeping, laundry, and indirect labor expenditures. Indirect labor costs include administrative costs, employee benefits, etc. Indirect costs usually are fixed and not controllable at the department level.

Fixed and Variable Costs

Costs are classified as variable or fixed in relation to volume:

- Fixed costs are those that do not change in response to volume; they are a function of the passage of time. These usually are the indirect costs allocated to the department. They also may include some direct costs, such as minimum personnel needs, equipment, supplies, and programs.

- Variable costs change as volume changes in a constant proportional manner. Most of these are direct costs, such as salaries and supplies.

At the nursing unit level, an example of direct costs would be the salaries of those involved in direct patient care. This may include both direct care activities at the patient's bedside and indirect ones such as documenting, planning, and reporting—all the activities that are part of the nursing process. Indirect costs would include the salaries of nursing management, clerical help, and those involved in nursing committees or other hospital committees. These salaries are considered as being paid for productive time. Benefits such as vacations and holidays, sick leave, or any time off with pay are considered nonproductive time and are allocated as direct expenses to the cost center. The amount of indirect care activities and nonproductive time is a cost that needs to be identified, analyzed, and controlled by nurse managers to improve productivity.

For example, Exhibit 2–1 presents calculations for a typical nursing unit. These figures identify the hours worked, hours of nonproductive time, and hours paid. These figures are shown as they occurred, and in relation to patient days. To put these figures into perspective, this pay period can be compared with the same one a year earlier, other previous pay periods, or averages over the most recent three years. Goals then can be set to improve productivity, which may include an analysis of nonproductive dollars and ways to decrease that expenditure. Factors such as controlling absenteeism or utilizing more part-time workers without benefits are considered at this point.

From studying Exhibit 2–1, the nurse manager also can discern that the actual hours worked per patient day exceeds the standard productivity range of 5.10 to 5.30 hours per patient day. Thus, the relationship of actual hours to the standard hours required needs to be evaluated. Possible reasons for this difference could be:

- The illness level of the patients on unit 14 has changed since the standard productivity level was set.
- There has been a change in physicians frequenting the unit, and some new doctors have different types of patients or write more orders than those working when the productivity level was set.
- The staffing mix is improper so that the hospital is paying for "down time" in worker categories that are limited in functions by licensing.
- The unit is overstaffed consistently.
- The current standard productivity level is unrealistic in relation to nurse expectations for patient care that have been established in the division and on this unit.
- The unit has extreme census swings because of decreased lengths of stay; thus, staffing averages are skewed by days in which there are many dis-

Exhibit 2–1 Departmental Productivity Reporting

PREPARED 02/12/86 14.22   01/26/86 THRU 02/08/86

DEPT 112—UNIT 14-MED/SURG

UNIT OF SERVICE: PATIENT DAYS   STANDARD PRODUCTIVITY RANGE: 5.10 TO 5.30 (HRS/PATIENT DAYS)

Reporting Criteria	Current Pay Period Pay No (16)		Previous Pay Periods (15/14/13)		Year-to-Date		Previous Three Years History Fiscal Pays		
	This Yr	Last Yr	This Yr	Last Yr	This Yr 1985–1986	Last Yr 1984–1985	1984–1985	1983–1984	1982–1983
Hours—Worked	1,972	2,092	5,666	6,379	29,824	33,797	54,150	58,412	59,423
Dollars	20,142	19,555	57,763	60,761	295,615	312,563	506,083	521,450	494,873
Hours—Non-Prod	213	237	1,273	1,219	4,782	4,997	7,253	8,075	7,569
Dollars	1,911	2,175	12,684	10,674	45,103	42,430	62,626	68,369	58,464
Hours—Paid	2,186	2,330	6,939	7,598	34,607	38,794	61,404	66,487	66,993
Dollars	22,053	21,731	70,448	71,435	340,718	354,993	568,710	589,820	553,337
F.T.E.—Worked	24.6	26.1	23.6	26.5	23.3	26.4	26.0	27.0	28.5
F.T.E.—Paid	27.3	29.1	28.9	31.6	27.0	30.3	29.5	30.7	32.2
F.T.E.—Budgeted	27.5	30.7	27.5	30.7	27.5	30.7	30.7	31.6	33.2
Patient Days	325	369	1,020	1,018	5,008	5,899	9,323	10,341	10,655
Actual Hrs Worked	6.06	5.67	5.55	6.26	5.95	5.72	5.80	5.64	5.57
Dollars (Hrs/Patient Days)	61	52	56	59	59	52	54	50	46
Actual Hrs Paid	6.72	6.31	6.80	7.46	6.91	6.57	6.58	6.42	6.28
Dollars (Hrs/Patient Days)	67	58	69	70	68	60	61	57	51
Hours—Variance	.76	.37	.25	.96	.65	.42	.50	.34	.27
Dollars (Wrk./Prod. Stud.)	47	19	14	57	38	22	27	17	12
F.T.E.—Equivalent (Hours-Variance)	3.0	1.7	1.0	4.0	2.5	1.9	2.2	1.6	1.3
Productivity %	87.4	93.4	95.4	84.6	89.0	92.6	91.3	93.9	95.1

Source: Used with permission of Welborn Baptist Hospital, Evansville, Ind.

charges and others when personnel is stretched to the limit when the unit is filled.

To better determine the nature of the problem, the nurse manager can analyze the data in relation to the information gleaned from the patient classification system to ascertain whether the productivity standard varied from the average hours of nursing care required by the acuity level of patients on a unit for a specified period. Where certain days of the week show extremes in census, the manager can use flexible scheduling to meet staffing needs while minimizing nonproductive paid hours.

While the calculations of patient acuity in relation to nurse hours can be done manually, as shown in Exhibit 2–2, it is much easier to evaluate with a computer. More information on patient classification systems, staffing, and costing of nursing care is presented in subsequent chapters.

INTERNAL ASSESSMENT

Pressure to make the nursing division more productive can be expected to continue, since, as noted earlier, the nursing staff salaries comprise the largest portion of the hospital budget. The time has come for nursing to reconcile the care-centered value system with the cost-centered value system. Nursing needs to know its price tag and to realize that the cost of optimal health in patients is more than the available national resources allocated to health care.

Nursing care has to be defined in terms of what it is and who will provide it. However, that is not to say that quality care cannot be given. Nurses are revising their working style and objectives to work smarter, not harder, and to realize that effective resource utilization is required. The days of "more is better" are gone, but in those days nurses did not really have to assess quality or efficiency. Did nurses really do a better job?

Traditionally, hospitals have been in the business of inpatient care—but traditional markets are declining. Inpatient services are decreasing and outpatient services of all types have increased. Nursing must not be bound to traditional methods that preclude total financial management; instead, they must explore nontraditional means of generating revenue.

When nurse administrators develop a new program or service that works, many other hospitals in the country probably would pay for a copy of a prefabricated model ready for implementation. What are these managers doing that has salable potential? Have they written excellent total patient care plans, complete with teaching formats and discharge instructions? Is their policy manual outstanding?

Do they have specialized nurses whose workshops or courses could be marketed? Have they found a charting system that really works? Do they have a creative nurse paging system, medication cart, or some piece of hospital-created equipment that is ready for market?

Can the staff from one of the profit centers or units be a part of the team that assesses needs, instructs, or provides services that attract satellite, feeder hospitals or industry to purchase services and/or use the hospital? If so, nursing is in the "intrapreneuring" business in which it can collect a percentage of the revenues generated from such endeavors. This money can be used to purchase equipment that saves nurse time or makes the work area more effective or more pleasing. It also can be used to pay for audiovisual aids to provide faster and better patient education.

COSTING NURSING SERVICE

Typically, the cost of nursing care has been buried in the room rate, along with other allocated charges from nonrevenue-producing cost centers. Under the prospective payment system, hospitals must identify their actual costs if they are to control them. The nursing division makes many decisions concerning patient needs, including allocating resources to maintain quality of care for patients. The future of nursing service, the key to improved productivity, and the maintenance of quality care depend on a data base that most hospitals have been developing. This data base relates the actual cost of nursing care to the patients' care needs within each diagnosis related group.

Efforts to break nursing costs away from room rates have been in the literature for some time. Massachusetts Eye and Ear Infirmary in Boston and St. Luke's Medical Center in Phoenix were among the first to charge patients for nursing services. The Hospital of St. Raphael in New Haven, Conn., presents its patients with itemized bills for nursing services. The charges are based on the amount of assistance the patients need in broad nursing categories such as bathing, positioning, feeding, and IV therapy. Other hospitals will follow. In Maine, a state law that became effective in July 1985 requires hospitals to break nursing charges out from other hospital charges and list them separately on patient bills. At the outset, those charges were based on average acuity levels, within systems such as those presented in Chapter 5.[7]

In an age of cost containment, in which institutions must compete for their share of the market, hospitals are turning to computerized accounting systems that can monitor cost on a case-by-case basis. Determining the cost of nursing care per patient on a daily basis is an important factor in pinpointing actual costs for an individual patient.

Exhibit 2–2 Daily Staffing Data Sheet

NURSING

			DAYS 7-3										EVENINGS - 3-11				

UNIT	HN	RN	LPN	NA/MHA	US	PROD. STAFF*	PROD. HOURS**	ACUITY LEVELS	CENSUS	UNIT	HN	RN	LPN	NA/MHA	US	PROD. STAFF*	PROD. HOURS**	ACUITY LEVELS	CENSUS
B-2								I___ II___ III___ IV___		B-2								I___ II___ III___ IV___	
C-2								I___ II___ III___ IV___		C-2								I___ II___ III___ IV___	
G-4								I___ II___ III___ IV___		G-4								I___ II___ III___ IV___	
OB-PP								I___ II___ III___ IV___		OB-PP								I___ II___ III___ IV___	
OB-L&D								I___ II___ III___ IV___		OB-L&D								I___ II___ III___ IV___	
NBN								I___ II___ III___ IV___		NBN								I___ II___ III___ IV___	
ABC								I___ II___ III___ IV___		ABC								I___ II___ III___ IV___	
NICU								I___ II___ III___ IV___		NICU								I___ II___ III___ IV___	
PEDS								I___ II___ III___ IV___		PEDS								I___ II___ III___ IV___	
PICU								I___ II___ III___ IV___		PICU								I___ II___ III___ IV___	
1400								I___ II___ III___ IV___		1400								I___ II___ III___ IV___	
CCU								I___ II___ III___ IV___		CCU								I___ II___ III___ IV___	
TCU								I___ II___ III___ IV___		TCU								I___ II___ III___ IV___	
CCU OPEN HEART								I___ II___ III___ IV___		CCU OPEN HEART								I___ II___ III___ IV___	
1500								I___ II___ III___ IV___		1500								I___ II___ III___ IV___	
ICU								I___ II___ III___ IV___		ICU								I___ II___ III___ IV___	
1600								I___ II___ III___ IV___		1600								I___ II___ III___ IV___	
Rehab								I___ II___ III___ IV___		Rehab								I___ II___ III___ IV___	
DSU								I___ II___ III___ IV___		DSU								I___ II___ III___ IV___	
ER								I___ II___ III___ IV___		ER								I___ II___ III___ IV___	
YSA								I___ II___ III___ IV___		YSA								I___ II___ III___ IV___	
ASA								I___ II___ III___ IV___		ASA								I___ II___ III___ IV___	
EDS								I___ II___ III___ IV___		EDS								I___ II___ III___ IV___	
OPEN M.H.								I___ II___ III___ IV___		OPEN M.H.								I___ II___ III___ IV___	
CLOSED M.H.								I___ II___ III___ IV___		CLOSED M.H.								I___ II___ III___ IV___	
ICU M.H.								I___ II___ III___ IV___		ICU M.H.								I___ II___ III___ IV___	
ADOL M.H.								I___ II___ III___ IV___		ADOL M.H.								I___ II___ III___ IV___	
								I___ II___ III___ IV___										I___ II___ III___ IV___	
TOTAL										TOTAL									

DATE_____

*Prod. Staff—Working Staff except head nurse and unit secretary.

**Prod. Hours—8-hour census − number of working staff persons.

Source: Adapted from form developed by Welborn Baptist Hospital, Evansville, Ind.

DIVISION

NIGHTS - 11-7

UNIT	HN	RN	LPN	NA/MHA	US	PROD. STAFF	PROD. HOURS	ACUITY LEVELS	CENSUS	24-Hour Totals	Average Census	Average Activity	Nsg Hrs-Patient	Variance from Standard	Paid Nonproductive Hours
B-2								I___ II___ III___ IV___							
C-2								I___ II___ III___ IV___							
G-4								I___ II___ III___ IV___							
OB-PP								I___ II___ III___ IV___							
OB-L&D								I___ II___ III___ IV___							
NBN								I___ II___ III___ IV___							
ABC								I___ II___ III___ IV___							
NICU								I___ II___ III___ IV___							
PEDS								I___ II___ III___ IV___							
PICU								I___ II___ III___ IV___							
1400								I___ II___ III___ IV___							
CCU								I___ II___ III___ IV___							
TCU								I___ II___ III___ IV___							
CCU OPEN HEART								I___ II___ III___ IV___							
1500								I___ II___ III___ IV___							
ICU								I___ II___ III___ IV___							
1600								I___ II___ III___ IV___							
Rehab								I___ II___ III___ IV___							
DSU								I___ II___ III___ IV___							
ER								I___ II___ III___ IV___							
YSA								I___ II___ III___ IV___							
ASA								I___ II___ III___ IV___							
EDS								I___ II___ III___ IV___							
OPEN M.H.								I___ II___ III___ IV___							
CLOSED M.H.								I___ II___ III___ IV___							
ICU M.H.								I___ II___ III___ IV___							
ADOL M.H.								I___ II___ III___ IV___							
								I___ II___ III___ IV___							
TOTAL															

SUMMARY

Nurse managers who succeed in balancing staff satisfaction/morale, quality care, and productivity standards effectively must be in touch with budgetary concepts and the rapidly changing trends that characterize the health care environment of the 1980s. Moreover, if decentralization is to work, managers from the first level to the top must have total responsibility and accountability for managing the nursing budget. It is only when nurse managers can control the purse strings that they can continually assess the monetary impact of their productivity improvement efforts.

Nursing managers need to be reasonably expert in financial management and health economics to improve productivity with an eye to cost containment and quality. Along with polishing these skills, the nursing division must assess the environment and the available resources.

Information needed to assess staffing resources effectively in relation to their ability to contract and expand with a variable workload includes:

- staffing mix and qualifications
- orientation and staff development programs
- salary and benefits
- use of flexible scheduling and part-time/casual staff
- staff turnover
- nursing care delivery systems
- staffing and scheduling patterns
- average patient acuity levels, nursing hours required, and average length of stay on various units.

This assessment involves the use of the patient classification system. Managers should be sure that this system meets their need to measure the workload accurately. Is the tool predictable, valid, reasonable when compared with staff and managerial judgment of the patient care/staffing situation, and able to reflect the intensity of care accurately? Managers should be sure that they are happy with their system or have contacted vendors for one better suited to their institutional needs before attaching nursing care costs to the system. It makes little sense to proceed with elaborate measurements, standard setting, and costing if the system is not geared to show staffing levels compatible with the administrators' philosophy of care as well as acuity figures that match actual patient experiences.

Once data are collected, nurse managers should develop a total productivity plan geared to meeting their goals in patient care and the needs of their staff. They should continue to monitor productivity data as a means of determining whether their many programs are working.

Rapid change in hospital nursing is a reality that will remain for a long time. Nurse managers no longer can deal merely with today's operations while allowing nonnurses to control financial data and costs/profits. To remain competitive and acquire the professional help and capital equipment needed to thrive, nurse managers must take charge of their budget.

NOTES

1. H.J. Berman and L.E. Weeks, *The Financial Management of Hospitals* (Ann Arbor, Mich.: Health Administration Press, 1982), 82–83.
2. Ibid., 35–40.
3. H.A. Black and D.E. James, *The Managerial and Cost Accountant's Handbook* (Homewood, Ill.: Dow Jones-Irwin, Pub., 1979), 847–51.
4. Charles T. Woods, "Relate Hospital Charges to Use of Service," in *Saving Our Health Care Systems* (Boston: Harvard University Press, 1982), 97–104.
5. J.E. Mistarz, "Cost Accounting: A Solution but a Problem," *Hospitals* 58, no. 19 (October 1984): 96, 99–101.
6. Benton Gup, *Principles of Financial Management* (New York: John Wiley & Sons, Inc., 1983), 210.
7. Scott Water, "What Happens If Your Hospital Bills Separately for Nursing?" *RN* 48, no. 7 (July 1985): 18–21.

BIBLIOGRAPHY

AHA. *Managing under Medicare Prospective Pricing*. Chicago: American Hospital Publishing, Inc. 1983.

Deines, Elaine. *Staffing for DRGs*. Chapel Hill, N.C.: W.L. Ganong Co., 1983.

Ethridge, Phyllis. "The Case for Billing by Patient Acuity." *Nursing Management* 16, no. 8 (August 1985): 38–41.

Hanson, Robert L. *Management Systems for Nursing Service Staffing*. Rockville, Md.: Aspen Publishers, Inc., 1983.

Higgerson, N.J., and Van Slyke, Ann. "Variable Billing for Service: New Direction for Nursing." *The Journal of Nursing Administration*, 12, no. 6 (June 1982): 20–27.

Riley, W.J., and Schafers, Vicki. "Nursing Operations as a Profit Center." *Nursing Management* 15, no. 4 (April 1984): 43–46.

————. "Costing Nursing Services." *Nursing Management* 14, no. 12 (December 1983): 40–43.

Schmid, Elsie. *Maintaining Cost Effectiveness*. Wakefield, Mass.: Nursing Resources, 1979.

Sovie, Margaret. "Amalgram of Nursing Acuity, DRGs, and Costs." *Nursing Management* 16, no. 3 (March 1985).

————. "Managing Nursing Resources in a Constrained Environment." *Nursing Economics* 3, no. 2 (March/April 1985): 83–94.

Staley, Marilyn, and Luciano, Kathy. "Eight Steps to Costing Nursing Services." *Nursing Management* 15, no. 10 (October 1984): 33–38.

Starling, Grover. *The Changing Environment of Business*. (Boston: Kent, 1980).

Walker, Diane. "The Cost of Nursing Care in Hospitals. *The Journal of Nursing Administration* 13, no. 3 (March 1983): 13–18.

ACTION CHECKLIST

1. Staffing requirements: How many people are needed and what is the best mix? What resources are available and what can be done with them?
2. Patient classification system: Does it accurately reflect the workload? Are the staffing recommendations correct?
3. Reporting systems: Are staff members charged to the cost centers where they actually work? Are there methods to collect and analyze unit cost data on a continuing basis?
4. Staffing and scheduling procedures: Are there established staffing and scheduling policies and procedures? Is there a centralized control system for staffing?
5. Staff education program: Does the continuing education program meet the developmental needs of the staff? Is the orientation program adequate? What are the actual costs of the program, including salaries, replacement on duty, preparation, equipment, and teaching?
6. Performance evaluation: Is there an effective criteria-based performance appraisal system in place? Does it measure the results of a person's work?
7. Decision making: Does staff participate in the decision-making process? Are first-line managers and staff nurses involved in the budgeting process and accountability for cost control?
8. Marketing: Does nursing market its services to physicians, to patients, and to the community?
9. Environmental awareness: Is there sensitivity to the business world at the nurse manager level? Is there an awareness of the changes in the environment?
10. Innovation: Is creative thinking encouraged? Are innovative ideas tried and rewarded?

Chapter 3

Budget

E. Marie Nelson

Real improvements in productivity require efficiency and effectiveness to be built into the budgeting process. When the nursing goals and objectives are not tied into the budgeting process, the chance of achieving them is decreased. When goals and objectives are prioritized by deadlines and criteria are established for acceptable achievement and costs for accomplishment, the nursing division is truly on a path in which productive efforts have been identified, budgeted, and targeted for success. Organizational priorities are obvious when a manager studies the budget. Programs that do not receive adequate monetary attention have a poor chance of success.

DEFINITION AND DESCRIPTION

A budget is a plan for the future stated in numerical terms. It covers the activities of all levels of the organization for a specified period. When the organizational goals and objectives are expressed in financial terms, expected costs and revenues can be compared to judge the institution's financial position and its level of productivity.

Although the final budget is translated into dollars and cents, not all budgets are expressed in financial terms. Personnel budgets indicate the number of employees and the skill levels required, or the number of staff hours needed to carry out the planned activities of the nursing department or program. However, acquiring adequate numbers of people is only the beginning. Staffing needs should be calculated so that the appropriate mix is available to achieve the quality of work desired. Supportive services should be incorporated so that available staff members have the skills and materials needed to function effectively and efficiently.

For example, patient classification systems typically measure nursing hours per patient over a 24-hour period. However, if supplies are not well located, nurses spend some of this credited time traveling the hallways instead of being with their patients. Moreover, if staff members are not prepared to meet patient needs, nursing departments can end up with the wrong person at the bedside to perform a task or can have a nurse with poor communication skills who is unprepared to provide the emotional counseling or teaching required. Improving this situation can require the hospital's administration or its education division to budget programs and money to bring services up to the desired standards. In other words, the budgeting process should bring various departmental services into harmony to achieve the desired work product.

Budgets always apply to a specified period. They usually are projected over a year but longer term ones for up to five years are common. The annual budgets are divided into shorter periods so that the allocation of resources can be compared with the quality of the staff output at regular intervals.

The budget is a blueprint for action. Each department of the hospital knows the results it is expected to achieve individually and collaboratively. When monetary figures are placed alongside these expected outcomes, the budget can become a yardstick for determining the success of programs or activities. All levels of management can and should utilize the budget as a tool for planning and control.

While patient acuity and census are parameters for assessing the adequacy of staff in direct care, they are less effective in judging levels of productivity in management or support staff such as infection control, supervision, quality assurance, or education. Thus, these support persons need to identify their own objectives and budgets within the constraints of hospital guidelines so that they also may be held accountable for the way they spend their time. Over the years, the measurement of indirect services has been less successful than that of staff persons performing direct patient care. However, the demand for cost containment and improvement in services requires this group to be monitored as a part of the overall departmental effort.

Budgets are a quantification of plans and are only as good as the plans on which they are based. They should not be mistaken for the plans themselves. They are merely a quantitative tool for evaluating performance and utilization of resources. Measuring outcomes against revenues and costs is important if those numerical assessments also incorporate the efficiency and effectiveness with which services are being performed.

For example, in one hospital, patient turnover and staffing ratios were excellent on paper. However, patients felt that the staff was surly and uncaring and many vowed to turn to other hospitals for future health care needs. In this case the productive goal of efficiency was accomplished, but the staff members were disgruntled and ineffective in achieving patient care goals. Thus, they were not truly productive since their efforts were working to thwart future business and keep staff unhappy. This is an example of a penny-wise and pound-foolish approach. Wise hospitals adopt plans that make the books look good both now and in the long term by looking at a combination of expenditures and quality of work. A budget that is effective is one that is monitored continually so that management and staff efforts can be maximized within the bounds of available resources.

The first step in developing a budgetary process that emphasizes a total approach to cost containment and to improved productivity is to select, to the extent feasible under the overall hospital budget system, the budgetary style that best fits the needs of the nursing division. To ensure continuity, the budgetary format in nursing must dovetail with the rest of the system.

BUDGET STYLES

Fixed or Static Budget

This is based on a fixed volume level such as number of patient days, patient visits, etc., to arrive at an annual budget total. Estimates are based on historical data and do not always allow for seasonal or monthly variations.Expected results can be compared with actual results; the difference is called a variance. If the cost is greater than planned, it is identified as a negative variance; if the cost is less, it is a positive variance. Figures can be misleading because, for example, decreased costs could be the result of reduced workload due to lower census, and thus not necessarily favorable for revenues. This is the simplest form of budgeting, but it is not easy to evaluate performance since there are no relevant ranges of volume established in the original plan.

Planned Program Budgeting System (PPBS)

This system links planning, program, and the budget. Since planning looks beyond the immediate year's budget, programs and budgets are projected over longer periods. Nurse managers must consider the external and internal environment when budgeting under PPBS. This system requires the development of programs based on the goals and objectives of long-term planning. With this type of budgeting, different projects aimed at the same goal can be evaluated on a regular basis. Future costs are identified for consideration, and decisions can be based on looking at the entire program over a period of years, rather than on short-term analysis. A modification of this method is recommended because the extreme use of PPBS is very time consuming.

Flexible Budget

This approach allows management to adjust the budget to meet actual changes in costs and activities. Budgeting for a specific workload on a nursing unit is not sufficient in the environment of the late 1980s. Flexible budgets show costs at different levels of activity.To forecast costs accurately at various workloads, it is necessary to distinguish between fixed, variable, and semivariable expenses. An important element of budget monitoring is a prompt, accurate reporting mechanism that informs the nurse managers of budgeted versus actual expenditures. This is necessary to identify problems and trends for future planning and budgeting.

Zero-Based Budget (ZBB)

This requires that each year's budget start from a zero base. All dollars spent must be justified. Established programs compete with new programs. Existing programs must justify their continued existence. Alternative ways of delivering programs are analyzed. An attempt is made to identify the costs of services and what the cost would be if these services were discontinued. First-line managers must evaluate the cost effectiveness of each activity they direct. Three major alternatives for each program are considered: alternative methods, volume of service to be provided, and varying levels of quality.

Upper management then ranks all programs. Resources are allocated to the projects having the greatest net benefit, regardless of whether they are established or new programs. In theory this should make budget control easier, since low-priority projects would be the first to be deleted if the budget needed to be reduced. This type of budgeting requires that first-line managers be fully informed of the long-range plans of the institution and have skills in cost-analysis techniques. However, the purest use of this method has proven to be too time consuming to be practical on an annual basis.

As hospitals attempt to deal with cost-reduction issues and competition, they will need to utilize styles of budgeting that will enable them to adapt to rapid changes and yet provide a structure for evaluation of long-term planning. They may choose to use combinations of these styles, or others, depending on their unique needs. Nurse managers must increase their knowledge of the budgeting process since they control a large proportion of hospital resources, making it important that they understand and use their budgets appropriately in operating their departments.

RESOURCE ALLOCATION

When resources are too limited to achieve all the objectives, their allocation through the budget will be controlled by the objectives that the institution prioritizes. Because decisions will be resource driven, those available must be identified and utilized efficiently. In the economically constrained health care environment, there is risk associated with such decision making and allocation. A systematic approach must be taken and analytical tools utilized to determine cost effectiveness and benefits. Moral, ethical, and social considerations also must be part of the approach.

Availability of resources can cause conflict when there is competition for limited resources and their division is perceived to be inequitable. Negative consequences can affect the overall performance of the organization. All departments should be involved in the processes of priority setting and decision making. Compromises can be made during the planning process.

To utilize budgeted nursing resources to the best advantage, nurses at all levels must participate actively and knowledgeably. Staffing systems must be verifiable and justifiable. To maximize nursing resources there must be good communication between the nursing and fiscal departments and administration.

The successful nursing department will be prepared to maintain quality with fewer resources. Strategies must be developed for cost containment, revenue enhancement, and increased nursing productivity. Nurses must become business oriented as well as clinically competent. Nursing care needs to be defined, measured, and costed. The relationship between nursing care and costs must be understood by administration and the public.

BUDGETING PROCESS

Ideally, the budgeting process should be set out in a procedure manual that describes the mechanics of the function. If not, this information may be included in a budget packet sent to managers responsible for developing budgets for their area. The packet should include an organizational chart, a chart of accounts, the forms, supportive data, the budget calendar, and the directions for completing the budget.

Generally the budget information goes to the nursing manager of each unit. As the unit budgets are completed, they are returned to nursing administration, where the master budget for the department is compiled and reviewed. It then is forwarded to top management for final review and, when accepted, becomes a part of the master budget for the institution. The budget plan has been developed.

MAJOR BUDGETS

Nurses should be knowledgeable about three major budgets—cash, operational, and capital equipment. Budgeting for the nursing department usually involves the cost of allocated resources for the services offered. Nursing is responsible within its own department for the operational budget, which includes salary management and a nonsalary portion that covers all of the expenses of running the department or unit, such as supplies, fees, dues, tuition, equipment, and other items. The capital equipment budget includes large pieces of equipment, remodeling projects, etc. The nursing department is involved with a portion of that budget.

Cash Budget

This budget, also called cash flow, is the schedule of cash receipts and cash disbursements and is handled by the finance department. Based on estimated needs, a minimum cash balance level is established. Hospital cash budgets usually are projected on a monthly basis. The format is standard. Each month begins with a starting balance, and expected cash receipts are added to it.

- Starting cash balance + expected receipts = cash available
- Cash available − expected payments = tentative balance
- Tentative balance − minimum balance = amount to be invested or, if a new balance, amount to be borrowed (minimum balance is a buffer for any required cash outlays)

The cash budget is not a primary budget. It is constructed from information obtained from the revenue, expense, and capital budgets rather than from operating decisions and projections.

Operating Budget

The personnel budget is the largest expenditure within the operating budget. Budgeting for a seven-day week and three shifts a day with the correct mix of personnel to cover a variable workload is no small task. The nurse manager first must have a projection of patient days. This usually is based on trends from the past and estimates for the future, influenced by what is occurring in the health care environment. Projections generally are broken down to unit level.

An accurate classification system can help in determining the number, type, and mix of full-time equivalents needed if it includes a system for workload measurement. Correct information on hours of direct and indirect care should be available. Staff members are allocated according to shift and mix of personnel needed to meet the hospital's standards. These standards should be based on knowledge of the institution, its geography, routines, and patient needs.

The first step is to establish daily staffing patterns based on the average workload. If there is a staffing system in place, this information is readily attainable; if not, the average acuity and census can be used as an indicator of the unit's projected activity and personnel needs. The higher the acuity, the higher the professional component of the staffing mix. Staff mix is dependent upon the method of delivery of nursing care. The ratio of professionals to nonprofessionals will vary according to the hospital's goals.

The next step is to estimate nonproductive time. How much vacation, holiday, and continuing education time is allowed for each employee? Will replacements be needed? Nonproductive hours (NPH) can be calculated for each person or based on an institutional average. This figure should include holidays, vacations, sick leave—any paid time away from work.

Employees considered indirect caregivers, such as the unit clerk, clinical specialists, the nurse manager (in most cases), or any other personnel assigned to the unit not engaged in direct patient care must be included in the budget. These employees are not included in the statistics of nurse staffing systems.

Following are definitions used in this process:

FTE = full-time equivalent, refers to a full-time position, usually 40 hours per week
Work week = 40 hours per week, usually 5 days
Work day = eight-hour shift
Shift = eight hours
Work year = 2,080 hours
0.2 FTE = eight hours per week
1.4 FTE = seven shifts per week
Hours per patient day (HPPD) = average hours of care per patient for 24 hours
Direct care = delivery of direct patient care
Indirect care = administration, education, clerical, and other support personnel
Direct and indirect hours = hours worked and paid for
Nonproductive hours (NPH) = hours paid for and not worked, holidays, vacations, etc.
Total FTEs = all paid hours in a week divided by 40

Following are calculations used in this process:

Average occupancy = number of beds × percent occupancy
Hours per patient day × average census = total nursing hours for the unit
Total hours per day ÷ eight hours = number of FTEs for 24 hours
Percent staff per shift × total FTEs = FTEs per shift
Percent staff ratio = professional to nonprofessional
Number of hours worked per hours in work week = FTE (eight hours ÷ 40 = 0.2 FTE)

5 East medical unit, Monday through Friday
Average daily census 21.0
HPPD = 5

	7-3	3-11	11-7	Total
Head nurse*	1			1
Registered nurse	4	3	3	10
Nurse's aides	2	1		3
Ward clerk*	1	1		2

*Head nurse and ward clerk indirect.

Multiply each category by 1.4 to find total FTEs in each category.

Multiply total FTEs by 2,080 to obtain hours worked.

Use average percentage for hospital NPH (5% is used here) to calculate replacement hours.

Use average percentage for unit overtime.

The annual staffing schedule based on the above daily staffing pattern should look like this:

STAFFING SCHEDULE

Classification	FTEs	Hours Worked
Head nurse	1.0	2,080
Staff nurses	14.0	29,120
Nurse's aides	4.2	8,736
Ward clerks	2.8	5,824
Totals	22.0	45,760
Replacement	1.1	2,233
Overtime	.5	1,040
Budgeted	23.6	49,033

If census varies on a daily basis, the same method can be used to develop variable staffing guides for direct care. This can be helpful in developing scheduling patterns. A good patient classification and staffing system will provide this type of information.

Other nursing department personnel budgets are based on other indicators of workload, such as number and type of procedures (surgery and recovery room), or number of visits (emergency room and outpatient departments). The staffing will depend upon standards set by the institution. Staffing in this area needs to be individualized to meet the hospital's needs.

Salary Management

As the unit leader and the central administrative staff plan their budgets to support the delivery of quality nursing services, it is imperative that they build daily, weekly, monthly, quarterly, and annual objectives into their calculations that make them more accountable. To do this, all activities need to be analyzed and prioritized so that the nursing division can see results from the project money and managerial salaries expended.

For most management staffs, this includes examination of how the job is done each day, followed by revisions of activities designed to produce a greater impact on staff or programs. It also includes a hard look at all of the time spent in meetings. Since some of the activities of management staff, and special jobs such as infection control, are not as quantifiable as providing direct patient care, creativity is needed in setting parameters for measuring success. Naturally, these guidelines and deadlines should be revised continually as needed.

The purpose of quantifying the qualitative aspects of the nursing division is to bring every individual and all activities into the arena of accountability. If this is not done, the productivity calculations, based strictly on patient classification systems, can be misleading and unreliable as predictors of work to be accomplished.

True accountability is achieved and resource utilization is maximized only when productivity is woven into all department efforts. This should not be an add-on process after decisions have been made. Instead, it should be an integral part of the total effort, beginning with the planning and goal projections and ending with evaluation.

For example, one supervisor noted a few items that interfered with her own productivity:

1. Her job overlapped that of the unit leader, duplicating efforts until the problem was evaluated and the two worked more cooperatively in how they spent their time.
2. She was wasting time in meetings, so the division reduced meetings and shortened long sessions that were not goal driven.
3. She found herself saying, "I guess I will go to the unit to see what is happening." After the productivity assessment, she formulated an action plan for accomplishing a specific goal before making unit rounds.
4. She gained control of the day by writing a brief outline of how time should be utilized. In so doing she cut down on nonproductive time and budgeted time for reading and keeping up with the paperwork.

Finally, the nursing division reorganized office duties to give supervisors more time to engage in true management.

Nonsalary Budget

The nonsalary budget includes the remaining direct expenses of the cost center. Its items are not charged individually to the patient; if they are, the unit should be credited with the revenue. These expenses are allocated to accounts. The nurse manager must know what items are included in each account. Trends from the past and plans for the future must be considered when planning this budget. Costs may be projected based on current prices with an adjustment on the total budget, or directions may be given to adjust cost on the basis of information from manufacturers and other sources. An example of a nonsalary budget sheet is shown in Table 3–1.

Table 3–1 Nonsalary Budget Sheet

Calendar Year 1986

Expense Class Number	Description	Actual Expense 1984	5 Months Actual 1985	Projected Expense 1985	Budget 1986
025	Professional fees				
031	Consulting fees				
032	Legal fees				
033	Audit fees				
034	IV solutions				
035	Medical supplies	$27,980	$13,344	$28,000	$30,000
036	Housekeeping supplies				
037	Linen supplies				
038	Blood supplies				
039	Oxygen				
046	Office supplies	6,686	6,037	11,000	12,000
048	Print shop	311	4,902	11,760	12,600
050	General supplies	41,209	670	1,600	1,700
056	Repairs & Maintenance				
059	Collection				
060	Other purchased services	6,296	1,416	4,000	5,400
061	Dietary	329	196	600	700
062	Outside services				
077	Lease expenses				
080	Print shop materials				
082	Utilities				
089	Dues and fees				350
090	Books and subscriptions	110	30	400	450
091	Outside training & travel			0	150
092	Tuition	84		468	702
	Totals	83,005	26,595	57,828	64,052

It is important to analyze each projection. For example, account 050 represents a change from stock supplies on a unit to an exchange cart system. The supplies now are costed out through materials management and allocated, rather than through the nursing unit. This department has a heavy workflow during the summer months, which must be taken into consideration when projecting for the remainder of the year as well as for the following year.

Capital Budget

A capital expenditure is a commitment of resources that is expected to provide benefits over a period of time—at least two years, and generally much longer. A hospital can have many types of capital expenditures. In the health care industry, the capital decisionmaking process can be complicated. The rapid changes in technology, the shifts in cost-containment regulations from government, and third party payers all have created an environment that requires careful evaluation of any financial commitments.

Within a hospital, more individuals are involved in decision making than in other industries: departmental managers, medical staff members, the finance officer, administration, and the board. The capital budgeting and decisionmaking process will vary from hospital to hospital, depending upon each facility's philosophy. The control of capital costs generally falls into three methods, requiring administrative approval for (1) all capital expenditures, (2) all purchases over a certain dollar amount, or (3) budgeted amounts allocated to a responsibility center for expenditure.

Different types of expenditures require different methods of evaluation. The initial investment may be a small portion of the total amount of resources that will be needed. Consideration must be given to the life cycle of the investment and the operational costs. It can be difficult to quantify the benefit of proposed expenditures in an industry whose product is service and that is heavily influenced by ethical and legal issues.

Nursing's involvement in the capital budgeting process will vary from institution to institution. Usually it becomes involved through requests for capital equipment, remodeling or replacement of existing equipment, or in projects that require nursing and affect its provision of care. As with the rest of the budget, nursing must know the hospital's overall goals to participate effectively. Plans must be coordinated with other departments. Communication upward, downward, and laterally is essential. Effective decision making requires planning and coordination in collecting and presenting valid data for the cost/benefit analysis of a capital expenditure proposal.

Analyzing the costs of a large expenditure will be beyond the scope of most health care managers; however, they must understand the process and be fiscally responsible for their departments. Nursing resources will be affected by most capital decisions because of the interdependent relationships between nursing and the other departments in the hospital. Nursing must consider the effect on other departments when proposals are planned. Nursing will play a vital part in the conversation and utilization of limited health care resources. Successful nurse managers will acquire the knowledge needed to understand and participate in the capital budgeting process. At the most basic level, nursing must be able to justify its budget requests with accurate data and consideration of alternatives.

To be truly productive, the nursing division must obtain the tools and equipment needed to save precious personnel hours. This process involves much more than flipping through a catalog until allocated dollars are spent. Instead, nursing must conduct studies to identify equipment that will attract physicians to the hospital, save valuable nurse time, and/or make the delivery of care safer. When the needs are known, they must be matched to the appropriate capital resource. The justification for the item must be sound and stated in numbers and business terms so that the nursing need can be conveyed clearly to those in charge of the institution's purse strings. While short-term savings have become the No. 1 priority in hospitals, managers must make a case for the impact that well-chosen expenditures can have on long-term costs.

BUDGET REQUESTS

There are several factors to consider before initiating a capital budget request. The final evaluation of the proposed investment will be based on the same considerations. Having done its homework before presenting the proposal will give nursing a considerable edge in justifying the proposal. Nurse managers must investigate the alternatives, consider other manufacturers, look at other methods to reach the goal, evaluate different parameters for the project, and consider the results of not making the proposal, or getting approval for it.

The added costs beyond the initial investment must be evaluated. Operating costs are an important factor if they are in addition to the present amount. Opportunity costs—the costs of investing capital in a proposal—are another factor. A question is whether income from other resources will be reduced or eliminated, because the loss of profits from another source must be considered as an added cost. Similarly, if resources are shifted from another service and a reduction in care occurs, any resultant loss of revenue must be considered as part of the cost. The cost of not making alternative investments and the loss of interest revenue from the cash allocated to the proposal should be part of the evaluation. Another measure of opportunity cost is the current liquidation value of the asset. Maintenance and replacement costs also must be examined.

Managers must be prepared to respond to such questions as:

- Who will benefit from this proposal, and how?
- What populations will be served?

- Are other resources for these services already available?
- How will competition affect volume and what will be the effect on cost and benefit?
- Does the proposal relate to the institution's purpose and goals?
- How can the benefit be quantified and measured?

Any project that cannot remain solvent is a risk that must be considered carefully. Unless a hospital is in good financial condition, it may not be prudent to subsidize programs. Prospective payment and a competitive market require hospitals to pay close attention to their capital budgets. Resources will have to be allocated and monitored carefully. Nursing managers must acquire a level of understanding of the concepts of budgeting that will allow them to communicate with financial managers. They also must develop the skills to plan and manage their budgets.

CONTROLLING COSTS

The budget is a plan that estimates amounts of resources to be used to produce a specific amount of services over a particular period. It is based on forecasts of activities for the coming year. The forecasts are based on data that are both constant and variable. In an era of rapid change, it is important to develop estimates at several levels so the cost of variations can be determined.

First-line supervisors are at the site of action for cost control because they have the greatest influence on the utilization of staff and supplies. It is essential that they understand cost structure and budget systems and receive the information needed to measure their own and their unit's performance and take corrective steps when costs are unjustifiably out of line. Nurse managers must be involved and informed as to the cost of health care delivery. The successful managers have the ability to plan, budget, control, and monitor their own unit's operations.

All nurses must become cost conscious since they are the keys to the hospital's ability to cope with limited resources. Their proximity to patients allows them to assess the clients' needs for supplies, equipment, and treatment. They know the situation on their unit better than anyone else. They can plan with the physician to use the most cost-effective approach to meet those needs.

To assist in controlling costs, the unit's staff members must identify the portions of the budget that they can control. This requires communication and frequent review of the budget and its monthly reports as part of the evaluation of all of the unit's goals and objectives. Cost control should become a routine part of the nursing process. Nursing must think in terms of the best care possible with the available resources rather than the best possible care regardless of the cost.

FORECASTING

Forecasting is a projection of operational plans into the future, an educated guess based on historical data and reasonable assumptions using the best information available. The purpose of forecasting is to aid in financial decisions. Its usefulness is judged by its contribution to effective decision making. Techniques have been developed to make projections that will aid in assessing the institution's financial needs.

Forecasting is a must in developing an effective operating budget. It helps guide planning. Forecasting techniques begin with the collection of data; for a nursing operating budget, this would include workload, patient volumes, supply usage, supply costs, nursing hours, etc.

These techniques include judgment, trend, and cycle; regression forecasting and the Box-Jenkins method of forecasting; and exponential smoothing. To learn more about each method and gain facility in using them, the reader is referred to Chapter 6 of Clark and Schkade's book (listed in the references).

The development of the nursing operating budget requires monthly information. While it would be easy to use the annual budget and divide it by 12, that method would not take into consideration seasonal variations, the changing numbers of days, weekends, and holidays in a month, or upward or downward trends over the year. The capacity for work does not change up or down easily. It is hard to reduce operations on short notice, but it is even more difficult to handle an increase in workload quickly. Building a productive work force requires time, training, and money. It is costly to adjust to the frequent short-term fluctuations that seem to be more prevalent with decreased lengths of hospital stays.

The time frame for the data is important; generally, a five-year period is recommended. Data for each month can be compared over that time. It is easier to evaluate trends over a 60-month period. If there has been a substantial change, historical data may not be valid. All changes must be considered when interpreting the data. The environment of the data collection period must be compared with the current environment. Intuition must not be ignored. Nurses usually have a good understanding of their surrounding situation and should interpret the data accordingly.

Graphing is a technique commonly used for displaying data for evaluation. Trends can be spotted readily when information is displayed on a graph. Nursing hours required in the past can be plotted and compared for a specific month over a period of several years as well on an annual basis. This information can be helpful in planning staffing and scheduling patterns as well as in developing the personnel budget.

Regression analysis allows administrators to make predictions or estimates of the value of a dependent variable from given values of an independent variable; that is, how will a dependent variable be altered by a change in an independent value? To do this, a mathematical expression in equation form is constructed to show the relationship between two variables:

$$Y = f(x)$$

For example, a manager may want to correlate the current rate of absenteeism and the cost of providing direct nursing care on a particular unit with the relationship of a seasonal census drop and profits of the nursing department, or correlate servicing Medicare patients in a certain DRG with profits. Readers are referred to the bibliography for books detailing the use of this technique.

Regression analysis is a statistical technique that can be used to determine the straight line that comes closest to all of the data points on the graph. It is a fairly simple process when using a calculator. This information along with other data can help in predicting seasonal changes as well as in identifying trends.

It is important for nursing to be able to forecast for its own department. To do this effectively, the department must have access to hospitalwide information. It also must be aware of national trends and changes in health care that will affect nursing. In some institutions this information is readily available and shared.

SUMMARY

Any business organization must make a profit to survive. Nonprofit institutions do not have shareholders to pay; any surplus income goes back into the organization for improvement and development. Profit is necessary for stability and growth, which are essential for survival. In order to survive, hospitals are looking for dependable sources of revenue. They are allocating resources to services that can support themselves.

The basic managerial objective of nonprofit hospitals has been the providing of a socially desirable and needed service to the public. For numerous reasons, resources once available to hospitals no longer exist. In the environment of the late 1980s, hospitals, like other businesses, must seek profits and try to avoid losses.

Effective budgeting skills thus are essential for health care managers. Under the old system of cost reimbursement, budgets were a way of justifying costs. Under the DRG-PPS system, the budgeting process assumes importance as a planning, evaluation, and control tool. It offers an opportunity to evaluate options and alternatives, using available data to develop plans for the future. The business of the hospital remains health care, but funds are limited for the old methods of delivery.

Proactive nursing managers will define the essential nursing services and develop productivity plans to provide them with limited resources. Nurse managers must participate in developing their unit and departmental budget and accept responsibility for monitoring it. Nurses must be concerned about the quality and costs of care, identify those costs, and define and market their services to the public.

BIBLIOGRAPHY

Berman, H.J., and Weeks, L.E. *Financial Management of Hospitals*. Ann Arbor, Mich.: Health Administration Press, 1982.

Clark, Charles, and Schkade. *Statistical Analysis for Administrative Decisions*, 3rd ed. Cincinnati, Ohio: South-Western Publishing Co., 1979.

Davidson and Weil. *Handbook of Modern Accounting*. New York: McGraw-Hill Book Company, 1983.

Deines, Elaine. *Staffing for DRGs: A Unit-Specific Approach for Nurse Managers*. Chapel Hill, N.C.: W.L. Ganong Co., 1983.

Finkler, S.A. *Budgeting for Nurse Managers*. Orlando, Fla.: Grune & Stratton, Inc., 1984.

Gup, Benton. *Principles of Financial Management*. New York: John Wiley & Sons, Inc., 1983.

Mathews, L.M. *Practical Operating Budgeting*. New York: McGraw-Hill Book Company, 1977.

Newman, W.H. *Constructive Control*. Englewood Cliffs, N.J.: Prentice-Hall, Inc., 1975.

Schmid, Elaine. *Maintaining Cost Effectiveness*. Wakefield, Mass.: Nursing Resources, 1979.

Terry, G.R. *Principles of Management*. Homewood, Ill.: Richard D. Irwin, Inc., 1972.

ACTION CHECKLIST

1. What marketable services can nursing offer in the hospital setting?
2. How informed are nurses about the cost of health care delivery in their work setting?
3. How can nursing managers communicate if they do not understand accounting language and the accountant does not understand nursing language?
4. Do nursing managers understand the budgeting process? Are they involved in the process in their department?
5. Do they understand the style of budget used in the organization?
6. Are the nurses in the department aware of cost, quality, and standards of productivity when they plan patient care?
7. Do these nurses seek information on the current status of the health care environment?
8. Do the department's goals address cost control and quality?
9. Are the nursing managers proactive, seeking information and planning for the future rather than reacting to crisis after crisis as the environment continues to change?
10. Have they set goals for where they want to be next year and five years from now? Have they developed a plan of action to attain those goals?
11. Do the nurses integrate goals of improving productivity into all phases of work activity?
12. Does the budget and productivity plan show how various other departments will contribute and interface with nursing care delivery and its programs?
13. How do nursing managers monitor productive efforts by those who do not provide direct patient care?

Chapter 4

Staffing and Resource Development

Joyce Rhoades

A discussion of productivity is incomplete without an in-depth review of staffing methods. It is unrealistic to believe that old staffing methods can continue without change. The characteristics of the nursing practice environment in the mid-1980s—including increased acuity levels, decreased lengths of stay, and fluctuating patient occupancy rates—have compelled managers to select staffing and scheduling strategies that are responsive to the needs of nurses and patients while also being cost effective. As hospitals weather the changes imposed by diagnosis related groups (DRGs), Medicare's prospective payment system (PPS), and changing financial incentives, managers are challenged to support an environment of health care delivery that is both effective and efficient while remaining within the reality of their nursing budget.[1]

When looking at ways to increase productivity and reduce costs, administrators always address the fact that 40 to 50 percent of the total organizational budget is expended for labor. Because nurses comprise about half of all employees in a hospital, their staff is the first item on the agenda. For many nurses, the adjustments and cutbacks of the mid-1980s have been equated with productivity in a negative context, since their work force has been reduced more times than that of smaller departments. It is important to convey to staff nurses that productivity is a positive process that required drastic initial adjustments in hospitals unaccustomed to operating within the new fiscal accountability requirements. The process also can be participative once these mandates change hospitals into more responsible businesses.

Some hospitals reduced registered nurse (R.N.) positions along with other cutbacks, then realized that meeting the goals of improved productivity and cost containment are possible only when they have enough licensed professionals to conduct the work efficiently. R.N.s are licensed to meet all patient care needs and can perform several jobs simultaneously when they are delivering services. Because of their increased skill level, R.N.s have flexibility in the work for which

51

they are qualified. This allows the hospital to make the best use of its staff. R.N.s' salaries are higher than those of other nursing personnel, but the costs of getting the job done actually can be less with a higher percentage of professional nurses. Hospitals are wrestling with how many professional nurses to employ and how many nurse extenders are needed to achieve a cost-effective, productive effort.

A major reason that patients enter a hospital is to receive expert nursing care. The successful hospital of the future will recognize this fact and work to define essential nursing services within the constraints of limited resources. To do this, each nursing division must address the questions of staffing mix, cost, and consumer expectations. Moreover, creating a positive work climate for employees is essential to avoid high costs in absenteeism, staff turnover, and apathy related to low morale.

Each nursing division needs a staffing plan that addresses the institution's values, mission, philosophy, and practice standards. Information must be generated on patient demographics (such as diagnosis, acuity, and census), category and mix of staff, and costs for salaries and benefits with an eye to improving productivity. The creation of organizational values that place a high priority on cost control and the provision of efficient, quality nursing care are vital.

In compiling this plan, managers need to send a clear message to staff members about their concern for them and about the mandate to provide quality care within cost constraints. The acceptance of these values is important to the very survival of the hospital in generating future business. This era is one in which teamwork and a feeling of ownership by all employees in the operation of the hospital is vital to business success.

Nursing managers can build this sort of positive corporate culture by being receptive to new ideas, supporting a high quality of work life, and encouraging staff participation in operations-level activities in cost control, quality assurance, and research efforts to get the most impact from the dollar.

For example, staff nurses who are involved in a decentralized operation where they are participants need experience and input into the utilization review process, in knowing the pricing of supplies and services, in setting policies and priorities, and in monitoring productive efforts through the quality assurance program. Employee input is an important part of getting staff to feel a part of the process and the business.

In planning staffing for improved productivity, the American Nurses' Association (ANA) suggests four questions that must be addressed by the nursing division:

1. For how many patients can one professional nurse plan, supervise, and evaluate care given?
2. How many associate nurses can one professional direct, supervise, and evaluate?

3. How many patients will require the direct care of a professional nurse and how much nursing time is involved in this care?
4. How can the autonomy of nursing practice and acceptance of accountability for results be fostered?

The ANA believes that the primary problem in determining staffing is to develop and execute a rational program. While this program must satisfy the needs of third party payers, other health care providers, and employees, it also must ensure that nursing care is safe, responsive to patient needs, and scientifically and technologically sound.[2]

ORGANIZATIONAL CLIMATE

Some savings can be realized in hospitals that foster a cooperative spirit among their departments. In striving for improved productivity, this effort is especially vital in avoiding duplication of efforts. For example, it is not unusual for the education department to have the mechanisms for providing staff development in place, yet nurse managers bypass them to do their own program. Such duplication is the result of poor communication and politics that must be addressed if a system is to cut wasted efforts.

Hospitals no longer can be a collection of individual turfs, where battles consume endless hours. Instead, wise hospitals are recognizing that their departments all are a part of the big business. Moreover, without true cooperation aimed at improving the total organization, costs escalate and productivity suffers.

Data Base

Managers need to educate staff members as to the cost of providing care in their clinical areas. To identify personnel needs, the nursing staff data base should include the following elements:

- staff profile of education and experience
- recruitment, orientation, continuing education, and retention program
- efforts in cross-training
- salary and benefits
- staff turnover
- nursing care delivery system, both current and ideal
- staffing patterns
- scheduling patterns

- availability and qualifications of the casual labor pool
- range and average patient acuity levels on units
- average length of patient stay on each unit.

The resulting data base, used in tandem with the hospital census, budget, and patient classification reports, provides essential information about the nursing staff, especially with regard to staffing mix and capabilities to meet fluctuating patient loads at a realistic cost.[3]

Quality of Care

The trend for some health care providers has been to respond to cost containment by decreasing the quality of patient service. This approach is in direct conflict with the needs and demands of consumers. According to Thomas J. Peters and Robert H. Waterman in *In Search of Excellence*, "Winners almost always compete by delivering a product that supplies superior value to customers rather than one that costs less." With the continuing reality of prospective payment, nurses must work to keep the focus on delivering safe, effective, quality care. Such a focus requires continual evaluation of how productive efforts are aligned with the budget and the values of the organization.

Cost savings will come from "turned-on" teams of professionals committed to providing excellence in service delivery. According to Peters and Waterman, "The single best way to reduce costs is to increase quality, if you go about it in a systematic way." The concept of doing more for less needs to be countered with the fact that no one used to measure the benefit of having a larger staff. Will quality suffer? No, if a creative, participative approach to care delivery is adopted that charges all employees with the task of working smarter, not harder.[4]

MONITORING STAFFING AND PRODUCTIVITY

To integrate goals of productivity and decreased costs into the staffing plan, the hospital needs a staffing and scheduling policy and procedure, productivity index standards, patient classification and acuity system, budgeted unit staffing standards, census data, position control, periodic workload measurement, and a *Monitrend* report. Welborn Baptist Hospital, Evansville, Ind., has allowed the use of its forms as examples applicable to most institutions.

Staffing and Scheduling Policy and Procedure

In a decentralized staffing system, it is essential to have guidelines for coordinating schedules that are followed uniformly by all profit centers and nursing units. When no master system or standard abbreviation system is available, misunderstandings can occur between various units and the nursing office. Moreover, if the payroll clerk misconstrues symbols, errors in paychecks are more likely. (See Appendix 4-A for a policy and procedure on staffing and time schedules and Appendix 4-B for a sample of an actual four-week work schedule.)

Productivity Index Standards

In measuring productivity, administrators have had difficulty in changing staffing from a census-based to an acuity-based system. When a hospital elects to move into an acuity-based system, the nurse manager should refer to the established hospital workload index figures such as those in Exhibit 2–1 (in Chapter 2). The hospital then applies these figures to each specific nursing unit with an eye on possible modifications because of special circumstances of that unit.

One of the most difficult staffing problems to reconcile is the wild swings in census that occur on some units. When the census soars, help is inadequate; when it plummets, there is too much help. Yet by averaging these up and down periods, staffing can look excessive. Staffing is done by the average population and demographic characteristics on a unit. However, staff members feel angry and overwhelmed when these average figures do not reflect the short-staffed days. These often unpredictable changes in census can be better managed if staff members are cross-trained for several work areas and if floating is viewed as a positive process. Other alternatives include the use of a bigger on-call labor pool or more part-timers to cover predictable days in which workloads are heavy. Flexible hour schedules and voluntary unpaid days off are other options.

To stay productive, the unit manager needs to be aware of the workload index daily, weekly, and monthly. Graphing of this index can help in noting patterns and in recalling the actual staffing situation at a given time.

Managers can calculate budgeted patient care hours from examining workload figures and by considering the special needs of the unit, the occupancy rate, and the characteristics of the patients. The budgeted hours of direct and indirect nursing care should be expressed per 24 hours. The indirect hours of the head nurse and the ward secretary are included in the calculations so that individual hospital figures can be compared with internal and external reporting/data in *Monitrend*.

The head nurse then calculates the actual staffing situation by using the form in Exhibit 2–2 (Chapter 2) to gather daily staffing data and the form in Exhibit 2–1 to summarize the productivity index. The policy and procedures for this process are presented in Appendix 4–C.

Minimum Staffing

A certain level and mix of staffing must be maintained on each nursing unit to meet the standards of safe patient care, to relieve staff members for meals and breaks, and to cope with unexpected emergencies. Calculations for this minimum staffing are available in Appendix 4–D and the procedure for completing this form in Appendix 4–E.

Monitrend **Report**

To compare the level of productivity in an individual hospital with other subscribing institutions, the American Hospital Association's Administrative Services publishes a computerized monthly *Monitrend*. This report compares the nursing division's financial, utilization, and productivity performance with its own past record and with that of other hospitals.

Nursing managers should review these data with caution, however, since hospitals may vary in what they report and in how specific services compare. For example, the cardiac care unit may be filled predominantly with older, multiple problem patients, while the unit in the other hospital in the area attracts young, fit patients. Of course, the productivity index would be affected by the differences in care for these two types of patients, even though the admitting diagnosis appears to be the same. Other factors that could influence results might include the presence and use of couriers rather than nurses to transport patients or the geography of a poorly constructed unit that compromises efficiency.

In general, the *Monitrend* data are good and provide a confidential network of information so that hospitals may make comparisons on productivity in medical-surgical, pediatric, psychiatric, medical and surgical intensive care, neonatal intensive care, subacute units, and obstetrical and newborn units.[5]

RESOURCES

A number of factors make staffing productivity a challenge. First, nurses do not control the admission and discharge of patients or the census. Moreover, physicians may schedule for their own convenience, so that their vacations can cause a precipitous drop in census and their return a sudden peak. Such physician habits can be predicted if the doctors understand the monetary impact on the hospital and agree to inform nursing of personal plans in advance. However, because illness often is unexpected, even physicians lack total insight into workload peaks.

Second, emergencies, automobile accidents, and whether a given patient will have a simple or complex myocardial infarction cannot be planned. However, physicians who perform elective surgeries can inform the nursing division of expected schedules. Obstetricians can list expected delivery dates. While such collaboration is not perfect, it can assist nurse managers in anticipating census so they can plan staff vacations. Physicians who have latitude in scheduling in-house patients for a procedure, such as an incision and drainage of a wound, can get better care for them by informing the nurse manager of the anticipated surgical time.

Because many physicians have been unwilling to cooperate and instead set schedules for their own convenience, it behooves nursing to become creative in showing them how this increases costs. When physicians cooperate, they should receive enthusiastic appreciation and perhaps an incentive something like "frequent flyer points" for bringing in a certain volume, changing rounds times, decreasing extraneous orders, or operating in off-peak hours. These points can be applied to gifts or to a monetary reward, such as a percentage of the savings realized by the hospital.

Third, research has shown that professional nurses are needed to provide the patient education, emotional support, and discharge planning mandated by shortened lengths of stay. Solid preparation of patients also results in a lower incidence of return to the hospital for complications and problems related to a poorly handled stay. For this reason, hospitals will continue to hire more professional nurses.

STAFFING METHODS

The trend in hospitals is away from centralized nursing administration toward a decentralized model that emphasizes participation of staff and especially professional nurses. Hospitals shifting from centralized control need to know that nurses require education and practice in what is expected before they can be valuable participants in decentralized management. This should be done in advance of the changes. At the same time, supervisors and head nurses need to be prepared to relinquish some of their control so that the changes are not threatening to, or sabotaged by, insecure managers.

Centralization vs. Decentralization

Decentralization is the assignment of decisionmaking accountability away from the central office and close to the operational level—in nursing, to the patient care unit level. While maintaining responsibility for overall operations of their departments, nursing middle managers acquire the opportunity to focus on more general issues and concerns.[6]

An important element in decentralization is the elimination of multitiered levels of authority, with concurrent increases in the number of middle management positions. The role of the head nurse assumes increased importance as the manager of patient care and related activities. Each unit staff participates actively in the determination of patient care quality and administrative procedures and is held accountable for decisions made. When managed properly, this can improve staff morale and produce feelings of enhanced importance and an increased willingness to contribute.[7]

Exhibit 4–1 compares centralized and decentralized methods of staffing that a nursing department should review before deciding which method best relates to its organization, philosophy, and needs.

The Decentralization Experience

Centralized staffing addresses the needs of the nursing division as a whole but is less responsive to the momentary needs of widely diverse specialty units in a hospital. Central staffing methods lack the in-depth data on any one unit to send the right category of appropriately trained personnel to a unit with special patient needs. This lack of such detailed information can mean that one unit can be severely understaffed while another is overstaffed. Because of the slowness of communication, the lack of flexibility frustrates staff members and causes productivity figures to be out of line. The lack of accountability at the unit level makes it

---

Exhibit 4–1 Comparison of 2 Methods of Staffing

Decentralization	Centralization
1. Maximizes unit staffing	1. Manages staffing of nursing departments as a whole
2. Minimizes or eliminates a centralized float pool	2. Maximizes utilization of float pool
3. Gives head nurse accountability for the entire staffing budget	3. Gives head nurse accountability for staffing budget on the unit
4. Gives head nurse responsibility for 24-hour staffing and scheduling	4. Gives head nurse responsibility for 24-hour patient care
5. Provides for contingency staff backup from companion or sister units, per diem (on-call) staff, increased hours of part-time staff, or overtime when shortages occur	5. Permits reassigning float personnel when shortages occur
6. Assigns selection of all unit staff members to head nurse	6. Assigns core unit staff selection to the head nurse
7. Provides that head nurse keeps updated record of current staff skills	7. Centralizes updated record of skills required
8. Puts decision making at the unit level	8. Puts decision making in the central office
9. Promotes relationships between sister units	9. Does not emphasize relationships between like specialties
10. Commits staff to making method successful.	10. Depends more on central office management for success.

too easy to place calls to the central office to pad staffing, or to dip into the float pool, where nurses' training may or may not meet the specialized unit's needs.

When staffing is controlled at the unit level, knowledgeable nurses close to the point of action can meet needs swiftly. Moreover, staff members learn to accept accountability for keeping their unit staffed so that they do not experience unnecessary shortages.

For example, one staff decided that weekend staffing was a crisis because nurses called in sick when the scheduled workers seemed adequate. As a result, weekends were understaffed and were a nightmare for those on duty. To solve this problem they decided that those absent on a weekend or holiday would have to give up a similar day for which they had been scheduled to be off duty. This reduced weekend absenteeism, enabled the unit to operate more safely, and made weekend work a better experience.

As each unit assumes responsibility for covering its staffing needs, it is more likely to contact sister units to arrange cross-training, building in flexibility for times of census changes. When staff members know before floating which units they may work, they can learn about specialized medicines and treatments in advance. For example, one head nurse printed a list of the 30 most common drugs administered on her unit. This list was given to potential floats so they could become familiar with the drugs before working on the unit.

Decentralized operations still can use on-call personnel, but these persons are assigned to areas in which they have the most competency. Then they can be called as needs arise. However, criteria for minimum work shifts and staff development need to be developed so that these float nurses remain safe to administer care.

One hospital that moved into decentralized staffing reported the following positive results:

1. improved interpersonal relationships between units in problem solving
2. improved staff morale, as measured by a survey
3. increased accountability and autonomy in head nurses
4. improved, more effective communications
5. shorter response time to operational detail
6. decrease in overtime and personnel utilized
7. more time for central directors to be involved in strategic planning and programming, research, and change that has long-term divisional benefits
8. decrease in the numbers of management staff needed.

ALTERNATIVE WORK SCHEDULES

Assigning personnel can produce overstaffing that can lead to complacency and low motivation or to understaffing, which is dangerous and demoralizing to the staff. Both conditions can be avoided through the use of alternative work schedules.

Alternative work schedules are beneficial because they provide needed help during peak workloads and allow nurses more flexibility in balancing job requirements with professional goals and personal interests. Some of the more popular scheduling methods include:

- 10-hour shift
- 12-hour shift
- work two 12-hour weekend shifts and get paid for 40 hours (no benefits)
- combination of eight and 12 hours
- job sharing
- part-time work.

When staffing is decentralized, some staff members may work on a nontraditional schedule, the others on usual hours. One staff nurse may work eight hours that overlap two shifts. For example, on a surgical floor, nurses rotated the right to work from 0500 to 1300. This meant surgical charts had to be checked only once, instead of twice, by someone on each shift, and all surgical patients would be cared for by the same nurse. It left the rest of the staff free to organize work for the postoperative load. Finally, this nurse posted the assignment sheet for the oncoming shift so that work could start immediately. Thus, early morning confusion was minimized and the unit avoided the peaks in activity that exhaust nurses and make them feel overworked, even after a crisis is abated.

Because any pilot staffing programs involve only the unit at hand, adjustments in what is tried can be based on the needs of the staff. In the centralized model, changes need to be more uniform housewide, which can stifle creative ways of using staff members more effectively to meet the needs of each unit or profit center.

10-Hour Shifts

Ten-hour shifts can be established in several ways. The most popular is the 4-40 in which staff members work four days a week for ten hours a day, a 40-hour work week. Some hospitals utilize a 7-70 combination in which nurses work seven 10-hour days for a total of 70 hours within a two-week period. These staff members may be given full-time benefits based on hours worked at less than 80 hours per two-week pay period. In some cases, with the 7-70, nurses are on seven days and off seven days. This does provide for higher continuity of care because the same nurses care for patients for seven days in a row. There is potential for increased burnout, however. Research is needed in this area to identify whether the fatigue factor creates burnout and affects productivity and quality of care.

Advantages of the 10-hour schedules include:

- decreased absenteeism
- reduced overtime
- decreased utilization of temporary personnel from outside sources
- lower turnover.
- greater verbalized job satisfaction
- improved staff communications
- better intershift patient conferences
- more time for inservice courses and other education
- improved continuity of care.

Disadvantages of the 10-hour schedules are:

- potential for misuse of overlap time
- potential for increased costs if nurse-to-patient ratio remains the same as eight- or 12-hour schedules (resulting in higher staff hours per patient day).

12-Hour Shifts

Twelve-hour shifts can be operated in a variety of ways, depending on the system established. The methods of scheduling within a two-week pay period are:

- seven 12-hour shifts
- seven shifts on and seven shifts off
- three shifts a week at 72 hours per pay period.

The first two options permit full-time nursing personnel to work 84 hours per pay period, providing for four hours' overtime, which usually must be paid at a time and one-half rate. Advantages of the 12-hour shifts are similar to the ten-hour shifts:

- decreased absenteeism
- lower turnover
- greater retention of staff
- improved recruitment
- decreased utilization of temporary employees

- increased opportunities for satisfaction of personal needs and interests
- improved job satisfaction
- higher staff morale.

Variations have been developed on the 12-hour shift. One is used when nursing personnel normally work eight-hour shifts during the week but twelve-hour shifts on weekends. Another variation is to work two eight-hour and two 12-hour shifts in a week, or 80 hours per pay period. A third variation to avoid the overtime requirement consists of six 12-hour shifts and one eight-hour shift worked per pay period, totaling 80 hours every two weeks.

However, different work schedules for personnel on the same unit can be disruptive to the organization and continuity of nursing care. Therefore, it is wise to be cautious in initiating flexible schedules and to minimize the number of different schedules on a given unit to one or two variations.

Disadvantages of these other systems include:

- potential for fatigue
- increased costs when overtime is paid for 84 hours per pay period (although it can be argued that retention of staff and resulting lower costs can offset the expense)
- initial adjustment period of four to six months for staff members and families.

The Weekend Alternative

The weekend alternative started at Baylor University Medical Center in Dallas. It usually provides for two separate staffing systems on one patient care unit. There is 40-hour coverage Monday through Friday with one set of staff and 24-hour weekend coverage with a second set. The Monday-Friday staff generally works eight-hour shifts, the weekend staff two 12-hour shifts. Both receive full-time pay and full-time benefits.

Some nursing departments use the weekend alternative schedule to supplement weekend assignments on units where nurses who traditionally work eight-hour, five-day schedules are required to work some weekends in addition to Monday-Friday. Weekend alternative staff members usually are exclusively responsible for weekend coverage and provide reinforcement to the rest of the staff. This system often is used to provide every other weekend off where it would not otherwise be possible because of a high number of full-time nurses.

Advantages of the weekend alternative schedule include:

- assurance of sufficient weekend staff coverage for the delivery of quality care seven days a week

- increased satisfaction with work schedules that meet personal needs and interests (especially for full-time students and single parents who do not have their children on the weekend)
- reduced absenteeism
- lower turnover and resultant cost savings
- decreased use of temporary nursing personnel.

Disadvantages of the weekend alternative are:

- potential for higher costs for the weekend staff
- increased turnover after a period of time (this has been reported in hospitals that maintain this method for long periods)
- loss of continuity of care on weekends

Eight 12-Hour Shifts

This option is increasingly popular, offering a four-day work week. It gives full-time employees a combination of two eight-hour shifts and two 12-hour shifts a week for a total of 40 hours in a four-day week. To reduce fatigue, no more than two 12-hour shifts are worked together, with the longest stretch not exceeding four days (40 hours). The advantages are the same as for the 10- and 12-hour shifts.

Job Sharing

Job sharing is a voluntary arrangement in which two persons share one full-time position. In some hospitals, job sharing is an alternative that provides for more flexible scheduling and permits nurses to feel they have more control over their work. For example, two R.N.'s could share a 40-hour position, one working 16 hours, or two shifts a week, and the other 24 hours or three shifts a week. The R.N.s would share full-time benefits divided on the basis of their hours worked. By using this alternative and prorating benefits, they would receive greater benefits than part-time nurses and also would be able to split the required weekend and holiday work time.

There are obvious advantages, including:

- incentives for nurses who enjoy bedside nursing but are tired of weekend and holiday work
- reduction in the use of temporary and per diem nurses
- decreased sick time
- greater productivity

- coverage for each job sharer for illness or extra time off that might be needed
- reduced turnover
- support through mutual interest in the job and shared responsibility.

Disadvantages include:

- increased costs for fringe benefits, employee orientation, etc.
- higher social security benefit payments by the employer.

Part-Time Supplement to Workload

The use of part-time staff helps nurses who want more time off for personal reasons such as raising children or continuing their education. It also provides a cost-effective way to provide staff coverage seven days a week. Part-timers often are able and willing to work an extra shift to fill either unexpected or planned coverage needs. This additional flexibility provides trained staff backup. It is imperative in the future that full-time and part-time staff ratios be established on a permanent basis on each unit if staffing is to be cost effective and flexible. In most institutions, seven-day coverage means a ratio of one part-time person to one full-time person, or a 50 percent ratio.

There is a theory that part-time nurses destroy the continuity of care. This has proved not to be true in many cases as long as the part-timers are assigned regularly to cover full-time staff members.

Float Pools

No nurse is equally skilled to work every unit in the hospital. Staff expectations for float pools are not reasonable. Where a float pool exists there is the expectation that there is float staff just waiting for call-ins to meet unexpected personnel needs. There is a tendency to manage staff less well when there is a float pool since there is an urge to use resources whether or not they are needed. Float staff members usually cannot provide the experience level needed. Such a staff generally is designed to meet peak activity periods. Because float personnel move from one area to another and often do not work the same unit twice in a row, there is disruption in continuity of care.

Per Diem (On-Call) Staff

Rather than utilize personnel from outside agencies, many hospitals have established a supplemental staff or registry of their own. This staff fills unexpected and planned needs for coverage for benefit days, vacancies, and unexpected swings in census or acuity.

Advantages of a per diem staff include:

- flexibility
- increased ability to control and maintain current competency
- use of experienced staff members who want to work fewer hours yet continue seniority status
- greater experience than agency nurses
- ease in ensuring quality
- easier recordkeeping
- variety of incentives, e.g., higher hourly salary if no benefits
- cost effectiveness.

Guidelines must be established for use of per diem staff. For example, these may require that nurses:

1. work the equivalent of one weekend out of four if needed
2. not refuse to work three consecutive times when called
3. cross-train for two areas
4. be available two shifts
5. have the same orientation as other full-time and part-time staff
6. be assigned a supervisor
7. participate in an evaluation feedback conference at least once a year or every 600 hours worked
8. Benefits:
   a. vacation benefits prorated on basis of hours worked
   b. option of higher hourly salary in lieu of benefits
   c. time and one-half pay on holidays worked
   d. salary increase every 2,080 hours worked
   e. market factor salary increases awarded on a par with other staff members
   f. vacation scheduled according to current nursing department policy.

Minishifts/Short Shifts

Hospitals must provide coverage during the peak workload times to cover meal breaks, when admission schedules are the heaviest, when patients are returning from surgery, etc. Minishifts are regular work periods of less than eight hours. Many times such shortened work hours are convenient for part-time nurses who can be on the job while their children are in school or while their spouses are at home to watch them.

CROSS-TRAINING

The American Hospital Association broadly defines cross-training as the preparation of individuals to function effectively in more than one area of professional responsibility. From a nursing perspective, cross-training refers to the preparation of registered nurses for care delivery for more than one clinical specialty in an institution.

Hospitals and nursing departments are responding to the fight for survival by resorting to business thinking, business language, and business personnel who make high policy decisions. As a result, nurses are being pushed to be more efficient workers, to be more astute managers, and to make better use of time and resources.

As part of the hospital economy drive, many nurses are being asked to be generalists—to be ready with the skills and flexibility to fill in almost anywhere they are needed in the hospital. Institutions no longer can afford nurses who are skilled in just one area. Nurses often find this a little disconcerting since the new environment comes after a period in which they were encouraged to develop an area of expertise. However, as noted earlier, no nurse can function well in all areas. An obstetrician would not be expected to do neurosurgery, or vice versa, nor could an obstetrical nurse work in a neuro unit or vice versa, without current knowledge of skills and nursing practice in that other area. Nurses cannot be expected to maintain competency in specialties that are not similar.

Therefore, hospitals should establish companion or "sister" units—cross-training groups or tracts that are comparable and related. Examples of cross-training groups include:

- obstetrics: postpartum and labor and delivery, newborn nursery, pediatrics
- neonatal intensive care unit and pediatric intensive care
- intensive care unit, coronary care unit, emergency
- medical surgical preoperative and postoperative units, medical units
- mental health units, substance abuse units, eating disorders
- day surgery and recovery.

Advantages of cross-training include:

- increased ability to deal with changes in census and acuity
- greater availability of qualified nursing personnel

- improved capability of nurses
- heightened professional satisfaction
- lower absenteeism and less turnover
- increased stimulation from exposure to more than one unit.

Disadvantages of cross-training include:

- increased staff stress in having to adjust to working more than one area
- need by sister units for staff when census and/or acuity are high at the same time on both units
- reduced continuity of care because of nurses being assigned only temporarily when workload requires (difficult to measure).

The cross-training program should provide for the same orientation to the unit as is provided all new employees. Inservice education and staff development activities are shared between nursing and education departments. Skill checklists for all specialty orientations should be completed, kept available for reference, and filed according to the hospital procedure.

PLANNING FOR STAFFING

Health care institutions have lost their ability to predict census. A comparison of previous months for the last three years may show that the only consistent factor is continual change, e.g., census declines, yet workload per patient increases. Predicting what is going to be happening in the next month or even days is extremely difficult, if not impossible. With professional review organizations, utilization review, and prior approval activities, even daily admissions cannot be predicted as they once were. What can be done? Hospitals can look at:

1. occupancy trends by day of the week
2. patient classification and acuity system—the most important data now available
3. the essential elements of managing staff
4. staff distribution by shift (the most common is days 55 percent, evenings 30 percent, nights 15 percent), when tests are done, when workload is the highest, etc.

CUTBACK PRIORITIES

Nursing often is the first target in a cost-reduction program. Nursing managers must support efficient, productive utilization of resources; analyze potential changes in staffing levels and staff mix; assess continuing education; and evaluate compensation in light of its impact on the quality of care. They then must find ways to provide patients with the best quality of care at the least possible cost. Effective use of nursing resources is important to help keep Medicare costs below the diagnosis related group (DRG) prices. It is important that hospitals address issues involving the quality of work life and not permit across-the-board cutbacks.

The process of reducing nurse staffing is not easy. Careful evaluation of the needed mix and number of persons before initiating cutbacks is imperative. Many hospitals have experienced rapid declines in census but higher acuity since the start of the prospective payment system (PPS). Adjusting staffing in such times is much different from accommodating a slow downward trend in patient census through attrition. It also is far more painful.

Approaches such as flexible scheduling, increasing part-time staffing ratios, etc., will work over time but may not meet the need when greater cost reduction is necessary.

As quality of care is reduced, a hospital's reputation suffers. In today's consumer-oriented society, a hospital cannot afford to provide mediocre nursing care so it faces the dichotomy of cutting costs while maintaining quality. Staff morale and productivity always are affected when reductions are drastic. Therefore, managers must make every effort to provide fair and equitable treatment and be responsive to staff needs.

Again, reduction of the number of professional nurses must be considered carefully. An inappropriate level of nonprofessionals, or too many professionals when nonprofessionals can meet the need, can reduce quality and flexibility to adjust to census/activity swings.

When cutbacks must be made, it is important that employees be informed as soon as possible of the hospital's financial situation to help them identify more closely with what is going on. A communication strategy should be established. Hospitals that know that cutbacks are imminent should plan employee education, including the following, beginning with first-line management. They should:

- inform staff as to what is happening at the facility and in the health care industry in general
- update employees regularly as to their status
- explain how staffing levels are established and identify staffing goals, and other data such as staff hours/patient days and projected occupancy levels
- define and explain the patient acuity and classification system
- ensure that nurse/patient ratios are understood
- post schedules and budgeted staffing on units
- inform employees as to expected standards of performance

- reinforce (or develop) criteria and weight values for performance appraisal
- outline what the hospital is doing to cut costs and ask employees for their input.

Important areas to be evaluated in the hospital as a whole when beginning a staff cost-reduction program include the following:

- making clear the mission and philosophy of the hospital and of nursing
- refreshing department staffs as to the goals of the institution
- ensuring the consistent, appropriate use of discipline in removing "dead wood" from the staff and in correcting personnel problems
- identifying productivity and staffing levels
- making sure human resource management data are current and available, e.g., turnover reports by category/department, etc.
- analyzing medical staff relationships and communications
- prioritizing any facility improvements and changes and evaluating them with staff input
- analyzing standards of performance and care for each department
- decreasing or eliminating overtime and increasing part-time staffing
- ensuring that the mix of professionals is at desired levels before any reductions
- developing a layoff policy and procedure and guidelines for management actions.

Hospital administration must never decrease staff benefits. Long-term employees will take this personally and will never forget.

EXPERIENCE OF A TYPICAL HOSPITAL

One of the best ways to understand such a situation is to examine in detail the experience of a typical hospital, in this case Welborn Baptist Hospital, a 491-bed facility in Evansville, Ind., one of three providing health care to a 120-mile region in Southern Indiana, Southern Illinois, and Western Kentucky.

Adjacent to the hospital is a physician's office complex, Welborn Clinic. Its physicians are primarily specialists covering nearly all areas of medical practice, plus some in family practice. The clinic-based staff provides the majority of medical staff membership for the hospital.

In the early 1980s, Welborn Clinic physicians began participation in a health maintenance organization (HMO). The emphasis on preventive medicine and outpatient service gradually began to affect the hospital's census. Staff levels were adjusted with attrition and cost-control measures such as minimal hiring, elimination of overtime, increased hours, monitoring of expenses, prioritizing of needs, etc. As census in the other hospitals in the area was not affected, Welborn administration and staff members were concerned about adjusting to their unique situation.

Over the next few years, the mix of patients in specialties varied greatly from day to day and month to month. Historical data no longer could be used to project census. Wide swings and peaks and valleys in both census and acuity created serious problems in managing staffing and scheduling. The high ratio of full-time staff and low numbers of part-time staff made it difficult to adjust to the variations.

Following implementation of the prospective payment systems, census reductions accelerated. It became apparent that further action had to be taken, so layoffs were considered. It was anticipated that the census and staffing levels would stabilize soon. Evaluation of staffing levels by department presented the following considerations:

- The existing size of staff was needed at peak census/workload times but not when valleys developed.

- Layoffs would present problems relating to recall and potential loss of trained staff members who were projected to be needed after the census stabilized.

- The anticipated mix of staff meant certain categories of personnel would be affected more than others, and community responses would be negative if this occurred.

- Hospital administration felt employees generally were supportive and willing to participate in a program that would secure the jobs of most of them, although some sacrifices might be needed.

- Administration determined that the reduction of staff varied at times from 5 to 20 percent of the total work force.

- The duration of the situation was not predictable, although it was not doubted that census would decline further.

The staff was divided. Certain departments, especially those that might be least affected (or not affected at all) recommended layoffs. Departments most likely to be hit supported either across-the-board cuts or elimination of certain nonprofessional categories of personnel, depending on the mix of staff and technology required.

By this time, the other area hospitals also were experiencing the effects of PPS and other constraints and began layoffs. The Welborn staff frequently expressed its feelings of insecurity. Hospital administration decided against layoffs and initiated a voluntary and mandatory staff reduction program based on productivity, staff hours/patient day, and patient acuity standards.

The flex program provided management with a tool to adapt staffing levels based on need on a shift-by-shift basis. Management on each unit/department was responsible for managing the program, using approved standards and the management guidelines to administer the program (see Appendix 4-F).

In addition to the flex program, a decision was made to permit current full-time employees to reduce hours to 64 or 72 per pay period with prorated full-time benefits based on hours worked. This reduction of hours was permitted on a permanent or a temporary basis. It also was decided to establish permanent full-time/part-time ratios upon which future staffing and new hires would be based. New hires also would be made on a part-time basis or on full time at 64 or 72 hours per pay period until equitable part-time or full-time staff ratios were achieved. This change proved to be positive as many staff nurses wanted to reduce hours but needed the full-time benefits. They seemed to find the extra day or two off a help since they felt better able to balance their personal lives and careers.

One year later, the amount of flex time had diminished. The majority of flex time was and had been voluntary, not management induced. Staff members were appreciative their jobs were secure and felt they had participated in maintaining a financially stable environment while providing quality care. Flex time overall was diminished greatly, and the ability to adjust to census and acuity variations had been established. Turnover during this period was very low in all hospital departments.

Management also reduced staff through evaluation and downsizing of positions with attrition, some reorganization, and either taking a temporary salary reduction or going on flex time.

SUMMARY

Attaining goals of improved productivity, cost containment, quality patient care, and job satisfaction among staff members requires nurse managers to assess all possibilities for utilizing staff wisely. The total staffing program needs to be proactive, responsive to census fluctuations, and defensible as a systematic effort. Quantifying staffing for direct patient care is probably the easiest area in hospital nursing to express numerically.

Since the nursing staff comprises a large portion of the hospital budget, getting a handle on controlling labor costs and staff utilization is vital to organizational viability. This chapter has reviewed the use of a number of forms that can make the decentralized staffing program more systematic, and discussed critical factors that are included in any well-formulated plan designed to improve productivity within reasonable cost constraints.

NOTES

1. American Hospital Association, *Managing Under Medicare Prospective Pricing* (Chicago: AHA Publishing, Inc., 1983).
2. American Nurses' Association, *Nursing Staff Requirements for Inpatient Health Care Services* (Kansas City, Mo.: American Nurses' Associaton, Inc., 1977), 3.
3. American Hospital Association, *Strategies: Flexible Scheduling* (Chicago: AHA Publishing, Inc., 1985), 1-3.
4. Thomas J. Peters and Robert H. Waterman, *In Search of Excellence* (New York: Harper & Row, Publishers, Inc., 1982).
5. American Hospital Association, *Monitrend Data Analysis Manual* (Chicago: AHA Publishing, Inc., 1983).
6. American Hospital Association, *Strategies: Nurse Involvement in Decision Making and Policy Development,* (Chicago: AHA Publishing, Inc., 1985), 3–4.
7. Ibid., 3.

BIBLIOGRAPHY

American Hospital Association. *Managing Under Medicare Prospective Pricing*. Chicago: AHA Publishing, Inc., 1983.

American Nurses' Association. *Nursing Staff Requirements for Inpatient Health Care Services*. Kansas City, Mo.: American Nurses' Association, Inc., 1977.

Brandon, Jeffrey A. "TEFRA: Impact on Hospitals, Nurses, Physicians, and Patients," *The Health Care Supervisor* (April 1985).

Deines, Elaine. *Staffing for DRG's: A Unit-Specific Approach for Nurse Managers*. Chapel Hill, N.C.: W.L. Ganong Co., 1983.

Hanson, Robert L. *Management Systems for Nursing Service Staffing*. Rockville, Md.: Aspen Publishers, Inc., 1983.

Harrell, Joanne S., and Frauman, Annette C. "Prospective Payment Calls for Boosting Productivity." *Nursing and Health Care* (December 1985).

Kirk, Roey. *Nursing Management Tools*. Boston: Little, Brown & Co., 1983.

Naisbitt, John. *Megatrends*. New York: Warner Books, Inc., 1982.

Peters, Thomas J., and Waterman, Robert H. *In Search of Excellence*. New York: Harper & Row, Publishers, Inc., 1982.

ACTION CHECKLIST

1. Staff Mix:
   a. What is the current staff mix?
   b. What is the staff mix goal?
   c. Have nurse managers discussed their goals with administration?
   d. Do they need to justify goals to administration?
   e. How long will it take nurse managers to achieve the goal?
   f. Have they projected cost, FTE, and productivity standard changes as staff mix is achieved?

2. Communications:
   a. How good are interdepartmental, medical staff, and interunit relationships? What duplicated effort can be omitted?
   b. Do nurse managers have a written plan for orientation for each specialty, with clear objectives and expectations?
   c. Are staff members aware of:
      1) mission, philosophy, and goals of the hospital and of the nursing department
      2) current happenings in the health care industry and hospital that have an impact on them
      3) current budget
      4) current census
      5) current acuity
      6) expected standards of performance
      7) current cost containment needs/efforts

3. Staffing and Scheduling:
   a. Do nurse managers have a written staffing plan?
   b. Do they have flexibility of scheduling?
   c. What should their part-time/full-time ratio be?
   d. What are current benefits costing in paid hours/patient day and overall in comparison to worked hours?
   e. Is there a workable system for classifying patients according to acuity?
   f. Are data available to do adequate monitoring and evaluation of staff?
   g. Are nurse managers knowledgeable as to staffing and scheduling policy and procedure? Do they follow it?

4. Personnel Policies:
   a. Are policies current regarding layoff, disciplinary action process, etc.?
   b. Are controls and standards for productivity monitored consistently throughout the hospital?

Appendix 4–A

Staffing and Time Schedules: Policies and Procedures

Section: NURSING DIVISION—GENERAL

Subject: Staffing and Time Schedules

I. Policy:
 A. Staffing:
  1. Patient care units are staffed 24 hours a day, seven days a week. Staffing is based on the census, acuity of the patient, and the staffing pattern of the unit. Staffing patterns shall be in compliance with federal, state, and local laws and regulations.
  2. Personnel in all areas must be assigned in a manner that minimizes the risk of cross-infections and accidental contamination.
  3. The staffing patterns shall provide for sufficient nursing personnel and for adequate supervision by qualified registered nurses. LPN's, nursing assistants, other nursing personnel, and ancillary personnel must be supervised by a registered nurse.
  4. Nursing personnel must reflect consideration of the nursing goals, of standards of nursing practice, and of characteristics of patient needs.
  5. Records and reports of both staffing patterns and patient needs should be maintained in the Nursing Administration Office. These reports should identify the staffing needs of each nursing care unit and reflect the daily staffing pattern.
  6. A registered nurse must plan, supervise, and evaluate the nursing care of each patient.
  7. All nursing staff will be expected to work on any assigned nursing unit. Every attempt will be made to keep the employee on his/her assigned unit, although this may not always be possible. Also, every attempt will be made to keep the assignment within his/her capabilities. Refusal to accept assignment will result in disciplinary action.

Note: Appendixes in this chapter are used with permission of Welborn Baptist Hospital, Evansville, Ind.

8. Nursing personnel temporarily assigned to a different specialty should not be assigned charge responsibility. The exception would be within the Medical/Surgical Units.
9. In the event of the need to change staffing requirements due to census, employee illness, terminations, or other emergency situations, the individual employee to be reassigned will be contacted as far in advance as possible.
10. Student nurses may be employed as per diem staff who work within unit secretary or nurse assistant job descriptions to provide minimum daily staffing on each unit.
11. Per Diem Staff Registry:
    a. May be taken off the registry if they do not work 20 percent of time requested.
    b. May be asked to cover vacation time, work some weekend shifts and some holidays.
    c. May be hired for a permanent shift or any shift.
    d. May be asked to attend two weeks' orientation in the Education Department. Additional orientation will be individualized and based on level of experience.
    e. May be asked to attend required inservices.
    f. May choose the area of nursing he/she would prefer to work.
    g. Will be assigned to work within the budgeted daily staffing whenever staff coverage is needed for vacancies, vacations, etc.
    h. Should provide information to supervision regarding the days and hours when available to work two weeks in advance of schedule's being posted.

II. Responsibility
    A. Management:
       Directors of Nursing, Assistant Directors of Nursing, Head Nurses, and Charge Nurses are responsible for scheduling and monitoring of overtime and budgeted hours. The Head Nurse is responsible for the 24-hour unit time schedule and assisting with providing 24-hour unit coverage.
    B. Employee:
       1. Request eligible benefit days within the established allowable time period.
       2. Keep track of benefit time both taken and not taken. Do not depend on Head Nurse or Director of Nursing to do this.
       3. Always check time sheet as soon as posted. Watch days off carefully for changes in routine days off, possible errors, etc.
       4. Notify Head Nurse of any benefit time or any time change in which the Head Nurse was not involved.
       5. Code time card to appropriate department when floating to another unit.

6. Never carry time card away from time clock unless Head Nurse signature is necessary.
7. Mark time schedule on unit when Nursing Service Office calls to units reporting that an employee will not be on duty.
8. Call unit to verify flex management (FM) days scheduled in advance.
9. Assigned Charge Nurse will mark "C" on time card in Distribution Code column.
10. Charge Nurse is to mark on unit time schedule when an employee is floated to another unit.
11. Employees are not to "punch in" earlier than approximately five minutes before their scheduled work periods begin, and are to "punch out" promptly at the end of their scheduled work periods. Employees are not to clock out prior to completion of assigned work. If unable to complete work prior to scheduled end of shift, the employee must obtain supervisory approval to complete assigned work.

III. Procedure:
  A. Staffing:
    1. General Facts, Sister Units:
       a. Staff Coverage—sharing between units, staff may be required to float to any nursing unit according to capability. If at all possible, staff will be requested to work only in sister units to provide minimum staffing needs whenever absenteeism or vacancies require it or to meet the acuity requirements of the unit. Staff will be utilized elsewhere only when unit census is low or staffing ratio is higher than normal. Staff will not be required to teamlead or be in charge outside area of specialty unless oriented and capable. Sister units are:
          • NICU, NBN, OB, Pediatrics, PICU, BC
          • Open MH, Closed MH, EDS, Adolescent Substance Abuse, Adult Substance Abuse
          • ICU, CCU, Emergency, RR, DSU
          • 1400, 1500, 1600, B-2, C-2, G-4, Rehab
       b. In Critical Care Units, staffing should be based on the following criteria:

Classification System	Nurse:Patient Ratio
Level IV	1:1 or 2:1
Level III	1:2
Level II	1:3

Patient load may be adjusted in Levels III or IV to accommodate flexible schedules, overlap time, and workload.

2. Procedural Steps for Under and Over Staffing:
   a. If, according to nurse:patient ratio, patient acuity, and minimum staffing, additional help is needed, the charge nurse:
      1) Should call Director of Nursing/Assistant Director of Nursing on duty for guidance.
      2) May carry out the following steps in coordination with the Director of Nursing/Assistant Director of Nursing:
         a) Call sister units to see if additional personnel are available to work.
         b) If no personnel available in sister units, call the Director of Nursing/Assistant Director of Nursing on duty to see if there is a nurse available elsewhere.
         c) If no assistance available at this point, obtain permission to call in staff utilizing per diem registry and part-time nursing staff. If no part-time or per diem staff are available, contact personnel scheduled to work next shift to come in early or call off-duty personnel until assistance is obtained. It is important that increased hours and overtime be used to provide peak time and minimum staffing standards only. No staffing may be scheduled above the budgeted basic daily staffing unless approval of the Director of Nursing/Assistant Director of Nursing is obtained.
         d) Ensure all personnel staffing changes are made and initialed in the Nursing Office and unit schedules.
   b. If, according to basic staffing ratio, the unit is overstaffed, the charge nurse:
      1) Should call the Director of Nursing/Assistant Director of Nursing on duty for guidance.
      2) May carry out the following steps in coordination with Director of Nursing/Assistant Director of Nursing:
         a) Call sister units to see if assistance is needed. If help is needed, send appropriate person to that area.
         b) If sister units do not need assistance, notify the Director of Nursing/Assistant Director of Nursing on duty.
         c) Initiate flex time procedure.
   c. If census/acuity of the requesting unit changes after assignments are made, the minimum of 4 hours' pay will be charged to the requesting unit.
   d. The assignment of staff to another unit is final by three (3) hours prior to the beginning of the shift. Staff may not be pulled back to the home unit unless negotiated agreeably between the two units.

B. Time Schedules:
   1. General Facts:
      a. Time schedules provide an equal and consistent distribution of personnel based on the census and staffing pattern of the unit.
      b. Time schedules are posted 4 weeks at a time. The schedules are posted no later than the second Monday of the current schedule.
      c. Special requests for days off should be communicated to the Head Nurse in writing. Whenever possible, every attempt will be made to honor the request. Should the request not be honored, the Head Nurse will communicate this to the employee along with the reason that the request cannot be honored. Should two people request time off at the same time, the employee's length of service will be given consideration as stated in the *Employee Handbook*.
      d. There should be two consecutive working days between scheduled days off.
      e. Each nursing unit will be scheduled with every other weekend off *when staffing ratios allow this to be done*. The schedule for each shift on each unit will be decided by the majority of the employees with approval of Nursing Administration. Every effort will be made to allow employees who desire a 6-2 rotation or every third weekend off to remain on this schedule.
      f. Regular part-time employees are scheduled to work every other weekend and every other holiday unless staffing need permits other scheduling.
         Absence on a weekend or holiday:
         1) If an employee is absent on an assigned weekend day/holiday, that employee may be scheduled to work an additional weekend day/holiday at the discretion of the Head Nurse as the needs occur.
         2) The time schedule will be marked "pay back" on the proper days.
      g. Personnel may be requested to work another shift to provide adequate coverage.
      h. Holidays: Holidays will be scheduled at the discretion of the Head Nurse. Requests for days off may be submitted in writing, prior to the posting of the four-week time schedule. Every effort to honor the request will be made. Time and one-half will be paid to all employees working the holiday—see *Employee Handbook*.
      i. Once the time schedule has been posted, there should be no time changes unless two people of the same category agree to change. It is up to the person desiring to change to find someone agreeable to change. If this is agreeable to both parties and the Head Nurse,

with approval of the Head Nurse or her delegate, the Head Nurse will make the appropriate time schedule changes on both unit and Nursing Office sheets and initial it.

NOTE: If the time change alters the staffing pattern, the Director of Nursing should be notified.

j. Vacations: (part-time; full-time employees)

1) Vacations will be scheduled a minimum of one week and a maximum of two weeks per request throughout the year January to January. Each Head Nurse will calculate the number of employees who will be scheduled for vacation per week throughout the 12-month period.

2) Each Head Nurse will list employees per length of service at Welborn Baptist Hospital.

On October 1 yearly, the Head Nurse will advise staff members that she will start the vacation scheduling the middle of October according to length of service. They must know at that time what their choices are (first, second, third, etc). The first two weeks of requests will be scheduled at that time. The second two weeks' requests will be scheduled after all first requests made. A master schedule will be plotted. The employee has to know his/her request when the Head Nurse asks or forfeit her/his turn. The employee's first and second choices will be granted before the third and fourth.

3) Five vacation days may be held by the employee to be used at random throughout the year. Request for these days must be submitted at least six weeks prior to requested time off. These requests will *not* take priority over vacations previously scheduled regardless of seniority.

4) Vacation requests must include the entire desired time off work, not just vacation days (flex time, holidays, etc.). If extra weekends are involved, the employee must trade or pay back a weekend that normally would have been worked.

5) Conflicts of vacations caused by employee transfers from unit to unit, etc., after scheduling has been done will be handled per Hospital policy.

6) Accrued vacation is paid out on termination. It is not pre-scheduled prior to eligibility date.

k. The Director of Nursing and the Evening/Night Assistant Directors of Nursing will schedule and assign the float nursing personnel.

l. Employees not able to work on a scheduled day are required *personally* to notify the Nursing Office by at least one hour prior to the beginning of the scheduled shift, or at an earlier time if at all possible to ensure adequate time to adjust staffing needs.

The secretary will transfer the phone call to the Head Nurse of the unit. The Head Nurse will determine if the call-in is justified and notify the Nursing Office of the call-in:

1) Employee's name.
2) Shift.
3) Nature of illness/absence.
4) Next scheduled day to work.
5) Instructions to notify daily of illness/absence.

If employee calls unit,the Head Nurse will notify the Nursing Office secretary. The secretary will notify the Director of Nursing.

In the absence of the Head Nurse, the secretary will transfer the caller to the appropriate Director of Nursing or Assistant Director of Nursing, who in turn will follow the same procedure. If no one is in the office to take the call-in, the employee *must* have the Director of Nursing/Assistant Director of Nursing paged. Failure of the employee to follow these steps could result in disciplinary action. If the employee calls in after the beginning of the shift, it could result in disciplinary action.

   m. Scheduling shall not exceed approved budgeted daily staffing unless justified by higher-than-average acuity with full occupancy and with approval of Director of Nursing.

2. Maintenance of Time Schedules:
   a. *All time changes must be made on both copies (Nursing Office and Unit) and initialed by the person making the changes.*
   b. Time changes should only be done by Directors of Nursing, Assistant Directors of Nursing, Head Nurses, Assistant Head Nurses, Charge Nurses, and Nursing Office Secretaries. (A limited number of employees should have access to the time schedule book.)
   c. Do not *call* time changes to N.O. unless absolutely necessary—they should be made in person.
   d. All changes should follow the same legend as the completion policy.
   e. When changes are made, be sure that the count number at the bottom of the category is also corrected.
   f. If two (2) units are involved with time changes, the unit asking for the change is responsible for documentation in all places.

3. Procedural Steps:
   a. Obtain ''Schedule of Hours—Nursing Department'' from Print Shop.

b. Send new time schedules to Nursing Office by the first week of the current time schedule.
c. Send original to Directors; a copy is returned to the Head Nurse for posting on units.

Complete form as follows:
   1) Enter name of unit, dates, and staff members on sheet in pen (all other entries are in pencil).
   2) Enter first and last name of employee, title, and agreed hours normally worked.

Example: Jane Doe, R.N. $\underline{\dfrac{80}{10}}$

             Ann Smith, N.A. $\dfrac{64}{8}$

   3) Fill in each square under date column using the following legend:
      a) Leave square blank if employee is on duty working the normal shift without any variations.
      b) D = day off
         S = sick
         V'85 = Vacation/Year
         B'85 = Birthday/Year
         N'85 = New Year/Year
         M'85 = Memorial/Year
         I'85 = Independence/Year
         L'85 = Labor/Year
         T'85 = Thanksgiving/Year
         C'85 = Christmas/Year
         PH#1'85 = Personal Holiday/Year
         PH#2'85 = Personal Holiday/Year
         JD = Jury Duty
         IS = Inservice (In-House)
         MC = Meeting/Conference
         LOA = Leave of Absence
         ML = Military Leave
         P = Personal Day
         FL = Funeral Leave
         FM = Flex Management
         FE = Flex Employee
         TP = Termination Pay
   4) Separate each category of staff by at least one blank line or a heavy marked line.

5) Write in square below each category in date column if another employee, other than names listed in left column, will be working that day (floats, staff from other shifts or units, etc.).

6) Total the staffing for each day and indicate number in square near bottom of sheet.

7) Indicate below that number if that category is " + " or " − " that day (if correctly staffed, leave blank).

8) If an employee is working a weekend day to make up for a weekend day missed, indicate "Pay Back" in the square.

9) If an employee is working hours that are not the normal working hours for that shift, write in time schedule to work. Example:

| 0545 |
| to |
| 1815 |

10) If several occurrences are scheduled in one day, clearly indicate all of them in the square. Example:

| Work 7 – 12 |
| & |
| 3H* Vac '85 |

| 2H FE |
| & |
| 6H PH'85 |

11) Indicate charge nurse by a small

| c |

in the right upper corner of the square (do not use "c" if Assistant Head Nurse or Head Nurse is the Charge Nurse).

12) Indicate that certain days are requested off by the employee with

| R |

in the right upper corner of square.

13) Indicate a part-time employee's hours by using all of the above data. Blank squares mean that she/he is on duty that day.

---

*H = hours.

14) Keep employees that are on LOA in their category section on the time sheet. Be sure the sick days and benefit days are used and marked appropriately before LOA actually begins.
15) Mark

> orient

in square when an employee is on nursing's budget for orientation and

> Ed.
> Orient

in square when at education department for orientation.

C. Overtime:
1. Increased part-time hours should be explored prior to scheduling overtime of full-time personnel at time and one-half.
2. All overtime requires the approval of the Director or Assistant Director of Nursing prior to scheduling the overtime. When overtime is needed, it shall be scheduled to cover peak work times rather than overlap at low staffed times.
3. Overtime, increased part-time hours, and per diem staff are not to be used to cover absenteeism routinely.
4. Every attempt should be made to increase part-time hours or use per diem personnel prior to scheduling overtime on a time and one-half basis.
5. If an employee anticipates the need for working overtime, that employee is to:
   a. Inform the Head Nurse/Charge Nurse.
   b. List on unit's overtime sheet the date, amount of overtime, justification, and sign.
   c. The Head Nurse (or designee) at the end of each week will send overtime sheets to the Director of Nursing, who will forward to the Nursing Office timekeeping secretary.
6. Failure to obtain approval of management for working overtime will necessitate disciplinary measures:
   a. Oral counseling after failing to have a written overtime request (two incidents).
   b. First written warning (three incidents).
   c. Second written warning (four incidents).
   d. Suspension, after second written warning (five incidents).
   e. Termination (six incidents).

7. *Employees are not to work past the time clocked out or written on the time card.*

8. Whenever possible, employees may eliminate overtime by leaving early or coming in late with approval of the Head Nurse/Nursing Administration.

D. Absenteeism:

1. It is important that all employees report to work as scheduled regardless of weather conditions or other personal difficulties.

2. Employees who are unable to report for duty as scheduled will not be paid for lost work time, unless:

   a. The employee requests a paid Personal Day, Holiday, or Vacation, *and;*

   b. The supervisor is able to approve the employee's request. *Important Notice:* It may not be possible for the supervisor to approve such short notice requests for benefit payments due to circumstances of employee absenteeism, heavy work schedules, or other reasons specific to the employee's department or work unit.

3. Department management may elect to reschedule employees to ensure that necessary work is performed or allow employees to make up work in circumstances where they can be productively engaged to support department needs. Rescheduled work should be permitted only where it serves interest beneficial to the Hospital.

4. Nursing will follow the Hospital Policy regarding disciplinary action on absenteeism.

E. Flex Time:

1. General facts:

   a. Flexible schedules are encouraged with approval of nursing and hospital administration. Schedules must be developed based on workload, acuity of patients, staff mix, and budgetary constraints.

   b. Staff will be asked to take time off when the census/acuity/staffing standards support the need for reduction of staff on a shift-by-shift basis.

   c. Records will be kept on each nursing unit documenting rotation of reduction of time, listing employees' names, dates of reduction, and number of hours reduced.

   d. Scheduled work time will not be reduced more than an average of 20 percent of agreed hours within a pay period unless employee agrees to or desires the reduction. It may be necessary to look at the work hours over a period of six to eight weeks due to rise and fall of workload to achieve this average. Supervisors are asked to avoid reducing work hours by more than 10 percent whenever possible. Reduction of staff greater than 10 percent must have approval or be on direction of the Director/Assistant Director of Nursing. Reduction of hours by employees who have temporarily reduced agreed hours will count as flex time.

e. When employees are requested to reduce hours, they will be selected on a rotating basis beginning with least length of service by category of personnel. If an employee is not on duty when rotation occurs, that employee will be selected on next occasion of need.

2. Procedural Steps:

a. On Shift: the Head Nurse/Charge Nurse will:

1) Consult with Director/Assistant Director of Nursing regarding staffing status.

2) Ask for volunteers to leave early on "FE" day.

3) If not volunteers, employees will be chosen to leave early on a rotating basis according to the procedure and records kept on each nursing unit on an "FM" day (management-initiated work scheduled adjustment).

4) Mark time schedule "FM" or "FE" on the nursing unit and in the Nursing Office.

b. Prior to Shift, the Head Nurse/Charge Nurse will:

1) Consult with Director/Assistant Director of Nursing regarding staffing status.

2) Notify nursing staff members making selection on a rotating basis according to the procedure and records kept on each nursing unit.

3) Mark time schedule "FE" or "FM" on the unit and in the Nursing Office.

Note: See Policies and Procedures: "Assignment of Nursing Care"
"Patient Classification System"
"Organization of Nursing Department"

See "Employee Handbook"

Appendix 4-B
Example of Four-Week Work Schedule

WELBORN BAPTIST HOSPITAL
SCHEDULE OF HOURS—NURSING DEPARTMENT

UNIT: _____
FROM: _____ to _____
        (date)   (date)

S	M	T	W	T	F	S	S	M	T	W	T	F	S	S	M	T	W	T	F	S	S	M	T	W	T	F	S

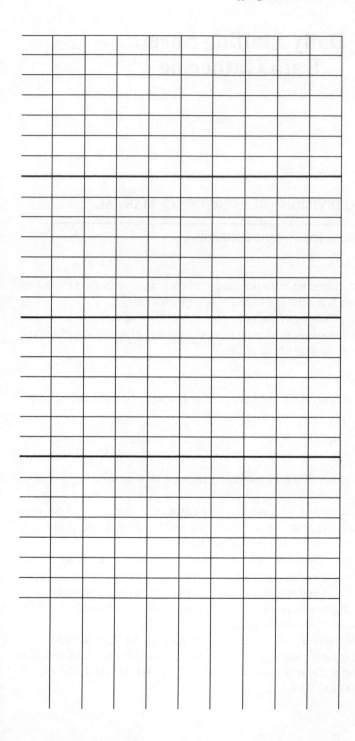

Appendix 4-C

Daily Staffing Sheet: Data Gathering

Subject: Daily Staffing Sheet—Data Gathering

I. Purpose:
   A. To provide adequate statistics and reference as to exactly how much nursing staff is available as needed at a given time.
   B. To provide productivity data for management services.
   C. To provide assistance to nursing administration in planning staffing at the beginning of the eight-hour shifts.

II. Responsibility:
   Directors of Nursing, Assistant Directors of Nursing, Nursing Office secretaries.

III. Procedure:
   A. General Facts:
      1. The staffing data for a particular shift are to be entered by the end of that shift.
      2. The Director of Nursing/Assistant Director of Nursing who does the assignments at the beginning of the shift will fill in the skill level, productive staff, and productive hours.
      3. Changes/completion of staffing are made by the supervisor of the area by the end of the shift.
      4. Subtract or add any increments of time greater than one hour.
      5. Head Nurses may check the computations, if desired, for their respective units by 0900 on the following day.
      6. Management Services will obtain a copy of the sheet at 0930.
      7. Nursing Office secretaries are to enter the patient census on each unit and the acuity levels on PICU, ICU, CCU, NICU, TCU, and OHRR at 1400 and 2200.

8. The Assistant Directors of Nursing are to enter the patient census on each unit and the acuity levels on PICU, ICU, CCU, NICU, TCU, and OHRR at 0600.

9. When calling the units for census, request the number of persons in each skill for the following units:

OB Post Partum
OB Labor/Delivery   } at end of each eight-hour shift

CCU
Telemetry   } at end of each 12-hour shift

10. Definitions of each column of daily staffing sheet.

   a. Unit: The nursing unit/area.

   b. Skill levels (H.N., R.N., L.P.N., N.A./M.H.A., U.S.): Obtain from counting the skill levels for each unit in the time schedule book except for OB-PP, OB-L&D, CCU, and Telemetry.

   For each skill level column

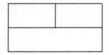

   1) Upper left-hand corner: Number of orientees (do not count orientees in total number of staff).

   2) Upper right-hand corner: Staff pulled or not going to be on duty as scheduled. + or − number of staff.

   3) Bottom half: Number of persons for the skill level EXCLUDING orientees on that unit (excluding nonproductive time). Any staff members working 12-hour shifts are documented as day or night according to 12-hour shift schedule; eight-hour shift staff members are documented as day/evening/night according to eight-hour shift scheduled.

   4) Productive staff: Total number of staff EXCLUDING orientees for that unit for that shift.

   5) Productive hours: Number of hours of staff working on that unit (do not include meetings, workshops, etc.). Multiply the number of productive staff by hours on duty, including Head Nurse and unit secretary.

   6) Acuity levels: Complete the number of patients in each acuity level. PICU, ICU, CCU, NICU, Telemetry, and Open Heart Recovery acuity levels are documented each shift (eight hours or 12 hours).

7) Patient Census   H   L   :   Total number of patients

on the unit at 0600, 1400, and 2200.

H = number of patients present on the unit at 0600, 1400, and 2200.

L = number of patients on LOA at 0600, 1400, and 2200.

NOTE: H & L should equal total patient census.

8) Outpatients: Number of patients not admitted to the hospital but receiving care, treatment, tests, etc. *Day Surgery Unit's patient census is placed in the Outpatients column.*

11. When checking the schedule book, make sure that the staff originally scheduled for a shift is actually working that shift. Do not count orientees as part of productive staff.

B. Equipment:
1. Daily Staffing sheet.
2. Computer/screen for patient census on PCS.
3. Telephone.
4. Pencil.
5. Computer/data staffing screen on MDAX.

C. Procedural Steps:
1. Initiate a new daily staffing sheet at 0600 by documenting appropriate date on sheet and placing on clipboard in Assistant Director of Nursing's office.
2. Complete the following columns for day shift at 0600 by recording the correct number for each unit:
   a. Skill levels: call OB-L&D, OB-PP, CCU, and Telemetry at end of shift.
   b. Productive staff.
   c. Productive hours.
   d. Acuity levels: only for PICU, ICU, NICU, CCU, Telemetry, and Open Heart Recovery, call the units.
   e. Patient census: may be obtained on the PCS computer screen.
   f. Outpatients: call DSU to obtain census.
3. Review the documentation for day shift at 1400 and make any changes as necessary.
4. Complete the following columns for evening shift at 1400 by recording the correct number for each unit (if on 12-hour shift, the staff and hours may not apply except for unit secretaries, nursing assistants, etc.).

a. Skill levels: Nursing Office secretary will call OB-PP, OB-L&D, CCU, and Telemetry at end of shift, obtain others from schedule book by nursing supervisor.

b. Productive staff.

c. Productive hours.

d. Acuity levels: Nursing Office secretaries will document on the daily staffing sheet according to the levels listed on the daily variable staffing sheet.

e. Patient census: May be obtained on the PCS computer screen.

f. Outpatients: Call DSU for census.

5. Review the documentation for evening shift at 2200 and make any changes as necessary.

6. Complete the following columns for night shift at 2200 by recording the correct number for each unit:

a. Skill levels: Call OB-PP, OB-L&D, CCU, and Telemetry at end of shift (Nursing Office secretaries will do).

b. Productive staff.

c. Productive hours.

d. Acuity levels: Only for PICU, CCU, Telemetry, ICU, NICU, and Open Heart Recovery—call units by Nursing Office secretary.

e. Patient census: May be obtained on the PCS computer screen; Nursing Office secretaries are to call the unit for verification of census.

f. Outpatients, if applicable.

7. Review the documentation for night shift at 0600 the following morning and make any changes as necessary.

8. Give the daily staffing sheet to the Nursing Office secretary.

9. Review of the sheet by the Head Nurses may be done if desired until 0900 of the following morning.

10. Total the columns by the Nursing Office secretary at 0900 on the following morning.

11. Copy the daily staffing sheet and place in the Management Services mailbox by 0930 on the following morning (Nursing Office secretary will complete this task).

12. Enter the actual staffing data onto MDAX's staffing data screens between 0800 and 0930 on the following morning (done by Nursing Office secretary).

13. File the daily staffing sheet in the daily staffing sheet notebook (done by Nursing Office secretary).

Appendix 4–D
Staffing Standards Form

NURSING UNIT STAFFING STANDARDS

Cost Center#: _____

Capacity: _____

Ave. Occupancy (last 6 months): _____

Projected Occupancy 1985-86: _____

Date Submitted: _____

YEAR _____

DAILY STAFFING/BUDGET REQUIREMENTS

Category	DAYS		EVENINGS		NIGHTS		Total FTE
	Daily	Required	Daily	Required	Daily	Required	
Total:							

Productive Staff Levels:

Total M-F Staffing Including HN & US: _____ × 8 (10 or 12) = _____ hr.

Total Weekend/Holiday Staffing: _____ × 8 (10 or 12) = _____ hr.

MINIMUM STAFFING STANDARDS

	DAYS	EVENINGS	NIGHTS
Census:			
Category:			

PATIENT CARE HOURS/PATIENT DAYS

OCCUPANCY	NUMBER OF PATIENTS	HOURS OF CARE PER PATIENT

Productivity Index _____

FTE Determination Legend:

  8-hr. shift: 1 position 5 days/week = 1.0 FTE

10-hr. shift: 1 position 7 days/week = 1.8 FTE

12-hr. shift: 1 position 7 days/week = 2.3 FTE

Appendix 4–E

Procedure for
Unit Staffing Standards

I. Purpose:
To provide a guideline for use of Nursing Unit Staffing Standards.

II. Responsibility:
Head Nurses and Charge Nurses.

III. Procedure:
A. General Facts:
1. The Nursing Unit Staffing Standards Form [Appendix 4–D] is used to provide guidelines for budgeting and management of staffing, productivity index, and minimum staffing (safety) standards.
2. A copy of the Nursing Unit Staffing Standards is kept on each nursing unit and in the Nursing Office.
3. These standards are to be utilized in conjunction with the patient classification and acuity systems to coordinate and adjust staffing on a shift by shift basis.
4. The following are appropriate figures currently used in determining FTEs while providing benefit coverage.

> 8-Hr Shift: 1 position 5 days/week = 1.0 FTE.
> 1 position 7 days/week = 1.5 FTE.
> 10-Hr Shift: 1 position 7 days/week = 1.8 FTE.
> 12-Hr Shift: 1 position 7 days/week = 2.3 FTE.

5. Staffing may not be decreased below designated minimum staffing standards nor increased beyond established budget without supervisory approval.

6. The Productivity Index should be maintained within 10 percent range above or below the standard. Staffing levels will be evaluated if this occurs.

7. The acuity of patients will need evaluation in conjunction with the productivity index.

B. Procedural Steps:

1. Categories of staff are listed in the first column, i.e., R.N., L.P.N., N.A., U.S.

2. The number of each category to be scheduled is listed in the daily column for each shift.

3. The number of FTEs needed to provide coverage for seven (or five or whatever is appropriate by day of week) days is listed.

4. List FTEs at the bottom and side of each column by category and by shift.

5. Total number of staff persons in daily columns should be added and multiplied by number of hours each person works in section marked Productive Staff Levels. Note: Weekend and holiday staffing may need to be addressed differently than Monday through Friday staffing when average census is lower on these days.

6. Minimum Staffing Standards section: List name of category in category column. List census in the appropriate sections for each shift.

7. Patient Care Hours/Patient Days: List occupancy percent in appropriate column: 100 percent, 90 percent, 80 percent, etc. List number of patients commensurate with percent occupancy listed.

8. Hours of Care Per Patient: Divide number of hours of care for 24 hours by the number of patients.

9. Productivity Index: Identify current average occupancy, number of patients, and hours of care per patient. The hours of care are listed in the top right-hand corner.

10. Productivity and Staff Levels were determined by shift, utilizing the completion of the data on the form in Appendix 4–C by Nursing Office staff (also see Exhibit 2–2). The data are entered in the computer and an analysis of productivity levels is provided daily and by pay period. See sample in [Appendix 4–D].

Appendix 4–F

The Flex Program

Section: PERSONNEL

Subject: Flex Time Work Hours
A Management Guideline

I. PURPOSE:
The purpose of this policy is to provide a mechanism to adjust employee work time consistent with short-term temporary fluctuations in patient census levels and departmental workloads.

II. POLICY:
Welborn Hospital schedules employees' work time based on projections of anticipated patient census levels and departmental workloads. On those occasions when projections are not realized, hospital management may notify specific employees within selected job classifications that there is insufficient work to complete the work day as previously scheduled and the employee will be sent home for lack of work.

This policy also permits individual employees to request a change in their scheduled work time in order to accommodate personal needs for time off. Such employee requests will be considered by department management and approved if possible.

It will be the policy of Welborn Hospital in circumstances where work schedules are modified by employee request or on Hospital management initiative to prorate all paid nonproductive benefit hours.

III. PROCEDURES:
Management-Initiated Work Time Reductions: On those occasions where departmental/unit work volumes have declined to a point clearly requiring a temporary adjustment in employees' scheduled work, management is obligated to notify employees promptly of necessary work schedule changes or job assignments. Department management is to give as much advance notice as possible of such work schedule changes in order to permit employees the

96

maximum opportunity possible to accommodate to changes in their work time. Employees must perceive any reduction in hours as a necessary and reasonable management action related to a change in department/unit workloads.

Considerations should be given to the following factors in selecting individual employees to relieve from work or alter previously communicated work schedules:

1. Which job classifications are most directly affected by the drop in patient census or departmental workloads?
2. Which employees have been required previously to reduce their work time to accommodate to a decline in the work to be performed? The hospital should avoid reducing employees' scheduled work time more than 20 percent in a pay period. Department management must ensure that reductions in scheduled hours are apportioned fairly within a job classification.
3. Are there any volunteers who want to reduce their scheduled work time? The 20 percent guideline is waived when employees voluntarily elect to reduce their scheduled work time. Department management may use a "signup sheet" similar to overtime assignment practices to identify volunteers.
4. Department management may elect to initiate a change in employees' work schedules for an indefinite period of time until the department workload volumes increase to permit scheduling regular work hours.
5. In circumstances where changes in employees' work schedules are to be made, the following classification of employees will be affected in sequential order:

   A. On-Call Employees
   B. Temporary Employees
   C. Probationary Employees
   D. All Other Employees (Full- or Part-time)

Any management-initiated hours reduction will not reflect negatively on the employees' attendance record. Accruals for all paid nonproductive benefit entitlements (vacation, holidays, and sick pay) will be prorated.

In order to record flex time adjustments accurately in an employee's work schedule, it will be necessary to code the timecard to ensure that any work schedule changes are formally recorded. The code for management-initiated work schedule adjustments will be FM.

Employee-Requested Change in Scheduled Work Time: Employees may request changes in their scheduled work time as personal needs may require. Each individual employee request will be considered dependent upon the department workload and job classification scheduling requirements. Such requests should be presented to department management as early as possible in order to permit a timely evaluation and allow for necessary adjustments in job assignments or other necessary factors.

There is no required form or paperwork needed to request a change in scheduled work time. All benefit accruals will be prorated.

All Hospital employees (regardless of status or classification) are eligible to request changes in scheduled work time. Approval is entirely dependent upon department management prerogatives. Employees must have approval in order to avoid having an absence charged against their attendance record when scheduled time is not worked.

Employees may request up to 100 percent reduction in their scheduled time during a work week. Employees who request more than four consecutive full weeks off from work without pay will be required to apply for a leave of absence.

In order to record flex time adjustments accurately in an employee's work schedule, it will be necessary to code the timecard to ensure that any work schedule changes are formally recorded. The code for employee-initiated work schedule adjustments will be FE.

Part-time employees also will be permitted to request a reduction in their scheduled work time. Benefits for part-time employees will be prorated consistent with present Hospital Benefit Administration Policies.

Proposed by: _____   _____
                  Personnel Department   Date

Approval: _____   _____
                  Executive Director   Date

COMMUNICATION:
Policy Distributed To: Date
A. Department Management   __3-22-84__
B. Employees   _____
C. Bulletin Boards   _____
D. Welborn Week   _____
E. Handbook   _____

BENEFIT ADMINISTRATION
for
FULL-TIME EMPLOYEES*

40-HOUR WORK WEEK/80 HOURS PER PAY

Employees working a 40-hour work week, or 80 hours per pay period, will accrue vacation based upon 80 hours per pay period. Sick pay will accrue at the rate of 8 hours per month, cumulative to a maximum of 192 hours or 24 days. First-day payment will be made if their accumulated sick pay credit is at 192 hours or 24 days. The other criterion for first-day payment remains the same as in the Employee Handbook. The holiday entitlement is *two* Paid Personal Days plus the standard seven holidays per year: New Year's Day, Memorial Day, Independence Day, Labor Day, Thanksgiving Day, Christmas Day, and the Employee's Birthday. Other benefit entitlements are: Blue Cross/Blue Shield, life insurance (one times annual salary), disability insurance, retirement plan, tuition reimbursement, jury duty, and bereavement pay.

36-HOUR WORK WEEK/72 HOURS PER PAY

Employees working a 36-hour work week, or 72 hours per pay period, will accrue vacation based upon the number of hours paid, including work and benefit hours. Sick pay will accrue at the rate of 7 hours per month, cumulative to a maximum of 168 hours or 21 days. First-day payment will be made if their accumulated sick pay credit is at or above 168 hours or 21 days. The other criterion for first-day payment remains the same as in the Employee Handbook. The holiday entitlement is *one* Paid Personal Day plus the standard seven holidays per year: New Year's Day, Memorial Day, Independence Day, Labor Day, Thanksgiving Day, Christmas Day, and the Employee's Birthday. Other benefit entitlements are: Blue Cross/ Blue Shield, life insurance (one times annual salary), disability insurance, retirement plan, tuition reimbursement, jury duty, and bereavement pay.

32-HOUR WORK WEEK/64 HOURS PER PAY

Employees working a 32-hour work week, or 64 hours per pay period, will accrue vacation based upon the number of hours paid, including work and benefit hours. Sick pay will accrue at the rate of 6 hours per month, cumulative to a maximum of 144 hours or 18 days. First-day payment will be made if their accumulated sick pay credit is at or above 144 hours or 18 days. The other criterion for first-day payment remains the same as in the Employee Handbook. The holiday entitlement is the

* Full-time employees are budgeted to work 32 or more hours per week (64/pay period).

standard seven holidays per year: New Year's Day, Memorial Day, Independence Day, Labor Day, Thanksgiving Day, Christmas Day, and the Employee's Birthday. Other benefit entitlements are: Blue Cross/Blue Shield, life insurance (one times annual salary), disability insurance, retirement plan, tuition reimbursement, jury duty, and bereavement pay.

FLEX TIME

Additional reduction of the above standard full-time schedules by "Flex Time" will affect the proration of benefit entitlements (Vacation, Paid Personal Days, and Sick Pay) proportionate with the reduction of hours. Management-initiated Flex Time reductions and approved employee-initiated Flex Time reductions will have no effect on the employee's attendance record.

WELBORN BAPTIST HOSPITAL

Benefit Accruals for Full-Time
32- and 36-Hour Work Week Schedules

Type of Work Period	1-4 Year Employees		5-14 Year Employees		15 Years and Over	
	Accrual Factor Per Hrs. Worked	Eligibility after 2080 Hrs. or 1 Yr.	Accrual Factor Per Hrs. Worked	Eligibility after 10,400 Hrs. or 5 Yrs.	Accrual Factor Per Hrs. Worked	Eligibility after 31,200 Hrs. or 15 Yrs.
32 hours wk. or 64 hrs. pay	.03846	64 hours, 8 days	.05769	96 hours, 12 days	.07692	128 hours, 16 days
36 hours wk. or 72 hrs. pay	.03846	72 hours, 9 days	.05769	108 hours, 13.5 days	.07692	144 hours, 18 days
40 hours wk. or 80 hrs. pay	.03846	80 hours, 10 days	.05769	120 hours, 15 days	.07692	160 hours, 20 days

Maximum Sick Leave Accumulation for First-Day Pay

*First-Day Sick Payment if
Accumulation at or Over*

Reduction from 40- to 32-hr. work wk., 64-hr. work period	144 hours, or 18 days
Reduction from 40- to 36-hr. work wk., 72-hr. work period	168 hours, or 21 days
40-hr. work wk., 80-hr. work period	192 hours, or 24 days

Employees changing from 40-hr. work weeks to 32- or 36-hour work weeks will be paid "first-day" sick pay if accumulated balance is at or above the new maximum for their respective category; i.e., 144 hours or 18 days for 32-hr. per week employees, and 168 hours or 21 days for the 36-hr. per week employees. No additional accruals are permitted until balance drops below maximum.

In the event the employee on a reduced work week schedule resumes a 40-hour work week at the expiration of the agreed hours, he/she will again accrue sick pay credit at the rate of 1 day per month cumulative to a maximum of 24 days.

Holidays

Work Week Hours	*Holidays*
32 hours	7 per year
36 hours	7 per year + 1 PPD
40 hours	7 per year + 2 PPDs

Other Benefit Entitlements

Blue Cross/Blue Shield
Life Insurance (one times annual salary)
Disability Insurance
Retirement Plan
Tuition Reimbursement
Jury Duty
Bereavement Pay

March 27, 1984

Chapter 5

Nursing As a Profit Center

The introduction of diagnosis related groups (DRGs) has forced hospitals to become cost conscious, and nurses have been scrambling ever since to find a valid way of measuring nursing costs and their relationship to productivity. The thrust has been to identify the intensity of care that patients require, the various direct and indirect nursing costs that relate to wise resource utilization in service delivery, the relationship between DRGs and nursing costs, and the total of nursing costs in relation to the cost for hospitalization.

However, some hospitals measure care with which they are dissatisfied rather than defining desirable and realistic goals for productivity and patient care standards before establishing the system for quantification. The ideal situation is to gain practice with costing out nursing services so that a defined level of productivity and quality can be produced instantly on the computer to compare resource utilization with results. The anticipated future goal is to establish nursing as a profit center whose budget is totally autonomous within the hospital system.

HISTORICAL ASPECTS

Historically, nursing costs have been buried in room rates, and nursing has been regarded as a cost center rather than as both a cost- and revenue-producing operation. Traditional accounting methods have lumped nursing costs with some of the general overhead costs of operating the hospital. This has produced estimates of nursing care higher than the costs actually are. Moreover, health care has begged the question of discovering what various levels of patient care really cost and what staff mix and numbers are required to achieve desirable standards of productivity.

In reality, McKibben reports, the total nursing labor expenses are about 11 percent of total hospital expenditures.[1] Walker writes that actual nursing costs were closer to 14 to 21 percent of total hospital charges in a study at Stanford University Hospital.[2] Thus, when nursing expenses are separated from room rate and hospital overhead costs, the actual money expended for nursing care represents a relatively small percentage of costs for hospitalization.

Responsibility Accounting

If one of the major reasons for patient admissions to the hospital is the nursing care (surgery and the use of very expensive testing equipment are among the others), nursing must take its proper place in the accounting process designed to measure this care. That means that nursing managers become responsible for costs, revenues, profits or losses, the quality of services delivered, and productivity standards in staff members. For example, the peer review organizations (PROs) in the states must judge the quality of care in relation to costs among area hospitals. Other third parties use this information to determine which hospital to use for Medicaid, insurance company, and local companies' patients. Nursing care is a large part of this expense, and its future revenues are contingent on the efficiency and effectiveness and the personalized service it provides to patients.

There are two types of responsibility centers—cost and profit. In the past, nurses were accountable for costs but had no responsibility for profits. This meant that nursing was viewed as a revenue drain, not a source of profit. It has been difficult for many nurses to understand just how productive they are because they have not had a budget to use as a yardstick. Now, awareness of their productivity in relation to costs and revenues should help them understand the financial impact of their efforts.

To truly be able to control costs, nurses must be given responsibility for both costs and profits. Cost thus can be compared with revenues to assess whether or not a profit has been made. When a deficit results, nurses also become accountable for corrective action. On the basis of viewing the full cycle of costs, productivity level of services delivered, revenues, and profits or losses, the nursing division can measure its real efficiency and effectiveness.

Managerial Responsibility

When hospitals switch their accounting for the nursing department to meet the DRG, prospective payment system (PPS), and PRO requirements, nursing administrators must be given more accountability and autonomy. This requires that nurse managers be equal to the task, which means that they must develop sophistication and skills in financial management. They then can support their requests for staff and supportive equipment and education with sound financial data.

Fiscal management means not only basic budgeting but also the ability to control expenditures and be accountable for nursing funds on a continuing basis.

Thus, as nurses at all levels become more participatory, they too must understand the relationship between resources utilized and the budgeting process. True control of nursing services is not possible until they are equipped to accept accountability.[3]

NURSING AS A PROFIT CENTER

The body of literature is growing on how to relate the cost of nursing to the intensity of the services it delivers and the productivity level of its staff members. Most of the current studies are attempts to relate nursing productivity to DRGs, since this is the national system in use.

Getting Started

The first step in producing revenues with actual reimbursement for direct care services is to place the nursing division and its centers in a system that gives them total accounting responsibility for their operation. One mechanism is to set productivity goals based on patient needs and to establish a price for this nursing care. This price is calculated for services that nursing provides to the hospital, and can be a basis for allocating money to the nursing department. Under this method, each DRG would be assigned a cost for nursing care. This cost could be multiplied by the number of admissions to determine what nursing generated in revenues. The figures for all DRGs could be added to produce the bottom line. The costs for delivering nursing services then are subtracted, leaving a net profit or loss.

Based on these calculations, a break-even point can be established to determine how many patients a unit must have for revenues and costs to be equal. In plotting the number of patients, the number is figured first on actual census, then on the effective census. The effective census is a multiple of patient care intensity. For example, some days, 12 patients on the unit can seem like 30 because of the severity of their illnesses. This actual census of 12 becomes an effective census of 30. Thus, the intensity of nursing services needed must be factored in. Costs then can be related not only to volume but also to the numbers when illness acuity varies.

In effect, these calculations show the hospital what the nursing department is contributing and what level of quality and productivity is available for a specific price—what nursing is selling in services to the institution. The calculations provide the nursing division with a realistic idea of what changes it must make to promote further profitability and productivity. Naturally, the total can be separated for study on the costs and profits of each DRG. Finally, when the DRG categories are analyzed, reasons for the expenses can be determined and appropriate changes made in costing and providing care.[4]

When profits occur as a result of special efforts by the nursing staff, the savings should be spent within the nursing department as an incentive for future cost containment. For example, in one hospital, innovative changes from staff nurses' working flexible hours resulted in a saving of $40,000 from reduced overtime and decreased numbers of per diem staff needed. The money was spent on a beeper system for nurses that reduced steps, as well as patient education software that saved nurses' time. These items had been requested previously, but had been on hold because of other budgetary priorities.

Issues in Costing

The problem in costing nursing care has been in finding a valid and reliable method that has wide acceptance. With the impetus of the Joint Commission on Accreditation of Nursing Services, patient classification systems have gained wide use in identifying staffing needs based on the intensity of care required. However, these same systems usually have not been as well utilized in the budgeting process, yet they can help match staff to patient needs, assess staff productivity, and develop a nursing budget while being aligned with DRGs.

Early efforts to establish a system for determining nursing costs by patient discharge resulted in Relative Intensity Measures (RIMs).[5] Because of practical problems in using them, many nursing divisions continued the per diem method of calculating costs.[6] However, since nursing managers had to have a system for valuing nursing in quantitative terms both within and among DRGs, problems of methodology had to be overcome. One early effort at meeting this need is described in a model by Curtin.[7] This method assigns dollar figures to a patient classification system so that a monetary figure can be derived for budgeting that reflects the patients' intensity index. The appeal of this approach was that a current method could be used to reflect monetary needs and expenditures according to varying needs of patients with specific conditions on actual shifts and measure productivity levels in staff members without the need to develop a different system. This permits the calculation of direct costs of providing nursing services in relation to the application of the nursing process to patient care.

In one hospital where major DRGs were analyzed in 98 cases for direct and indirect nursing costs, about 60 percent of the total went for direct care, and 40 percent for supportive services and administrative costs. Nursing accounted for 17 percent of the total hospital costs per patient but varied widely according to DRG. In this study, the extreme problems of some patients, whose stay exceeded the average, accounted for 34 percent of all nursing costs.[8] The cost of nursing care varies for each DRG studied, depending on the acuity level, the mix of staff used, the manner in which physicians prescribe treatment, and the way calculations are made.

After direct costs are known, the nursing division still must account for the indirect costs. These include the use of support personnel, nursing administration, nursing supervision, and education. The indirect costs lend themselves to much analysis, since changes are needed to make these services effective, efficient, and open to accountability.

SEVERITY OF ILLNESS STUDIES

The federal government has noticed that the DRG system, based on medical diagnosis, is not accurate enough in predicting total patient costs and appropriate levels of staff productivity and mix because it omits illness acuity. To rectify this problem, the Health Care Financing Administration (HCFA) has funded research on some projects seeking to provide a better measure of severity of illness. The major projects are summarized as follows:

- *Horn's Severity of Illness Index:* This is an expensive, subjective system that is not computerized. It is based on the use of trained raters who assign a numerical value of 1 to 4 to patients based on seven subscale ratings—stage of diagnosis, complications, comorbidity, response to treatment, recurrence of symptoms, and number and nature of nonoperative procedures.
- *Patient Management Categories* (PMC): This system is computerized and uses the Uniform Hospital Discharge Data Set (UHDDS). However, it has been criticized because of its ''cookbook approach'' to medicine. After patients are grouped by diagnoses, comorbidities, and multiple diagnoses, a group of physicians decides on the most effective course of treatment. Then dollar values are assigned to services needed.
- *Acute Physiology and Chronic Health Evaluation* (APACHE II): This system does not use UHDDS and is limited mainly to critically ill patients. It uses an analysis of 12 physiologic variables to assess the severity of illness. For example, blood pressure and certain laboratory values are evaluated upon admission.
- *The Medical Illness Severity Grouping System* (MEDISGRPS): This system also is more applicable to seriously ill patients but it does use UHDDS. This method involves the assigning of points by trained raters from chart abstracts on physiologic condition and clinical problems. From these data, patients are assigned to one of four categories, according to whether or not they have certain characteristics.
- *Disease Staging:* This computerized system uses UHDDS and is a popular choice because of its accuracy in predicting resource consumption. In this method, patients are staged into four groups by whether they have a simple

problem without complications, a problem in one system or organ, one involving multiple sites, or one that is terminal.[9]

However, it is felt that these systems still fail to solve the problem of predicting intensity and type of nursing services required since they are based only on medical diagnoses. Now is the time for nursing to formulate an acceptable system that integrates medical and nursing care needs.

PROGRESS IN NURSING SYSTEMS FOR PRICING

Efforts in pricing nursing services are becoming widespread. A few of the better known projects are highlighted here. No matter which system a hospital adopts, nursing managers are cautioned to make the monitoring of productivity and quality of care a continual quality assurance priority, lest the model provide ineffective, inadequate, or unorganized nursing services and plug in the wrong finances.

Riverview Medical Center

One example of encouraging work to formulate a realistic system for pricing nursing services has been done at Riverview Medical Center in Red Bank, N.J. This hospital tested its system in its own hospital and six others, and planned to extend testing to others that met the testing criteria. The goals of this method are to establish a computerized base for nursing reimbursement by:

1. finding the relationship between total hospital charges and nursing care costs
2. determining the average hours and costs of providing direct nursing care for each DRG by using a commercially prepared factor evaluation method
3. assessing the range of costs and hours within DRGs for patient care
4. adding any other factors or criteria that will make resource intensity measurement more effective.

In this system the nursing workload is assessed and is measured as one hour equaling one nursing care unit (NCU). Point values are assigned to patient care needs (PCUs), with one point equaling 6.5 minutes. These PCUs are calculated for direct physical care, indirect nursing care, and teaching time. To the sum of direct care is added a 15 percent constant for interruptions and delays, an average of 14.5 minutes of patient teaching and emotional support per day, and a constant of 38 minutes for administrative activities. Time for administrative activities is added regardless of the patient's illness intensity.

This system allows the hospital to predict the PCUs per clinical area and to assign dollar values to these units for determining costs and revenues. When total nursing costs are calculated, these figures are increased by adding a hospital mark-up factor, spread across all departments, and a departmental overhead fee. This system was being tested only on acute care units, not in critical care, until refinements could be made.[10]

Strong Memorial Hospital

Another example is Strong Memorial Hospital, in Rochester, New York, which has led the way in developing a nursing patient classification system that is reliable and valid for that hospital, attested by its having been in place since 1978. Its studies can be replicated over time and across institutions. In the most recent update, the four categories based on intensity of nursing services were converted to actual hours of care.

Through this computerized system, total patient costs can be calculated by combining nursing acuity data with data generated from the prospective payment system. Detailed accounts of this work may be found in *Nursing Management*.[11,12]

University Hospitals of Cleveland

The University Hospitals of Cleveland have been developing a computerized nurse information system that is applicable to costing, decision making at all levels, changing needs of patients, productivity of each nurse, and patient assignments in relation to the nurse's individual skill and education. This system of nurse/patient summation is premised on nursing diagnoses developed by the North American Nursing Diagnosis Association, and has been tested on its staff, which is predominately registered nurses.[13]

In one study comparing two wards, Halloran found that a higher R.N. staff resulted in lower costs for nursing care. On the surgical unit, 42 percent of the staff were R.N.s, on the medical unit, 72 percent. The costs of delivering direct nursing care were $25 less per patient day on the medical unit than on the surgical unit. This difference was attributed to the fact that registered nurses were more productive in providing direct care than were fewer R.N.s who assigned direct care to nursing assistants. If the proportion of R.N.s were increased across the 30 medical and surgical units in this hospital, Halloran predicted a saving of $273,750 annually in salary expense.[14,15]

Halloran's work in measuring the productivity of R.N. staffs should continue to be monitored. Most hospitals are planning to increase the numbers of registered nurses and working to measure nurse effectiveness in relation to nursing diagnoses and the nursing process.

St. Mary's Hospital and Health Center, Tucson, Arizona

A committee of professional nurses and outside consultants developed an acuity system for this hospital that allows nursing to put a price on eight acuity levels. In their extensive studies, they found that the average cost of a caregiver was $16.17 an hour and indirect nursing costs $2.85 for a total of $19.02 an hour.

In this system, one relative value unit (RVU) for medical-surgical nursing was $70, for critical care $210. In one month, the total medical-surgical revenue for room, board, and nursing was $1,350,768, for critical care $254,065. Thus, the total amount collected for room charges was $1,604,833. Typically, 50 percent of this amount would be attributed to nursing, which would have been $802,416.50. However, when nursing revenues are calculated according to acuity levels, the amount attributed to nursing became $901,646.[16]

UTILIZING A VENDOR

Not all nursing divisions have expert researchers on staff to help in converting their patient classification system to a computerized method that lends itself to costing nursing care. Lacking such aid, some hospitals have sought assistance from the growing number of vendors available in this field. One of the most complete systems has been offered by MDAX. With the permission of MDAX and Welborn Baptist Hospital, an overview of the experience is presented next.*

When Welborn interviewed vendors to assist it in identifying nursing costs, it used a set of objectives in assessing which company could best meet its needs:

1. Find a vendor who could adapt the current information system programs, data, and patient classification system, since the hospital was satisfied with the existing system.
2. Computerize the patient classification and acuity system so that unit staff input was possible.
3. Provide a mechanism for generating relevant and timely reports to all levels of administration.
4. Identify costs of nursing care data with specific information on the level of the persons providing care and the actual amount of time required for caregiving.
5. Allow a breakdown of costs into direct and indirect care components.
6. Identify costs according to the prospective payment system.

---

*Many other vendors, notably GRASP and Medicus, are also well regarded. The MDAX system is used as an example to illustrate the usefulness of all such vendors.

7. Provide a mechanism for comparing budgeted staff costs with acuity levels on each nursing unit.
8. Develop reports that outline historical data by DRG.
9. Provide reports and tools to assist with budgeting based on acuity and nursing costs per DRG.
10. Standardize nursing costs and acuity data so that networking and comparisons with other health care delivery organizations is possible.

THE MDAX NURSING INFORMATION NETWORK

Of all the companies interviewed, Welborn decided that only the MDAX Corporation's Nursing Information Network (NIN)* met all of these requirements. Though MDAX was a new company, its founders and staff were experienced health care professionals with expertise in nursing and information system development. The company soon grew to service more than 50 systems.

The implementation and development of Welborn's system took nine months, with the major emphasis on system usage and management reporting education for the nurse administrators, unit managers, and unit staff. As of this writing, the system had been implemented for one year, generating staffing and costing information for budgeting purposes. To ensure that patients are receiving the care suggested by this system, a comprehensive quality assurance effort (also one of the MDAX NIN modules) was instituted to establish and measure standards of care.

The MDAX NIN system uses a process that classifies each patient daily, placing them all in one of four types. Each patient type has a range of nursing care hours and an associated acuity value that reflects the relationship between each category. A Type II patient is given an acuity of 1.0, while Types I, III, and IV have values of 0.5, 2.5, and 5.0, respectively. These values demonstrate the relationship of one patient type to another in terms of nursing workload. For example, a Type III patient represents two and a half times the workload of a Type II patient.

The relative index of workload (RIW) is calculated for each nursing unit by multiplying the number of patients in each type by its associated acuity factor and summing the total. This process converts the census by patient type into the number of equivalent Type II patients, thus providing the basis for comparative analysis. The acuity for the unit is determined by dividing the RIW by the census. This statistic, therefore, describes the average intensity of workload per patient on the unit.

With the use of a valid, reliable, and standardized workload measurement method, internal and external comparative data can be developed easily. Within

---

*This section and its tables were written by Teresa J. Jacobsen, Director, Nursing Marketing and Research, MDAX Corporation, Chicago.

the department each unit can be compared against its history, the budget, and other units. External comparisons can be made at the unit specialty level or organizationally against similar institutions.

The critical focus for enhanced utilization of comparative data is the development of profiles that describe both the internal and external data bases. The MDAX concept of ''profile management'' provides the link among DRGs, nursing cost, and productivity management. It gives managers a mechanism that signals the need for intervention when it is appropriate, dramatically improving the quality of nursing's concurrent utilization management of DRGs.

Two profile models are compiled for nursing management—by DRG and by nursing unit. Within a specific DRG, the acuity and workload are tracked by patient throughout the entire length of stay. Information, including budget and actual costs, actual staffing, primary physician, ICD-9 code, and even nursing diagnoses, is captured. As a result, nursing costs can be calculated and variances identified per DRG.

The use of RIW is advantageous because it translates the patient's needs for nursing care into comparative units of measure. Per unit of workload, the number of hours (HR/RIW) given or dollars ($/RIW) spent in providing patient care become productivity and cost control measures. The relationship between productivity and cost is vital since first-level managers in nursing may control $400,000 to $1.5 million a year in staff resources. The nurse manager's ability to allocate and control resources with regard to the interrelationship between daily staffing and dollars available (the budget) has an impact on the bottom line. Managerial performance against the unit's budget is the key measure of managerial effectiveness in today's environment.

The nursing cost formula can be expressed as follows:

$$\text{Nursing Cost} = \text{LOS} \times \text{Acuity} \times \$/\text{RIW}$$

The variability of nursing cost per patient can be explained by an examination of the cost components. Length of stay (LOS) and acuity are variable components, of which acuity is a measured component that cannot be influenced. Length of stay, however, can be influenced greatly by nursing when effective utilization management is combined with the concepts of profile management. The nursing cost per unit of workload ($/RIW) is the fixed component directly controllable by management.

The MDAX NIN promotes management of all three cost components through the management reporting module. On a daily basis, managers are provided with comparisons of today's acuity and $/RIW against budget, along with the averages of these variables on a period and year-to-date basis. The NIN Nursing Cost Analysis module provides a detailed description (Table 5–1) of $/RIW split into

Table 5-1 NIN Nursing Cost Analysis

BUDGETED NURSING COST/RIW
For Fiscal Year 1985 Beginning 1/1/85

Unit Code Name	Budget			Unit Cost		Allocated Cost		Total Dollars/Year	$/RIW Per Day Analysis				
	Census	Acuity	RIW	Direct	Non	Overhead	Indirect		Direct	Non	Overhead	Indirect	Total
3W	24	1.50	35.7	$ 496,336	$113,239	$ 26,272	$ 7,457	$ 643,303.55	$38.09	$8.69	$2.02	$0.57	$49.37
4C	23	1.20	28.1	422,411	88,958	20,691	5,873	537,932.41	41.16	8.67	2.02	0.57	52.42
4W	25	1.30	32.4	475,339	91,553	23,870	6,775	597,536.83	40.15	7.73	2.02	0.57	50.47
5E	34	1.40	48.2	681,391	113,029	35,450	10,061	839,931.60	38.75	6.43	2.02	0.57	47.77
ER	0	0.00	0.0	0	0	0	0	0.00	0.00	0.00	0.00	0.00	0.00
L&D	0	0.00	0.0	0	0	0	0	0.00	0.00	0.00	0.00	0.00	0.00
MCCU	5	3.80	18.6	255,871	58,710	13,661	3,877	332,118.73	37.76	8.67	2.02	0.57	49.02
NICA	18	1.50	26.7	391,401	85,564	19,634	5,572	502,171.50	40.19	8.79	2.02	0.57	51.57
NUR	10	1.50	14.6	206,230	38,262	10,721	3,043	258,256.54	38.78	7.20	2.02	0.57	48.57
OB/PP	17	1.00	17.0	241,723	52,231	12,482	3,543	309,979.05	39.04	8.44	2.02	0.57	50.07
PEDS	10	1.60	15.5	201,459	52,555	11,371	3,227	268,612.81	35.72	9.32	2.02	0.57	47.63
SCCU	5	4.20	19.8	262,386	49,772	14,582	4,139	330,878.65	36.28	6.88	2.02	0.57	45.75
SSC	12	1.80	22.1	256,173	57,033	16,273	4,619	334,098.04	31.74	7.07	2.02	0.57	41.39
TELEM	11	1.90	20.0	278,911	61,200	14,726	4,179	359,015.95	38.19	8.38	2.02	0.57	49.16
Totals	193	1.55	298.6	4,169,631	862,107	219,733	62,365	5,313,835.65	38.26	7.91	2.02	0.57	48.76

Definitions:
Direct —Direct Care Costs   Nondirect—Other Unit Costs
Overhead—Departmental Costs Including Administration & Education
Indirect —Allocated Costs from Nonrevenue-Producing Areas

Source: MDAX Corporation, Chicago.

four categories: Direct Care, Nondirect (Unit Based), Nursing Overhead, and Indirect Allocated Costs.

The MDAX DRG and unit profiles describe the nursing costs equation (LOS, $/RIW, Acuity) as parameters for management control. Analysis of the minimum, average, and maximum values for each cost component provides a framework to monitor activity. Exceptions to the profile are identified easily for management investigation and resolution.

Since total costs are a product of LOS × Acuity × $/RIW, a change in the mix of DRGs will not cause a problem with nursing costs since the mix of reimbursement changes with it. Yet a change or variation in acuity or LOS within a DRG will affect nursing costs dramatically as it increases or decreases the consumption of resources. Since changes in any of the variables will have an impact on costs, nursing will have to change the $/RIW to control expenses. Knowledge of the direct, nondirect, overhead, and indirect cost components allows nursing to make reductions in areas outside of direct patient care.

In summary, through the utilization of the MDAX NIN system, resource allocation is enhanced by the ability to compare and control both productivity and costs via unit and DRG profiles (Tables 5–2 through 5–4, Figure 5–1). This concept of profile management reflects a four-point plan for nursing:

1. *Daily Nursing Cost per RIW:* A weighted index of resource consumption links nursing workload to nursing costs. When the cost per RIW is monitored within the unit profile, total expenditures will be at or below budget. The index serves as a guide for future decision making through tracking of actual decisions against the budget (daily and year-to-date).

2. *Average Acuity by Nursing Unit:* Although average acuity will vary daily, experience indicates over time that acuity remains within certain boundaries. Analysis of variances can be used as an indicator of acuity ''creep'' and the need for management attention.

3. *Nursing Workload and Cost per DRG:* Monitoring the workload per DRG may serve as a predictor of changes in the case mix, an important component of the hospital's fiscal strategy. Variance from established limits may signal RIW creep and the need for management action. The RIW methodology enables management to separate the true nursing costs components per DRG into fixed ($/RIW per day) and variable (acuity per DRG, average LOS).

4. *Relationship of Productive to Nonproductive Time:* Nurse managers need to monitor the relationship between productive and nonproductive time each pay period throughout the year. Reductions in costs cannot be accomplished by increasing nonproductive time.

By having timely, accurate, and complete information concerning acuity, workload, and costs by unit and DRG, nursing will be able to respond proactively and appropriately to increasing fiscal constraints.

Table 5–2 Workload Analysis by Day of Stay

DRG: 14 Specific Cerebrovascular Disorders Except TIA

Day	Tot. Wkld.	Numb. Pat.	Avg. Wkld.	$/ RIW	Cost /Day
1	$41.00	12	$3.42	$48.24	$164.82
2	34.50	12	2.87	48.24	138.69
3	27.00	12	2.25	48.24	108.54
4	30.50	12	2.54	48.24	122.61
5	31.50	11	2.86	48.24	138.14
6	28.50	10	2.85	48.24	137.48
7	19.50	9	2.17	48.24	104.52
8	21.00	8	2.62	48.24	126.63
9	19.00	8	2.37	48.24	114.57
10	19.00	8	2.37	48.24	114.57
11	17.00	7	2.43	48.24	117.15
12	17.00	7	2.43	48.24	117.15
13	18.00	6	3.00	48.24	144.72
14	16.00	6	2.67	48.24	128.64
15	17.50	5	3.50	48.24	168.84
16	15.00	4	3.75	48.24	180.90
17	10.00	3	3.33	48.24	160.80
18	10.00	3	3.33	48.24	160.80
19	10.00	3	3.33	48.24	160.80
20	10.00	3	3.33	48.24	160.80
21	7.50	2	3.75	48.24	180.90
22	7.50	2	3.75	48.24	180.90

Specified Conditions:
  MD Code: ALL ICD-9: ALL
  N-Diag: ALL Option: ALL
  Data Range From 1/31/85 to 3/8/85
  Data are Based Upon 12 Patients

Source: MDAX Corporation, Chicago.

FURTHER CONSIDERATIONS

There are other important factors to consider when applying existing patient classification systems to costing. The system generally may estimate care for a category without actually defining what each patient really needs or the level/ quality of service the hospital plans to deliver. Many hospitals also base the system on what a patient should get, rather than what services it actually delivers. While this is helpful in determining how staffing should be built, it is unfair to bill a patient for services not provided.

Table 5–3 Cost Detail by DRG

DRG: 89 Simple Pneumonia & Pleurisy Age >69 &/or C.C.

Patient Number	Gov. LOS	LOS	Total RIW	Avg. RIW	$ RIW	Daily Cost	Total Cost
0736744	8.50	1 –	2.5	2.50	$48.24	$120.60	$ 120.60
0735530	8.50	5 –	6.0	1.20	48.24	57.89	289.44
0735134	8.50	6 –	6.0	1.00	48.24	48.24	289.44
0734772	8.50	5 –	6.5	1.30	48.24	62.71	313.56
0732974	8.50	8 –	7.5	0.94	48.24	45.22	361.80
0732818	8.50	4 –	12.5	3.12	48.24	150.75	603.00
0731190	8.50	8 –	22.5	2.81	48.24	135.68	1085.40
0730234	8.50	8 –	18.5	2.31	48.24	111.55	892.44
0730218	8.50	7 –	17.5	2.50	48.24	120.60	844.20
0730093	8.50	13 +	31.0	2.38	48.24	115.03	1495.44
0729533	8.50	24 +	45.0	1.87	48.24	90.45	2170.80
0729475	8.50	7 –	17.5	2.50	48.24	120.60	844.20
0727339	8.50	9 +	11.0	1.22	48.24	58.96	530.64
0726513	8.50	23 +	48.0	2.09	48.24	100.67	2315.52
0726224	8.50	11 +	26.0	2.36	48.24	114.02	1254.24
0724476	8.50	6 –	7.5	1.25	48.24	60.30	361.80
0723106	8.50	5 –	25.0	5.00	48.24	241.20	1206.00
0719286	8.50	2 –	10.0	5.00	48.24	241.20	482.40
Total 18		152	320.50	2.11			
Average		8.44 –	17.81	2.11	48.24	101.72	858.94
Std. Dev.		10.17	21.53				

Specified Conditions:
  MD Code: ALL ICD-9: ALL
  N-Diag: ALL Option: ALL
  Data Range From 8/28/15 to 3/8/85
  Data are Based Upon 18 Patients
  Below: 13   Above: 5   Outlier: 0

Source: MDAX Corporation, Chicago.

In most systems, scores for patient services are added and the client is placed in one of four to six categories. At this stage, patients in the same category would be billed the same amount, even though the actual services received individually may vary. While this collapsing of data into fewer categories is helpful in staffing, it is a question whether actual points tallied for care should be used for billing purposes. The work with total points has been unrealistic, but the use of computers should make the handling of such data easier.

Table 5–4 Cost Summary by DRG

DRG	Num. Pat.	Avg. LOS	Avg. RIW	Avg. RIW /Day	Cost per RIW	Cost per Day	Total Cost	Nurse % of Medicare
14	12	13.08	35.58	2.72	$48.24	$131.20	$1716.54	0.00
15	9	8.89	14.61	1.64	48.24	79.29	704.84	0.00
18	2	9.00	24.50	2.72	48.24	131.32	1181.88	0.00
22	1	6.00	8.00	1.33	48.24	64.32	385.92	0.00
24	1	3.00	7.50	2.50	48.24	120.60	361.80	0.00
28	1	1.00	1.00	1.00	48.24	48.24	48.24	0.00
32	1	5.00	2.00	0.40	48.24	19.30	96.48	0.00
39	4	2.00	3.50	1.75	48.24	84.42	168.84	0.00
42	1	2.00	3.50	1.75	48.24	84.42	168.84	0.00
45	1	1.00	1.00	1.00	48.24	48.24	48.24	0.00
65	1	1.00	2.50	2.50	48.24	120.60	120.60	0.00
76	1	17.00	19.00	1.12	48.24	53.92	916.56	0.00
77	1	4.00	4.00	1.00	48.24	48.24	192.96	0.00
78	1	3.00	3.00	1.00	48.24	48.24	144.72	0.00
79	3	12.33	37.17	3.01	48.24	145.37	1792.92	0.00
82	2	14.00	21.00	1.50	48.24	72.36	1013.04	0.00
87	5	10.00	23.20	2.32	48.24	111.92	1119.17	0.00
88	1	9.00	9.50	1.06	48.24	50.92	458.28	0.00
89	18	8.44	17.81	2.11	48.24	101.72	858.94	0.00
90	1	5.00	3.00	0.60	48.24	28.94	144.72	0.00
92	1	8.00	9.00	1.12	48.24	54.27	434.16	0.00
94	1	12.00	45.00	3.75	48.24	180.90	2170.80	0.00
96	5	10.00	17.80	1.78	48.24	85.87	858.67	0.00
99	4	10.25	18.62	1.82	48.24	87.66	898.47	0.00
100	1	5.00	6.50	1.30	48.24	62.71	313.56	0.00
101	2	8.00	10.25	1.28	48.24	61.81	494.46	0.00
110	4	15.75	27.13	1.72	48.24	83.08	1308.51	0.00
112	2	14.50	26.50	1.83	48.24	88.16	1278.36	0.00
113	1	4.00	5.50	1.37	48.24	66.33	265.32	0.00
114	1	24.00	106.00	4.42	48.24	213.06	5113.44	0.00
116	3	14.00	30.17	2.15	48.24	103.95	1455.24	0.00
121	9	10.22	26.83	2.62	48.24	126.63	1294.44	0.00
122	4	11.50	24.63	2.14	48.24	103.30	1187.91	0.00
123	2	14.50	62.50	4.31	48.24	207.93	3015.00	0.00
127	14	7.86	12.11	1.54	48.24	74.33	584.05	0.00
130	4	6.75	8.00	1.19	48.24	57.17	385.92	0.00
132	5	6.40	13.60	2.12	48.24	102.51	656.06	0.00
134	3	10.67	12.00	1.12	48.24	54.27	578.88	0.00
135	1	2.00	3.00	1.50	48.24	72.36	144.72	0.00
138	5	2.60	4.50	1.73	48.24	83.49	217.08	0.00
140	19	6.37	11.74	1.84	48.24	88.91	566.19	0.00
141	1	13.00	12.00	0.92	48.24	44.53	578.88	0.00
143	3	7.67	13.17	1.72	48.24	82.85	635.16	0.00

Source: MDAX Corporation, Chicago.

Figure 5–1 Workload Analysis by Day of Stay

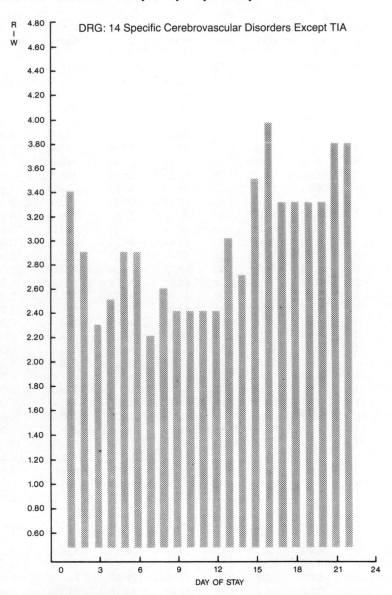

Specified Conditions:
    MD Code: ALL ICD-9: ALL   N-Diag: ALL   Option: ALL
    Data Range From 1/31/85 to 3/8/85   Data are Based Upon 12 Patients

Source: MDAX Corporation, Chicago.

If the acuity level indicates a certain average care time per patient, but the nursing unit is short of staff or in need for time management skills to boost productivity, do all patients receive the same percentage of cuts in care delivered? How can bills be adjusted to reflect understaffing or overstaffing in relation to services actually provided? This obviously requires more study. Work is still at the macro level, but computers should assist nursing in making these refinements as studies progress.

Another problem is that many systems do not distinguish the level of personnel delivering the hours of care. Yet skill level makes a large difference in the depth and totality of services and in reducing duplicative efforts. For example, on most calls to the patient room, the nursing aide finds it necessary to go get the nurse. Thus, two persons must go into that room to get the job done.

Units with more licensed nurses cut down on such duplicated effort, especially when updated job descriptions make more appropriate use of ancillary personnel. Moreover, as the intensity of patient illness increases, more services probably are delivered by the registered nurse because those services require an R.N. More study is needed to assess the relationship of acuity and skill mix to each DRG since the level of care should be considered when patient costs are charged to individual clients.

The next question is how to allocate indirect costs to each patient. Some say they should be allocated evenly over the length of stay, others that costs should be linked to the total number of points that a client accrues in the patient classification system for services delivered. While these indirect costs are constant in a nursing department, studies are needed to determine whether some patients require more indirect time than others.

For example, a critically ill patient requires more time from the head nurse and the ward secretary because of the increased numbers of orders. Other patients may require more time from supervisors or clinical specialists when their condition upsets visiting family members or when unusual family circumstances increase teaching and support time. Does this even out over time or should special charges be initiated for indirect services that exceed a preset limit?

If all of these studies show that the differences in costs are minor, then perhaps an average cost per patient is justified. If they show wide discrepancies in services within direct and indirect categories, then some adjustments are in order before patients can be billed equitably for care received.

Of course, to know what services actually have been delivered, attention must be given to upgrading documentation, along with the study of quality assurance tools to measure what is done. In documentation, nursing probably is in its worst interim phase, since it is new at being concerned with productivity and unaccustomed to streamlining charting to capture the essence of the work effort. While documentation needs have risen, the system for capturing information still is largely manual and very time consuming. Checklists and standard forms and plans can help. However, what is really needed is more work on dictation systems—and eventually computerized systems that minimize manual writing functions.

SUMMARY

This chapter has reviewed the status of pricing nursing as a beginning to making the nursing budget autonomous. However, pricing nursing is only one part of the pie; the rest is to establish standards of productivity and research/quality assurance to monitor patient care constantly and make continuing improvements in nursing service delivery as a means of gaining consumer approval both now and in the future.

Establishing a system for accomplishing this mammoth task is consuming most nursing managers since it forces them to look at the total process of care delivery in relation to accountability. Because this task is overwhelming to accomplish manually, the system chosen needs to build in all factors and be computerized.

NOTES

1. R. McKibben, "Registered Nurses' Wages Have Minor Effects on Total Hospital Costs," *Nursing Management* 13, no. 12 (December 1982): 12–22.

2. Duane Walker, "The Cost of Nursing Care in Hospitals," *The Journal of Nursing Administration* 13, no. 3 (March 1983): 13–18.

3. Rachel Rotovitch, "The Nursing Director's Role in Money Management," *The Journal of Nursing Administration* 11, no. 11–12 (November–December 1981): 13–16.

4. F.A. Shaffer, *Costing Out Nursing: Pricing Our Product* (New York: National League for Nursing, 1985).

5. Tax Equity and Fiscal Responsibility Act of 1982, P.L. 97–248.

6. Paul Grimaldi and Julie Micheletti, "RIMS and the Cost of Nursing Care," *Nursing Management* 13, no. 12 (December 1982): 12–22.

7. Leah Curtin, "Determining Costs of Nursing Services per DRG," *Nursing Management* 14, no. 4 (April 1983): 16–19.

8. W.J. Riley and Vicki Shaefers, "Costing Nursing Services," *Nursing Management* 14, no. 12 (December 1983): 40–43.

9. Leah Curtin, "Integrating Acuity: The Frugal Road to Safe Care," *Nursing Management* 16, no. 9 (September 1985): 7–8.

10. Joan Trofino, "A Reality-Based System for Pricing Nursing Service," *Nursing Management* 17, no. 1 (January 1986): 19–34.

11. M.D. Sovie, M.A. Tarcinale, A.W. Vanputtee, and A.E. Stunden, "Amalgam of Nursing Acuity, DRGs and Costs," *Nursing Management* 16, no. 3 (March 1985): 22–42.

12. A.W. Vanputee, M.D. Sovie, M.A. Tarcinale, and A.E. Stunden, "Accounting for Patient Acuity: The Nursing Time Dimension," *Nursing Management* 16, no. 10 (October 1985): 27–36.

13. Sovie et al., "Amalgam,"

14. E.J. Halloran and Marylou Kiley, "Case Mix Management," *Nursing Management* 15, no. 2 (February 1984): 39–45.

15. E.J. Halloran, "RN Staffing: More Care, Less Cost," *Nursing Management* 14, no. 9 (September 1983): 18–22.

16. Phyllis Ethridge, "The Case for Billing by Patient Acuity," *Nursing Management* 16, no. 8 (August 1985): 38–41.

ACTION CHECKLIST

1. Does your patient classification system accurately reflect the actual workload?
2. What have you done to begin pricing nursing care?
3. Does the system lend itself to multiple uses of staffing, budgeting, and pricing nursing care?
4. How do various vendor systems compare with your system in relation to data production, ease of use, cost, and relevance to your total needs?

Part II

Results Oriented Management

Chapter 6

Understanding Top Management

Many hospitals have reorganized under corporate umbrellas as a means of coping with the new mandates for cost containment and increased productivity. In doing so they have created the vice president of nursing, a power position that extends the role of the traditional nursing director to one with more accountability for balancing fiscal aspects with productivity.

To be effective in being a top hospital executive, vice presidents of nursing need to reflect on ingredients for staff satisfaction, improved productivity, maintaining the quality of patient care, hospital values, institutional survival strategies, power acquisition, plans for success, ways to develop support systems, and means of increasing profits within the responsiblity centers of nursing that are developing.

INGREDIENTS FOR EFFECTIVENESS

In their book *Leaders: Strategies for Taking Charge*, Bennis and Nanus conclude that society has too many managers and not enough leaders.[1] They say that, "Managers are people who do things right and leaders are the people who do the right thing." To be a leader in this new era, nurse executives need to have vision and focus and operate from a results-oriented agenda.[2] Along with these attributes, they need to have a good sense of timing and be good communicators who can translate vision to peers and subordinates and inspire confidence and trust for plans of action. This process of inspiring the nursing division to become committed, motivated, and more productive will require these executives to spend the bulk of their time in working effectively with and through others.

Contemporary Issues

Because the role of vice president has expanded, there are certain issues that such executives will encounter. Nursing is the biggest department in the hospital but traditionally has had the weakest administrative support and the least real autonomy. To succeed at making nursing profitable, productive, and proactive, nurse executives must command adequate power commensurate with the responsibilities of the job. To do this, they need to acquire sophistication in business, accounting principles, human resources management/labor relations, computer application, research skills, communication strategies, statistics, and politics.

In some hospitals, leaders who have worked to polish skills and extend political power by networking with hospital administration, physicians, other health care professionals, community groups and leaders, and board members have suffered subtle sanctions as the power potential in nursing has threatened other vice presidents or even the hospital president. Subsequent problems have included the great stress of restricted autonomy, in which the president must approve even the simplest nursing actions or expenditures. Simultaneously, the nurse executive still needs to present a positive image to the nursing staff that does not reflect the political strife. Unfortunately, this can result in the nursing department's blaming the executive for not providing necessary positions, monies, or permissions.

For example, in one hospital the vice president for nursing, who faced the problem of having a motivated staff, put forward a number of proposals to enhance productivity. However, discouragement ensued because the executive did not have an autonomous budget or authority to approve implementation of these worthy projects. Thus, the staff became apathetic because the excitement generated over the possibilities of improving productivity and adding resources ended when the projects were placed indefinitely on hold.

The problem in this all-too-common situation is that hospitals cognitively realize that motivating staff toward greater participation and productivity will result in the generation of new ideas, yet they are not entirely ready to abandon the paternalistic, centralized management approach that stifles results-oriented people and outcomes. A serious look at this dichotomy is imperative, since it works against productive efforts.

Many nurse executives find that their jobs are grueling, imposing unreasonable time and energy demands. While some of this goes with the territory, many tasks can be delegated. However, some nursing leaders, skilled at being "martyrs" and primed to gain personal power despite its consequences for the division, can have difficulty letting go of matters that they should delegate. Executives vary in their success in utilizing and developing others and must assess this issue on an individual basis. However, until this problem is overcome, true productivity that can result from maximizing resource utilization in a decentralized operation cannot occur.

According to Stevens, each hospital is in a different stage of growth and development.[3] As a result, nurse executives cycle through five roles in meeting the demands of improved productivity and creative programming in their division and their institution. Because executives vary in ability, they may feel more successful at times and less effective at others in the roles of innovator, expander, refiner, stabilizer, and revolutionary.

Executive Roles and Skills

Innovator

In breaking old patterns and embarking on new creative approaches to improving productivity and containing costs, the nurse leaders as innovators can be timely. However, innovation without a strategic plan can result in great departmental disruption and a negative outcome if the innovator lacks a sense of timing, coordination with others, and a means of following up on new methods and programs. In its extreme form, the innovator approves numerous projects simultaneously without ensuring plans for their survival.

For example, one nursing division decided to purchase a van from which nurse practitioners and other disciplines could provide revenue-generating mobile mass examinations for local industries. However, no plan was written for maintenance of equipment and the vehicle, and when the hospital's census climbed, the nurses were pulled back to unit staffing, leaving the program inoperable. In additon, the revenue from the project was funneled back into the general operating budget instead of being used for expansion of the program.

Expander

Expanders broaden programs and work to diversify services to better meet the contemporary needs of consumers. The role of the expander has been valuable in diversifying programs and maximizing resources so that losses can be minimized. Expanders need to be good communicators and politicians, but they also must understand the realilty of the business cycle; that is, advertising and new programs can catch on slowly. Thus, adequate budgeting for up to five years is needed to allow a program to grow.

Where this is not understood, administrators start a program, provide a brief testing period, then withdraw support before their ship comes in. The net result is that staff members feel insecure about moving into new ventures that may collapse, leaving them without the option of returning to their traditional jobs, which may have been filled by someone else.

Refiner

Where a hospital is excelling in innovations and expansions, staff energies can peak and work at cross-purposes without the aid of a refiner who can assure cohesiveness and thorough integration of programs across the system.

For example, in one hospital eyeing improved productivity, the key was to improve the quality of work life and health in nurses as a means of stimulating employee motivation. Several departments and nursing units began to create programs for accomplishing this end, but there was no communication and coordination between these isolated approaches. As a result, nursing units and other departments such as physical therapy, psychiatry, and dietary became angry about duplicated efforts.

What was necessary was a central coordinator, or refiner, who could monitor individual efforts and bring them together in a cohesive whole while preserving the enthusiasm that employee groups felt toward their contribution.

Stabilizer

The role of the stabilizer has particular importance in this health care revolution, when rapid change causes employees to feel unsettled and uncoordinated efforts cause them to clash. The truly productive, cost-effective system needs a stabilizer to blend the divergent ideas and people smoothly as they generate the plethora of ideas necessary to operate the hospital successfully.

Revolutionary

The role of the revolutionary also is one whose time has come. Particularly in hospitals with a conservative, slow rate of change, an executive is needed to revamp the division and try new methods that will improve productivity. Some hospitals are hiring this type of nurse leader to clear out the deadwood, streamline policies and procedures, and implement exciting new programs that improve the facility's business position.

However, revolutionaries should realize that they may be sacrificed in the process, even though their originally unacceptable ideas eventually win full support several years after these executives are gone.

Some nurse executives take jobs temporarily to achieve this end. But for those who want permanent employment, the need for revolutionary change needs to be tempered with some of the other roles that foster stability and change over a longer period. When revolution is needed, but the nurse executive does not want the blame, a consultant can be hired to get the wheels turning and leave quietly in the role of scapegoat.

Exhibit 6–1 can be used by nurse executives to analyze the roles they play best and the ones that need improvement in relation to the needs of the nursing division.

HOSPITAL VALUES

Success as executives requires nursing leaders to blend roles with the needs of the system. Because it is the top administrators who set the standards and policies

Exhibit 6–1 Executive Roles and Skills

Directions: Nurse executives should review the following roles and skills to determine which ones are comfortable and which require further development. They then match skills to the situation that exists in their hospital or nursing division to determine their degree of effectiveness.

Role I—Innovator

Traits: Creative role emphasizing new ideas, methods, or programs.
Skills: Ability to set new goals, to be visionary, to try new ways of operating.

Role II—Expander

Traits: Growth role emphasizing expansion in the breadth and numbers in the division.
Skills: Effective communication skills, wise use of networks, and facility in capitalizing on political relationships to advance desired goals.

Role III—Refiner

Traits: Microorganization role to provide more cohesiveness in the department through the effective interface of systems, policies, procedures, and protocols.
Skills: Logic, ability to fit pieces together to improve the whole effort.

Role IV— Stabilizer

Traits: Peacemaking and diplomatic role that results in balancing and blending factions and interest groups within the division.
Skills: Excellent problem-solving abilities with people, effective crisis manager.

Role V—Revolutionary

Traits: Revamping of existing operations and mechanisms so that the division operates differently.
Skills: Ability to weed out people and procedures that are not appropriate, ability to evolve a new system.

---

of performance and productivity for all other levels, it is important to view action mandates in relation to hospital values. The hospital system has been undergoing rapid changes in relation to its values. Values can be defined as conceptions of what is desirable or a belief in what should be attained at the ideal level.

Macro and Micro Levels

Values in hospitals have shifted both at the macro and micro levels. At the macro level, executives realize that more stringent management is required because of decreasing resources to accomplish quality patient care and to improve productivity. At the micro level, institutional and divisional effectiveness is affected by the fact that consumers, staff personnel, and others have changed expectations in relation to what the hospital should do.

In the macro arena, forces outside the hospital (governments, insurers, public pressures, etc.) have indicated a strong desire for quality care and increased productivity without higher health care budgets. This has meant that hospital executives have had to find unique ways of providing better service by increasing resource utilization and implementing innovations in service delivery suitable to both consumers and employees. These mandates have led to the altering of the administrative structures in many hospitals to enhance accountability for the way services are delivered.

Many nurse executives have been involved in making macro changes in operations to meet the demands of the new era. Examples of these changes include decentralization, primary or modular care, participatory management, increased quality assurance, risk management, computerization and quantification of services, and marketing.

However, some difficulty is being encountered at the micro level, where the impact of rapid value shifts on individuals still is marked. Because the time lag between value changes and the implementation of effective programs has been short, employees often have felt that the system is unresponsive to their personal and professional needs in delivering quality services. Consumers similarly are afraid that they will be victims of cut-rate medicine. Thus, while macro system changes are being put into place, nurse executives must deal with micro events involving individual responses to changing mandates and systems.

Making Choices

There are three approaches for coping with micro changes: Executives can ignore the problem, solve the symptom, or work with the value change directly. The first two are brush-fire methods that do little to help the system in the long run. However, such approaches have been popular in hospitals. Many times fad management techniques have been put into place to gloss over problems.

For example, the nurse executive provides a course for supervisors and unit managers in participatory management without reference to actual problems on the units. The executive then directs managers simply to implement the concept. Of course it does not work, because analysis of the situation and thoughtful strategy have been omitted. Failure to analyze the situation is an effective way to overlook the changing values in health care that prompted action toward participatory management in the first place.

The last method, working with the value change directly, requires managers to analyze both macro and micro forces involved before effective programs can be implemented. The system, by blending individual and hospital values, can work to seek individuals' support of its goals. Areas requiring attention to the individual include accountability, standard setting, realistic productivity levels, professionalism, team spirit, and integrity.

Accountability for meeting productivity goals and containing costs must be recognized as a dominant value in hospitals. To meet the goals of reduced costs, improved quality of care, and improved productivity, employees need to know that the hospital is interested in results. Subsequently, top management must underscore that priority with a new system of rewards for those who comply with the mandates.

To be accountable, executives need to know the standards against which they and/or their programs are being judged. That involves the definition of philosophy, standards, and goals delineated in this book.

Employees will need to be encouraged to operate professionally through actions and behaviors to effect the necessary changes. Moreover, they will need to abandon the trivialities of discord and strive to be team players. However, to accomplish these goals, top managers need to have integrity and consistency in their approaches to employees. This means that their relationships with employees need to be based on factual, consistent, and honest interactions.

In summary, micro value changes need to be addressed along with sweeping changes if hospitals are to be successful in their efforts toward efficiency and effectiveness in health care delivery.

HOSPITAL SURVIVAL STRATEGIES

Short-term survival is the goal of many hospitals, but those that will thrive for many years must couple these efforts at existing with strategies for long-term realignment within the total health care delivery system. In hospitals and nursing divisions alike, there is conflict as to how the future should be approached.

Conservative leaders who have succeeded in the past have relied on tried-and-true methods that have brought them through earlier crises. While those strategies worked in relatively stable periods, they can inhibit progress in the 1980s' environment of change.

While action must be rational and planned in relation to the total system, there has to be room for flexibility and innovation that is not built into most management strategies in hospitals. When administrators fail to confront changes squarely, they can miss opportunities for institutional growth and survival. Such errors work to erode the hospitals' power base and growth potentials.

For example, now is the time for experimentation with decentralized staffing and alternate work schedules, such as those identified in Chapter 4. It also is time to challenge microtechniques that mire down efforts to improve productivity by prodding middle and front-line managers to challenge staff nurses who do things "the way that they have always been done—just because." Nurse leaders know that unessential procedures must be eliminated if they are to meet goals of improved productivity and staff acceptance of altered work roles.

In addition to helping staff nurses improve their jobs by using wise time management skills, nurse leaders can assign clinical specialists to provide critical assessments of what stays and what goes. For example, one author attacks infection control, urine catheters, wound soaking, disallowing competent patients to self-medicate, IV tube changing, and routine vital signs rituals. When each of these areas is examined, that writer says, there are scientific indications for abandoning practices that are national in scope, and instead implementing newer, data-based methods.[4]

POWER ACQUISITION

The power of the nursing department in gaining control over its budget and in improving and monitoring productivity depends on the success of the nurse executive in constructing a plan and then being politically effective in the powers of persuasion and negotiation.[5] (See Exhibit 6–2.)

Development of the plan will require clear direction in relation to client satisfaction, business relationships, productivity, innovation, people development, budget goals, strategic plans, quality-of-care objectives, organizational climate, and marketing. Ideas for the development of this plan are detailed throughout this text.

Once the plan is known, the leaders are ready to acquire the power necessary for achievement of the desired goals. To be able to convince others, executives must believe in their own ideas and in themselves as power brokers. Gone are the days where this could be a passive process. Now, with limited resources, these executives must realize that nursing is competing with other divisions of the hospital for a pool of limited resources. Thus, the power brokering process will have to be one of trade-offs and compromises.

Political Process

Politics is the process of getting things done. This is accomplished through the art of persuasion and negotiation.[6] Persuasion is getting others to agree with one on ultimate goals and ways of attaining them. Negotiation is a process in which nurse executives seek advantage in dealing with others as they get them to cooperate in reaching goals. When the process of persuasion and negotiation breaks down, paralysis occurs.

For example, even though the administrative team agrees that it wants quality patient care at the lowest cost, it cannot act until its members agree and work together in a united effort to reach this goal. A large part of getting this agreement is in the skillful, documented presentation that nurse executives can make to significant others.

Exhibit 6–2 Techniques in Negotiation

1. Never underestimate your opponent. If you realize what is going on, assume that your opponent can draw the same conclusions. Be sure that your plan is complete and reasonable.

2. Plan to give adversaries an agreeable deal but expect to gain support for the essential parts of your plan.

3. Plan your strategy with an eye on timing your presentation effectively in relation to hospital events.

4. Deal from a position of strength. When possible, get the group to negotiate from your proposal, not its. Always phrase your questions in a way that prompts a positive response from others.

5. Be thoroughly prepared and versed in all applicable factors and be able to show that you have lined up support and gained approval for what you are doing. Strive for approval on the general plan before moving into specifics. Be the moving force in introducing the issues involved in your plan.

6. Practice anticipating responses from others and plan your answers in advance. Learn to be comfortable with group tension and silence. Practice refocusing the group on what you need to discuss when it avoids necessary issues.

7. Have giveaways that can be used to help you negotiate what you need.

8. Listen attentively.

9. Phrase all comments in a nonpersonal business style. Accept criticism and suggestions in a positive manner, while continuing to assert the critical portions of your proposal.

10. Bluff and gamble if you need to in an effort to show that you are not desperate but are willing to wait for the best solution. If you need to convince the others further, stop the meeting and work outside it until you gain the support to convene again.

11. Keep your sense of humor and work to maintain a clear perspective about your purpose in relation to the organization.

12. When you win, stop. Don't say another word.

The process begins as nursing leaders analyze those whose influence is needed to reach their goals for improved productivity. The first step is to analyze all the characters in the act as to their political and emotional connections, prior commitments that would augment or detract from the alliance with the objectives, and methods of approach and persuasion that would be acceptable to each person involved. Next, the executives view the relationships that need to be influenced to gain the support of each individual and decide how to influence the key persons to win support for the division.

Divisional goals then are analyzed with the aim of finding trade-offs. The executives should know exactly what they must have in permissions as well as help from others or resources to get the job done minimally, and then ideally. Where are compromises feasible? What can be offered to the other parties for the concessions needed from them? Why should they want to agree to nursing's ideas?

Finally, nurse executives should convert their divisional goals to business terms that can be illustrated on charts, graphs, transparencies, and slides. Because the decisions have to make sound business sense, these plans must be developed solidly to present to the president and the board. Hospitals are worried about survival and cannot afford to take risks that are unsound. Nurses who strive for increased divisional autonomy and budgetary control must understand this concern and work within it.

Techniques for Success

Laying the groundwork can be a time-consuming process in gaining adequate power to facilitate the productive efforts of the nursing division. This process also must allow adequate time for others to get used to what nursing executives are doing. A good sense of timing is imperative. Successful strategies can include doing a number of preipheral things for significant others. Because people want something in return for concessions made, nursing leaders can begin by establishing an "emotional bank account" with each of the principals. In this account one builds credits with others that can be used when support and concessions are needed. As with a financial bank account, executives will want more credits than debits. How are those credits established?

Nurse executives should assess what projects are essential to the hospital's leadership. They then should do their part in helping each principal achieve an important goal. They should build relationships that can result in effective coalitions throughout the usual administrative meetings.

For example, nurses in one hospital were very critical of dietary, and dietary responded in a negative fashion. The nursing vice president seized this problem and turned it to advantage by encouraging staff members to be supportive of dietary. As relations between the two departments improved and credits built in the emotional bank account, the vice president was able to induce dietary to cooperate in a program in which clear liquid choices were improved and more items were made available for postoperative patients on the unit. Thus, there was less waste of salty, cold broth and rubbery Jell-O as more palatable choices were made available.

This effort was beneficial from a cost standpoint and effective in decreasing the patient complaints that had angered staff members. The improved morale and communication aided both departments in being more productive, since they spent less time quarreling and seeking food for patients who had rejected the original choices.

During this process of compromising and making trade-offs for success, it is important that nursing executives reconcile their responsibility to the hospital with that to their department. While the needs of the nursing department must always be a prime consideration, because of the executives' primary advocacy role such efforts cannot seem to be defensive or self-serving. If the leaders' efforts seem to be directed toward getting more power in nursing, their effectiveness may be undermined by a competitive relationship with other vice presidents, who also seek control and power. Then worthy goals may be sacrificed in the power struggle that ensues.

At times, nursing executives may have to (or want to) share the credit for any advances with other members of the administrative council. If the nursing department gets the needed resources, this sacrifice is worth it as the whole hospital benefits.

In some hospitals where power struggles are brutal, nurse leaders have lost control of the nursing staff in the outpatient department, which can cause intra-departmental policy differences that interfere with continuity of care. This power distribution can be particularly damaging if the outpatient business generates a profit, which would be helpful to nursing if it were acquiring autonomy for its own budget. If viewed in the context of the future, the loss of these revenues for nursing is significant since the largest projected area of growth in hospitals is in outpatient services.

There is a fine line between political effectiveness and failure stemming from ego involvement that goes beyond the business goals being negotiated. For some leaders, this feeling of capturing power in nursing stands in the way of the formation of effective working coalitions. However, success in efforts with other administrative leaders is the beginning of the team-building effort that also must occur at the top of the organization as an example to all employees.

Nursing executives, in addition to their role in the administrative council, must work at building other important relationships. That will mean inclusion on the medical board and the board of trustees.[7] To gain the experience and power necessary to be a functioning member of these groups, nurse leaders may want to get on some community boards, both to gain experience and to develop alliances with some of the important hospital supporters in the community. Selecting the persons and boards that would be timely takes a plan; otherwise, these efforts can be diffuse and nonproductive.

Once adequate board skills and key relationships have been established, nurse executives should study the medical board to align themselves with key physicians and identify important issues that require the support of nursing. The building of an effective physician-nurse alliance then will be contingent on the ability to offer timely trade-offs and be businesslike in all transactions.

For example, physicians feel the threat of governmental and third party intervention in their medical decisions. That can put them in an unprecedented position of insecurity, so they may be more amenable to working cooperatively with nursing now than ever before. Insight into these feelings can be discovered in

American Medical News,[8] a publication of the American Medical Association, which deals with these matters in almost every issue.

When cooperation is assured, physicians need to be diplomatically oriented as to how their work style affects nursing costs and the productivity/work life of staff members. If cooperation does not seem to be forthcoming in all physicians, nurse executives should begin with the ones where the opportunity for success seems to be best and reward them with enthusiastic support so that others may follow their lead.

It must be remembered that control of physician orders and schedules is one of the biggest keys to improving nursing productivity. Once the relationship is effective between a physician and the vice president of nursing, it is important to transfer some of this positive interchange so that it includes other nurse leaders and staff members.

Similarly, positive relationships with members of the board of trustees require a pattern of good decisions; mature, businesslike behavior; and an understanding of how this group works. Effectiveness with the board depends on nursing leaders' personality, fairness, persistence, and ability to influence individuals. This influence stems from personal relationships with board members and from coalitions formed with community leaders. Nurse executives need a great deal of practice in affecting board relationships since this is a new area of involvement for most of them, but it is one that is vital to gaining program support.

DEVELOPING NURSING SUPPORT

Efforts to gain power and resources for the nursing division consume a great amount of time, research, and effort, so the vice president often is less involved than ever in the daily management of the department.[9] To fill the void, there is a team of middle managers that generally includes directors of nursing and the evening and night administrators. This team also may include a nurse office manager, who coordinates the functions of that office and special supportive divisional projects. However, who will be involved in this group and how their labors will be divided depends entirely on what works best for the division.

Because of the emphasis on cost containment and improved productivity, the relationship between the vice president and the middle and front-line managers must underscore the need for them to set a good example in using time and resources effectively. A plan for such exemplary behavior must include personal goal setting as well as cooperative goal planning with others that maximizes the use of networking.

Middle Management

Middle managers must be kept informed about and involved in the establishment of productivity and cost-containment goals for themselves and the entire nursing division. They constitute the group that will translate those goals to front-line managers for implementation and will convey input from the work force back to the vice president. It is vital that these managers show staff members that they are working hard in their behalf to be a partner in reaching the goals of productivity and cost containment. Problems can arise when this middle management team does not fully support the vice president of nursing. In such cases, the resultant petty power games can work to dilute the effectiveness of the entire division.[10]

Middle managers need enough power and autonomy to be able to translate divisional goals into the areas for which they are responsible. They also need the educational and experiential background to be able to personalize divisional goals to their department and work to facilitate the efforts of each center. This ability must be adequate for them to build unit or center leaders and to be able to facilitate problem solving designed to meet productivity challenges creatively. To be the ideal leader, middle managers must function as consultants, educators, and facilitators in linking unit goals with both the department division and with hospital efforts in general. Old authoritarian power relationships will not work to build decentralized centers and avoid costly duplicated efforts within the department.

In some hospitals, problems develop when the vice president becomes frustrated in the new job and pushes problems onto middle managers. In such cases, the middle managers spend a great amount of time in limbo because they must negotiate and renegotiate their power base constantly. In effect, there is a centralized power system based on the vice president, with middle management jobs established to function under a decentralized power structure. As a result, the middle managers have no clearly delineated function or power and thus always feel that their efforts are crisis management.

This process may give the vice president the same sense of control as existed in traditional nursing departments, but it reduces middle managers' effectiveness. This ineffectiveness trickles down to the front-line managers, who are constantly informed of the bottleneck in nursing administration. Problems with system ineffectiveness and frustration thus are reinforced. This also may include the bypassing of the nursing director, with the vice president consulting directly with the unit managers. As discussed earlier, these are among the problems with micro values that have resulted from the macro changes in hospital systems.

Nursing divisions that function in a cost-effective, productive manner are those with middle managers who are competent in clinical matters and adept at management functions. Team play is critical at this level, since it sets the tone for the whole division and each department. When traditional supervisors are unable to develop the requisite skills to function as directors in the division, they need to be replaced by those who can be new era managers. Clear delineation of those roles is critical to the smooth operation of the division. Part of the problem in some hospitals is the lack of clarity as to just what the nursing directors' functions are. Thus, they are pulled back into crisis management in daily patient care, a role that effectively keeps them from doing the real job of a middle manager in a decentralized system while infringing on the territory of the unit manager.

For example, one old-time supervisor talked decentralization but practiced authoritarian leadership. She hugged the time schedules, spent time handling patient problems best suited to the unit leader, and destructively changed unit leader evaluations of staff members in an unconscious effort to preserve the accustomed, comfortable prior supervisory role. When she retired, her replacement, a new-era manager, delegated, facilitated, and supported unit leaders. Unit morale increased as staff members got the green light to move forward with ideas for improving productivity, and the new leader had time to work more on people building, future goals, and programs that would continue to enhance morale, productivity, creative programming, and cost effectiveness in the department.

While the evening and night administrators are in middle management roles, they tend to be more concerned with immediate coaching and counseling of employees and current problems in the administration of patient care. Directors of nursing are responsible for strategic planning and for the entire department. Directors need to work cooperatively with the evening and night administrators to resolve problems on the other shifts.

In many hospitals, the evening and night administrators report to the directors. However, there is substantial uncertainty as to what functions they should have in the decentralized operation, since many of their traditional activities, such as staffing, are handled now by the unit manager with a central staffing secretary as a hospitalwide coordinator. As their facilitative and mentoring role becomes better defined, they also need to work on positive relationships to enhance the efforts of each unit manager.

Unit Manager

Unit managers need clear direction and the feeling that they are positively aligned with middle and top nursing management. Otherwise, time spent in meetings to get enough power to do the job is borrowed from time on the unit or center that is desperately needed for planning creative programs, improving the staff's productive efforts, monitoring quality and efficiency of care delivery, working personally to develop and support staff, budgeting, and contributing to the marketing plan goals.

INCREASING PROFITS

Most nursing executives spend much of their time identifying, measuring, and controlling costs. Instead of chasing costs, it is time to adopt a philosophy that increases opportunity for dollars expended. Before trying to cut costs, it is important to view the desired performance standards and productivity enhancement goals. Next, a value needs to be attached to each item in the context of overall goals.[11]

There are four cost categories: productive costs, supportive costs, policing costs, and waste. In deciding what the quality indicators will be for each category, a decision must be made as to what is worth controlling and what is more trouble than the effort to monitor it. The problem or point of the effort should be delineated clearly in advance to avoid generating reams of data in which important answers are buried deep. Essentially, there are a few activities in every responsibility center and effort that account for the bulk of the costs. Before choosing a wide variety of quality assurance items to monitor, it is important to decide what factors provide the best picture of the level of productivity, the quality and documentation of services, the performance and morale of staff, and the cost of services.

The costs for each measured item are determined next. Within those costs, nursing executives can decide at what point further expenditures do not produce adequate returns. They often can identify places where minor adjustments could result in large savings. Sometimes this process gets painful, as when a traditional program must be cut because it does not fit into the context of where the nursing department is moving. After the major activities are analyzed and costed out, the nurse leader may selectively choose other items to assess.

One area involving productive costs and waste that can serve as an example is the national practice of report between two shifts. While a number of methods have been tried, most staff members give report in their own way. Thus, it can stretch out to an hour and still fail to include significant items. To make better use of staff time and provide a smooth start on the new shift, report needs to be analyzed, streamlined, made the subject of inservice workshops, and monitored.

This effort starts by studying all of the report methods available, discussing possibilities with staff members, establishing criteria for an adequate report with a deadline of perhaps one minute for most patients, giving all staff members instant instruction in the practice of new methods, and measuring the effectiveness of the change.

This changed report can be measured by:

- the reduced overtime for the offgoing shift
- the decrease in incidents and dry IVs when the floor is left uncovered for long reports
- the gain in staff time for patient care
- the reduction in delays in getting patients to surgery or other departments
- the satisfaction level of staff members
- the decrease in patient complaints at the end of the shift

- decreased anxiety and untoward incidents in the first hour of the oncoming shift.

Nursing executives should think about the goal of being one of the first units in the hospital and nation to overcome this perennial problem.

Meetings

One of the mysteries in most nursing departments is why there are so many meetings, since few persons like to attend them and they tie up a large group that could be working on the units. The number of meetings bothers everyone, yet they continue. These meetings exaggerate the support costs and waste in the nursing budget.

Ideally, meetings should be designed to pool ideas, share information, discuss resource utilization and movement toward goals, benefit members from peer stimulation, gain group support, and solve problems. In reality, they often rehash events that have occurred already. Instead of being proactive, they are bogged down with discussions that have little value for what is being done now or in the future. To check this out in their own division, nursing executives can simply write down the number and types of meetings, what is discussed, how long they take, and what they have to do with further action on important goals. The results will be depressing—and a stimulus for reform.

The real reasons that people go to meetings are to relieve loneliness, avoid individual decisions, get a break from work, get in on what is happening politically, gain status, talk, share problems, or just because there is a meeting. Through these meetings, managers meet important people, learn meeting skills, find a forum to test their ideas, gain friends by supporting issues unimportant to themselves, are included as decision makers, and sometimes coerce others before the group. However, meetings usually become ends in themselves and rarely result in productive problem solving.

How can that be changed? Meetings have to be assigned a cost value and a purpose. Alternative methods for achieving goals need to be discussed. Where meetings are necessary, each topic on the agenda needs to be analyzed thoroughly and presented in relation to accomplishing a specific goal.

The cost of an item can be calculated by multiplying the meeting time required by the cost of the salary and time of each person in the room. That cost should then be added to the budget for accomplishing each activity in the nursing department. By placing a monetary value on meeting time assigned to each project, nurse executives establish accountability as a priority.

To make meetings worthwhile, those presiding need to balance the mandate of pushing the sessions to reach decisions with the need to ensure fair play. To do this, they must avoid excessive talking, inhibiting discussion, offering too many suggestions or leading the group, and rushing the meeting so fast that the group process is negated. Everyone in the group needs to be involved as appropriate without dragging the meeting out. Through the facilitation process, the leader in effect becomes the group servant, focuses it on its tasks, suggests alternatives, protects members from attack, encourages participation, helps everyone win, and coordinates premeeting and postmeeting logistics.

Thus, instead of being nonproductive, meetings become forums for sharing ideas and projects that presenters have prepared. They also become springboards for action and effective networking within the nursing division. If the division is not using meetings in this way, now is the time to analyze why. Is it because unit managers are trying to play power games and sidestep the way things go through the system? If so, nurse executives may be dealing with the problem of being very centralized in management while appearing to be decentralized in function. This issue must be solved before meaningful decentralized projects can move forward.

The benefits to be derived from meetings should go beyond the needs of participants. Staff members have to work harder to fill gaps when managers go to meetings, so managers should bring back meaningful information. When this is not done, staff nurses may feel that they carry the productive load of the hospital on their backs while their management team is drinking too much coffee in meetings. When this resentment grows, staff members may decide to slack off in their work and in their participation in unit projects because of the apathy and lack of team commitment they feel.

This problem exists in many hospitals, and at varying levels on each unit, depending on the personality of the leader. It is significant as a major deterrent to productive effort. Some leaders say that the golden rule and consideration of the feelings of others is unfortunately the first thing to be omitted in times of increased workloads and stress.

However, units that excel in feeling positive about their job, their peers, and the quality and quantity of their work effort learn to value the small kindnesses that can make the biggest difference of all in meeting improved productivity and cost containment goals.[12]

SUMMARY

To achieve goals of improved productivity and cost containment, managers need to begin by taking a hard look at themselves, their skills, and their effectiveness in human relations and in facilitating and guiding the work of others. Because hospitals have major problems in clearly delineating the goals of each level of manager and giving them the necessary budget and power to accomplish their jobs, this area requires serious scrutiny. Otherwise, figures of productivity, on paper, limited to direct care can be meaningless and simple changes possible through thoughtful commitment and action by the management team can be overlooked.

Decentralization is a large step forward in improving productivity, but it takes a great deal of planning, education, experience, and monitoring if it is to work in reality as it looks on paper. Where planning and coordination are evident, decisions can be made close to the point of action without losing the feedback mechanism essential to keep the department integrated as a whole.

Moreover, as the nursing staff develops skills in improving productivity and implementing ideas that benefit the whole hospital, the division will acquire the credibility that will induce top administration to share the purse strings.

NOTES

1. Warren Bennis and Burt Nanus, *Leaders: Strategies for Taking Charge* (New York: Harper & Row, Publishers, Inc., 1985).
2. J.M. Carter and Joan Feeney, *Starting at the Top* (New York: William Morrow & Company, Inc., 1985).
3. Barbara Stevens, *The Nurse as Executive* (Wakefield, Mass.: Nursing Resources, 1980), 200–201.
4. F.L. Huey, "Working Smart," *American Journal of Nursing* 86, no.4 (June 1986): 679–783.
5. Arbraham Zalenznik and Manfred Kets de Vries, *Power and the Corporate Mind: How to Use Rather Than Misuse Leadership* (Chicago: Pluribus Press, 1985).
6. Leah Curtin, "Political Savvy," *Nursing Management* 13, no.3 (March 1982): 7–8.
7. Everett Johnson and Richard Johnson, *Contemporary Hospital Trusteeship* (Chicago: Pluribus Press, 1983).
8. American Medical Association. *American Medical News*.
9. R.E. Brown, *Judgment in Administration* (Chicago: Pluribus Press, 1983).
10. R.J. Plachy, *When I Lead, Why Don't They Follow?* (Chicago: Pluribus Press, 1978).
11. Peter F. Drucker, *Managing for Results* (New York: Harper & Row, Publishers, Inc., 1964).
12. Winston Fletcher, *Meetings, Meetings: How to Manipulate Them and Make Them Fun* (New York: William Morrow & Company, Inc., 1984).

ACTION CHECKLIST

1. How does top management function at the hospital?
2. What skills or changes are needed to acquire adequate authority to do the job better?
3. Wht is the relationship like between the vice president and the senior nurse managers? What are some ideas for improving this relationship?
4. What is the relationship between middle managers and front-line managers? What can be done to improve this relationship?
5. How effective has the hospital been in accomplishing decentralization and staff nurse participation in decisions?
6. What are five things that should be done to operate the department more effectively?

Chapter 7

Front-Line Management

Achieving the goals of productivity depends heavily on the effectiveness of the unit leader. Some nursing leaders have suggested that true productivity that integrates all factors in productivity evades realization until working models become available. Curtin and Zurlage have constructed a comprehensive model that bears close analysis by all front-line managers, since it incorporates a mathematical model with the major factors to be considered in achieving nursing productivity.[1]

However, this productivity index still requires national definition of desired outcomes, ways to measure them, and means of collecting essential data. While nurse managers can study and work toward the implementation of this model and others that will be forthcoming, front-line managers still are left with the pressing priority of making their units productive and cost effective now. Whatever model nurse leaders adopt, basic problems at the front-line level must be identified and resolved to attain productive work patterns.

Succeeding at achieving greater productivity requires adherence to four fundamentals: clear goals and standards, commitment, quality feedback, and organizational support.

Before unit managers or head nurses can direct the productive efforts of their staffs, they must identify a specific plan of the goals, standards, and priorities on their units. Not all standards are new, but they have to be written to ensure inclusion in the total plan. For example, under the goal of facilitating early patient discharges, a standard might say that bedfast patients will be turned and given skin care every two hours. This step, of course, prevents problems that can prolong the hospital stay.

This productivity plan must include the staffing and patient care data available through the computerized patient classification and staffing system, methods for meeting the human needs of staff members and patients/families, ways that all hospital resources can be blended into the efforts of the unit, and specific plans for monitoring the effectiveness of the plan.

In formulating this plan, unit leaders can benefit from the assistance of the quality assurance director and consultation with a nurse researcher. Time and money spent at this point is cost effective since it prevents the expenditure of resources and efforts in fruitless directions.

Once goals are established, the unit leader and staff must make a total commitment to achieving them. The creative efforts of the entire staff are required to deal with the many changes in evaluating time management and quality in patient care delivery, charting, meeting in committees, changing cumbersome policies and procedures, fostering a positive climate of team spirit, and improving customer relations. This further underscores the importance of decentralization, since the unit leader cannot accomplish all of these productive changes without staff involvement.

Monitoring and feedback systems and deadlines must be designed before the productivity plan is initiated, so objective data are available to evaluate whether or not the program is staying on course. Such feedback can include:

- simple logs to learn what category of employee runs off-unit errands and does patient transporting, including the frequency and length of those trips
- random audits of charts to look for special results or patient outcomes
- surveys of staff and patients to assess the quality and effectiveness of the efforts
- bedside patient care audits
- comparisons of treatments and lengths of stay when some category of patients is receiving a given method of nursing care while other patients are not.

Costs also can be assigned to each nursing treatment regime and evaluated with the final patient outcome for each treatment method.

The unit leader needs organizational support if the productivity plan is to succeed. This organizational support varies in each nursing division and even on different units in the same hospital, because of political and personality factors. This involves questions such as:

- Is this unit leader given autonomy to run a decentralized operation?
- Does the leader have an adequate budget to construct a total plan for productivity and get assistance in creating monitoring tools?
- Is the unit leader provided with the educational support to understand how every management and staff effort can be assessed in relation to its fit with the total productive effort?
- Does the leader have the skill and direction to mentor all staff members so they can make meaningful contributions to the total productivity program?

To understand how realistic daily implementation of the front-line manager role affects productivity, it is important to review the factors inherent in this job. Some unit leaders have found it valuable to establish a support group with unit leaders in related areas in meeting the new productive challenges of this era.

THE TRADITIONAL ROLE

Most systems that assess productivity, top management expectations for more direct patient care with less resources, and responsibility for coordinating communications with all hospital publics converge at the point of the front-line manager. Because this unit level has always been the place to test the "proof of the pudding," this front-line leader has one of the most stressful jobs in the hospital.

Under the traditional system, the unit leader manned the desk and knew every detail about immediate needs on the unit. Caught up in moment-to-moment decisions and activities, this person had great difficulty finding time and getting needed consultative help in managing the unit, as well as devising a systematic plan for making needed improvements.

By the mid-1980s, this role had been changing slowly so that unit leaders would have days when they did not manage the traffic of the unit but were free to work on management projects related to it. This transition has been difficult for some, who may feel threatened in leaving the old, comfortable role and moving into strategic planning for which many deem themselves unprepared.

While most unit managers have had some courses in management and basic budgeting, they may lack the education and experience needed to construct a pragmatic, cost-effective productivity plan with measurement criteria in conjunction with the nursing staff, and then sell this plan to administration, whose support they require.

For example, in one obstetrical unit, nurses who had attended numerous conferences were excited and well equipped to construct a plan for improving staff utilization and attracting a larger number of patients to the hospital. However, their plan was not implemented because the marketing executive did not agree with extending the hospital advertising campaign to the obstetrical unit at that time. Moreover, the staff committee was not given adequate guidance and administrative approval to make its pilot plan operational. Thus, the politics of the system undermined the effort.

The emphasis on improving productivity, building the participative management role of registered nurses, and providing quality care in a shorter hospital stay has caused front-line managers to realize that the traditional role of the head nurse must include the support systems needed to effect change.

THE CHANGING ROLE

Many unit or center managers have assumed 24-hour accountability for their units. They also have become more involved in strategic planning, staffing, budgeting,[2] research, productivity, computerizing the unit, and quality control. Thus, the definition of operating the unit has extended to include responsibility for both its immediate and long-term management.[3]

For many managers, assuming these new functions has created a need for continuing education to bridge their skill gap. Courses in business skills, accounting, marketing, legal aspects, and computers need to be augmented with those that emphasize such people-building skills as motivation, conflict resolution, change theory, and participative management.

Changes in unit leaders' roles have involved their authority, accountability, advocacy, and management style.

Authority

On the surface, many hospitals have a decentralized operation, but in reality may not have changed the way they function. Centralized leaders still may be counteracting true autonomy and productivity at the unit level by withholding vital information or by keeping red tape in the system that blocks true decentralized functions. Thus, good ideas for improving productivity that require policy changes can get mired down in red tape.

For example, one unit created a flow sheet that denoted patient progress in relation to the care plan in a quick, systematic format. The unit documented how this flow sheet would decrease documentation time so that the registered nurse could function more productively. However, the central nursing office blocked the change by saying that this form would cause confusion and lack of standardization for nurses from other areas who might float to this unit to work.

Obviously, if improved productivity were the honest objective, a continuing education bridge could have been constructed to assist new nurses or those from other units in utilizing the form if the pilot test revealed a significant improvement in nurses' productive efforts.

Some unit managers are not given the information necessary to know the direction and issues of the entire hospital. This becomes especially frustrating when decisions about the hospital and their unit appear in the news media before the unit manager is aware of an event or plan. While some of this breakdown in communication is caused by the hospital's need to keep its plans private to maintain a better competitive position with other agencies, the problem also can be caught up in a power struggle within administration.

At times, information that could be shared more widely is kept confidential simply because traditionally it has not been made available to the unit leaders, whose input is necessary because of its relevance and its importance in establishing the unit as a cost-effective, productive operation. When unit leaders do not handle these problems in a mature manner, they may feel an us-them relationship with higher management. This destructive process dilutes productive efforts in the hospital.

Red tape also can frustrate leaders, who may be unable to manage the unit productively because of the need to attend frequent meetings to gain permission for action and to keep abreast of politics that can affect power within the system. Red tape also can be a disguise for the bigger problem of overlapping roles and resistance to change.

Even though this problem is not new, many unit leaders say they spend far too much time in courting and convincing an often outdated central supervisor on the need for implementing a new idea. This process undermines their effectiveness as leaders with staff members since the latter have difficulty understanding why a productive idea that is well written and supported can be stopped arbitrarily by the nursing office.

In many hospitals, there still is a power struggle between the unit leader and the supervisor, whose roles overlap. While the message to the unit leader is to act, there is a penalty when departmental directors or supervisors perceive such action as threatening to their role. It is essential to free head nurses to be productive, to clarify roles, and to develop collaborative relations with the departmental director and the shift supervisors. Then, their combined efforts can provide a constructive environment for staff members and for the provision of productive, cost-effective patient care delivery. Head nurses' "people problem" with higher-ups cannot be quantified, but it can be the underlying reason why unit leaders cannot seem to resolve some of the poor habits and work patterns that stifle productivity.

On the other hand, such perceived problems in authority also can be a convenient excuse for not making progress. Seasoned leaders who understand change theory know that it is not wise to continue to bang one's head on a concrete wall; unresolvable problems and ideas should be put on hold, while elements that can be changed are worked on.

For example, all unit leaders have sufficient power to build a positive attitude in staff, to mentor staff members in better ways to organize and document work and make assignments, and in faster ways to do an in-depth job of counseling patients and providing patient education. They also have the freedom to excite their staffs as to the advantages of everyone's helping the others to best finish the workload on the unit. It does not take a policy change to bring sunshine and enthusiasm to staff members, but it does take a working knowledge of how to work effectively in guiding others.

Nurse leaders should remember that some of the delay and review in making policy changes is a healthy systems check to be sure that such actions are not spurious or half-baked and that the hospital itself does not end up in chaos from rapid moves that do not fit into its total picture.

Accountability

Accountability at the unit level has changed. Unit managers now are responsible for supervising the delivery of quality care to patients in a more productive, cost-effective manner, and facilitating the efforts of each staff member. However, where job authority and resources do not match this increased responsibility, the unit leaders feel frustrated.[4]

For example, the most commonly heard question at a productivity workshop is, "How can my staff members participate in planning for productive change or working on their personal projects that will help the unit when we are only staffed well enough to barely get the patient care done?"

One answer is to divide each nurse's project into small achievable pieces in which 20-minute work segments will make a difference. For example, in reviewing all procedures for patient safety, effectiveness, and cost reduction, one step—catheter care—could involve researching a leading textbook to find the procedure for catheter care, speaking with the infection control nurse to learn the essential requirements for managing catheter care, or calling the librarian for a literature search.

The key is to construct a project outline of steps, each with a deadline. When small steps are put together, they produce information adequate to more effective and cost-wise procedures.

Another answer is to construct a rotating list, with all nurses taking a turn at working on their own projects when census shifts free up short periods of time. This "turn" list needs the support of all staff members, since they must be committed to cover the work of the freed nurse, whose project should benefit everyone on the unit, and in turn have opportunities to develop their own projects.

The workload has changed because more patients have severe illnesses so the length of the hospital stays has decreased and staffing needs have been altered. Hospitals need more professional nurses to manage the more complex patient problems and sophisticated treatments. Many unit leaders thus must change the staffing mix and the job descriptions to better meet today's challenges. Despite the changes, some long-term employees may remain on the staff in traditional roles.

For example, some hospitals are letting the number of licensed practical nurses (L.P.N.s) decrease through attrition. Since L.P.N.s are limited in nursing process skills, documentation abilities, and skill level, registered nurses on the unit may be carrying an undue load to compensate. This impedes the staff's ability to improve its productivity and can cause R.N.s to burn out. While hospitals owe loyalty to hard workers who have been in the organization for a long time, they must devise educational updating efforts and work on outplacement of L.P.N.s so they can hire more professional nurses.

Where nursing assistants remain, R.N.s may find that the old aide role is not supportive of the new demands. When aides finish routine care and mealtime assistance, they may take numerous breaks, while the registered nurses run at a more frantic pace. The nursing assistants and L.P.N.s often feel threatened and resentful of the changes and create morale problems each time they are asked to perform added errands or modify old work patterns.

Obviously, these roles need to be redefined and working hours need to be reevaluated so that these helping persons can be utilized more effectively. In the meantime, many unit leaders complain that time credited for R.N.s' "direct patient care" often is spent in running to the pharmacy for an IV additive or in getting liquid refreshments for patients.

Why don't R.N.s delegate these functions if ancillary personnel take so many breaks? Because they do not like handling the hostility and the problem of continually trying to motivate these persons to work. Thus, they give up, do it themselves, then find they are short of time or in need of overtime to complete their own work.

Correction of these problems requires changes in staffing. It also calls for education in conflict and leadership skills for staff nurses faced with these problems. The continuing support and guidance of the unit leader is essential if these obstacles to productivity are to be hurdled.

There also is a great ethical and legal necessity to be certain that patients have received physical care, psychosocial support, and educational information to be discharged safely from the hospital. Accomplishing this in a shorter time frustrates nurses, who feel torn between direct care and paperwork. Head nurses must change that environment to assure patient care with the least amount of wasted time, resources, and effort.

Specifically, this means that unit leaders need to work with staff nurses and network with other hospital units to devise checklists, flow sheets that minimize writing, standard care plans with discharge components, and patient handouts that ensure a complete approach for each client. Nurses then need help in learning how to write meaningful notes that accurately summarize a patient's condition and progress in relation to the plan of care. Units using such an approach save time in documentation, improve their position for potential legal cases, and have a clear plan in mind that facilitates early discharge and added safety for patients.

Accountability also includes networking with other health care professionals whose work can augment the achievement of productivity and cost containment goals (Table 7–1). For example, physician orders are the single most important factor in determining cost of patient services. Head nurses therefore need to build collegial relationships with physicians and between staff members and physicians

Table 7-1 Protocols by M.D. for DRG 90, Including Costs for Treatment "C"

M.D.	Patients Treated	ALOS		Cost/Discharge		Profit/(Loss) "C"	Discharge No "C"	"C" Costs
		"C"	No "C"	"C"	No "C"			
1	6	46.7	28.0	$10,568	$5,702	$ (4,250)	$ 450	$ 4,700
2	3	46.7	34.8	10,231	7,416	(3,557)	(762)	2,795
3	13	38.9	27.7	8,595	5,856	(2,058)	374	2,432
4	67	34.6	21.6	7,376	4,320	(937)	1,968	2,905
5	2	95.0	20.6	21,928	4,596	(15,268)	1,618	16,886
6	12	17.9	12.8	4,827	2,990	1,492	3,209	(1,717)
7	15	27.4	15.4	6,804	3,618	(465)	2,573	3,038
8	19	48.6	32.1	11,275	7,033	(4,772)	(633)	4,139
9	0	—	17.2	—	3,861	—	2,656	—
10	27	35.2	22.7	9,028	5,574	(2,242)	866	3,108
Other	4	52.8	31.6	13,683	7,400	(7,023)	(903)	6,120

Comments:

1. Treatment "C" represents a specific intervention that has a highly effective impact on patient care but an adverse impact on the length of stay (LOS).

2. Patient care should be analyzed to determine whether this same positive effect can be attained with a less costly intervention.

3. If not, is this an area where patient well-being is prioritized over economics? If so, cost containment and improved productivity will be needed in other areas to offset the expense of "C."

4. This table is an example of how comparisons for one DRG can be made across the physicians who admit patients to the unit.

so that unnecessary orders are minimized and the efforts of health care specialists are best coordinated.

Finally, accountability extends to intricate details of management that affect the bottom line: a systems analysis to streamline paperwork, ordering, supply charges and availability, patient scheduling, and gaps between testing time and the availability of results. Unit leaders also must be concerned with analyzing staff, unit, and patient needs, provisions for meeting those needs, and quality control mechanisms for testing how productively current strategies are working.

For example, the emphasis in charting is on patient response to treatment, as well as comparative discharge planning throughout the hospital stay. After the question of what is to be done is answered, careful implementation of methods to meet these needs should follow, with subsequent monitoring to be sure that everyone complies with the plan. Chart audits and checks on patient care, as well as management by walking around (MBWA) are useful ways to be sure that standards of quality are met.[5]

Similar study is needed on productive methods in staffing and scheduling. For example, in one hospital the head nurse was spending an undue amount of time on weekend schedules because absenteeism had increased, especially among those who had subsequent days off or for those with special plans. To solve this problem, the leader established a schedule of some nurses who worked only on weekends and a rule that regular staff nurses who missed work on a weekend would have to sacrifice a similar day later when they were scheduled to be off. This simple step dramatically reduced absenteeism on weekends, and improved productivity.

The bottom line is that as quantitative, computerized systems are instituted, the responsibility (accountability) for budget control becomes a daily concern of unit or center managers as well as of the central administrative office. Such control goes far beyond staffing patterns to include all details of unit operation that need to be identified and monitored for the itemized billing in addition to large categorical assignments based on patient acuity.

Budget control is more than pouring over staffing ratios. It also requires unit leaders to study ways to simplify nursing procedures and decrease the cost of supplies without compromising the quality of care.[6] As hospitals institute monetary rewards and profit sharing for such efforts, the impetus will be greater to ferret out the many ways that staff members waste supplies, time, and energy in traditional nursing practices. In succeeding at this detective job, creative leaders will make the process a challenge and a game that has the important stakes of improving the quality of patient care.

The Advocacy Role

Head nurses act as mediators who connect resources with staff and patients/families. They need to be the new era leaders who facilitate communication with all staff members. They must cope with staff members' needs for security, fair treatment, involvement in decision making, and assistance in staying current with both the regular unit and the units to which they may be floated.

Leaders also need to have the respect and personal knowledge of each staff person. When problems occur on the job or in the staff members' personal lives, the leaders should be supportive and helpful in connecting these individuals with appropriate resources.

For example, Mary X was reporting respiratory infections and flu quite often. Her leader pointed out the illness pattern and the increased sick time, and worked with Mary to modify her work schedule and assist her with time management techniques to minimize stress. Mary confided some personal problems to the leader and received a referral to a qualified counselor, who assisted her in getting her life in order. As a result, Mary became a much healthier, productive employee.[7]

Unit leaders play a large advocacy role in assuring that patients and families have what they need from nursing and available resources in the health care delivery system. That role begins with setting, adapting, and amending patient care standards and developing written guidelines and instructions that can be given to patients to clarify their understanding of what is happening to them. It continues as the leaders work to enhance staff members' expertise in utilizing and documenting the nursing process. Where staff members lack coursework at the baccalaureate level in communication techniques, psychiatric nursing, and community health nursing, the leaders must supplement their skills on an individual basis.

Patient advocacy also includes keeping staff members posted on the resources in the hospital and community that might be helpful to patients and families. The wise use of these resources can mean the difference between patient safety, maximum value of therapeutic intervention, and satisfaction with the illness experience or an unnecessarily negative experience. This process involves effectiveness in networking.

For example, nurses need to know what other departments (such as dietary or social services) can provide to patients and families in need. They also should become skilled at the type of discharge planning that matches patient needs to postdischarge services. In one hospital, this need was met through the use of selective rounds with physicians, pharmacists, social workers, dieticians, chaplains, physical therapists, nursing home representatives, and home health care nurses. Other specialists were included as needed.

The counseling role is an important component in productive service delivery for patients and families whose life styles change in response to major illness. Services can involve individual counseling between the nurse and patient/family, as well as group sessions for needs of like diagnostic groups. The idea here is to identify informational needs as well as support systems for patients and their families. Getting the right services to the client by mentoring staff nurses in this process can result in improved productivity because of the increased speed of recovery and the availability of needed help after discharge.[8]

Management Style

The management style of leaders in the new era involves balancing humanism with the entrepreneurial system. People building is a major part of this role, which is designed to get all nurses interested and involved in providing cost-effective, productive, quality patient care. A major component of this process is the mentoring role.

Traditionally, unit leaders quietly made individual rounds on all patients to assess nursing care. However, some leaders now make concentrated rounds on a small group of patients with the staff nurse responsible. As they walk and talk, they discuss care planning strategies, problems, and progress that the staff nurse will implement, and ways to achieve goals most efficiently. Less experienced nurses can watch the senior nurse leader communicate with patients and work through the steps of the nursing process. These rounds build the skills of less experienced nurses while clarifying the expectations for nursing care.

For example, in one case, the nurse had difficulty in getting into a discussion with Mr. J about his personal reaction to the diagnosis of terminal cancer. The nurse leader demonstrated interviewing techniques to facilitate this discussion and pinpoint special problems, then introduced the staff nurse as the person who would continue to work with Mr. J. This experienced approach minimized the time required to get into a meaningful discussion and clarified the important points of care for the staff nurse while involving that individual as the primary caregiver.

The real problem here is that getting the nurse to the bedside is not enough, even though this is termed direct patient care in patient classification systems. The problem is what that nurse does when interacting with the patient:

- Are conversations meaningful and goal directed in terms of patient care?
- Can the staff nurse identify major problems and determine effective strategies for helping the patient overcome these problems?
- Does the nurse know how to maximize family support systems?
- Can the nurse plan care so that there is continuity in the effort?
- Is the nurse effective and efficient in essential patient teaching and counseling?
- Does the nurse effectively communicate the merits of nursing services delivered?
- Is all of this captured in chart documentation?

All of this is what nurse leaders mentor staff nurses to learn. When staff nurses are not effective in these operations, care suffers, costs rise, and patients may decide to choose another hospital for their next illness.

Delivering and taking credit for excellent care and incorporating patient teaching and motivation into other tasks is a subtle process. When staff nurses do this well, they get more job satisfaction and patients benefit from more productive use of the nurses' time.

For example, Jill was a staff nurse who had a chronic health condition for which she had been hospitalized frequently. What distinguished her from other nurses was her heightened sensitivity to what patients were experiencing. Instead of going into the room and silently checking the patient and the intravenous drip, she took every opportunity to say something personal, make clear that she was checking on the person, and include a small item of patient education with every contact.

Patients felt that other nurses blurred in identity but often specifically named Jill as their nurse and one who took a special interest in them. Jill did not spend more time with patients than did other nurses, but she made known what she did, made sure that the patients knew why she was there, and used every contact to prepare them for discharge. As a result, her patients felt more comfortable and secure, rarely needing to put on their call lights.

Jill's type of approach is what nurse leaders should strive for in developing the skills of their staff members.

Leaders also should emphasize the importance of staff nurses' viewing each other as peers and working together as a team. When problems or care challenges occur, they need to be encouraged to network and utilize each other effectively. The leader should assist staff nurses in working with the myriad resources in education and other departments. Such small steps in efficient resource utilization are important, and often overlooked, opportunities that can make a large difference in productivity.

The unit leaders need to encourage brief, well-organized conferences at which staff members become involved in resolving patient care problems, in maintaining nursing competencies, and in sharing in decisions about managing unit productivity.[9,10]

SUMMARY

The role of unit managers in improving productivity is a tall order that extends to the style with which they approach every detail of operations. This style requires personal strength, confident leadership, and a quiet way of developing the entire staff to meet its responsibility of functioning automatically in a productive manner in everything it does. Regardless of the productivity model selected, the subtle people building and recognition of how to work smart in little ways is an area that bears examination.

As the strengths of the nursing care program are identified and improved, the leaders also emphasize staff-assisted methods for streamlining costs. Research becomes an important part of this effort, which strives to keep improving the delivery of nursing services and the satisfaction level of everyone involved, while documenting what is working.

NOTES

1. Leah Curtin and Carolyn Zurlage, "Nursing Productivity: From Data to Definition," *Nursing Management* 17, no. 6 (June 1986): 32–41.

2. Barbara Lang Rutkowski, "Now All Eyes Are On You," *Nursinglife* 5, no. 2 (March/April 1985): 30–32.

3. Sarah Becker and Donna Glenn, *Off Your Duffs and Up the Assets* (Rockville Center, N.Y.: Farnsworth Publishing Co. Inc., 1985).

4. Howard S. Rowland and Beatrice L. Rowland, *Nursing Administration Handbook* (Rockville, Md.: Aspen Publishers, Inc., 1985).

5. Barbara Lang Rutkowski, "Problem Solving," *Nursing 85* 15, no. 2 (February 1985): 89–92.

6. C.G. Meisenheimer, *Quality Assurance: A Complete Guide to Effective Programs* (Rockville, Md.: Aspen Publishers, Inc., 1985).

7. Arthur D. Rutkowski and Barbara Lang Rutkowski, *Labor Relations in Hospitals* (Rockville, Md.: Aspen Publishers, Inc., 1984).

8. Barbara Lang Rutkowski, "The Nursing Approach to Better Time Management," *Nursinglife* 4, no. 5 (September/October 1984): 52–57.

9. Barbara Conway-Rutkowski, guest ed., "Patient Compliance: A Symposium," *Nursing Clinics of North America* 17, no. 3 (September 1982).

10. Barbara Lang Rutkowski, "6 Steps to Building Your Confidence," *Nursinglife* 6, no. 1 (January/February 1986): 26–29.

ACTION CHECKLIST

The following points should be pondered as ways of being more effective front-line managers:

- Reality never lets nursing leaders down; their own expectations, distortions, and demands on reality do.
- The need to have perfect control and power results in great tension. No one knows everything. It is important to be a learner, not an authority; to get involved; to feel comfortable in admitting that sometimes one does not know what to do.
- Leaders obviously will be criticized at times. The question is how they can keep from passing the feeling on to staff.
- Leaders face a similar problem of what to do when blamed for things beyond their control.
- Leaders must determine how to do their part in streamlining their goals to fit with the total nursing division and hospital plan.
- They must figure out how to find the time to work personally with each staff member to build skills and solve individual problems.
- They must analyze how they are going to make ancillary roles more supportive to the functions of professional nurses.
- They must learn how to resolve the problems that occur in this transitional period for L.P.N.s and nursing assistants.
- They must develop techniques for assisting staff in utilizing more productive methods in time management.
- They must learn how to keep a healthy distance between themselves and staff and still be viewed as effective facilitators.

Chapter 8

Understanding Nurse Motives

Since the prospective payment system was introduced in hospitals, dramatic changes have occurred affecting nurses. Suddenly, they have been faced with demands to increase productivity and contain costs, but many do not understand how this can be done without compromising the quality of patient care. Most nurses came into the profession because of a deep desire to help and nurture others. Until the early 1980s, they could hire more and more people to achieve their ends.

However, nurses were continually plagued by their lack of autonomy, the martyrdom socialized into the profession, the problems of being a "female" occupation, the problem of not running nursing like a business, and infighting—all of which kept them from enjoying their rights to professionalism and working productively within the role for which they were educated.[1]

The health care revolution has stunned them and caused them to examine all of their personal and professional motivations for being a nurse and for working in the new atmosphere, where improved productivity is a priority. Many believe the nursing profession can regroup to solve age-old problems and become a business that can provide more satisfaction to members, while meeting productivity goals. However, first there must be a realistic self-appraisal, then some basic changes.

NURSE RESPONSES

When the impact of diagnosis related groups (DRGs) first hit hospital nurses, their overwhelming reaction was fear and insecurity. The job security that once had been a hallmark of the profession began to be affected by declining censuses throughout the country and cutbacks or unpaid days off, depending on how a particular hospital approached the situation. Since that initial shock wave, the picture has cleared. While workloads still are heavy, many hospitals are hiring registered nurses again.

According to an American Nurses' Association survey of its Council on Nursing Administration, several trends were evident:

- Hospitals reported they were relying more heavily on R.N.s because of their ability to handle the more complicated tasks involved in patients with more severe illnesses.
- Eighteen percent reported laying off R.N.s while 32 percent said licensed practical nurses (L.P.N.s) and aides had been most severely affected.
- Many hospitals reported they were reaching their reduced staffing goals through attrition.
- Many hospitals said they were cutting hours and employing part-time workers to decrease their labor costs.[2]

In Chicago, these trends were mirrored by the *Chicago Reporter*, which found that aides and L.P.N.s were the groups hardest hit by layoffs,[3] primarily because of hospitals' decisions to replace "team" nursing with primary or modular nursing. Hospital budgetary concerns, coupled with changes in patient workload and a philosophical shift in nursing, also were factors.

Because shifts in hospital nursing occurred so quickly, there was a rush to identify productive standards, implement patient classification systems, and decide where reductions in caregivers could be made on a daily basis. This trend angered nurses because patients required more assistance than that allocated by paperwork projections. Where the past was characterized by busy days followed by slack days when staff members could recuperate, the middle and late 1980s became a time in which slow days saw staff members being sent home without pay or transferred to busier work areas.[3] Nurses also became concerned with ethical aspects of their practice and with standard setting to be sure that patients were getting safe care.

The suddenness of this need to modify traditional nursing practices exacted a heavy emotional toll. Some nurses wondered about changing professions or jobs, others about the problems of allocating enough time for patient care and the mounting chores of documentation. Their specific concerns include:

- discomfort with the decreased quality of care
- stress because of increased responsibilities
- frustration over the nonnursing duties that stand in the way of patient care
- ethical and legal concerns over safe practice
- discouragement over dispensability and job insecurity
- worry that the changes may not result in equivalent or better care.

They hear administrators telling them that improved productivity is important because the hospital is "their" business, yet nurses have not seen concrete changes in the system of overt and covert awards to make this statement relevant to them personally. Why should staff nurses be involved and motivated to make the hospital the most productive business that it can be? Because, according to the Women's Bureau in the U.S. Department of Labor, most adult women are employed and will continue to stay active in the work force for many years. Thus, an investment in bettering the way nursing care is delivered is one that will pay personal dividends in many ways for years to come.[4]

Hospitals have responded to the new mandates by reorganizing staff, increasing the documentation of expenses, expanding computer services in nursing, and changing the style of delivering services. Efforts are under way to motivate and involve all nurses personally in making the hospital the most efficient, effective business that it can be.

Emotional Responses

For many nurses, the initial impact of these changes has been a continuing cycle of grief. Grief over the loss of familiar patterns is expressed in the same way as in response to death.[5] In the beginning, many nurses denied the reality of what improving productivity meant to them by actions and words such as, "This can't be happening to me," or "This change will blow over like so many others."

As hospital responses to prospective payment continued, denial was replaced with anger. Managers found that staff members were blowing up over minor incidents, resisting the notion of quantifying patient care and improving productivity in service delivery. Nurses often said that patients were not widgets on an assembly line, so treating them as consumers in a business would undermine nursing dangerously.

Some nursing managers became depressed and frustrated because they could not seem to ease staff tensions and anger. They found that they could not always predict what changes would occur next in response to declining census and demands for improved productivity and cost reduction. When staff members accused managers of not knowing what would happen next and what would be a permanent change, the leaders felt anxiety at their own lack of control. Some abandoned their managerial role by saying, "I don't know what *they* will make us do next." This diluted the effectiveness of the executive team by creating a gap among front, middle, and top managers. Meetings became one way that managers felt they could escape the pressures of dealing with staff members for a little while. However, managers' absences from the unit caused even more anger in nurses, who already felt frustrated over the heavy workload, earlier discharges, and mounting paperwork.

The next stage of response was bargaining, with staff members trying to perform admirably in hopes that drastic census declines, days off without pay, or layoffs would pass them by. However, the reality of declining census, the increased workload caused by shortened lengths of stay, greater acuity, and budget cuts continued.

When it seemed that these changes would be permanent, many nurses became depressed about their helplessness and felt like they were the victims of the entire health care revolution. At that point some became very concerned about what would happen to them and expressed such negative emotion that it interfered with productive work efforts. They also believed that nothing one individual could do would make any difference to the hospital. At times, when staffing was adequate, nurses still responded as if it were not. Managers worried and worked for new ways to motivate their staffs.

Nurses who would never have agreed to work a few tours of night duty volunteered to do their part. Still, small efforts seemed to make little difference in returning things to the way they were: every time things seemed better, there were new rumors of cutbacks or there were changes in documentation or scheduling. Thus, small incidents would trigger new grief cycles and the anger would begin anew. The new cycles would discourage unit managers even more, especially if they had thought they finally were making progress in convincing staff members how productive work strategies could be compatible with making the workload more reasonable and the quality of patient care acceptable.

While these emotional reactions are still occurring in varying degrees in staff members, depending on the situation in a particular hospital and the approaches of management, some nurses have moved on to the stage of acceptance. In this phase, they accept the losses and work to find ways of coping with the inevitable. With the help of enlightened managers, these coping strategies can be both positive and progressive.

Ages and Stages

Even though many hospitals have identified the occurrence of grief cycles in their nurses, there are other reasons for the varied responses in individuals, who are reconciling improved productivity with job satisfaction and quality patient care. Certainly, nurses must be dealt with individually because of the variations in their psychosocial and financial needs and adjustment patterns.

However, a common major factor is the age of the nurse. To gain insight into this factor, nurse managers may wish to read *The Corporate Steeplechase: Predictable Crises in a Business Career,* Blotnick's account of how 5,000 Americans coped with careers over a 25-year period.[6] Although these involved persons in many types of business, there are striking similarities with which nursing can identify.

According to Blotnick, the personal and professional crises that most people face are predictable. While no two people react in exactly the same way, an understanding of typical obstacles and responses at various ages can provide direction in preventing problems and facilitating movement toward improved productivity and team cooperation.

People in their twenties tend to take risks readily and respond dramatically to what they want in their careers. This immaturity can result in morale problems in a staff and in problems with peer working relationships. A unit staff with a number of young members may remain in a state of constant upheaval.

For example, in one critical care unit, staff members were ready to walk off the job in reaction to the strict and insensitive approach of their nurse manager. By the time other intervention took place, the situation had deteriorated so that tempers flared over minor problems, nurses had developed cliques, one shift was openly critical of the others, disciplinary efforts of the manager were scoffed at since the young nurses felt they could always go elsewhere, overlapping 10-hour shifts resulted in a party-like atmosphere in which patients were disturbed and work was minimal, and those acting professionally were ostracized by the cliques. Managerial control was lost.

To regain control of this unit and restore a reasonable degree of productivity, the hospital made major changes, including replacing the nurse manager, separating individuals to eliminate cliques, and guiding staff members toward more positive, professional, and productive efforts.

During their thirties, people settle down. Success on the job depends on how well they have learned to work with others. To capitalize on this age-related trend, mature nurse managers must build a sense of team spirit. This spirit of everyone helping each other is a simple but critical ingredient in improving unit productivity. While everyone has an assignment, the motto should be, "No one is finished until everyone is done." In other words, the work of nursing is a shared job for all members.

Hospitals find that each unit or center varies in its ability to convey this message. One quick way of determining whether this spirit exists is to ask nurses which units they enjoy floating to and which ones they would rather not work on. Generally, they want to go where there is a friendly work relationship among nurses that extends to mutual team support and shared enthusiasm about the quality of work. Units where this feeling does not exist tend to be those where it is "everyone for themselves," and mature nurses are missing. Where this vital team camaraderie is missing, productivity suffers and staffing always seems short, even when it should be adequate.

During their forties, some people have great momentum and take pleasure in their accomplishments. Others try to blend into the system because they believe that they have invested too much time in their careers to make serious errors now.

The danger at this age is in doing what is expected instead of utilizing experience and skill in making the system more productive and cost effective.

People at this age who have talent should be encouraged to be self-starters in making the changes needed in hospitals. To accomplish this, those in their forties should be provided with enough positive feedback that they are encouraged to be motivated and innovative in finding ways to maintain quality while being productive. Negative feedback when a project fails, or messages that indicate a manager's territory is threatened, can cause productive efforts to cease.[7]

During the decades of their fifties and sixties, workers can be a great asset or a severe liability. If they work to remain flexible and current and have a positive attitude toward younger staff members, they can serve as role models in working smarter, not harder. If they adopt a "know-it-all" attitude or a defensive posture, they should expect the system to push them into early retirement.

One factor to study in making a unit or center staff more productive is the ages and stages of its members. When possible, it is advisable to provide a mixture of all ages so that the positive aspects of each can be amplified.

Ethical Dilemmas

It is no secret that America is graying and that some patients in hospitals have had their lives prolonged by advancements in technology. On the other hand, the health care system is expected to make cutbacks that can directly affect the oldest patients, whose resource consumption is greatest in the last days of life.

Issues of who gets, who pays, and what is a reasonable quality of care are at odds with early discharges of ever sicker people and when technologic advances should be denied to a patient. Horror stories of hospitals' turning away poor persons and planning to cut charity cases appear frequently in the media. So serious are these issues that many major newspapers frequently carry articles on the right to life, right to die, or ethical aspects of care. This emphasis attests that society is upset and is reexamining its values, just like the nurses who are striving to meet the needs of these ill people through more productive work strategies.

However, knowing the problem does not help the nurses immediately, since it is they who must set priorities of care and face the sick and dying each day. Moreover, when the workload accelerates, it is the nurses who must assume ethical and legal responsibility for delivering safe care while working with available resources. Nurses are beset by resolving the conflict between altruistic and realistic goals. Limiting time for care for a dying person who has no family is heartbreaking. A nurse in school would have only one patient, but in hospital practice that dying patient is only one of several very ill ones in the workload. Finding time to give the type of quality care nurses can live with, while balancing the need to finish their other work, is a key concern of many hospital nurses.[8,9]

Managers need to assist staff members in putting ethical issues on the table as the nurses collectively work toward setting treatment protocols, standards, and work methods that minimize their being caught between choices of what is right and what is unacceptable. Because nurses are prepared to be involved in decision making in patient care, they also resent physicians who restrict their practice, especially when it means that patient information or care suffers. Reflecting this widespread feeling, *The Wall Street Journal* in 1986 carried an article titled "Nurses, Tired of Answering to Doctors, Begin to Treat Patients on Their Own."[10]

LAWSUITS ARISING FROM ETHICAL ISSUES

When managers are not proactive in their effort to establish more fruitful nurse-physician relationships and to solve ethical dilemmas in practice, those problems can snowball until they lead to employees' filing legal actions.

As nurses have strived to resolve ethical issues, several of their cases have gone to court. These suits consume a great deal of energy and exact costly legal fees for the hospital's defense. Wise management is vital in stopping these problems before they can crystallize, thus minimizing the time that leaders must spend in nonproductive activity as well as the costs that offset productivity efforts in the entire hospital. Several examples of nurse lawsuits are discussed to highlight nurses' concerns.

Guarantee of Free Speech

Pamela Sue Jones, an intensive care nurse at Memorial Hospital in Houston, won her lawsuit on First Amendment grounds. She was discharged after she wrote an article on ethical conflicts inherent in a physician's refusal to write a "no code" order in a hypothetical case in which the patient wanted to be allowed to die. At a preliminary hearing, the hospital relied on a Texas statute of termination, which gives an employer the right to end employment for unstated reasons. The hospital contended that it had legitimate unspecified reasons, which had no relationship to the Jones article. On that basis the hospital won dismissal. Jones appealed.

In the appellate court, the hospital's defense again was based on the Texas statute, along with federal courts' interpretations of the Constitution as a document not protecting Jones's freedom of speech when promoting personal interests. The hospital also argued that the Constitution protects employees only from a state's actions, and not from those of a private employer such as the hospital.

The court ruled that constitutional rights are guaranteed in both public and private institutions, that the Texas statute is preempted when it usurps freedom-of-speech rights, and that ethical dilemmas in right-to-die decisions are public issues, not just Jones's issues. The court remanded the case to the lower court for additional hearings. (677 S.W.2d 221 (Texas 1984)).

The important point in this case is that nurses facing right-to-die issues need to have constructive communication and grievance systems to resolve their personal and professional values. This can help them feel better emotionally so they can continue to work effectively. When this forum is missing, nurses turn to less desirable means (such as lawsuits) that are more costly to the hospital.

Discharge for Nurse Ethics

In a lawsuit alleging wrongful discharge, Corinne Warthen refused to dialyze a terminally ill patient, who was a diabetic, bilateral amputee suffering from multiple system failure. On an earlier occasion, dialysis had to be stopped because of a cardiac arrest and heavy internal bleeding. When the nurse was asked to dialyze this patient again, she refused on the grounds of "moral, medical, and philosophical objections," and her request was granted by the unit coordinator. Later she refused again to dialyze this same patient even after a meeting with the physician, head nurse, and unit coordinator at which she was told that the family desired to keep the patient alive through dialysis. Warthen was given a disciplinary warning, then was fired for insubordination.

The lower court dismissed the case on the hospital's motion for summary judgment because patients must be treated by physicians and their orders must be carried out. On appeal, the nurse based her action on the American Nurses' Association Code for Nurses. The appellate court upheld the discharge, saying that the state has a basic interest in the preservation of life and that all patients have a basic right to expect that medical treatment will not be terminated against their will. It held that the nurse's use of the Code placed her personal interests above those of the public, which has a right to expect nursing care in a hospital. The New Jersey Supreme Court refused to hear the case on appeal. (*Warthen v. Toms River Hospital*, N.J. Super. Ct. App. Div, 1985, 118 L.R.R.M. (BNA) 3180) [11]

Because of this decision, Nurse Warthen sacrificed an 11-year job at Toms River Community Memorial Hospital because of what she intended to be a sincere effort based on the Code, which says at 1.4:

> If personally opposed to the delivery of care in a particular case because of the nature of the health problem or the procedures to be used, the nurse is justified in refusing to participate. Such refusal should be made known in advance and in time for other appropriate arrangements to be made for the client's nursing care. [12]

While all cases should be reviewed individually, hospital managers have the right to operate the business without interference from nurses whose personal ethics impair public rights. This issue is highly controversial and will recur more frequently as ethical decisions collide with health care cutbacks.

Wise managers will work to provide nurses with educational and emotional support in making ethical decisions so that issues do not need to reach the courts. This will require a concerted effort to work collaboratively with nurses, physicians, and families. Moreover, it will require the establishment of a dedicated hospital ethics committee that can provide prudent guidance to staff members on all such issues in patient care. Where management does not make the effort to assist nurses, entire staffs can be divided. Such negative emotions can consume nurses to the point that they become too upset to work productively with others in the best interests of the patient.

Protected Concerted Activity

As goals of improved productivity and cost containment have become widespread, nurses have become disturbed about the quality and standards of patient care in some situations. To reconcile this problem, they need to be active participants in discussing the reality of the workload in relation to the quality of service they will provide. In some health care agencies that have been remiss in involving nurses in the setting and monitoring of patient care standards, and in correcting deficiencies that they identify, nurses have resorted to legal means to rectify their problems.

This is an undesirable outcome since lawsuits consume the efforts of management and result in untoward feelings among other staff members. For example, what channel do nurses have in hospitals for registering concerns about the manner in which a physician is treating or ignoring patient problems? If the politics of the institutional structure do not allow immediate resolution of this concern, how can managers help nurses in coping with their dissatisfied or angry feelings?

In one case in which staff members were dissatisfied with standards of patient care, they resorted to the use of Section 7 of the National Labor Relations Act, which relates to "protected concerted activity." In *Autumn Manor Inc.*, 268 N.L.R.B. 29 (1983), two nursing home employees were held to be not engaged in protected concerted activity when, pursuant to a subpoena, they testified in a licensing hearing before the Kansas Department of Health and Environment. Testimony centered on patient safety and care, including such actions as the slapping of a balky patient on the back and the unsanctioned distribution of cookies belonging to one patient among other patients. While this testimony helped the Kansas agency in fulfilling its statutory functions, the department ruled that the actions had no direct relationship to the working conditions at the nursing home and thus was not protected concerted activity. The statutory mandate of the hearing was ruled to be patient care, not working conditions. Thus the discharge of these employees for giving testimony was not unlawful under the Act.

As of late 1986, this and other cases had not included the quality of patient care in the definition of protected concerted activities. Thus, the National Labor Relations Board has made it clear that it will not consider the way physicians direct care or the standard of care being delivered as a part of Section 7, "protected concerted activities." However, employees are learning that two or more of them, or one who is acting as the spokesman for the group, cannot be disciplined or discharged for complaining about wages, hours, and/or terms and conditions of employment to management or to an appropriate body.

An example of successful action culminated in the N.L.R.B.'s ruling in *Misericordia Hospital Medical Center*, 246 N.L.R.B. 351 (1979), in which nurse Cafaro complained to the Joint Committee on Accreditation of Hospitals (JCAH) on her group's problems with conditions of employment. She was discharged for this action but was returned to work under the protection of Sections 7, 8(a)1 and 8(a)(3) of the Act.

Class Action for "Whistleblowers" Denied

In seeking a forum for their discontent, another group of employees tried to become a class of "whistleblowers" to get legal protection for airing complaints. The U.S. Court of Appeals in Richmond denied employees of a state mental health facility the right to qualify as a class of whistleblowers for protection against alleged discrimination.

In part in an attempt to prevent the installation of a new hospital administrator, employees registered complaints of patient abuse through institutional channels, the media, and the American Civil Liberties Union (ACLU). The ACLU induced an investigation. At a committee hearing, the complaining employees refused to testify on substantive issues and responded by limiting comments to "name, rank, and serial number."

The hospital administrator responded to this refusal to testify by suspending and later discharging the employees. They then claimed protection under the conspiracy provisions of the Civil Rights Act of 1871 and contended that they were a "class of whistleblowers" discharged for exposing wrongdoing by the hospital administration.

In rejecting the claim, the Appeals Court ruled that although whistleblowers are protected under the freedom-of-speech rights of the First Amendment as state employees, the group did not qualify as a class under the Civil Rights Act of 1871 because it did not have "discrete, insular, and immutable characteristics" of such a class, such as race, age, or sex. The court held that the group deserved no special treatment since compensation awarded to employees does nothing to remedy patient injuries, and actual injuries did not occur to the employees involved. (*Buschi v. Kirven* 4th Cir. Richmond, 1985, 120 L.R.R.M. 3059).

As of late 1986, whistleblowers enjoyed protection in Michigan, Connecticut, and Maine if they made reports to public bodies of unlawful conduct and assisted in any subsequent investigations. Public employees receive statutory whistleblower protection in California and Illinois.

However, a preventive solution is to conduct periodic audits on the quality of patient care to spot problems and initiate corrective action before harm is done to patients, the institution, and employees' morale. It also is important to be sure that any subsequent employee discharges do not violate a contractual provision between the workers and the hospital or are contrary to a public policy. Once again the relationship to productivity is clear. Employees distressed about the quality of patient care cannot work wholeheartedly to improve the hospital's business and to be positive in their relations with the public.

BREAKING THE CYCLE

When work becomes a war between the "innocent individual" and the ogre of a hospital, it is easy to justify any shortcomings in the work effort by rationalizing. Some of the most overworked excuses are:

- That is not the way we do it.
- That is not my job.
- No one authorized it.
- You forgot to remind me.
- I did not see the memo.
- We need more people.
- I was too busy to do it.
- That was lost when we reorganized.
- I couldn't do it because I was in a meeting.
- I did not understand what you meant.

In their efforts to overcome what seems to be a lack of productive efforts, managers can compound the problems through punishment. When a nurse speaks up, the manager is passively hostile, even though words such as "Let me know if you have more ideas" sound positive. As a result, nurses become defensive reporters, saying only what the managers want to hear. Neurotic behaviors develop, as nurses perform in anticipation of punishment through verbal abuse or harsh discipline. Finally, creativity is squelched as nurses begin a pattern of job escape in which they "just do the job and leave" or dream of how they might move to a better situation.[13]

None of these behaviors improves productivity. Productivity is possible only when there is a proper balance of quantitative measures and positive interpersonal relationships that result in the correct utilization of people, materials, and systems in a dynamic balance. Achieving this goal requires the willpower, drive, and tenacity to implement and publicize these concepts.

The first objective in making the productivity program work is to resolve the problems that are bothering staff members. Only when they believe that quality of patient care and of work life is important to management do they feel inclined to work through the painful, difficult process of changing job patterns and procedures to promote productivity and cost effectiveness.

While it would be ideal if there were a way to shortcut the time-consuming process of appealing to staff members and including them in the process of change, there is not. Group work takes much more time than it would for the manager alone to create programs, but group commitment saves time during the implementation process, when everyone has pride of ownership in the improved work climate and productive gains.

Teamwork

It is time that everyone took personal accountability for becoming productive members of the team. That means putting petty differences aside and accepting responsibility for working cohesively with others. When this concept is raised, some nurses say that they cannot be team workers because their unit operates so that each person has a discrete assignment. However, teamwork begins with the commitment of one person to make this goal possible.

That commitment does not require a change in policy but does mean a different way of thinking. It ends the right of nurses who are "waiting to be asked" and puts professionalism where it should be—with the individual nurse. It means that nurses must make a strong commitment to brighten their own corner of the world by being positive with clients, families, peers, and other health care professionals, to offer assistance to co-workers when there is time, and to experiment with various ideas to improve productivity and the job for everyone.

This effort is contagious, although management must be more patient with some nurses, who can be slow in learning to do their part. It also means that team members need to develop a mature relationship in which they can air problems and complaints before they snowball, and feel responsible for being emotionally supportive of each other. Managers also have to be willing to institute timely educational programs or support sessions to help team members through difficult situations, and to stimulate teamwork. This may mean that outmoded work methods or policies must be discarded for newer ideas that get the job done better, but this process can turn into an exciting challenge where the work climate is supportive.

One difficult factor in overhauling the system into one that is more cost effective and productive is that there can be no sacred cows. Each task and responsibility needs to be analyzed collectively to make improvements that will work better for everyone. At times, making positive changes that interfere with comfortable habits is stressful, but the effort is worth it.

To establish shared goals, nurses need to adopt group norms that everyone adheres to. The idea of this group sharing is to voice problems, brainstorm solutions, and learn to work together. Once the team spirit takes hold, the resultant enthusiasm makes working life the way it should be. As morale improves, nurses are more successful in being positive with physicians, other departments, and clients and in performing more productively.

However, the success of this approach is contingent upon the manager's willingness to relinquish total control and to support participative efforts by staff members to deal with ethical issues and experiment with ideas that improve work.

As managers progress in building a team on the unit or in the center, they will find that trust among members grows. When that happens, nurses feel freer to relate their inner irritations and seek solutions before problems are magnified out of proportion. This process of team building can develop much like the sense of group grows in the field of psychiatry.

Reviewing the work of Robert Freed Bales, the father of group theory and methods, can be helpful in understanding this process. Networking with psychiatric nurses to share these insights with staff nurses on other units can help each group understand the growing pains that occur as they learn to be a real team.[14]

Cautionary Note

In trying to stretch staffing to cover all contingencies through improved productivity, managers need to be cautioned not to allow dangerous safety problems to arise. For example, staff members sometimes stretch themselves too thin but do not call for help until the last minute. Thus, the needed help does not have adequate time to get to the unit and meet the needs. This is foolhardy and can cause serious problems that scar nurses and endanger patients.

It is important, of course, to avoid asking for help when it is not necessary since other units or workers called in on time off become angry when the need does not justify their rushing to provide aid. It also is important to note whether overload is limited to a short period or the entire shift.

For example, sometimes a code blue on a busy unit can make the nursing staff short for an hour. In such cases, the assistance of a central supervisor or a nurse for a short time may be all that is needed to get the staff through the peak period. Some hospitals have a float person who can be moved about to assist various units for such periods. Even intravenous nurses might have this code duty assistance added to their jobs. However, that means that nonurgent IV starts in other areas would have to be done by the nurses on the unit. The cost effectiveness of this resource person would have to be evaluated.

There still are days when staffs truly are understaffed and need more help. What managers have to address is improving productivity through smart work strategies so that these instances occur less often and complaints about short staffing are not related to poor organization of the workload.

SUMMARY

Improving productivity and achieving cost-effective quality care requires nurse leaders to appreciate the relationship of nurse concerns and emotions to the total work effort. Such projects succeed best where the managers support a positive, constructive climate in which nurses feel supported in their problems and assisted in their efforts to work together in delivering the best level of quality care for the resources allocated.

Without sensitivity to the staff nurses, even the most glorious plans on paper can be doomed to fail.

NOTES

1. Barbara Lang Rutkowski, "Attitudes Toward Nurse Unionization in Kentucky as Perceived by Selected Administrators" (Ph.D. diss, Indiana University, 1984).

2. ———, *DRGs: Impact on Employee Relations in the Health Care Industry* (Washington, D.C.: Bureau of National Affairs, Inc., 1985), 22–23.

3. Ibid., 23.

4. Leonora Alexander, *Women's Bureau: Meeting the Challenges of the 80s* (Washington, D.C.: U.S. Government Printing Office, 1985).

5. Elizabeth Kubler-Ross, *On Death and Dying* (New York: Macmillan Publishing Co., Inc., 1969), 100.

6. Srully Blotnick, *The Corporate Steeplechase: Predictable Crises in a Business Career* (New York: Facts on File, 1984).

7. Stanley Milgram, *Obedience to Authority* (New York: Harper & Row Publishers, Inc., 1973).

8. Teresa Stanley, Sr., "Ethics: Who Is the Moral Agent?" *AORN Journal* (September 1984): 331–332.

9. Joyce Thompson and Henry Thompson, "Ethics," *AORN Journal* (February 1984): 157–158.

10. "Nurses, Tired of Answering to Doctors, Begin To Treat Patients on Their Own," *Wall Street Journal*, January 1, 1986.

11. Arthur D. Rutkowski and Barbara Lang Rutkowski, "Nurse Lawsuits Claiming Wrongful Termination for Following Professional Code of Ethics," *Health Employment Law Update* (May, 1985):1.

12. Katherine Carey, "Refusing to Follow Orders: What's the Cost of Saying No?" *Nursinglife* (July/August 1985): 52–56.

13. R.M. Greene, *The Management Game: How to Win with People* (Chicago: Dow-Jones-Irwin, Inc., 1969).

14. Robert Freed Bales et al., *Symlog: A Manual for the Case Study of Groups* (New York: The Free Press, 1979).

ACTION CHECKLIST

1. What have you done to encourage teamwork on your unit?
2. How do you assist nurses in resolving thorny ethical problems that are part of their hospital practice?
3. How active is your ethics committee in identifying issues, constructing supportive plans of action for assisting individuals with specific ethical dilemmas, and formulating policies that optimize the quality of patient care?
4. Are you able to accept constructive criticism and plans that differ from your own without retaliating against staff members involved in these activities?
5. What can you do to make your unit the most desirable area of work in the hospital?
6. What formal mechanisms exist for legitimate complaints about the quality of patient care?
7. What research tools—e.g., employee surveys, patient questionnaires, or productivity audits—have you constructed to make quantitative measurements of the impact of your positive work climate on productivity and cost containment? (Don't forget to include figures on absenteeism and staff turnover in this assessment.)

Chapter 9

Strategies for the Transition

Decentralization is the order of the day. Everyone is talking about how decentralization will help improve productivity. However, talking about achieving the ideal situation and doing it are two different things. Such changes move beyond the theoretical to the real world. While staff nurses have to undergo self-examination and make changes to accept accountability, so do managers. Until managers create a climate that fosters creativity in improving productivity, staff nurses will find their attempts to do so will continue to be stifled and punished. One thing is certain: When managers have to accomplish more with less, the creative ideas need to flow.

DECENTRALIZING MANAGEMENT

Decentralization often is termed horizontal management because it aims to flatten the hierarchy to allow nurses to take the initiative in making changes for more productivity. This process does not occur overnight because many managers stand to lose power and control. While staff nurses gain more decision making power, managers need to be retooled to accept a different way of operating. The very way that managers motivate, facilitate others, and assert themselves is quite different when power is shared. All of this can be threatening to their sense of personal worth. However, with a supportive vice president of nursing who also offers meetings and classes to ease this transition, the change to decentralization can succeed.[1]

Transitional Problems

Moving toward decentralization requires self-honesty on the part of managers. While most see themselves as fair and democratic in approach, their actions do not always mirror their words. When staff creativity and decision making are minimal, that situation reflects the fact that the members actually are reacting to the messages that the manager is sending. Managers who try to change but fail to make democratic decisions because of their lack of confidence in themselves adopt a wishy-washy approach that keeps staff members frustrated and off balance as to what is expected of them.

Managers who feel this threat tend to be low key in their approach and may even verbalize a commitment to the democratic approach. However, the outcome can be unfavorable when staff nurses act on this superficial permission.

The Egocentric Ogre

For example, in one hospital the nursing supervisor of a division set up meetings to obtain staff input for shared decision making in improving productivity. While she sincerely thought that she wanted feedback, she really intended that such feedback be a positive affirmation of her leadership skill. When staff nurses became comfortable in the meetings and voiced their true opinions, this leader became openly agreeable but quietly resentful.

Nurses who expressed criticism were ostracized behind their backs and were rated more harshly in the next performance appraisal because of the leader's input into their unit managers. Once word got around about the consequences of such honesty, staff nurses continued to be quietly frustrated and ceased their complaints, constructive change efforts, and enthusiasm. The supervisor concluded, erroneously, that things were better and that the meetings had resulted in shared input that resolved productivity problems. However, the structure of control within the division remained the same, even though there were decentralizing changes on paper.

To this day, no staff nurse or manager on that unit will make a decision without running even the simplest things by this supervisor. Yet the supervisor continues to say that all she lends is support and that they cannot think without her.

This defensive behavior is destructive because it puts the leader in a win-win situation and the staff in a lose-lose posture. Such a leader often can say yes, no, and maybe to the same question, depending on who she is conferring with. Because this type of leader often works sub rosa, she affects group process by behavioral rewards for those who support her views. She often relates personally to some group members to move them to support her view. Through this system of divide and conquer, she keeps the unit staff tense and indecisive while indirectly exerting firm authority over the unit.

The real message is: "Decide anything you want to, as long as I agree. If you are wrong, I told you so. If you are right, it is because the whole thing was my idea." The result is that trust among nurses is minimal, and individuals resort to placing their own interests above the good of the group. Yet the leader feels good because she is, after all, just as indispensible as she perceives herself to be. Hungry egos are those that are never fully satiated.[2]

Fortunately, not all managers are this manipulative and destructive. However, when there are such managers in a system, they must be identified. When they are counseled about their behaviors, they need to be given constructive support for change. If that change is not possible, they should be replaced with the type of person who represents the new era manager, committed to finding better ways to ensure quality patient care while improving productivity and containing costs. Otherwise, staff members will continue in their nonproductive habits and lack of enthusiasm because they do not know how to band together to change the situation without suffering personal retaliation, assuming that they can even determine exactly what is wrong in their situation.

BUILDING A POSITIVE CLIMATE

To create an atmosphere for creativity and increased nurse participation, managers must be consistent in setting boundaries, verbalizing clear instructions, providing consistent discipline evenly to all, and allowing nurses to express ideas without fear of retribution.[3] When this pattern remains in place for a period of time, trust is built. To determine where they are in relation to the trust of their staffs, each manager should ask:

- Are people defensive around me?
- Do I get the truth from my staff, even when it is not what I want to hear?
- Does the staff feel free to criticize me justifiably?
- Do others give me suggestions?
- Do I take the time to explore the feelings of those around me?
- Are job turnover and absenteeism high in the area? If so, why?
- Do nurses from other units enjoy spending the day on my unit?
- Have key people in my department left?
- Do I respect the decision making abilities of my staff members?
- Are my staff members good at generating ideas and unique solutions to productivity problems that they feel free to implement experimentally?

If managers answered some of these questions negatively, they may be facing a problem of trust with their staffs.

Instead of focusing on what is wrong, trusting leaders who are team players concentrate on what is right. They feel like team players, and that message comes through loudly to their staffs. When they give credit to others and admit their own imperfections, they have truly cast off the need to be martyrs.

Trusting others is the only way to decrease interpersonal stress and improve productivity. Making the system great requires more effort and input than one person can accomplish. Managers who accept these premises soon learn that their unit or center excels in enthusiasm, warm peer relations, and success. Moreover, the honest respect that they gain provides them with more power than they ever had by incessant tooting of their own horns.

Turnaround Strategies

Once managers become motivated to be facilitative leaders, they can look at any positive change in staff and feel good about it. While that is indeed positive, it may not work in moving the center or unit on to goals of increased productivity, decreased costs, or other improvements. Why? Because sometimes the true problems underlying the situation are unknown and may be symptoms of even deeper causes.

Thus, as managers work toward fostering trust in staff and making the group a team, they need to analyze their units' situation objectively to discern the real problems that block productive efforts. This requires a problem-solving approach, and probably the type of survey that they would do as a part of a marketing analysis of the units. Such an analysis is time consuming, but the results can be worth it. Organized action against the real problem can save time wasted in attempting to move without a plan. The results of the team effort also are more likely to result in a satisfying outcome.

This type of problem analysis requires objectivity and some expertise, so some units hire outside consultants to assist. They can provide insights because they are not involved emotionally in the situation. However, consultants must be chosen carefully so that this process can be handled constructively.

Reinforcing Personal Worth

Simultaneously with team building, managers must build the members' self-esteem. To understand this process, it is helpful to look at the work of Maslow,[4] which by extrapolation demonstrates that nurses cannot work productively as team members when they are deeply worried about personal, physical, psychological, or safety needs.

Managers may use performance appraisal conferences to gain insight into each staff member's degree of confidence and self-esteem. When this is known, it is important to find ways to help them feel important and satisfied with their work. Some of this need consist of no more than managers giving simple recognition for nurses' efforts. Leaders should abandon the traditional approach in which "no news was good news" and replace it with positive affirmations of staff actions.

This people-building effort must be a very high priority if all other efforts at improving productivity are to be successful. Because many managers already feel overloaded and unable to muster enough psychological strength to expend this level of energy constantly, they need to turn to the staff.

A good beginning is to reinforce the fact that most nurses are at work more than they are at any other place during the day. In the work environment, they expend most of their effort and energy and need to receive positive strokes to enhance their satisfaction with the demands of nursing, which go far beyond simple remuneration. In a manner of speaking, the staff is a family, and work is most satisfying when it is viewed as an environment of a home away from home.

Believing this message results in nurses' personalizing decorations, extending homelike courtesies to patient guests, and making the unit a personal part of themselves. Thus, managers need to solicit the help of each staff member in making a contract with the others to provide sincere warmth to each other.

For example, to maximize the efforts of float nurses to the unit, each member on one unit agreed to make one kind comment and two helpful comments to each staff person who was helping for the day. On that unit of 12 staff members, that was 36 interactions with each float nurse. The result was that float nurses functioned better, no one person felt burdened by the responsibility of making newcomers welcome, and nurses from other units requested this one as a work choice.

Not all efforts at building self-esteem need to center on sincere compliments or praise. Some should be directed toward constructive criticism, carefully expressed. When criticism is constructive, the manager has cared enough to analyze a problem, then work privately with the member to seek solutions. Well-managed and sensitive approaches can help staff nurses feel that they are growing and developing in the ability to be more productive.

Some efforts should be geared toward noticing nurses as persons. For example, in one hospital, managers approach returning nurses who have been absent to say that they were missed, and to decide whether special counseling or scheduling is needed to minimize absenteeism in the future. This counseling effort is constructive and makes staff members feel that their contribution counts. It also nips in the bud potentially chronic problems that can reduce productivity. In this same hospital, managers make a point of personally thanking any staff member who works overtime or floats to another area because they are conscious of the success that has resulted from these simple ways of recognizing the importance of each individual.

When nurse managers work to build esteem over time, the examples they set are mirrored by other staff members. As a result, the attitude of the entire team becomes more positive. It is understood that work on this unit is a positive experience: ''We thank you for what you do, and we will pitch in to help when you need it.''[5]

Maintaining the Energy

Being positive, attentive managers takes its toll. It is difficult to work under the pressures placed on them in the crisis situation created by the health care revolution. Thus, managers and staff members both need total life game plans that emphasize balance.

While the development of these plans is highly individual, most need to include balanced diets, exercise, positive personal relationships, fun, interesting avocational pursuits, support groups to resolve personal problems, and time management strategies to fit everything together into a more productive work effort. Sometimes it is wise to use time allotted for continuing education to find courses that augment positive personal life strategies.[6]

DEVELOPING CREATIVITY

Creativity is a way of developing ideas and products beyond immediate or original problems. Through creative efforts, nurse managers strive to solve problems and think of new ideas that get results in their efforts to be more productive, while providing a high quality of nursing care to patients.

Teaching Creativity to Managers

Some people feel that creativity is a special talent that cannot be taught: Either you have it or you don't. Others say that everyone has latent creative talents that can be nurtured and developed. Following the latter premise, a number of programs have been developed in business and in universities to cultivate creativity—and these efforts have been very successful. Among those promoting creativity courses are countless consultants, Stanford University in a course called "Creativity in Business," and the American Management Association in numerous seminars.

Historical Perspectives

Creativity efforts received a big boost when Alex Osborn launched the Creative Education Foundation in 1954 and taught the brainstorming technique that he later discussed in his book, *Applied Imagination*.[7] William Gordon, formerly a Harvard engineering professor, also was a forerunner who built a consulting practice around the concept of synectics, a technique using metaphors and analogies to promote inventiveness in problem solving. This effort was supported by published works of writers such as Moustakas in *Creativity and Conformity*, who explained the costs of conforming and the importance of being a whole person true to one's total being.[8]

While many approaches have been tried, most have commonalities. A number of creativity promoters have been focusing on developing the right hemisphere of the brain to balance left-sided functions of logic and analysis.[9,10] However, the best approach probably is a combination of methods that work best for the individual. This eclectic approach, taken by the Center for Creative Leadership in Greensboro, N.C., takes shape as "targeted innovation."[11] This one-week course costs $1,200. Participants learn and practice many techniques on actual business problems. Beginning with exercises about the whats and wherefores of a cardboard box and ways to market panty hose to men, the CCL teaches how to use techniques such as guided imagery and group work to foster creative expression of ideas and use the diversity of group members to advantage. For example, through guided imagery a leader may help participants imagine themselves on a lush, tropical island where a sage bolsters their self-confidence. In discussing the mental journey, participants describe the experience, including a description of how a goal was achieved.

Application to Hospitals

In Search of Excellence asserts that leaders must do more than allow creativity; they must actively encourage it if they are to improve productivity and assist employees in feeling satisfied with their work efforts.[12] There are several ways to accomplish this that can be applied to hospitals.

First, bureaucratic red tape must be minimized so that promising projects can get the approval and materials needed to progress. This simplification is a natural outcome of the decentralization process. However, managers are cautioned to keep some safeguards and controls so that adequate research and relevance to total hospital strategic plans is maintained in creative endeavors.

Another idea is to give nurses the right to develop good ideas as a reward. This is accomplished by selecting a committee to review ideas for promoting improved productivity. Other ideas include improvement of patient teaching or documentation, revamping nurse work schedules, or devising a more productive method of discharge planning. Nurses whose proposals are approved are freed from staffing to pursue the effort and are given the necessary funds and equipment to go forward.

While some of these projects may not succeed, nurses should not receive negative feedback for failures. Negativism puts a damper on future efforts. Sometimes finding out that something is not workable is valuable in identifying limits of what can and should be done in the unit or department. When suggestions sound promising but are too incomplete to investigate, the staff member may need support in developing the concept further.

For example, in one hospital nurses discerned that double charting was common when they first charted on a paper towel that they pocketed, then transcribed those notes to the chart later. They decided that a total program was needed to assist nurses in taking charts around on medicine carts, then writing final notes as they interviewed patients and provided care. This project was resisted at first by physicians, but later progressed to include unit-by-unit inservice workshops and follow-up by a peer on each unit. The result was improved productivity and an easing of the workload for the registered nurses.

It is time to refocus on the concept of clinical ladders. Some excellent practitioners make mediocre managers and should be allowed to progress up the ladder toward more sophisticated patient care practices. The height of this ladder is the clinical specialist, who has the experience and education to mentor less seasoned nurses and solve problems in direct clinical care.

One unique approach to clinical ladders includes a bidding system in which nurses choose to be at Levels I, II, or III:

Level I: This is for beginning nurses, whose clinical skills need development, and staff nurses who choose to limit their roles to being positive team members in the administration of routine care.

Level II: This is for nurses who agree, through a contract spanning one year, to accept responsibility for mentoring new staff members, conducting a specified number of staff and patient educational sessions, and contributing to the improvement of productivity on the unit, such as a total plan for the care of a specialized type of patient.

Level III: This requires more experience and a greater commitment to the development of the unit/center and to the resolution of its problems. Nurses striving to get the added pay and recognition of Level III work need to develop a 12-month plan for what they will accomplish in productivity improvement while containing costs and promoting quality in patient services delivery. Nurses with the most suitable plan are selected for Level III jobs as they open.

Level IV: This is for clinical specialists.

In this bidding system, nurses elect their level annually so that they can determine whether or not this is the right time in their lives to make the necessary commitments. When they cannot meet the responsibilities of added goals, they return to a lower level with a corresponding salary reduction. Through this system, nurse burnout is minimized and productivity and individual incentives are maximized. Moreover, this plan eases the unit managers' burden of being responsible for all progress.

Being Courageous

It takes a lot of courage for nurse managers to convince the hospital system that they have ideas for promoting productivity that are worth pursuing. Seeing an idea all the way through, overcoming the inevitable resistance to change, is hard work that takes great dedication—it is not easy to be creative. Being creative requires self-confidence, a way of convincing others that an idea is necessary, a sense of humor, and a desire to do the lion's share of the work in making the concept succeed. When someone sponsors an effort, managers should express their gratitude. To get creative persons to step forward, perhaps the hospital can follow the suggestions of Gifford Pinchot III in establishing an award for "meritorious defiance" so that employees know that its management has a sense of humor and an honest desire to encourage innovation.[13]

NONTRADITIONAL RESOURCES

Two types of resource persons are available to nurses who want to make positive changes in their center or department—the clinical specialist and the nurse consultant.

The Clinical Specialist

An entire body of literature has been written about what clinical specialists are and what they do. The function of the clinical specialist needs to be viewed now in relation to how the application of expert knowledge and skill in patient care results in cost effectiveness and the ability to make the health care delivery system more productive and responsive to patient and staff needs.

While some clinical specialists already are practicing in ways that make them invaluable to hospitals, others are functioning mainly as physicians' assistants since that is where the traditional rewards have been. Clinical specialists now must justify their existence to keep their place in the hospital system.

Since they have graduate preparation and extensive expertise as practitioners, they are in a prime position to do some of the essential research in patient care designed to give the safest, most productive, and best quality of care at the lowest costs. Their efforts also can include the writing of grants or the setting up of experimental programs to obtain reimbursement for services. An example might be convincing a health maintenance organization that reimbursed, quality patient education results in fewer readmissions for inpatient care. This type of project alone can offset the costs of their salaries.

However, clinical specialists also should assume accountability for patient education and mentoring of staff members to assist them in performing at the highest level of competence within available resources. This can include helping develop staff members' creative ideas into mature projects in which the clinical specialist is the mentor. Because of their research background, these persons can aid staff members in capturing data that show the quantitative productivity of their activities.

The problem in this role has been one of power conflicts between clinical specialists and the head nurses or supervisors, who have the line power to get results. Whether clinical specialists can be effective in a consultative role has long been debated. It is to be hoped that that problem can be put aside as collegiality improves with the more facilitative type of manager that is part of the new era.

Keeping clinical specialists on track requires the setting up of a support system in which they network with other clinical specialists and managers to function more effectively. In addition to their contacts with management and other clinical specialists, they need to have ties to the local collegiate program so they can continue to develop their expertise in practice, research, communication, teaching, and change strategies.

Consultants

A growing number of excellent nurses have opened their own private consultation practices and also are beginning to be used in hospitals.

For perspective, it should be noted that one hired generalist in a management support role can be an expert in only so many fields. This person's full-time salary must be paid, even when the individual's ideas are not revolutionary and their impact on the system is minimal. What is needed to assist the management team in improving the system are a number of productive ideas and fresh enthusiasm. This is where nurse consultants come in.

Some nursing departments have allocated money for the equivalent of a budgeted position to hire temporary independent contractors who have a specified dedicated purpose in the system. Because these people do not get paid if they do not produce, the money expended for their services is entirely productive. When used wisely, these consultants can be objective in:

- analyzing change
- writing a plan for a major productivity project
- working to resolve interpersonal problems among staff members
- observing the system for productivity problems, with the responsibility for making recommendations

- facilitating group work
- providing timely, expert educational programming.

Consultants also can make changes and comments that those in the system cannot communicate effectively, since the outsiders can accept blame without needing to remain to get involved in the personal politics. However, to be effective, they also must be oriented at the outset to the system's problems, activities, and power struggles.

When their work is done, other consultants can be used to accomplish different missions. Another advantage of consultants is that they are not paid to sit through meetings, nor do they get employee benefits.

SUMMARY

Hospitals moving away from a centralized structure pass through a transitional period in which staffs are not wholly decentralized. At that point, timely projects to improve productivity have not been in effect long enough to measure the final outcome. However, to keep the positive momentum going, managers and staff should emphasize team building, foster creativity, provide support to each other, and utilize available resources wisely.

NOTES

1. H. Ura et al., *Nursing Leadership: Theory and Process,* 2d ed. (New York: Appleton-Century-Crofts, Inc., 1981).
2. Daniel Levinson, *The Seasons of a Man's Life* (New York: Alfred A. Knopf, Inc., 1978).
3. Arthur D. Rutkowski and Barbara Lang Rutkowski, *Labor Relations in Hospitals* (Rockville, Md.: Aspen Publishers, Inc., 1984).
4. A.H. Maslow, *Motivation and Personality* (New York: Harper & Row, Publishers, Inc., 1970).
5. Eastwood Atwater, *Psychology of Adjustment* (Englewood Cliffs, N.J.: Prentice-Hall, Inc., 1979).
6. D.B. Ardell and M.J. Tager, *Planning for Wellness: A Guidebook for Achieving Optimal Health* (Dubuque, Iowa: 1982).
7. Alex Osborn, *Applied Imagination* (Out of Print.)
8. C.E. Moutakas, *Creativity and Conformity* (Princeton, N.J.: D. Van Nostrand Co., Inc., 1967).
9. G.B. Leonard, *Education and Ecstasy* (New York: Dell Publishing Co., Inc., 1968).
10. Bob Samples et al. *The Wholeschool Book* (Reading, Mass.: Addison-Wesley Publishing Co., 1977).
11. Center for Creative Leadership (Greensboro, N.C.: Center for Creative Leadership, 1985).
12. Thomas J. Peters and Robert H. Waterman, *In Search of Excellence* (New York: Warner Books, Inc., 1982).
13. Gifford Pinchot III, *Intrapreneuring* (New York: Harper & Row, Publishers, Inc., 1985).

ACTION CHECKLIST

Nursing managers in the transitional period should:
1. Work to set up a mechanism that encourages creativity by all staff members.
2. Build a system of rewards and a way to allow innovators to proceed with their ideas.
3. Reward action-oriented nurses who work diligently to achieve the personal and organizational goals that they have set.
4. Regard failures as learning experiences that are inherent in risk taking.
5. Assist innovators in understanding the system so that the obstacles they face can be minimized.
6. Help staff members enjoy a sense of accomplishment in working toward goals.
7. Assist nurses in minimizing the importance of getting credit personally so that getting the job done for the good of the system becomes an acceptable reward.
8. Provide a constant objective for innovators so that they do not stray from productive activities or lose their motivation to proceed.
9. Assist project innovators in tying ideas to the business mandates of cost effectiveness, improved productivity, and maintenance of quality in patient care delivery.
10. Provide a supportive environment in which nurses learn to network and use all resources to advantage as they work to improve productivity and work strategies.
11. Assist all team members in learning to support each other as an essential step in meeting the demands of this health care revolution.

Part III

Setting Standards of Performance

Chapter 10

Risk Management

With the advent of diagnosis related groups (DRGs), the new era in hospital care requires quality assurance and risk management efforts to be blended with marketing efforts, program development, patient care delivery standards and methods, and improvements in productivity and cost containment. Hospital survival depends on developing prudent quality assurance programs while minimizing legal liability in managing nurses and patient care.

RISK MANAGEMENT

Hospitals have been barraged with lawsuits since the 1970s from a public angered by the damage resulting from professional negligence. Guided by hospital insurers and the desire to minimize legal liability, hospitals formulated risk management programs whose purpose is to protect themselves and their caregivers against losses.

Staffing and Security Concerns

This effort includes patient care delivery as well as problems of environmental safety, infection control, and hospital security. For example, does the hospital have annual classes on "Saving Your Back" in which proper body mechanics are taught and practiced by every employee? Are nurses aware of the dangers of exposure to fumes, medications absorbed through the skin, and hazardous materials or patient conditions that require special precautions? Do nurse managers make periodic checks of staff practices by examining incident reports and monitoring routine practice to be sure that the nurses are adhering to safe standards? This is important in reducing illness and nonproductive days resulting from staff injury or sickness.

189

Do nurse leaders reinforce security precautions with staff members to make sure unauthorized persons do not have access to charts and do not have the opportunity to treat or remove patients? For example, strangers abducted a baby from one institution and did pelvic exams on elderly women in another by posing as hospital staff workers. Where efforts to avoid infection, protect staff members from injury, and protect the security of patients is inadequate, unit leaders can work cooperatively with the infection control nurse and the risk manager to institute programs and audits in these areas.

Liability in Patient Care Delivery

In studying the implications of risk management control and productivity, nursing managers soon discover that patient care practices that result in lawsuits more than erase a multitude of effective cost-containment practices. Thus, unnecessary risk is a factor that needs continual monitoring to prevent problems.

Awards in malpractice cases have soared. This crisis situation has resulted in some physicians' refusing to perform certain duties, such as delivering infants, because of the great risk of legal liability.[1] Some predicted that Congress would have to act to establish malpractice award ceilings to limit the spiraling cost of health care.

Efforts to resolve this problem have occurred already at the state level, particularly in Florida, Michigan, and California. Other states are also considering action to cope with this problem. As such measures are enacted, many experts believe that physicians will be able to write more streamlined orders since they will not be as worried about going to the extreme of practicing defensive medicine. Such reduced orders will greatly aid nurse productivity.

Areas of Nurse Liability

Because of the increasing illness level in patients, the decreased length of hospital stays, improved productivity mandates, and the burgeoning responsibilities of nurses in today's hospital, they must become more cognizant of the factors that limit legal liability.[2] Historically, nurses were involved mainly in lawsuits related to "custodial negligence"—that is, where they had a duty to protect the patient that was breached. The most common form of this problem is patient falls, so many early programs were geared to improving patient safety. A study by Swartzbeck at Veterans Administration hospitals showed that patient falls accounted for 73.8 percent of 1,140 incidents in three time periods, and suggested ways that nurses could cope with the problem.[3] A program titled Code Orange at Lakewood Hospital, Lakewood, Ohio, involved the formation of a Risk/Falls Committee to study the problem, identify high-risk fall candidates, and suggest helpful strategies. The article reporting this includes the patient guidelines criteria established for such patients.[4]

Nurse professionals are expressing great concern about the growing possibility of being sued for other areas of practice, particularly in the face of demands for increasing productivity.

This writer has found it beneficial to provide three-hour workshops to nursing divisions, given four times in two days so that all staff members can attend. These define and explain nurses' legal responsibilities. Each definition is illustrated with actual cases. By the end of the program, participants realize what is required of them and how to succinctly chart the important parts of the nursing care process. They also feel better psychologically since they have replaced near hysteria with facts.

For example, one easy way for nurses to know whether their charting is adequate is to pretend that they were reading their notes in a courtroom two years hence. Are the notes complete without further explanation? Do they explain what was done in a quantifiable way that anyone can understand; that is, the abdomen was 45 cm. at 1000 and 50 cm. at 1200? If the notes do not seem right, have nurses utilized peer critiques to better express themselves?

Major concerns of nurses are the problems of keeping current with new medication administration mandates and monitoring implications, the difficulty of properly utilizing new equipment that is being introduced at a rapid rate, and the fear of floating to a different unit where specialized skills are required.

While staying current is the responsibility of each nurse, managers and educators need to assist nurses in providing safe care through timely, brief inservice classes or workshops, and in often having educational videotapes available on all shifts that can be viewed when nurses find the time. In one setting, each staff nurse took responsibility for bringing a bulletin board clipping on a relevant treatment or drug and for presenting a ten-minute summary on relevant practice to other nurse peers. This reduced the burden on any one person while increasing the knowledge shared. Obviously, when nurses work together to identify how to stay current while being productive, they can be of substantial help to each other.

Nurses also worry about the so-called ''wrong tube'' errors because many patients have more than one intravenous line and perhaps an arterial line, along with feeding and drainage tubes. The problem occurs when a harried nurse picks up the wrong tube to inject a substance, or injects excessive or wrong drugs. Because of the immediacy of reaction, patients may experience adverse outcomes before corrective interventions can be implemented. Death has occurred in some cases in which lipids were injected into arterial lines in error.

The solution is to color code the ends of various tubes and to dye tube feedings blue in a standardized way to minimize the possibility for error. An additional solution is to have more registered nurses on the staff, since these problems are aggravated by poor staffing and by the fact that licensed practical nurses usually are barred from assisting with some intravenous treatments. To provide for prompter aid, a beeper-type call system also is needed so that the unit secretary can locate nurses quickly.

Because of the traditionally greater number of lawsuits involving operating room procedures, nurses in that area have been conscious of the need for careful practice for a long time. Emergency room nurses also are vulnerable because of the difficulty of documenting all aspects of care in hurried situations.

One recommendation for emergency room nurses is to separate nursing histories, care plans, interventions, notes, and discharge instructions from those of the physicians by preparing a form with different pages for each discipline. Otherwise, notes crowded on a single page can be inadequate in their brevity and hard to associate with the responsible individual. Preprinted discharge instructions also help nurses in providing consistent information that is documented while improving productivity by minimizing the individual writing of instructions.

Other areas of nurse liability include failure to (1) monitor a patient, (2) take proper action when a problem is evident, (3) report the problem to the physician and administration, and (4) chart. Nurses also are being held accountable for making proper assessments of a patient's condition and for intervening correctly. Because patients now are discharged more quickly from hospitals, nursing responsibility has extended to include adequate patient education and discharge planning.

Floating

The concern that many nurses currently express about providing safe care while floating in a different specialized unit has become a major issue. However, wide swings in patient census and the need for improved productivity in the nursing division make such floating a necessity. With some preplanning by unit leaders and staff nurses, floating can be made into a safe experience for both nurses and patients. How? The head nurse on each unit needs to:

1. Identify special skills required on the unit in a written format.
2. Collect reading materials that can be used by new nurses in the area.
3. Prepare a list of common procedures and medications with a bibliography so that prospective nurses can study before working (copies of the materials can be kept in the library to be checked out).
4. Videotape an orientation to the unit, complete with physician preferences, a sample of when major activities should be accomplished, and variations on policies and assignment methods specific to this unit.
5. Network with like units to arrange orientation times for nurses who will be working in the area.
6. Construct a skills checklist for each new nurse to ensure quality in patient care delivery.

7. Establish a standard that specifies the minimum amount of time a nurse should work in the area to be able to function safely there.
8. Specify the limits of assignments based on nurse experience.

Nurses who expect to float to different areas have responsibility to:

1. Identify skill deficiencies so they may be corrected prior to working.
2. Participate in getting oriented to these different units.
3. Allow time for reading key materials so as to become safe and current in providing care and administering medications.
4. Tell the head nurse responsible on the unit where assistance is needed.

Where leaders and staff nurses cooperate to make the floating experience more rewarding, productive, and safe, the legal liabilities can be minimized. The need to create this type of program is urgent since floating will continue to be a necessity in hospitals trying to utilize staff wisely as a part of their total effort to improve productivity.

Documentation

Since chart documentation is the proof that nursing care was given, much of the attention to reducing legal liability has been directed to that activity.[5,6] Managers face the problem that, with increased workloads and decreased use of overtime, nurses often give care that is uncharted. When malpractice cases go to court, the hospital's and nurses' defense is being based increasingly on the nurses' notes.

However, many staff nurses frustrated with the choice of giving care or completing voluminous records, elect to forgo their charting responsibilities. When confronted, they blame short staffing. Sometimes inadequate staffing is the problem, but more often it is one of needing to improve productivity, which can be done by instituting some important measures. Nursing managers should:

- Place charts in proximity to patients at the bedside or on medication carts so that nurses can chart care as it is given.
- Establish a system for assigning major care plan reviews to nurses.

For example, one hospital has an assignment board, with the nurses on each shift responsible for seven patient charts apiece. They must review those seven charts every 48 hours to be sure that the care plan is up to date and that at least one comprehensive note has been written noting patient progress in relation to the plan. Additionally, they need to make relevant notes about the care given and patient/family response in their original workload.

Every effort is made to give the nurse as many of these "seven" patients in the workload as possible. The reasonable time written into policies for this comprehensive review can vary according to the type of patients in a given unit or center. For example, long-term orthopedic patients might have a 72-hour review, intensive care patients more frequently. This method has improved charting greatly and has eased the strain of total charting on everyone.

Nurse managers also should:

- Develop checklists, flow sheets, and preprinted patient instructions that minimize nurses' writing, while guaranteeing a uniform quality of care.
- Work with individual staff members to help them in managing their time more effectively.
- Assist staff members in learning to write brief, comprehensive notes that tie the care plan into interventions and results.
- Work with staff members to develop standards of care that guide them in providing effective care at the required productivity level.
- Be sure standard care plans are available for the most common problems in the unit or center.
- Ensure that treatment protocols are written to aid nurses in performing their jobs more productively.
- Establish a method to use in ensuring that staff members comply with current policies and procedures.
- Analyze how this effort feeds into the performance appraisal process.

To assist staff members in being more aware of their charting practices, it is helpful to collectively audit a patient chart as an exercise in determining its defensibility, as if it were the only representation of care that could be used in court. When the nurses see how much explanation is needed to make sense out of their notations, they usually are motivated to improve. This motivation should be used to improve the criteria followed in performing concurrent patient care audits and chart audits, as a part of the quality assurance effort. Of course, incorporating the requirement for adequate documentation into the performance appraisal process can stimulate improvement.

The Challenge

The public and third party payers are not willing to continue paying for services unless they are effective, efficient, and safe, so care must be designed wisely and monitored continually to meet the demands of quality and improved productivity while minimizing legal liability and adverse public reactions.

Quality assurance efforts and risk management have different focuses, but share the common goal of trying to attain and maintain quality in patient care services. In the risk management process, problems are identified, analyzed, and evaluated in relation to the prevention of liability, damage, and subsequent loss. Large hospital insurers[7] send knowledgeable persons to examine the institution's practices and to recommend ways to reduce potential liability in cooperation with the risk management program. Accepting their suggestions is a prudent way to attempt to keep insurance premiums more reasonable.[8,9,10]

The focus of quality assurance is on setting standards of care with measurable criteria to evaluate the delivery of services at the prescribed productivity level. Together, risk management and quality assurance efforts work to identify and solve problems in productivity, quality of care, and cost containment.

QUALITY ASSURANCE

Through the quality assurance effort, nursing care is studied and revised at the departmental, unit, and individual levels to respond to the continuing need to improve productivity, contain costs, and ensure satisfactory patient care. To achieve this type of integrated program, all nurses should have the opportunity to assume responsibility for quality assurance efforts at the center or unit level and should be acquainted with the functions of the departmental and hospitalwide program. This is one of the best ways to learn about the concept and the monitoring mechanisms and to become more cognizant of individual practice through continuing informal audits.

Quality assurance standards are mandated by the Joint Commission on Accreditation of Hospitals (JCAH) and seem to be getting more comprehensive as time goes on. While JCAH accreditation is optional, most hospitals choose it because accreditation is a necessity for receiving Medicare funds, sponsoring internship and residency programs, and eligibility in some Blue Cross plans. The nursing audit of patient care is only one part of the total quality assurance effort that must also be done individually and collectively by all departments and physicians. It does not replace the need for other types of supervision and monitoring in service delivery.

Assessment of the adequacy of nursing care involves outcome, content, processes, resources, and efficiency.[11]

Assessing the Adequacy of Nursing Care

The primary thrust of the quality assurance effort is geared toward determining whether the desired patient outcome was achieved in the most productive manner by the time of hospital discharge.

Keys to a Positive Assessment

Some questions to be answered to produce a positive assessment include:

- Were staff members satisfied with the quality of care? What suggestions do they have for improving care to this type of patient in the future?
- Did the patient learn new health care information, ways to apply information, or improve/acquire self-care abilities?
- Did the consumer have the opportunity to make decisions and to participate in the planning, implementation, and evaluation of care? Was the patient adequately informed of problems, principles, and treatments underlying care?
- Did the patient get the best possible result psychosocially and physically in relation to the condition?
- Did the treatment improve the patient's ability to function in work and personal roles?
- Was the patient's quality of life increased by the hospital treatment?
- Was the consumer guided to needed personal and health care services required by the condition in a manner that optimized productivity and economy for the patient and the hospital?
- Was care delivered in a manner that resulted in a profit for the hospital? Could care have been provided in a more productive or cost-effective manner without compromising the result for the patient? Would additional resource expenditures have resulted in a better outcome for the patient?

If the outcome was not optimal, nurse managers should analyze whether they have audited the care for problems and worked to correct deficiencies. Untoward outcomes, especially where staff/patient relations were strained or the cost was high for the result, are more likely to result in lawsuits.

Auditing High-Risk Cases

It is helpful if the following points can be audited by nursing and then by an interdisciplinary committee in high-risk cases:

- Valid patient complaints: After investigation, an acceptable apology and solution should be offered to the patient. In one hospital, complaints that remain unresolved for 24 hours result in a free stay for that day.
- Admission or further treatment for adverse outcome following care in the hospital or outpatient department: The chart and care plan should be examined for evidence of a failure to prevent, treat, or diagnose a problem. Ways to avoid such problems in the future should be developed.

- Admission for complication or incomplete management of a problem present on a previous hospital admission: Admission notes, diagnosis, consult notes, and prior admissions within the past six months should be analyzed.
- Hospital-incurred incidents related to falls, drug errors, or transfusion reactions: The chart and incident reports should be checked to evaluate the problem and take corrective action.
- Infection not present on admission: The infection control nurse should be consulted for information on solving this problem.
- Unscheduled transfer from general care to a special care unit: Progress notes and nursing notes should be checked to find the reason for the transfer.
- Transfer to another hospital: It should be determined whether the transfer was for administrative reasons or for treatment unavailable at the hospital. Dissatisfaction with service requires more investigation.
- Operation to correct a perforation, laceration, or injury resulting from an invasive procedure: Progress notes, nursing notes, and operative information should be checked to help rectify this problem.
- Cancellation or repeated diagnostic study because of improper preparation of the patient: Laboratory and radiology reports as well as nursing and progress notes should be studied to identify the problem.
- Unplanned removal of a body part injured during surgery or unscheduled return to the operating room: Chart documentation should be examined to evaluate the reason for these events.
- Physiologic deficit at discharge that was not present upon hospital admission: The chart, the patient's condition, and the circumstances should be reviewed to determine the reason for this adverse outcome.
- Length of stay exceeds the geometric mean established by the prospective payment system, or the cost of treatment exceeds that normally allocated for such treatment: The chart should be analyzed to determine whether the cause was medical or nonmedical and whether or how it could be prevented in the future.
- Codes and abnormal births: Any cardiac or respiratory arrest and all babies with an Apgar of 4 or less should be investigated to determine the circumstances.
- Outpatient or emergency room treatment required to resolve an unplanned problem arising from a recent hospitalization: Inpatient records should be checked to determine the cause of the problem.
- Death: A mortality review should be conducted.

When studying a particular patient, it is important to determine whether the individual received the type and amount of care, or content, necessary to resolve the medical and nursing problems. A comparison of care given in relation to the hospital or unit standard of care can provide important information.

Validity and Follow-Through

In assessing the nursing process, it is important to evaluate the validity of, and follow-through on, care plans. Successful plans should include appropriate, personalized revisions, notations about progress, and evidence as to whether the approaches produced the desired result for the patient.

A study of the process of providing services can help prudent nurses devise creative methods for involving patients in care, giving treatments more productively, and finding better ways of networking with other departments and agencies. Well-kept records allow an audit committee to review an entire group of charts in a given DRG to assess methods used, patient progress, length of hospital stay, and personal factors that can affect productivity. By looking at a group of like patients simultaneously, the committee can determine which nursing measures produced the best impact for resources expended. This allows the committee to arrive at suggestions for changing nursing practices to improve the quality and productivity of the service.

An evaluation of resources is important in determining whether needed professionals, services, supplies, and equipment were available for patient care. It also allows nurses to assess the environment as to whether policies, procedures, and physical surroundings are the best possible to facilitate cost-effective care of the desired quality.

In assessing productivity, nursing centers and units need to be concerned with the cost-benefit ratio of providing care. The goal here is to find the best way of giving the desired care without expending resources excessively.

The Care of the Elderly Patients

For example, in one unit of elderly patients, many of whom required assisted feedings, the audit revealed that it took ten minutes to feed each patient and that staff members felt an urgency to rush each patient. The feeding times coincided with staff meal breaks and created problems for nurses in getting to the cafeteria before closing time.

In analyzing the situation, it was found that staff members put these patients into their chairs at 1000 and returned them to bed just before the lunch hour, thereby necessitating individual assistance for each one. After brainstorming these audit committee findings, the staff decided to revise the times that patients were placed in chairs to coincide with meals so that some of them could be wheeled to the unit conference room for a communal lunch. Eight patients then could be handled by two staff members, who felt more relaxed in allowing each patient sufficient time to eat. Music and flowers were added to the scene to create a better atmosphere.

Patients who could help themselves minimally were free to do so as staff members fed the others.

This experiment resulted in a more satisfactory mealtime experience for the patients and improved staff productivity. Because staff members were better able to take their own meal breaks, they approved the plan.

Types of Audits

The first step in the auditing process is to establish criteria against which the desired quality of care and standard of productivity can be measured. These criteria should cover structural, process, and outcome standards. They are easiest to use when placed in a checklist format in which compliance is marked by a simple yes or no.

Structural Audits

Structural audits usually involve a study of how effectively the center or department is set up administratively to provide the desired type of nursing care. Such factors as staffing, staff educational services, chart forms, and policies and procedures may be reviewed by noting time for completion, frequency of omissions or undesired results, and comments from staff members, other disciplines, and patients.

For example, in one hospital the care planning method was complicated, time-consuming, and inadequately inserviced. As a result, compliance with the charting method was inadequate and staff complaints were numerous. The audit led to corrections through changing the charting method, altering policies, and increasing staff education and support.

Because many hospitals tend to plaster new ideas on top of outdated practices, the time spent in structural audits can work well in streamlining administrative mechanisms underlying care.

Process Audits

Process audits focus on how care is being delivered. Standards for staff performance and expectations in providing care need are assessed. Process audits focus primarily on how nurses work and are task oriented. In assessing work methods and quality of effort, nurse managers with an eye on productivity can find better ways of teaching and achieving desired nurse performance.

For example, in some hospitals the admission history and assessment is expected to take 20 minutes. While a brief note is required at admission to ensure that patients' needs are met, a detailed assessment with a beginning care plan is required within 24 hours. In studying the admission process, auditors should ask:

- Are staff members really able to spend 20 minutes on this process?
- Do they use this time wisely by writing a final copy of the assessment and history as they take it at the bedside?
- How long does it really take to get the completed form on the chart?
- Do the admission data, when complete, provide caregivers with all the information needed to work effectively with the patient?
- Is the form practical, or does it need revision?
- Are nurses given adequate inservice training to use the forms as intended?

Outcome Audits

The study of outcome criteria is the most common type of audit and correlates with the JCAH requirement of audit at the time of discharge. Outcome criteria are written from the patient's perspective.

For example, at discharge patients with head injuries should be able to name six symptoms of increased intracranial pressure that require them to notify their physician, or be able to provide a simple reason for taking each medication. If patients cannot do this, a review of the nursing care is needed to discern why they were not at the desired point by discharge. Questions to be answered include the following:

- If staff members feel they did not have adequate time to accomplish this, would a patient instruction sheet help, or does the work assignment need reorganization to allow this objective to be completed?
- If staff members provided the education, but the patients were unable to grasp it, does the chart documentation show the nursing effort and the problem in patient reception, and does it specify discharge follow-up mechanisms to provide a community support system for this deficit?

Audit criteria for nursing service should be established in coordination with the total plan of care, although each discipline should evaluate its own contribution to the total process. In addition to a quality assurance (QA) committee in nursing, the hospital should have a committee to assess total patient care, with representatives from all disciplines.

While the development of specific audit criteria and methods for conducting the audit are beyond the scope of this book, explicit directions and resources are provided by Rowland and Rowland[12] and by Meisenheimer.[13]

Relating Audits to Productivity

Nursing must be able to show how follow-up is arranged for each of the standards set. While nurses' doing the best they could was once acceptable, this era of increased accountability and improved productivity requires them to specify what standard of care is safe and adequate. Such standards are written to meet the staffing level and mix needed on the unit.

Audits or measurement criteria assess compliance with the service that is supposed to be provided. As audits show compliance, staff members receive feedback about being on the right track; where deficiencies appear, nurses can construct improved methods for correcting the problems.

As the results of audits accumulate over time, nurses will have the data to study the impact of various service measures on a large group of patients, then address the need to change historical routines. For example, if auditing the adverse response to anesthesia and surgery in patients, managers can begin to question whether or not vital signs every 15 minutes times four and every 30 minutes times two makes sense after a patient has returned to the unit from the recovery room. Is there some reason why these vital signs cannot be taken at 30-minute intervals over a two-hour period?

When such questions are raised and answered, nurses will have a statistical basis for making decisions about their care routines in light of the need to improve productivity. Where time is wasted, it can be redirected to other activities that will result in wiser resource utilization of nursing time.

As nurses view this auditing process as one that can improve their jobs by eliminating or revising needless activity, they will realize how valuable this activity can be. Once they internalize the value of auditing, nurses will feel more prone to construct sophisticated tools to make the data-gathering process worthwhile.

SUMMARY

Risk management and quality assurance programs are important aspects of the total productivity program. The risk management process assists nurses in identifying, analyzing, and evaluating problems in an effort to prevent accidents and avoid losses. Success in this area is important to the financial integrity of the hospital system.

The process of quality assurance is one of setting standards of care commensurate with desired productivity standards and of establishing the means for measuring service delivery against preset criteria. This auditing process is important in letting nurses know how well they are meeting the standards. It also is a valuable research mechanism that measures data in the effort to decide how nursing practices can be improved to better meet the goals of increasing productivity, containing costs, and delivering quality patient care services.

NOTES

1. Dan Sperling, "Fear of Suits Drives Obstetricians Out," *USA Today* (August 27, 1985): 1.

2. P.D. Rheingold, "How to Know a Good Medical Malpractice Case." *ABA Journal* 17, no. 11 (November 1984): 71–74.

3. E.M. Swartzbeck, "The Problem of Falls in the Elderly," *Nursing Management* 14, no. 12 (December 1983): 34.

4. D.D. Fife, Phyllis Solomon, and M.A. Stanton, "A Risk/Falls Program: Code Orange for Success," *Nursing Management* 15, no. 11 (November 1984): 50–55.

5. Barbara Lang Rutkowski, "How DRGs Are Changing Your Charting," *Nursing 85* 15, no. 9 (October 1985): 49–51.

6. _____, "DRGs: Now All Eyes Are on You," *Nursinglife* 5, no. 2 (March/April 1985): 30–32.

7. _____, "Risk and Insurance Management," in *AMA Management Handbook*. ed. Russell Moore (New York: American Management Association, 1970).

8. Joseph Davis and Barry Bader, "The Systems Approach to Patient Safety," *QRB Special Edition* (Spring 1980): 47–56.

9. C.K. Van Sluyter, "Organizing for Patient Safety and Liability Control," *QRB Special Edition* (Spring 1980): 57–59.

10. Gerry Stearns and L.A. Fox, "A Three-Phase Plan for Integrating Quality Assurance Activities," *QRB Special Edition* (Spring 1980): 26–29.

11. Wisconsin Regional Medical Board, "Assuring Quality of Nursing Care," *Nursing Administration Quarterly* (Spring 1977).

12. Howard S. Rowland and Beatrice L. Rowland, *Nursing Administration Handbook* (Rockville, Md.: Aspen Publishers, Inc., 1980), 36–96.

13. C.G. Meisenheimer, *Quality Assurance: A Complete Guide to Effective Programs* (Rockville, Md.: Aspen Publishers, Inc., 1985).

ACTION CHECKLIST

1. What are the five most common problems that result in patient/staff accidents or untoward outcomes?
2. What risk management efforts have been instituted to correct these deficiencies?
3. What programs are in place for preventing staff injuries, illnesses, and exposure to hazardous materials and diseases on the job?
4. Have the nurses had a recent update in their legal responsibilities of nursing care?
5. What measures are being taken to improve patient care documentation in the hospital?
6. How will managers involve all of their staff members in participating and contributing to the quality assurance process?
7. Do all of the staff members get the opportunity to participate in a specific audit of charting or patient care?
8. Do the auditing forms lend themselves to pooled research efforts on a specific group of patients?

Chapter 11

Qualitative Standards

Improved productivity and effective care delivery are impossible if nurse administrators do not realistically face the goals they have set in relation to available resources. Patient classification systems have measured hours needed versus hours of indirect and direct care provided. But what is being measured? Getting nurses to patients is only half of the battle; the rest is being sure that the nurses can do what is needed at a level compatible with the standards.

The setting of organizational, departmental, and center philosophies and goals forms the basis of identifying what should be done and what can be done realistically. Four other factors also are important: resources, reasonable performance, directions, and audits.

REALISTIC EXPECTATIONS

Resources

In developing standards, resources are a primary consideration, since without resources, adequate authority, and guidelines for action, employees can fail to meet personal, professional, and center or unit standards in performance.

For example, if nursing managers have established a standard for rehabilitating the postmyocardial infarct patient that requires one hour of professional nurse contact a day, have they budgeted enough nurses to carry out this standard? If not, nursing care expectations need to be modified to be realistic in relation to staffing. Furthermore, if nurses have not met to agree on the exact course this patient guidance will take, patients may not receive the comprehensive rehabilitation instructions that the unit leader has in mind. Instead, each patient's program will be contingent on the skills, ideas, and time available to the nurse involved. The quality and comprehensiveness of the effort thus will be inconsistent.

Reasonable Performance

Once resources are evaluated, the next step is to be certain that all support systems and standards emphasize reasonable behavior and performance consistent with center and departmental objectives.

For example, it would be unreasonable to ask staff members to provide community education courses on abortion if they work in a Catholic hospital because of the conflict between the system and this issue. It also is unreasonable to ask licensed practical nurses to do significant patient teaching and emotional counseling for recovering myocardial infarct patients since they are not prepared for indepth nursing interventions of this type.

Inconsistent outcomes can be expected where behavioral expectations are inconsistent with values or preparation of the employees involved.

Directions

Directions are the cement that provides simplicity, clarity, and continued guidance to be certain that staff members understand what is expected and how to do it. For example, in one hospital a nurse was asked to revise the nursing admission form. Assuming that she had blanket permission, she constructed a new and elaborate form and obtained input from peers. The staff was excited about the new form. However, the director, upon returning from vacation, was upset about how far this nurse had gone in the process. The nurse, who had spent many hours on the new form, was devastated.

All of this could have been avoided if the director had given specific directions, which should have included limits of the assignment, areas open to this nurse's discretion, deadlines for completion, follow-up meeting dates at which further guidance would be given, budgetary limits, and an orientation to system requirements for changing the form.

This illustrates a common problem in hospitals: Harsh feelings and failed efforts often are related to the fact that the leader has provided sketchy directions for a project when the individual really had well-established ideas as to how the project should be done. Clear, complete communication is vital in hospitals that aim to save the time, resources, and energy of staff members while avoiding unnecessary conflict.

Audits

The auditing process also allows managers to be certain that performance is in line with standards and that program modifications are made as needed. This auditing process should be designed during the planning stage of the project so that nurses know the criteria for assessing success and feel supported by the knowledge that periodic follow-ups and guidance are built into the process.

The idea of setting standards and clear plans of action may be relatively new to many hospitals. While these efforts offer nurses a method of ensuring consistent, quality care for all patients, they require a lot of work to develop. However, only when standards are developed in terms of the time required to implement them can nurses assess what they realistically can do for patients in the work hours available.

Nurses have resisted the setting of standards because the emphasis of compacting patient care into a shorter period is a new experience and they have clung to the notion of "being all things to all people." As a result, many become frustrated when idealism and reality seem to be so far apart. The result in many settings is that nurses simply do the best they can. Such an approach is frustrating, because the issues of "What is enough?" and "What do they expect and what do I expect?" are not on the table for nurses and managers to discuss and resolve. Yet the government, other third party payers, and consumers rightfully are concerned with getting quality for dollars expended.

The trends in health care, the issue of qualitative standard setting, and evaluation of compliance are receiving wide attention in journals, from accrediting bodies, and by the nursing profession.[1] The process begins with a review of the total situation in relation to staff, unit strategies, and patient/family care priorities. Next, standards are written and criteria for compliance are specified as quality indicators. Finally, compliance is measured and programs modified—and the cycle is repeated.

Quality control is a continuing, deliberate process essential to the provision of efficient and effective care. Standards of care must be set judiciously since each requires periodic auditing and has legal implications.

ESTABLISHING STANDARDS

Defining and Writing Standards

A qualitative standard is simply a level of performance in staff or a set of conditions in a nursing center deemed acceptable by an authority. When nurse managers set the level of performance, they must avoid using such words as "minimal" or "marginal" since they could be judged against their own standards in a negligence case. Instead, they should write a standard of care that complies with accrediting requirements, practices in local health care agencies, and adequate service levels as identified in the literature.[2,3,4] However, these standards should not be rigid and unattainable.

An example is the SOAP format: *S* (subjective information), *O* (objective information), *A* (analysis), and *P* (plan of action). If a standard says that all nursing notes will be written in a SOAP format, when accreditors or hospital quality assurance committee members pull random charts to assess compliance, managers (and nurses) receive a fail mark if a single chart is not written according to this format. If a standard states that all newly diagnosed diabetics will have specific instruction on when and how to give insulin and what to know about hypoglycemia and hyperglycemia, such instructions must be documented. If not done, the managers or nurses may have some problems defending their care if accused of causing patient damage from inadequate discharge instructions.

To avoid problems, nursing managers should:

- Refer to standards in written documents as guidelines that are implemented to the extent possible in relation to individual patient needs.
- Set most compliance mandates for standard guidelines at less than 100 percent so that there is room for human error, subjective decisions, and omissions.
- Establish standards that nurses and managers agree on as acceptable and possible with available staff and resources.
- Strive to use negative and positive charting or quality assurance notations to explain deviations, special circumstances, and employee/patient response to interventions, depending on the standard.

Determining Compliance

Once the standard guidelines are established, criteria are written for determining compliance. These criteria are critical elements selected to judge acceptable performance and to show that the desired quality is being met or not met.

For example, a newly diagnosed diabetic or family member will be able to administer insulin safely by the time of discharge as indicated by a return demonstration and explanation of the injection procedure. That procedure should be written so that a copy is available in the center and in the patient discharge materials. If the patient/family is unable to administer insulin, a note must be written in the chart that includes some type of postdischarge follow-up designed to ensure safe administration. Because this ability is required for minimal, safe discharge, some mechanism of complete compliance must be established.

For example, where quality indicators (such as discharge outcomes, which require the patient or family to identify what insulin is, how to give it, what it does, and what symptoms require them to notify their physician) indicate a problem, the discharge note must include such factors, along with a referral to the public health department.

Standard setting implies accountability. Fear of accountability and inexperience in standard setting have caused many nurse managers to avoid putting standards in writing. However, standards do not need to be fancy; they need only express what the center is trying to accomplish so that everyone has a clear basis for knowing what is important. Managers desiring optimal performance should encourage standard setting and compliance.

For example, a common standard would require that the patient's response to the nursing care plan be reflected in the progress notes at least once every 24 hours. Nurses who chart to integrate patient responses to care planning, and revise plans accordingly, should be rewarded verbally on a regular basis and tangibly during the periodic performance appraisal process. In short, accountability is nurses' being answerable for their actions; where no effort is made to identify clearly the priorities of the system for which staff members are accountable, the quality of care suffers.

Quality assurance also is the process of setting standards and taking action to be certain that they are met. It is fruitless to attempt setting standards without a plan for implementing and monitoring them to be sure they are appropriate and produce the desired results. Thus, once managers identify a priority—such as a specific, total ambulation program for a certain type of postoperative patient—they need to have a place on the flow sheet to chart that this activity has been carried out. They then need an audit tool to judge the effect of ambulation on the patient's general condition and progress.

A review of numerous audits on patients can demonstrate whether the ambulation schedule is (1) adequate, (2) charted, (3) possible with current staffing, (4) possible with the type of patients, (5) helping patients improve faster, and (6) affecting the length of the hospital stay. The results of this audit make it possible to affirm the standard or modify it in light of the findings.

TYPES OF STANDARDS

While standards may be delineated in a number of ways, for purposes of improving practice they are identified as structural, process, and outcome:

- *Structural standards* are "thing oriented" and are the foundation of all other standards. Structural standards define the set of conditions and mechanisms basic to the provision of care under the identified criteria.
- *Process standards* are "action oriented" and define actions and behaviors in providing care.
- *Outcome standards* are "results oriented" and identify the final result of direct or indirect care.

Nurses who have difficulty in delineating process standards may find it easiest to skip to outcome standards as a means of identifying the final result, then turn to the process or "how-to" category. When the ultimate destination or objective is not defined, almost any route will do. That is part of the frustration related to poor delineation of standards.

STRUCTURAL STANDARDS

Structural standards define conditions and mechanisms that facilitate desired staff functioning, systems operation, and patient care delivery. They always are written in the hospital's policy format and should be coded for easy retrieval. Each of these policies should be written to interrelate meaningfully with other policies so that they result in a framework from which all other standards can be developed.

Structural standards are written first for the nursing department, then made more specific at the unit or center level. When the standards for those two are in fact more specific, nurses have a greater power base and more autonomy, as well as accountability, in their operations. Conflicts with physicians can be minimized where unit policies and decision directives are formulated jointly with the doctors involved. Naturally, more generalized units such as general medical-surgical floors are less elite in their mission, have more physicians with whom to contend, and generally have less power over policies and specific standards than does an oncology center or intensive care unit.

For example, in the case of "do not resuscitate" orders, the intensive care units in many hospitals regularly triage patients into four groups in which group I gets a complete code while group IV receives only supportive comfort measures. Thus when the patient arrests, clear policies of nursing responses are known in advance. However, on the general units, where numerous physicians have patients, nurses still have trouble in getting some of the doctors to write clear orders for nursing action. "Slow codes," and half-hearted resuscitation orders are inadequate since the nurse is required to resuscitate the patient fully unless there is a physician's order stating otherwise. Moreover, no-code policies should include an expiration time, so that patient conditions and wishes are reevaluated periodically.

A structural policy with appropriate physician approval and education is needed to provide nurses with a protocol in coding patients who have arrested. Until this policy is formulated and enforced, nurses are caught in a major professional crisis and upheaval about how to handle an arrest situation in a terminal patient. This issue was selected here because it is a major problem on many nursing units that are caring for increasingly sicker and older patients and the no-code question arises frequently. With the advent of the profit/loss centers concept, every unit must strive to become more specific in standard setting as a means of enhancing care delivery and communications among the professionals.

Other examples of structural standards involve:

- the patient population
- the environment
- physician support
- supportive services
- staff credentialing
- nursing responsibilities
- staff quantity, level, and quality
- equipment and supplies
- safety and health
- infection control
- educational resources
- fiscal policies
- personnel policies.

Most nursing departments and centers already have structural standards that explain the general nursing hierarchy, who does what, infection control policies, etc. However, a number of these mechanisms may not really be working to enhance nurse productivity. For example, the policy on maintenance of equipment may be so vague that equipment is not checked or fixed in a timely manner. A nurse who needs a wheelchair may have to go to another unit to find one that is not broken. Of course, implementation of this structural policy needs to be checked regularly so that functioning, safe equipment is available in a specific location. Otherwise, valuable nurse time is wasted.

In evaluating structural policies, nurse administators or managers should ask themselves:

- Do staff nurses have what they need to get their jobs done?
- Do any hospital policies impede the work flow or strain timely interchanges among departments?
- What nursing policies require undue paperwork or contain obstacles that need to be streamlined or deleted?
- What staffing, scheduling, and assignment policies facilitate or impede getting staff members to the work area when they are needed?
- What can be done to improve the general nursing division organization to maximize productive work efforts by each member?

Such questions should be asked at every level of the organization and particulary should have input from staff nurses who know the pros and cons of each policy.

There are several reasons for such a review:

- Managers/administrators and nurses legally can be held to the policies they have written. Thus, if actual practices differ from what is written, the policies should be revised, dated, and initialed by the vice president of nursing and the center director, as appropriate.
- These standards should be reviewed with an eye on increased productivity to be certain that they are comprehensive yet devoid of requirements that result in inefficiency or unwarranted resource expenditures.
- These structural standards should be utilized to maximize the acquisition of sufficient power and resources to execute responsibilities and performance at the desired level in the total department and at the center/unit level.

For example, the administrator may decide that all staff nurses will have a baccalaureate degree in nursing by 1995. That information would be reflected in the section on staff credentialing. However, this goal may never be met if at the same time resources are not allocated to attain it. A policy may be needed that provides a way for a current employee to be assigned to appropriate work shifts and possibly receive some monetary incentive or tuition assistance to make going to school possible. The manager's efforts may even need to include the establishing of a special program in cooperation with the local nursing program through which course offerings are made more flexible and accessible to employees in exchange for some type of package offer.

In short, for each item specified, whether it be specialized certification, cardiopulmonary resuscitation (CPR) proficiency, continuing education to maintain licensure, updated performance practices in patient care, or the planning of services by a registered nurse, managers should be certain that they have established a reasonable budget and mechanism to make compliance with the policy possible.

PROCESS STANDARDS

Process standards have a variety of formats, including job descriptions, procedures, protocols, guidelines for using nursing tools, standards of performance, and statements of standardized care plans. While each of these standards is different, they all specify expected action and behaviors on the part of either the nurse or the patient in defining appropriate care or its implementation.

Procedures

Procedures typically are written in a separate notebook and detail various psychomotor skills, such as how to insert a Foley catheter, care for an intravenous infusion line, or assist with a bronchoscopy. While all hospitals have such procedures, problems can occur when the book is not complete, when procedures require unneeded steps or equipment, when the instructions are not clear, or when the procedures have not been updated to meet current performance criteria.

Problems can develop when units differ in their interpretation of the same procedure and the float nurse, not specifically oriented to this difference, is admonished for an error. As hospitals become decentralized, it is critical to provide some central consistency for procedures and to identify areas in which differences should be interpreted to nurses who are not regularly assigned to an area.

For example, on one unit, differences and specialized points of information were videotaped by the regular staff for use in orienting persons to the unit. The tape included physician preferences and idiosyncracies, unit routines that are unwritten, comments on specialized policies and procedures, and patient care priorities for the major diagnoses. The tape was marked so that orientees could move quickly to a certain point for the information they sought. The advantage of this method was that new persons could be more comfortable with standard practices on the unit while regular staff members, freed from redundant lectures, felt more positive about answering individual questions after the learner had watched the videotape.

Procedures also are important in containing costs. Each procedure should be reviewed with an eye to eliminating unneeded steps and containing expenditures by the choice of equipment and supplies. The cost of performing each nursing procedure then can be estimated more realistically as a start in compiling specific charges and costs for care.

For example, the clinical specialist on the surgical unit might experiment with various ways of creating an absorbent abdominal dressing at the lowest cost. The choice of dressings decided on could then be put into the procedure and explained in inservice training as a means of saving money. The amount of savings could be projected and compared with current practices by determining the average number of dressing changes for certain surgical cases multiplied by the number of cases in the year. In similar fashion, most other procedures can be investigated and costed out by nurses, including the infection control nurse, who has the latest information on standards.

Protocols

Protocols (plans of treatment) are written to define what specifically is to be done for a certain category of patients. These protocols involve three levels of action: dependent, independent, and interdependent. Protocols define nursing management for patients on noninvasive and invasive equipment; in therapeutic, diagnostic, or prophylactic interventions; in psychologic or physiologic states; and in using nursing diagnoses:

- Dependent protocols require delegation of care through physician orders, such as the treatment of unconscious diabetic patients.
- Independent protocols identify autonomous nursing functions that can be initiated without physician orders, such as nursing diagnoses and action in maintaining skin integrity.
- Interdependent protocols include both dependent and independent actions by nursing personnel, such as patient education for the use of pacemakers or in home care of diabetes.

One particular problem, which in one hospital resulted in a losing lawsuit, was the inconsistency of the neurological assessment protocol from one area to another. In intensive care, the use of a flow sheet made the completion of a neurological examination self-evident. That was not true on the general unit, where the flow sheet was unavailable and the exact conduct of that nursing assessment was not detailed, nor was the nursing action charted clearly. Thus, the plaintiff won by contending successfuly that important parameters of patient assessment were omitted, delaying needed medical intervention.

Guidelines

Guidelines are written to explain the use of a nursing tool. Examples include the nursing data base or nursing history, nursing progress notes, standard care plans, medication sheets, transfer or discharge forms, and various nursing flow sheets. Guidelines should be written for each form that is used in the nursing department and should be a subject of inservice training for staff members to be certain that everyone understands the use of the element involved. These guidelines should be available on all units and in all centers for ready reference.

It is important to make guidelines specific enough that audit criteria may be derived from them. These guidelines thus serve as the base for evaluating nursing care. When quality assurance audits find deviations between guidelines and actual practice, nurse managers need to determine whether the practice differs from what is written or whether nursing staff members need further inservice training or follow-up in utilizing the materials in accordance with guidelines.

For example, in one situation, the Glasgow Coma Scale was incorporated into the neurologic checklist. However, in auditing patient flow sheets, the nurse manager found that several new nurses used the scale incorrectly. One nurse consistently checked ''3,'' which indicates brain death, when she should have checked ''7'' for the patient's higher functional state. This finding obviously made the charting inconsistent and indicated a need for further staff education.

Documentation of nursing care is a weak point in most hospitals since busy nurses often give care a priority over recording what was done. Legally, if care is not charted it has not been done. With the increased number and costs of lawsuits, managers must assist staff members in wise time management; in writing clear, succinct, complete notes; and in developing as many tools as possible that provide checklists and flow sheets that minimize writing. Pennies saved in cost containment are expended rapidly through the loss of just one major lawsuit premised on inadequate documentation.

It is to be hoped that this era of automation will cause hospitals to assist nurses in computerizing documentation to save time and make notations more complete. While some systems are available that allow this function either at the central station or at the bedside, further work is required to make them practical, cost effective, and efficient.

Standards of Care

The standards of service can be both general and specific in the patient care plan. Many units and centers begin by using nurse specialty standards developed by groups affiliated with the American Nurses' Association, and later writing more detailed standards for general and specific patient care. Others meet as a group and determine what they believe patients need.

Examples of general standards of care include:

- Patients admitted after midnight will not receive a routine linen change and bath unless their condition warrants it.
- Each patient will have at least one care plan item related to discharge planning, learning needs, and specific care related to the diagnosis. These items will be addressed in the nursing progress notes no less often than every 24 hours in 75 percent of the cases.
- Patients/families capable of doing independent personal care and feeding will receive a ____percent discount on the daily room rate.
- Seventy-five percent of the time, flow sheets for patient routines will indicate that restrained patients have had their circulation checked and that restraints have been released at least every four hours to allow appropriate exercise.
- Seventy-five percent of all pain medications will be followed with a mark in the appropriate ''effective'' column on the medication administration record.

If the pain medication was ineffective, an explanatory note will be written in the nurse's notes.

- Ninety percent of the time, patients will receive pain medication within five minutes of the request when the request is appropriate and orders are available.
- Ninety percent of the time, the registered nurse will have 25 minutes to complete the admission assessment and initiate the care plan.

In writing standards for specific patients, nurse administrators/managers may want to begin with a major problem or diagnosis that is most prevalent in the area, then:

- List necessary physical, emotional, learning, and discharge planning needs.
- Enter beside each item what level of employee is required, the time needed, and a method for auditing to determine whether nurses are complying with this standard at least 75 percent of the time.
- List desirable items for each specific standard that should be done if time permits.
- Negotiate needs versus resources until the items settled on are realistic and appropriate.

Many new books are available that outline care for most diagnoses. It is prudent to purchase two or three to compare approaches and make a good start on establishing the standards for the patient care area. The titles of these books can be obtained from advertisements in nursing journals and in the library reference book, *Medical Books in Print,* which lists current books.[5]

Standard Care Plans

A popular approach to decreasing the perennial problems that occur in maintaining comprehensive, updated care plans is to use preprinted standard care plans. This is effective in producing permanent records of plans, improving the quality of planning, and getting the job done consistently.

The standard care plan can be very sophisticated, and need not be written from the beginning, since so many care plan books are on the market to assist hospitals in compiling a sound program for each type of patient problem. While standard, published forms are available, staff members generally feel more commitment to a plan to which they have contributed. These plans can be personalized by leaving space for individualized comments and actions.

OUTCOME STANDARDS

Outcome standards simply express the results that should be achieved by some end point, preferably in behavioral, measurable terms. The use of outcome standards is appropriate in patient or staff education programs, in staff development efforts, and in nursing care planning. Where outcome standards are specified, nurse managers will need behavioral objectives and a method for reaching the desired outcome.

Goals are written in two ways to achieve outcome standards. First, the goals are written in relation to the nurses, explaining what they should accomplish by a certain time. When total success is not possible, nurses can write goals in terms of action verbs designed to minimize, reduce, maintain, or restore functions. For example, "The nurse will improve patient mobility by discharge." This standard will apply more often with the admission of older, sicker patients for whom small improvements are major milestones.

Second, the outcome goal may be written in terms of what the patient will achieve or do by a preset time. Such goals can be further divided into what the patient or family will do, what physiologic progress can be expected, what psychosocial goals will be accomplished, or what conditions or plans must be in place to ensure safe, competent, self-care or other-directed care in the postdischarge period. These patient outcomes are stated only as desired ends that can be evaluated as done or not done. No mention is made of the process by which these outcomes are to be attained.

For example, the nursing outcome goal might be to teach Mr. J to self-administer insulin safely by the time of discharge. To check on progress, a nurse auditor could rightly ask what was being done each day to reach the goal; that is, the process standards could be evaluated. However, no matter what the quality of teaching by the nurse, the patient still has to be motivated and able to reach the outcome as planned.

The second parameter of evaluation (the outcome assessment) would be to see if the patient accomplished the treatment. If patient learning was not successful, the nurse would need to delineate an alternative plan of interventions, thereby altering the process that would result in Mr. J's getting correct doses of insulin as specified by the physician. Appropriate charting would be required to specify special needs or patient deficits to protect staff nurses against discharging the individual with improper instructions or assistance and to improve chances for third party reimbursement when further health care intervention beyond the hospital is required.

To write outcomes for patients, the four-column care plan format is preferred, as follows:

Care Plan

Nursing Diagnosis	Nursing Goal	Interventions	Patient Outcome

QUALITY ASSURANCE

To be sure that the nurses are working both efficiently and effectively, the standards that are written in relation to personnel and patients must be scrutinized periodically to be sure they accomplish what is intended. Dates for periodic review should be set, in advance, when standards are established. The desired review dates should be marked on the calendar and recorded in the quality assurance committee efforts. While reviews of some items can be extensive and time consuming, most standards can be evaluated rather quickly if criteria for success are specified.

For example, patient response to pain medication should be noted 75 percent of the time in the chart. To simplify recording and auditing, some hospitals are adding a column to the medication administration sheet that requires initials for whether or not the pain medicine was effective. If it was not effective, a note must be written in the nurses' notes, according to the policy guidelines accompanying the use of the form. Five charts can be selected at random each month for a quick review of this checkoff or an appropriate note. Nurses are encouraged to be creative in finding shortcuts to planning, providing, charting, and auditing care so long as they maintain the desired level of quality.

When an audit of the standards reveals noncompliance, the staff should commence problem solving to determine the reason. Adjustments then need to be made either in the standard, in the work strategies for meeting the standard, or in the education/preparation of those involved. These adjustments should be recorded in unit quality-assurance minutes.

As this demonstrates, standards are not carved in stone. They are guidelines that assist in identifying when an adequate job is being done. When the guidelines are not realistic or are not implemented or monitored properly, they can become an impediment to success. If used properly, they can enhance communication among staff members, with other health care professionals, and with patients and their families, while ensuring the highest level of care for resources expended.

SUMMARY

To operate a productive nursing division that prides itself on quality patient care, standard setting is a must. To be sure that standards are implemented as intended, the nursing division also must make certain that adequate resources and means of accomplishment are provided, along with a continuous monitoring system to be sure that things are progressing as they should.

An essential process in becoming more productive is to scrutinize all structural, process, and outcome standards to be sure that they have been streamlined, updated, and accepted by the parties involved. Structural policies are the skeleton of the system, process policies are the "how-to-do-it" ones, and outcome policies are the end result.

For example, an adequate "do not resuscitate" policy that physicians use properly is an example of a structural policy. Evaluation of how the nurses proceed through the code or the no-code situation is process assessment. The rehash of how the code or no-code went, and the result for the nurse and patient, is an example of an outcome policy. The monitoring process and materials are part of the quality assurance effort.

NOTES

1. C.G. Meisenheimer, *Quality Assurance: A Complete Guide to Effective Programming* (Rockville, MD.: Aspen Publishers, Inc., 1985).
2. American Nurses' Association, *A Plan for Implementation of the Standards of Nursing Practice* (Kansas City, Mo.: ANA, 1980).
3. _____, *A Social Policy Statement* (Kansas City, Mo.: ANA, 1980).
4. Joint Commission on Accreditation of Hospitals, *Accreditation Manual for Hospitals*, 1986 ed. (Chicago: JCAH, 1985).
5. *Medical Books and Serials in Print* (New York: Bowker, 1985).

SUGGESTED READINGS

Cantor, M.M. *Achieving Nursing Care Standards: Internal and External*. Wakefield, Mass.: Nursing Resources, 1978.

Donnelly, G.F., Mengel, Andrea, & Sutterley, D.C. *The Nursing System: Issues, Ethics and Politics*. New York: John Wiley & Sons, Inc., 1980.

Hetherington, R.W. "Quality Assurance and Organizational Effectiveness in Hospitals." *Health Services Research* 17, no. 2. (Summer 1982).

Phaneuf, Marie, *The Nursing Audit: Profile for Excellence*. New York: Appleton-Century-Crofts, Inc., 1972.

ACTION CHECKLIST

1. Analyze how effective they are in delegating projects to staff in terms of identifying realistic resource utilization ideas, providing clear directions, requiring reasonable performance, and providing essential guidance and monitoring.
2. Determine what plan and timetable they have for reviewing their structural, process, and outcome standards.
3. Ask staff members to name five policies that enhance their work productivity most and five that hamper it. Compile the results of this poll to identify the priority policies with which to begin.
4. Identify specific staff members interested in assisting with policy changes or standard development and invite them to participate in the process.
5. Distribute to staff members material on setting general and specific standards for patient care. Then ask them to assist in identifying ten general standards and one specific patient type for specific problems.
6. Call medical records to get an analysis of the types of patient conditions that are admitted most often to the unit. From this list, it becomes easier to select priority areas for beginning patient standard development.

Chapter 12

Quantitative Standards

Pacquine R. Fairless

The time is ripe for nursing to blend its efforts in achieving a high level of productivity and pricing its services accordingly. Chapter 11 covered qualitative standards. This chapter, on quantitative aspects and patient classification systems, is centered on the more measurable aspects of care, patient needs, and what staff members are required to provide that care. To price nursing beyond a general categorical figure, both quantitative and qualitative aspects must be included.

In blending these two measurements, the questions are:

- What exactly can the patient expect as a standard of care in Level II?
- How does this standard change when the patient pays more money because of being placed in Level III?
- Do different patients pay the same amount for varying care within the same level?

THE CHALLENGES INVOLVED

Personnel and staffing costs are not fixed but vary according to the nursing decisions made in relation to patient needs. The government has not dictated what nursing will do but has included a sum for nursing care in each diagnosis related group (DRG). This challenges hospitals to identify nursing services, price them, and continue to reduce costs of providing care by developing more productive work strategies.

As census changes require staff reductions, the remaining nurses often divide added tasks. However, unless the acceptable standards of care are identified for each patient, basic service delivery is left open to intuitive determination and practice. As computer programs are developed, it is possible to write standards into care units for selection in treating each patient. For example, modules can be written for common problems in nursing care such as vomiting, problems in sleeping, moderate anxiety, confusion, incontinence, or cast care.

Another approach is to construct an "average" patient model for a specific DRG or medical diagnosis as a means of assigning hours and typical costs. The patient could be assumed to be having a cholecystectomy. Nursing could develop approximate costs from admission to discharge for an uncomplicated patient, then for a complex case such as a partially mobile, elderly person with secondary diagnoses.

A third approach combines these methods, identifying typical care for a cholecystectomy patient and writing modules related to nursing diagnoses that can be added to basic costs to arrive at a sum that is more representative of nursing care delivered.

For example, a patient is admitted for gallbladder removal who is elderly, confused, moderately impaired in breathing capacities, partially mobile, dependent for feeding, and grieving over the recent death of his wife. By determining the appropriate nursing care units, the hospital can price the time and individual staff members required to give cost-effective, productive nursing care.

Interventions can be written for these modules and a price assigned after the cost of the caregiver is determined. When a patient needs care, the nurse need only check off what units were required, and the nurse manager can identify the cost of care for that shift. If Mr. A needed meal assistance by a nursing assistant at $2.50 per meal, and the day shift helped with two meals, the cost would be $5. If his casted leg needed to be checked for neurologic integrity, warmth, and circulation by a registered nurse, the time could be estimated, and a charge of, say, $2.75 could be charged for each check. With computerized nursing care programs, these care units or modules are programmed into the system for ease in checkoff and addition of costs.

How does this work when the government has set ceilings on costs? Costs for each patient still can be added to a routine hygiene care expense. At times, the cost for a given patient exceeds the amount budgeted because of the intensity of services required—particularly since outlier cases consume the most resources of typical patients in a DRG. While costs can be excessive for some patients requiring an unusual number of care units, they are balanced by more normative costs for others.

At some future date, when an intensity index is figured into the DRG system, there may be a way to recoup some of these costs. Until then, nurse managers must identify the costs, work to streamline these care costs through productive use of resources, and distribute staff members so that their mix is appropriate to deliver the type of services needed on specific units.

By breaking nursing care into these additive units, nurse administrators can compare the average cost of care provided for each patient in a DRG and determine whether the services cost more on one clinical unit than on another for the same type of patient. From these comparisons, it is simple to determine whether there is a difference in the rate of progress between patients cared for by different staffs. Where the cost of delivering service is consistently beyond budget, nurse administrators can begin to make decisions about what elements will remain and what will be deleted.

For example:

- Will family members need to stay or provide sitters at night for confused patients?
- Will community health nurses have to teach new diabetics how to administer insulin because the cost of doing this for inpatients is too high?
- Will physicians need to teach pulmonary exercises to preoperative patients in their offices to minimize teaching time in the acute care hospital?

These are the questions that must be raised as nurse administrators make decisions about what care can be provided profitably for a fixed cost.

DEFINITIONS OF QUANTITATIVE STANDARDS

To better understand this process of writing care units, it is essential to define quantitative standards. These are measurable, valid criteria used to ascertain a degree of accomplishment. The need to establish standards to maintain a safe and productive nursing staff according to patient type or needs is not a new concept. The American Nurses' Association (ANA) *Standards for Organized Nursing Service* identifies the need for developing quantitative standards for the nursing department.[1] There are three standards relating to staffing:

Standard I states that:

> The division of nursing has a philosophy and structure that assure the delivery of high-quality nursing care and provide means for resolving nursing practice issues throughout the health care organization. (p. 3)

Standard II explains that:

> The division of nursing is administered by a qualified nurse executive who is a member of corporate administration. . . . The nurse executive participates in fiscal management decisions to assure resources to provide consistently effective nursing care. (p. 4)

To ensure quality of care, nurse administrators must have control over the staffing of the nursing units. Nurse administrators are held accountable for the quality of care delivered but vary in their authority to determine and maintain staffing systems to provide the care.

The last ANA point on staffing is Standard IV. It states:

> The division of nursing ensures that the nursing process is used to design and provide nursing care to meet the individual needs of patients/clients in the context of their families. . . . Nursing staffing patterns and assignments are made by use of a system that determines patient requirements and priorities for care, and matches those requirements with the knowledge and skills of nursing staff. (p. 5)

It is the responsibility of the nurse administrators to have a methodology identified for the productive utilization of nursing personnel according to the care needed by patients and the competency level of the staff members. In other words, nursing administration must establish and maintain a staffing system that is specific and objective to patients' needs.

The Joint Commission on Accreditation of Hospitals (JCAH) addresses the issue of establishment and utilization of quantitative standards for staffing.[2] Standard III for the nursing service department states:

> Nursing department/service assignments in the provision of nursing care shall be commensurate with the qualifications of nursing personnel and shall be designed to meet the nursing care needs of the patient. (p. 97)

In the interpretation of the standard, the JCAH comments:

> A sufficient number of qualified registered nurses shall be on duty at all times to give patients the nursing care that requires the judgment and specialized skills of a registered nurse. Nursing personnel staffing shall also be sufficient to assure prompt recognition of any untoward change in a patient's condition and to facilitate appropriate intervention by the nursing, medical, or hospital staffs. In striving to assure optimal achievable quality nursing care and a safe patient environment, nursing personnel staffing and assignment shall be based at least on the following:

> A registered nurse plans, supervises, and evaluates the nursing care of each patient; To the extent possible, a registered nurse makes a patient assessment before delegating appropriate aspects of nursing care to ancillary nursing personnel; The patient care assignment minimizes the risk of the transfer of infection and accidental contamination; The patient care assignment is commensurate with the qualifications of each

nursing staff member, the identified nursing needs of the patient, and the prescribed medical regimen; and Responsibility for nursing care and related duties is retained by the hospital nursing department/service when nursing students and nursing personnel from outside sources are providing care within a patient care unit.

The nursing department/service shall define, implement, and maintain a system for determining patient requirements for nursing care on the basis of demonstrated patient needs, appropriate nursing intervention, and priority for care. Specific nursing personnel staffing for each nursing care unit, including, as appropriate, the surgical suite, obstetrical suite, ambulatory care department/service, and emergency department/ service, shall be commensurate with the patient care requirements, staff expertise, unit geography, availability of support services, and method of patient care delivery. (pp. 97–98)

The state board of health, such as in Indiana, requires that standards be available to measure the nursing workload and to provide adequate staffing. Indiana State Board of Health (ISBH) Regulations for General and Special Hospitals—HHL 42 states in part:[3]

10.2 Administration of Clinical Services
   (a) (6) Patient needs shall be used as the basis for staffing patterns. (p. 6)
10.3 Nursing Services
   (c) A written organizational plan for nursing service shall be developed and made available to personnel.
   The plan shall include:
   (1) Staffing pattern for nursing personnel throughout the hospital.
   (2) Delineation of functions for which nursing service is responsible.
   (3) Specifications of positions required to carry out functions.
   (4) Designation of lines of communication with nursing service. (p. 7)

Each of these regulatory entities (ANA, JCAH, ISBH) recommends that quantitative standards be developed and utilized for adequate, productive staffing based on patient needs.

QUANTITATIVE STANDARDS AND PRODUCTIVITY

Once the general standards for the nursing division are in place, the nurse manager has the challenge of writing standards for direct patient care. The goal of these standards is to provide the highest level of patient care possible within the realistic economic and productive capacities of the nursing staff. In the DRG era, most hospitals have tackled this problem by implementing a patient classification system that divides consumers into several broad categories based on the nursing care they should receive.

These systems, used primarily at the outset to justify staffing, now are used to equalize staffing mix and numbers among nursing units or centers according to the severity of patients' illness. Some hospitals assign a price to the broad levels of care in their system.

When the concept of standards is plugged into these patient classification systems, the nursing division, instead of merely checking off items (such as complex feeding) writes a standard stating what is done for the patient in this category. This standard shows the process or procedure for helping, identifies the desired outcome, and assigns a cost. The total process thus becomes a care unit. By identifying nursing interventions as care units, the nursing division can better isolate what is done for patients, how much it costs, and how it can be done more productively and economically.

PATIENT CLASSIFICATION SYSTEMS

While the proper use of patient classification systems is the key to identifying, measuring, and pricing nursing activity and productivity, many hospitals operate the systems simply to meet the requirements of regulatory agencies. To better understand available patient classification systems and methods of calculating staff needed, it is helpful to review what is being done.

In the past, two methods were used to determine the required nursing hours:

1. the nursing hours/patient day, comparing this hospital with other institutions with similar bed size and patient population
2. the number of hours needed as identified by time and motion studies performed by the management engineering department.

Many nurse administrators have used a formula to define the required nursing hours in a 24-hour period based on nursing hours/patient day and census:

> nursing hours/patient days × patient census/unit = total nursing hours required/unit ÷ 8-hour shifts = number of staff needed in 24 hour/unit.

The problem with this formula was that it did not account for the acuity (degree of severity) of each patient or the skill mix of the caregivers and the shift distribution. The nurse manager used gut feeling as to the mix required and distribution of the mix per shift. Many times the gut feeling was correct; however, hospital administration did not always accept the validity of those feelings as justification for the desired personnel budget.

With increased emphasis on cost containment and productivity, nursing administrators have had to reevaluate their methodology for determining the personnel budget using patient classification systems. The system's effectiveness is dependent on the support it receives from nursing and hospital administration.

An objective, effective patient classification system contains the following components:

1. flexibility
2. utilization by nursing personnel
3. compatibility with nursing philosophy and productivity goals
4. capability of justifying why nursing hours/patient day do not comply with the budgeted figure
5. ability to be tracked to provide staffing and acuity patterns.

Many systems involve three components: patient classification system, management reports, and quality monitoring tools. These form an information system enabling the nurse manager to respond to changes in patient population, quality of care provided, and planning of future use of nursing resources. These components are discussed next.

Definition

A patient classification system is a method that is used to determine the severity of illness for each patient in a particular defined area or service. The severity of illness is translated into nursing workload, which defines the staffing needed to provide the nursing hours required within a specific period of time. In other words, a patient classification system is a way to categorize patients based on identification of care needs through assessment.

Types

Although there are numerous types of patient classification systems, the three used most often are the (1) descriptive , (2) checklist of nursing tasks, and (3) patient needs styles.

Descriptive Method

This is probably the oldest method used. In it, the nurse assigns the patient to a category that best describes the level of care needed. Standards are written to describe the various levels of categories. The narrative descriptions of categories are very general in nature. A predefined nurse-to-patient ratio required to achieve these standards is used to determine the nursing personnel needed.

The problem with this type of system is the subjectivity of the nurse's evaluation of the severity of the patient's illness. It has been found that nurses do not consistently interpret the same patient's illness the same way. An example of a descriptive patient classification system is presented in Exhibit 12–1.

Checklist of Nursing Tasks Method

The checklist of nursing tasks method is based on descriptions of activities that have been identified and sometimes timed using the industrial engineering

---

Exhibit 12–1 Descriptive Patient Classification System

Category I: Minimal Care

Patients who are convalescing and no longer require intensive, moderate, or maximum care. These patients still may need supervision by a nurse in the course of a day, even if only at infrequent intervals. This care group also includes patients who require diagnostic studies, minimal therapy, less frequent observations, daily care for minor conditions, are awaiting elective surgery, have difficulty arranging transportation between home and hospital, and those whose home environment temporarily makes discharge undesirable or impractical.

Category II: Moderate Care

Patients who are moderately ill or are recovering from the immediate effects of a serious illness and/or an operation. These patients require nursing supervision or some assistance ambulating and caring for their own hygiene. They may be ambulatory for short periods.

Category III: Maximum Care

Patients who need close attention throughout the shift; that is, complete care patients who require nursing to initiate, supervise, and perform most of their activities or who require frequent and complex medications or treatments.

Category IV: Intensive Care

Acutely ill patients who have a high level of nurse dependency, including those requiring intensive therapy and/or intensive nursing care and whose unstable condition requires frequent evaluation with adjustment of therapy.

Note: The category best describing the patient reflects the patient type. The nursing division may set the hours of care required by each patient category.

approach. Each activity pertinent to a particular patient is given a weight to show the degree of time to perform the tasks. The weights are summed to give a total for each patient. The total determines the patient type (Exhibit 12–2).

The problem with this type, as with the descriptive style, is the subjectivity of the nurse. In both types, the staffing is determined by the nurse's assessment of the patient and assignment to a level. One nurse's assessment can differ from another's for the same patient; so, too, can nursing tasks and the method of performing them. There also are differences from unit to unit. With this lack of consistency, the validity and reliability of these types of patient classification systems are questionable.

Patient Needs Method

The last type of patient classification system to be examined is based on patient needs (a section is shown in Exhibit 12–3). It identifies nursing resource requirements according to patient's dependence on nursing personnel. A list of patient needs has been identified, with weights assigned to the needs or indicators. These weights have been validated through time and motion studies. Each patient's selected indicators' weights are totaled. The person is assigned to a patient type corresponding to the totaled score. An acuity factor is assigned to each patient type that translates the workload of all the patient types into a relative workload comparable to a central frame of reference, such as the Level II patient. The workload thus is expressed in relative terms.

In a system using four patient types, the total workload for patient types I, III, and IV would be expressed in workload terms relative to the most common one— Type II. Desired hours that the nurse should provide for one unit of workload are identified by nursing administration. That workload plus the desired target nursing hours per unit of workload provide the total nursing hours required for caring for the patients. The total hours divided by eight hours yields the number of staff persons required to accomplish the required nursing hours for the unit's patient needs.

Within the system, the skill mix needed for each patient is identified, as is the shift distribution of the staff. With these two tables, the appropriate staff mix for each shift is identified. The tables of skill mix and shift distribution may vary from institution to institution, depending on the nursing department's philosophy of care delivery.

This system is more valid and reliable because it is based on patients' needs that are the same within the institution as well as between institutions. It permits one hospital to compare itself with others. It defines the patient types in hours of required care rather than by terminology of "self care," etc. This objectivity of definition of patients is more measurable than terms such as "self care."

Exhibit 12–2 Checklist of Nursing Tasks Patient Classification System

	Points	Check If Applicable
Nutrition & Elimination		
1. Eating: Self	1	
Assist	2	
Feed	3	
2. Fluid Balance:		
Intake	2	
Output	2	
Bed Weight	2	
Standing Weight	1	
Levine	2	
Hemovac	1	
Encourage Fluids	2	
Restrict Fluids	2	
3. Bladder: Voiding	1	
Catheterize	2	
Strain Urine	1	
Foley	2	
Clinitest	1	
Acetest	1	
Testape	1	
4. Bowels: Regular	1	
Colostomy	3	
Enema	2	

	Points	Check If Applicable
Mobility		
1. Activities:		
Complete Bedrest	4	
Turn	3	
ROM	3	
TCDB	1	
Dangle	2	
Bedside Commode	2	
BRP	1	
Chair	2	
Ambulate	2	
Up ad Lib	0	
2. Mode of Transfer:		
Stretcher	2	
Wheelchair	2	
Cardiac Chair	2	
Bed	3	
Bath & Skin Care		
1. Bath		
Self	0	
Assist	2	
Complete	3	
Bedbath	3	

Education
1. Routine _____ 1
2. Reinforcement _____ 2
3. New diagnosis/complete teaching _____ 3

Safety
1. Bedrails: Half _____ 1
   Full at HS _____ 2
   Full constantly _____ 3
2. Restraints _____ 3

    Total Points _____

    Tub _____ 2
    Sitz _____ 1
    Shower _____ 1
2. Mouth Care _____ 2
3. Positioning _____ 3

    Total Points _____

Total Points Column 1 & 2 _____

Type I = 0 – 18 points Requires 0 – 3 hours of care
Type II = 19 – 36 points Requires 4 – 6 hours of care
Type III = 37 – 60 points Requires 7 – 10 hours of care
Type IV = 60+ points Requires 11+ hours of care

Exhibit 12–3 Patient Needs Classification System

Patient Types

Type I   Patient requires 0 – 2 hours of direct care at the bedside.
Type II   Patient requires 2 – 4 hours of direct care at the bedside.
Type III Patient requires 4 – 10 hours of direct care at the bedside.
Type IV   Patient requires 10 or more hours of direct care at the bedside.

Sample of 3 Indicators' Definitions:
Partial immobility: Patients requiring nursing assistance to initiate physical movement because of casts, restricting IV's, and restraints; patients requiring nursing assistance because of obvious slowing in ability to perform activities of daily living.
Total feed: Patients unable to feed themselves, require constant supervision during the meal.
Monitoring: Patients being monitored mechanically as well as those requiring frequent visual observations (every 15 minutes or more often). Does not routinely include patients on IVAC.

For example: From totaling the patients' indicators and assigning the points to a patient type, the following numbers of patients have been identified:
Type I patient = 3
Type II patient = 4
Type III patient = 2
Type IV patient = 1
Total census = 10 patients

Relative workload index:

(# Type I patient × acuity factor) + (# Type II patient × acuity factor) + (# Type III patient × acuity factor) + (# Type IV patient × acuity factor)
$(3 × .5) + (4 × 1.0) + (2 × 2.5) + (1 × 5) =$
$1.5 + 4.0 + 5.0 + 5.0 = 15.5$

The census is 10 patients ; however, the nursing workload is equivalent to the unit's having 15½ Type II patients.

Totaled nursing hours required:

Desired target hours = 4 hours per unit of workload
Desired target hours × relative workload index = total nursing hours/24 hours.
    Thus, 4 hours × 15.5 = 62 hours.
Number full-time employees required in 24 hours (based on 8-hour shifts:)

Total nursing hours ÷ 8 hour shift = total #
    full-time equivalent employees needed in 24 hours
        $62 ÷ 8 = 7.75$

Source: Department of Health and Human Services, HRS 76–25, 1974.

Relating Patient Needs Method to Care Units

Most hospitals are moving toward a system based on patient needs. However, as Exhibit 12–3 indicates, simply putting a price on the Level III patient, for example, who receives 4 to 10 hours of nursing care in a 24-hour period is far from a definitive statement as to what actually is done in that time.

For example, if standards were developed, the nurse would know that this patient would have vital signs taken a minimum of four times, be checked hourly, and benefit from having care tailored to specific needs in several of the nursing care units or modules. The patient may need the standard care unit for Level III monitoring, intravenous therapy, complete feeding, Foley catheter care, stool incontinence, restraints, cardiac monitoring, or care specific to the DRG, until modules add up to four to ten hours of nursing care a day. However, until such standards are clearly delineated, nurses only know that four to ten hours of care are credited to a patient in this category; they do not know what that care actually is.

Because it is obvious that a patient needing four hours would receive less care than one needing ten hours, the standards will assist nurses in identifying care and cost differences between the two extremes. In defining care to this point, nurses profit immediately by understanding how they will use time productively to meet patient care needs. In the long term, nurses benefit by working on a system that may result in different benefit payments in the future, as broad categories are broken into more homogenous groups. As patient needs are identified, time can be spent on writing standards for nursing interventions in care units, or modules, that can be personalized by adding an "other" item to the schedule.

By evaluating these care units concurrently and when treatment is completed, nurse managers can determine better what services are needed to produce the best result in the most productive manner. Thus, the direct hours of care per patient take on meaning as nurses appreciate what standard of care is involved in each needed intervention. Only when care can be closely approximated at this level will nurses have a better handle on how their budget is being expended and where opportunities for profit lie.

As these care units are costed by DRG or nursing diagnosis and by the average hourly salaries of the skilled persons required, cost of coverage for nonproductive days (vacation, holidays, etc.), indirect/administrative and overhead expenses, the nursing department gains better insight into its total budget. It can determine its costs through the quantitative standards based on the patient classification system. That system can provide the data on hours of care required for each patient by day, entire length of stay, nursing diagnosis, and unit. Moreover, the costing mechanisms become defined well enough to determine the amount of revenue that the nursing division is producing.

Benefits

A benefit of a nursing information system is the various management reports it can generate to assist nurse managers in controlling the staffing and unit budgets. When nurse managers monitor these reports, they can make decisions based on current and historical data that are valid and reliable. The information in the reports is presented in a format and terminology understandable by nursing and hospital administration. When staffing changes are made, feedback on productivity and nursing costs is provided.

The last component of the nursing information system is quality monitoring. This is used to determine the results of usage of nursing resources. It assists in determining whether standards are attained. Through identification of strengths and weaknesses, nursing administrators can provide corrective actions to reward or to improve performances.

SELECTION OF A SYSTEM

In evaluating the nursing information system, the nurse administrator should consider the following questions and document the responses:

1. What is the end result to be achieved?
2. How will the classification system assist the nurse managers in meeting the mandates of improved productivity and cost containment?
3. Does the system reflect the philosophy and goals of the nursing department?
4. What is the present method of capturing specifics on nursing workload and assigning staff?
5. Does the classification system meet the requirements from external regulatory agencies (e.g., JCAH)?
6. What educational support is available from vendors?
7. What are the qualifications of the personnel implementing the system?
8. What is the reliability/validity of this method? What is the research on its development?
9. Is the system flexible enough to be tailored to the nursing department's needs without changing the basic structure of the system? If not, the nurse administrator should determine whether a change in the system would create a flaw in its validity and reliability.
10. Does the system have the capability of being used to cost nursing services via DRG? Nursing diagnosis?
11. Can the system be used on personal computer or mainframe?

12. Is the suggested staffing reflective of direct caregivers, indirect caregivers, or both?

DEVELOPING A SYSTEM

In modifying an existing classification or developing a new one, five steps have been identified by Hoffman:

1. Formulate patient care goals and objectives.
2. Examine existing methods.
3. Perform a time-motion study to ascertain the compatibility of the desired system with actual practice in the nursing division, using the desired method as a standard for comparison.
4. Conduct pilot tests of the completed time-motion study and establish the system's validity on two to three units for two months.
5. Start phasing in the system, after the pilot study has been operating successfully for a month, on other nursing units until all of them are using the system.[4]

The pilot test is important in identifying problems that need to be resolved before implementing it for all nursing. As each unit uses the system, more modifications may be needed; however, these must be major. Minor changes from unit to unit decrease the consistency of data and the accuracy of the system. With each step, the staff should be oriented prior to implementation on the nursing unit.

The nurse administrators should consider the advantages and disadvantages of developing or adapting a patient classification system. Some advantages of developing a tool within an institution are:

- The system is tailored for that particular institution.
- There is increased loyalty to utilizing the system because it was developed by the staff.
- The indicators of patients' needs better reflect the hospital's standards and activities.
- The weights or point system indicate the time needed to achieve needs for that facility's population.

Disadvantages of developing a system include:

- There is reinvention of the wheel.
- The process is very time consuming.

- Its validity and reliability must be verified.
- It is very difficult to compare data and results with other institutions.

Vendor System

When an existing system is used, the vendor usually has corrected many of the problems and inaccuracies already. Support and educational systems are available. The nurse administrator should examine what is to be accomplished with the patient classification system, what ones exist, and what ones would be applicable within the institution's goals and philosophies. In weighing these considerations, a decision can be made whether to develop or adapt an existing system.

Patient Classification System and Productivity

One of the byproducts of a patient classification system is increased productivity from nursing resources. This is accomplished through proper utilization of the assigned staff. Understaffing as well as overstaffing of a unit reflect improper management of time. Understaffing creates an increased workload and demand on the staff that cannot be handled in the designated shift. Anxiety increases, producing frustration among the staff members. Overstaffing creates too much free time for the staff, which wastes personnel.

Proper staffing allows time to perform the necessary tasks, produce more work, and provide the desired care to patients. The patient classification system not only suggests the number of staff members needed to meet patient needs but also the proper mix to accomplish the identified workload. Caregivers are more satisfied when there is adequate staffing, number, and mix. In turn, the hospital administration is content because money is being used wisely and more than likely within budget.

Role of the Computer

An information system that controls and manages nursing resources will collect and process a substantial amount of data. If this is done manually, feedback is slow and untimely. Computers can facilitate the system. With the aid of a computer, nurse managers can control staffing and scheduling in a more accurate and timely manner. Data and management reports needed for such control can be available on the same shift in which the material is collected. Interaction with the computer allows nurse managers to see the effect that the changes in staffing will have on the budget.

If patient acuity changes from shift to shift, the managers can enter the data and receive information on suggested staff within that shift. They can monitor patient

acuity and nurse workload patterns throughout the year, permitting better development of budgets in which nursing has increased control. The automated data for
the nurse managers are retrieved, compiled, summarized, and presented in a
meaningful and comprehensive format in a timely fashion. The reports are tailored
to meet the managers' needs. The speed of obtaining the data enhances their
controlability.

Selection Process

Many vendors selling patient classification systems naturally claim theirs are
the best. The decision as to which system to use is difficult. Nurse managers
should be aware of overselling by vendor representatives. In selection of the
software and equipment, the following plan may be useful as a guideline:

1. Select a task force.
2. Gather data about the institution, e.g.:

   a. philosophy
   b. goals and objectives
   c. average daily census
   d. number of staff members
   e. levels of patient acuity, if available
   f. departmental designs
   g. administrative structure

3. Document how the staffing system and personnel budget are operated now.
   Do not assume any step to be known. It helps to use algorithms to demonstrate the manual workload.
4. Send out letters of inquiry to vendors requesting information about their
   systems. Evaluate the information received:

   a. thoroughness of the vendor's approach: management and technical
   b. degree to which the vendor's proposal meets the priorities and manual
      workflow identified in the data-gathering process
   c. identification of the system specifications
   d. installations made elsewhere by the vendor—references/experiences
   e. qualifications of the vendor's implementation staff, nurse consultants,
      and technical support
   f. vendor's financial stability
   g. total cost of the system: what it includes in the way of software, hard-
      ware, installation, maintenance, phone calls, expenses for implementa-
      tion and support team, etc.

5. Select vendors from which more in-depth information is desired. Write them, providing data about the institution: manual workflow, utilization of the system, etc.
6. Review the proposals received. Select four to five vendors that meet the specifications. Request on-site visits to their plants or offices, if possible; if not, request the name of a key person(s) from whom information may be elicited. Do a reference check on the vendors' performance in other installations. Reevaluate each vendor's proposal and past work performances.
7. Select the vendor appropriate or able to meet the needs of the nursing department.
8. Negotiate the contract with the aid of the hospital counsel. Know the fine print in the contracts. Clarify whether the proposals sent to the institution will become part of the final contract. Request that all cooperation the vendor expects from the nursing department be in the contract.

Selecting the vendor, software, and system configuration can be a stressful project. Ball and Hannah listed several points to be remembered during the selection process:

1. Document tasks that must be accomplished; provide a time table for their accomplishment.
2. Assign responsibility for tasks, categorizing each one.
3. Ask for clarification as needed.
4. Identify the nursing department's (or hospital's) limitations.
5. Follow up on each assigned task to completion; this can make a difference.
6. Anticipate and resolve problems before they become a crisis, using help from other experts.
7. Do not be anxious about possible failure.[5]

Quantitative standards offer one method to justify the need of personnel costs. To deliver quality patient care in a productive manner, qualified nursing staff is required. To maintain the required staffing, there must be guidelines to measure attainment of budget and productivity goals. Quantitative standards assist in achieving goals.

SUMMARY

Quantitative standards need to be incorporated into the patient classification system. There are various types of patient classification systems, with the type based on patient needs the most popular. Future progress in pricing nursing, providing quality patient care, and improving/defining productivity will require nursing divisions to construct standards or units of nursing care (modules) that define how the range of hours in an acuity level is utilized in caring for specific patients.

Computer systems are available so that when a nurse enters a care unit in the system, charting and billing are part of the automatic process. For the present, however, much of the pioneering work on specifying, pricing, and charting such standards will be manual. That manual documentation can be eased with the use of flow sheets and having charges accessible at the point where care is provided.

NOTES

1. American Nurses' Association, *Standards for Organized Nursing Services* (Kansas City, Mo.: ANA, 1982).

2. Joint Commission on Accreditation of Hospitals, *Accreditation Manual for Hospitals 1985* (Chicago: JCAH, 1984).

3. Indiana State Board of Health, *Indiana State Board of Health Regulations for General and Special Hospitals—HHL 42* (Indianapolis: Indiana State Board of Health, 1977).

4. F.M. Hoffman, *Financial Management for Nurse Managers* (Norwalk, Conn.: Appleton-Century-Crofts, Inc., 1984).

5. M.J. Ball and K.J. Hannah, *Using Computers in Nursing* (Reston, Va.: Reston Publishing Company, Inc., 1984).

BIBLIOGRAPHY

Gillies, D.E. *Nursing Management: A Systems Approach.* Philadelphia: W.B. Saunders Company, 1982.

Haas, S.A. "Sorting Out Nursing Productivity." *Nursing Management* 15, no. 4 (April 1984): 37–40.

Huckabay, L.M. "Patient Classification: A Basis for Staffing." *Hospitals, 1982* (New York: National League for Nursing, 1981).

Jelinek, R., and Pierce, F. "A Nursing Systems Approach." *Public Productivity Review* (September 1982): 223–240.

Jelinek, R.C., Zinn, T.K., and Brya, J.R. "Tell the Computer How Sick the Patients Are and It Will Tell How Many Nurses They Need." *Modern Hospital* (December 1973): 81–85.

Johnson, K. "A Practical Approach to Patient Classification." *Nursing Management* 15, no. 6 (July 1984): 39–41, 44, 46.

Lewis, E.N., and Carini, P.V. *Nurse Staffing and Patient Classification.* Rockville, Md.: Aspen Publishers, Inc., 1984.

Norby, R.B., and Freund, L.E., and Wagner, B. "A Nurse Staffing System Based Upon Management Difficulty." *Journal of Nursing Administration* 3, no. 11 (November 1977): 2–24.

Sovie, M.D., Tarcinale, M.A., Vanputee, A.W., and Steunden, A.E. "Amalgam of Nursing Acuity, DRGs, and Costs." *Nursing Management* 16, no. 3 (March 1985): 22–28, 32–34, 38, 40, 42.

Staley, M., and Luciano, K. "Eight Steps to Costing Nursing Services." *Nursing Management* 15, no. 10 (October 1984): 35–38.

ACTION CHECKLIST

1. Is the current patient classification system suitable for staffing, budgeting, and pricing?
2. Does the current patient classification system accurately reflect productive nursing time?
3. Is the patient classification system computerized? If not, are materials being written in such a way that they lend themselves to future computerization? Has a comparison been made of costs for continuing to function without a computer?
4. Are costs being estimated in relation to nurse productivity and quality of care for each DRG and major nursing diagnoses?
5. Has a start been made on developing units of nursing care, or modules to provide standards, productivity/quality of care goals, and pricing on care clusters?

Part IV

Human Resources Management

Chapter 13

Performance Appraisals

Selecting the right employee to do the job is a critical first step in the human resources management program that underlies a productive, cost-effective operation. The choice about what is "right" refers to the nursing department's performance standards. These standards must be defined, then audited continually for each employee during the formal performance appraisal process, and daily as a means of keeping performance in line with productive standards and goals. This chapter reviews commonly used techniques and performance standards to aid in this process.

APPRAISAL TECHNIQUES

Performance appraisal systems can be selected by organizations to either motivate or categorize employees. When employee motivation and improved productivity are the primary objectives, the hospital designs the system to appeal to employees, involves them in setting performance standards, assists them in "owning" the job, and coaches them in wise resource utilization and time management.

The most common method for implementing this style of appraisal involves the management-by-objectives (MBO) system. At the other end of the continuum is the method used to compare employees with each other as a means of selecting workers and defending personnel decisions. The purest example for this employee comparison is the rank order method. Most appraisal systems incorporate both of those purposes. To evaluate the form that the nurse administrators are using now, it is helpful to consider the performance appraisal techniques available.

MANAGEMENT BY OBJECTIVES

With the emphasis on decentralization and self-management by professional nurses, the MBO method has become popular. According to Cecilia Golightly of

Saint Joseph's Hospital in St. Paul, Minn., implementing a successful MBO type of form requires total involvement of head nurses and staff along with careful assistance and monitoring to be sure that it measures behaviors that management and peers have identified as essential.[1] These measurements should include skills and strategies for promoting a positive work environment and providing, documenting, and monitoring an up-to-date, safe, quality level of patient care while improving productivity and containing costs (see Exhibit 13–1). The ability of staff members to work cooperatively in sharing the workload is a key aspect of improving productivity.

In a typical MBO evaluation, the middle manager and employee jointly plan goals that the latter agrees to achieve over a specified period. When that time elapses, the two meet again to review success (or failure) and to establish new goals for the upcoming time period. Ideally, the conversation about goals and the assessment of progress should not be limited to these formal reviews but should be held on a continuing basis. When this interaction functions as it should, motivation and feelings of personal commitment are enhanced in both the employee and the manager. However, this mutual goal sharing requires managerial preparation in the institution's own directions and its resource utilization strategies so that employees set objectives that complement the hospital's progressive business strategies.

Once objectives are set, the manager should jointly revise them continually with the employee to best meet the changing needs of the patients, the employee, and the work milieu. When possible, managers can take advantage of peer networking, in which staff members benefit by sharing goals and working collectively on mutual interests and problems.

For example, in intensive care and cardiac critical care in one hospital, the staffing was planned for an "average" census. However, when the units filled to capacity, staffing was inadequate to care for patients. Both staffs were concerned and met to consider all options to resolve the problem. They determined that they could best cover this census peak by having the freedom to modify work hours among eight-, ten-, and 12-hour shifts, according to the census. Because these

---

Exhibit 13–1 Sample Items from MBO Format

1. List ten objectives describing accountability and rate the employee from 1 to 5 (weakest to strongest) on each.
2. Identify three job priorities and write a goal, action steps, deadline, and measurement criteria for each one.
3. Identify any significant changes in performance since the last review.
4. Describe areas that need to be improved and provide an action plan for each one.

units were decentralized, this flexible, ever-changing pattern could be accomplished without affecting other parts of the hospital. Both staffs voted to participate in flexible shifts when either unit filled to 80 percent or more of capacity, and to assist in cross-training medical-surgical unit nurses to function in high census periods. Criteria were established to measure the cost effectiveness of this strategy, and a diary of untoward events was kept to compare the occurrence of incidents with various levels of staffing coverage. Group expectations were established for individual nurses, who wrote specific commitments to do their share in their MBO type evaluation method. This plan was successful in coping with periods of high census, but staff learned that prolonged periods of high census required additional nurses to avoid excessive fatigue and errors in patient care.

The MBO method is well suited for decentralized settings and for nurses who require little supervision since it is objective and participatory. Users feel that it elevates morale and encourages nurses to be more productive (see Exhibit 13–2). The system is prospective and concentrates on what the employee is doing, as well as on negative aspects of performance or retrospective behaviors. Nurses feel that this method encourages them and their managers to build a stronger working relationship because of their joint participation in establishing, monitoring, and evaluating performance goals.

Exhibit 13–2 Orienting Individual Goals to Productivity

The following are factors employees should consider when helping improve productivity:

1. Relationship of individual efforts to long-range center or departmental goals
2. Relationship of individual efforts to cost containment
3. Innovation
4. Ways to boost individual or unit productivity
5. Individual efforts in improving patient education and discharge planning
6. Measures to create, maintain, or restore cohesion among staff
7. Individual ways of overcoming a center or departmental problem
8. Individual efforts toward applied research
9. Ways to induce growth and motivation in self and others
10. Production of a needed form, method, or tool helpful in improving patient care or staff efficiency
11. Ways to improve the quality of services
12. Ideas to help services expand
13. Methods for improving continuity in patient care or center/department functioning
14. Specific ideas to enhance communication
15. Establishment of a system to improve quantitative or qualitative analysis of effort
16. Ways to improve relationships with patients, families, staff members, and other health care providers

The MBO method also works well in managerial performance appraisals and in assessing the effectiveness of nurses at various steps on clinical ladders. For example, the role of the assistant head nurse too often has been only to relieve the charge nurse two days a week. The MBO format is ideally suited to helping this senior, better-compensated nurse in identifying performance goals and projects that are of more benefit to the unit and can be implemented on a regular basis. Moreover, the joint planning with the head nurse can assist these two in better defining ways to divide leadership duties and coordinating job efforts.

There are disadvantages to using the MBO method that can be overcome by utilizing some of its items along with another type of system in designing a program. For example, a standard rating scale could be combined with a small MBO section in which individual employees could set personal goals that complement unit and hospital goals. Problems in using this method correctly arise where managers have not been well grounded in how to (1) write the goals, (2) operationalize the strategic plans of the hospital and center or department, (3) motivate and communicate effectively with the employee, and (4) weight various key items in the evaluation process.

For example, if a nurse is punctual, perfect in attendance, and meticulous in giving medications and doing technical nursing care but has a poor attitude and depresses staff morale and productivity through a negative relationship, leaders should ask:

- How is performance weighted on each item?
- How can they defend themselves against discrimination if they heavily weight interpersonal relationships for this nurse but minimize its significance for other nurses?
- Could they discharge this nurse for reasons of attitude yet justify keeping someone else whose technical performance is less adequate?
- How do they make standards of performance equitable and consistent for all?

This last is done by setting specific performance standards that involve nurses' attitudes for each important area of performance. For example, a staff nurse expresses an interest in bringing critical new information to the entire staff by preparing a five-minute inservice talk for use during report each month. Such a positive attitude would earn a plus in the performance appraisal.

Because it is individualized, the MBO format requires a great deal of time and must be written in relation to the employee's ability to do the job. Because of this, some hospitals have found it more effective to modify this format to "management by exceptions" so that objectives are prioritized to encourage positive behaviors and eliminate negative ones. However, it is important not to include personal traits unrelated to the job on this type of loosely structured form.

For example, one nursing student who weighed more than 300 pounds claimed she was "pressured" to sign an agreement under which she would lose two pounds a week or voluntarily withdraw from the nursing program at Salve Regina College in Newport, R.I. When she did not accomplish this goal, the college refunded her tuition money with a note that she had withdrawn voluntarily. She filed a $2 million lawsuit alleging breach of contract since she was meeting all of the criteria required to get her degree, such as being an honors student, not being a discipline problem, and complying with all college regulations. In disputing the right of the nursing program to set "health and medical requirements," she said that the hospital where she had worked as an aide had offered her a job after graduation. Having completed three years of the program, Ms. Russell transferred to another college. (*Russell v. Salve Regina College,* 85–628B.)[2] In November 1986 a U.S. District Court upheld her right to go forward with her case. This case is an example of the need to avoid non-job-related items in the MBO format.

Other disadvantages of MBO are its tendency to set such specific goals that it is difficult to determine their meaningfulness to others in the organization. Sometimes the system lacks the specific points necessary for defending personnel decisions, making it hard to establish an objective basis for such actions as transfers, promotions, raises, layoffs, discharges, etc.

One compromise would be to use an MBO-like, self-appraisal method in which both managers and employees write a version on a preset form, then discuss likenesses and differences. This combines interactive features and possibly goal setting. It also can include more precise rating items and be more standardized for ease in comparing employees if the nursing division sets guidelines requiring the evaluation of certain key behaviors in all performance appraisals.[3,4]

RATING SCALES

Traditionally, the most popular form of performance appraisal has been the rating scale. Traits, criteria, and performance techniques are itemized with a numerical or written scale linked to each item. These items include attitude, attendance, job knowledge, work quality, problem-solving ability, productivity, organization, documentation, adaptability, leadership, and ability to work well with others. While the rating scale may have as many as 15 gradations, many feel that three is best: "exceeds performance standards," "meets performance standards," and "does not meet performance standards." This eliminates the difficult decision of comparing "good" and "very good."

About 70 percent of all employees will meet the standard for each item if it is realistic. For example, attitude—a difficult area to evaluate precisely—could be measured by establishing a standard of performance such as:

1. Works collaboratively with peers, other disciplines, and agencies to operationalize and document the nursing process in assigned patients 80 percent of the time.
2. Extends courtesy to patients and families so that no more than two valid patient complaints are registered against this employee over a six-month period.
3. Volunteers to assist other team members with their work assignments when the individual has free time of 15 minutes or more.

The advantage of rating scales is the ease, speed, and low cost of their construction and use. Moreover, they are applicable to a number of different jobs and need only minimal skill to complete. However, when traits are left general, such as "leadership," it can be difficult to relate them in a meaningful way to job performance. Some experts feel that major categories should be subdivided.

For example, leadership could include:

1. ability to inspire improved performance in subordinates and associates
2. creative application of new forms and methods to patient care
3. skill in getting patients and families to comply with the plan of care.

A weight then can be assigned to each item, according to its job significance, and specific standards can be written to establish criteria for each item.

Rating scales have the disadvantage of rater error. Managers may not be familiar enough with an employee's performance, except in isolated situations, or may have a personal bias toward an individual. This bias could result in unreasonably high or low ratings, or a middle-of-the-road rating that sidesteps controversy.

Ratings can be made more specific by requiring that they include a critical incident and/or an exception to each normative behavior to support the assessment. Some managers supplement the rating scale with MBO sections, skills checklists, essay techniques, or critical incident diaries.

Skills Checklist

To devise a skills checklist, nurse managers should itemize the important behaviors desirable in adequate performance and identify specific time intervals for observing the work of each employee. For example, a checklist can be devised to audit concurrent bedside conditions in patient care or to audit five charts for compliance with charting policies and procedures for every staff nurse at least every three months. Managers can utilize such lists in making periodic checks on the quality and safety of care to be certain that individual employee assessments are based on comprehensive, concrete work behaviors.

Records also can be kept of employee initiative in participating in unit projects, in willingness to float, and in efforts to improve time management skills to enhance productivity. The types of critical behaviors that can be documented to support evaluation can be made specific and somewhat standardized to relate to important unit and divisional goals.

Essay Rating

This is the most open-ended type of method and is characterized by its subjectivity and difficulty in construction. Managers who write well can produce a more meaningful essay on employee performance than those who have difficulty in composition. Moreover, this can easily veer off from the employee's ability to do the job onto personal traits. Such deviations can result in discriminatory practices.

Because this method encourages an evaluation of strengths, weaknesses, learning needs, and major aspects of performance, it can be used to promote communication between manager and employee. However, because of its focus on individuals, it does not lend itself to a comparison of employees in a category when making personnel decisions. Users are encouraged to combine essays with a more objective method or to use detailed guidelines for specific aspects of performance.

Critical Incidents

Some hospitals have experimented with individual tracking by keeping a diary of positive and negative events on each employee. This method is said to provide a fairly accurate idea of how the employee performs. However, it may lack critical incidents or documentation in all of the areas on which performance opinions should be based. Managers also may recall negative or extremely positive behaviors more readily and weight them unrealistically. There also is a tendency to accumulate a laundry list full of negative incidents and unload them all at one time on the employee. Such an evaluation does little to encourage nurses' development.

However, the keeping of critical incidents has an important place in the performance appraisal process when the events are used as a part of another method to illustrate rating decisions and when guidelines are used to ensure that the sample of behaviors for each nurse is representative of the general work performance over time. In participative management, nurses may be encouraged to identify critical behaviors in their own performance to illustrate the type of work that they do. The two lists of behaviors then can be compared and discussed.

One hospital unit found a very creative way of building a "Kudos Book" of critical incidents. A book was provided in the nursing station for use by all staff members. They were instructed to write an anecdote about a peer when that individual found a creative way to improve the quality or safety of patient care, make staff members and patients feel more satisfied, contain costs, or boost productivity. These records were used as a way to enhance nurses' job satisfaction, as a pool of ideas that were shared with other units, and as a basis for rewarding merit in staff members.

BEHAVIORALLY ANCHORED RATING SCALES (BARS)

To overcome the drawbacks of other rating methods in not identifying specific behavior or relying on rater subjectivity, the behaviorally anchored rating scale (BARS) method was initiated (see Exhibit 13–3). In this method a vertical scale is constructed that is equated with specific standards, from worst to ideal, on a specific job-related trait. By selecting the statement that most accurately describes an employee, the nurse manager arrives at a point value for an item. Because all persons in one job category are compared on the same behaviors, this method reduces rater bias.

Exhibit 13–3 Behaviorally Anchored Rating Scale (BARS)

Rate the registered nurse on the ability to document patient care.

Outstanding performance	Care plan, nursing notes, use of problem-oriented method, and nursing process excellent. Results of intervention and patient follow-up exemplary.
Good performance	
Slightly good performance	Above items meet minimal audit criteria.
Neither good nor poor performance	Above items completed. Needs further work on charting policy and nursing process.
Slightly poor performance	Above items completed at times. Quality of work is marginal. Little patient follow-up.
Poor performance	
Extremely poor performance	Care plans rarely done, nursing process and problem-oriented method not followed. Nursing notes unrelated to care plan. Rare evidence of outcomes of interventions and patient follow-up.

The BARS method is very sophisticated and expensive to create since it requires a behaviorally anchored analysis of all critical job behaviors. Once it is agreed what the critical behaviors of each task are, and the rating statements reflect varying levels of performance, this system can provide an objective, quantitative measurement based on actual job behaviors.

MSS and NARS

Spinoffs from the BARS method include the mixed standard rating scale (MSS) and the numerically anchored rating scale (NARS).[5] In the MSS method, behavioral information is coupled with directions requiring the rater to decide whether an employee is better than, worse than, or like the descriptions. In the NARS method, a statement is presented, with directions to circle the numerical value that best ranks the employee. An example appears in Exhibit 13-4.

OTHER METHODS

A number of other methods should be mentioned. Some of their concepts can be incorporated if the hospital decides to critique all performance appraisals as a group to determine their cost. However, for obvious reasons, some are unsuited to individual performance appraisals.

For example, if improved productivity is a priority, a checklist of items could be devised that pinpoints that factor. The head nurse and all employees then could be challenged, through this documented method, to show how they had improved productivity. Employees could be given monetary awards for merit.

Weighted Checklist

One way to accomplish this is the Weighted Checklist. This is an exhaustive job analysis that is not as job specific as BARS. By totaling points given to checklisted

---

Exhibit 13-4 NARS on Communication with Patients

Directions: Circle the value that best describes the employee's performance.				
Trait	*Weak*	*Satisfactory*	*Good*	*Outstanding*
COMMUNICATION: Explains all treatment and care-related items thoroughly to patients.	1–2	3–4	5–6	7–8

items, the manager arrives at a numerical value. This method is easy to use but expensive to develop. One of its advantages is that varying numerical weights can be assigned to emphasize the importance of one item over another. While the total scores for two employees could be the same where every item has the same number of points, the meaning of certain categories should vary.

For example, in an unweighted version in which all categories are equal, Nurse A had 15 points, placing her in a satisfactory category; her strength in attendance balanced her deficit in providing safe care to patients. This means that her performance was unsafe and unsatisfactory, despite the rating. This method could focus on one specific strategic goal, such as improved productivity, to reward outstanding employees.

Forced Choice Checklist

Another expensive method to develop is the Forced Choice Checklist. This contains as many items as are required to describe job performance fully. For each behavior, a set of statements is presented that requires the rater to select the most or least applicable to the specific employee. Each statement is given a value, and totals for performance are calculated after completion of the form. This method is objective, job-related, and quantifiable.

Paired Comparison Ranking

A simple but time-consuming process is termed Paired Comparison Ranking. In this method, Nurse B is compared with Nurse C and ultimately all others in the center on each job behavior. Points are assigned for ranks relative to peers. The problem with this method is that the nurses' performances are not actually described, and they may be the "best of the worst," or could rank last in a different group of employees.

Alternation Ranking

A similar method is Alternation Ranking. Here managers pick the best and worst performer on each trait until the work force is divided into two groups. However, criteria for distinguishing one from the other are missing and, at best, managers know who good and poor performers are.

Forced Distribution Ranking

In Forced Distribution Ranking, the manager is told to rank employees so that 10 percent are rated excellent, 20 percent good, 40 percent average and 30 percent below average. While this method, a form of bell curve, is expedient, it may not apply where there are a number of excellent employees and marginal workers have been weeded out through the disciplinary process. However, where this technique is used in a general way on a divisionwide basis to give managers a broad perspective, strong nurses can be identified. They can be asked to mentor weaker nurses to raise the total standard of performance.

Peer Review

Peer Review is used particularly in higher educational institutions with professional groups. In this method a panel of peers compares each employee with set criteria to arrive at an evaluation. Confidentiality is required so that decisions can be discussed honestly. Disadvantages of this method are political or personality considerations and the fact that remarks and notes may be discovered legally if the employee files a charge under federal or state discriminatory statutes.

Assessment Centers

Assessment Centers constitute another expensive, sophisticated method that lends itself to the identification of potential managers. In this method, job situations are simulated through in-basket exercises, tests, written work, interviews, and the performance of sample job duties. By adding up points for various areas tested over several days, managers can construct an evaluation that can help in determining latent or natural leadership skills.[6]

RATER RELIABILITY

The performance appraisal process, dreaded by most managers as negative and time consuming, can be made more positive when they are given adequate education and training to conduct evaluations. Too often, managers are merely told to evaluate employee performance while getting little formal assistance in how to do it. Moreover, the link between individual performance and the unit's goals may be overlooked.

Educational seminars should relate the relevance of the performance appraisal method to the effectiveness of the organization, the marketing image, and the potential for increased productivity in individuals. Managers should be cautioned about the rights of employees and the importance of keeping the evaluation job-related. The discussion also should cover what points to consider in each category.

The most helpful part of such seminars is the opportunity to practice the skills acquired. Various nurses can be videotaped or involved in a skit that is then rated by the group, using the hospital's evaluation method(s). Results of the rating can be compared and discussed. Many workshop leaders feel that forcing managers to correct errors publicly before a group can be less effective than using a structured format, in which results are given quietly after general discussion. More formalized, structured programs tend to cover more information in a shorter period and give participants the guidance they seek from the workshop leader. Less structured group formats tend to raise tension levels in response to feelings about not learning something concrete for time invested.

New managers may require follow-up and assistance with the first few evaluations. All managers should use another rater occasionally to be sure that appraisal criteria are uniform and fair. This peer consultation is particularly important when a difficult evaluation is at hand. Assistance and miniworkshops should be provided at nurse executive meetings on conducting interviews, developing and maintaining a highly productive team effort, investigating and administering discipline, motivating employees, and setting appropriate communication strategies for managers. This should be a continuing effort, since success in these skills is one of the most important abilities in operating a superior nursing center or department. Managers also can administer self-tests (Exhibit 13–5) that, if their answers are candid and objective, can reveal their own strengths and weaknesses and point them in the direction to improve their performance.

Situations that need to be emphasized in these simulations include:

- *Just-Like-Me:* Raters tend to rate persons higher who are similar in type and behavior to themselves. It is important that raters (1) know a job's performance standards before beginning an evaluation, (2) are certain that all criteria are job related, (3) value employees for their work efforts, not their similarity to the rater, and (4) insist that problem employees be assessed by several raters.

- *Halo/Horns Effect:* Raters tend to rate an employee similarly in all categories because of marked behavior in one area. In the discussion after the exercise, points should be developed to show how different items may be unrelated and why discussion of a person should be delayed until after the rating is completed.

- *Contrast Effect:* Raters, when assessing an average employee after a very good or very poor one, tend to compare the two persons rather than relating their behaviors to established performance standards. In the discussion, raters should be encouraged to keep copies of the job criteria and critical incidents beside the performance appraisal when they are completing the form and should not rate employees in an order that would encourage evaluation by contrast. Comparisons between individuals can be made after the appraisal decisions are completed.

- *First Impression:* Sometimes an early behavior that is inappropriate can color decisions on areas of acceptable behavior, or vice versa. To avoid this

Exhibit 13–5 Self-Test for Managers

For each item, indicate how you are doing in employee development. Write (A) for "I am good at this," (B) for "Could use some improvement," and (C) for "Immediate Action Required."

_____ 1. All of my employees have written objectives detailing specific unit objectives over the next three months.

_____ 2. All of my employees have developed a realistic challenge to strive for.

_____ 3. All of my employees have one specific objective for improving their performance that will lead to center and departmental improvements.

_____ 4. I am good at keeping my employees informed of new developments that could alter their individual efforts.

_____ 5. I have continuing dialogue with my employees that gives them assistance and feedback on how they are performing.

_____ 6. My employees feel that they have input on most center/departmental decisions.

_____ 7. I emphasize the importance of the business approach, quality inpatient care, and the satisfaction of the consumer to my employees.

_____ 8. My employees would say that I was fair and up front.

_____ 9. My employees respect me as a person and a manager.

_____ 10. My employees have a positive feeling about their individual contributions to the center, the department, and the hospital.

_____ 11. My employees feel free to suggest new methods and ideas, and have the freedom to try more productive work methods.

_____ 12. My employees feel free to discuss disagreements and negative events with me without fear of retaliation.

_____ 13. My employees are working up to their level of capacity.

_____ 14. Employees are satisfied with the way that I exercise discipline.

_____ 15. I have a written plan for unit progress derived from group input that has staff support.

problem, raters need to maintain anecdotes and periodic skill checklists between appraisal sessions, then read them in random order much later when emotional involvement with them is less intense so that they can be objective in the evaluation, which should be a summary of behavior over time.

A final exercise is to record the exact behaviors seen in a situation, then relate them to the required job behaviors/standards. Analysis of the group's work shows tendencies toward positive and negative leniency.

The literature is mixed on the success rate of decreasing rater errors because most are systematic and related to the evaluator's personality and ingrained biases. To deal with this problem, hospitals should institute programs for all managers emphasizing the importance of objectivity and of methodical follow-up. The significance of rating fairness can be further underscored by top management when it includes this factor as a part of middle managers' own performance appraisals.[7]

ESTABLISHING RATING CRITERIA

Managers can use several ways of documenting behavior. The most common is general observation, with examples. While this is the least time consuming, it is the most subjective because of the lack of criteria for making regular, comprehensive evaluations of the nurses. This method can be more systematic by observing work more directly and by devising skills or audit checklists for use on a particular category of employees. This can be augmented by keeping a diary of exceptions—both positive and negative—to usual work behaviors.

The important point is that behaviors should be categorized according to specific performance standards and that managers need to carefully prioritize the relative importance of various standards. For example, accurately assessing patient status and needs every two hours and keeping the charge nurse informed about changes would have a greater relative weight than attending 80 percent of the inservice programs during the year.

The relative weight of each item is established through trial and error. If an employee accurately assesses, reports, intervenes, and evaluates patient care, the manager may think that worth 20 percent of the total points on the evaluation. When three levels—exceeding, meeting, or not meeting a standard—are used, points of 4, 2, and 0 can be assigned to these three groups. Thus, the final evaluation on a nurse exceeding the standard is done by multiplying $4 \times 20 = 80$ to calculate the relative points for this item.

Points and relative weights are figured similarly for each item on the performance appraisal until weights equal 100 percent. Because the evaluation is converted to numbers, comparisons can be made across employee groups for purposes of making personnel decisions and rewarding merit pay. If categories are weighted wrongly, the nursing division can alter the relative weights of each item.

SETTING PERFORMANCE STANDARDS

Now that the tools for measurement have been delineated, it is important to determine what to measure. The first step in setting the measurement standard is in writing the job description (see Exhibit 13–6). However, job descriptions probably should be changed to job description guidelines, since they cannot include all behaviors nor can they be perfectly current with organizational needs. This point is illustrated in the case of *Bouzianis v. U.S. Air Inc.*, in which U.S. Air Inc. won because its managers were not held to rigid standards in handling discharges.[8]

Exhibit 13–6 Job Description Guidelines

A. Purpose of the Job
   1. Explain why the job exists.
   2. Justify each duty, adding more where needed and removing some to other jobs as justified.
   3. Define key relationships between this job and others in the department, the hospital, and outside organizations or people.
   4. Describe conditions that should exist if this job is to be performed optimally.
B. Scope of Responsibility, Accountability
   1. Identify key result areas in which performance will be measured.
   2. Describe major duties and/or assigned personnel.
   3. Explain the accountability of this job to others.
   4. Delineate the physical parameters of responsibility.
   5. Identify any budget decisions or limitations.
C. Degree of Authority
   1. Identify the scope of freedom to determine methods for achieving job results.
   2. Explain relationship of this job to others in terms of individual and joint accountability.
   3. Describe the opportunity for development in this job.
   4. Delineate the scope of this job in relation to resources, time, and autonomy.
D. Objectives
   1. Describe the objectives that individuals will be required to set in relation to performance appraisals for specific time periods.

The focus of most "job descriptions" is tasks rather than results. They no longer are appropriate in this era of running hospitals like businesses. Tasks are means to an end. Given room, nurses often can devise creative methods for accomplishing goals. Thus, managers must make a basic decision: Will rewards be tied to compliance with tasks, as in the past, or with results?

In other words, should a merit raise be based on items such as attendance, when being there is required anyway? Should certain items be required just to keep the job, while pursuits designed to improve such elements as team morale, patient care and satisfaction, promotion of new business, or generation of increased profits be linked to rewards? These are basic decisions that need to be reexamined in an organization that is seriously regarding quality and improved productivity in an era of cost containment mandates.[9]

Once the job guidelines for each category have been decided on, performance standards can be established. Managers should start by explaining the guidelines to employees as dynamic job descriptions designed to provide general parameters of acceptable performance. This can be done in a series of center meetings, so that center, departmental, and hospital objectives and performance standards can be discussed.

Once a working list is written, managers should confer with the personnel director and the nursing director to be certain that these standards are appropriate for the job categories involved in relation to local hospitals and criteria in other parts of the nursing division.

Managers and staff then finalize area priorities that will be used to evaluate the effectiveness and adequacy of individual performance. After considering area standards and priorities, each employee works with the manager to establish related individual performance standards in the form of temporally defined objectives that are realistic, objective, and obtainable for that job (see Exhibit 13–7). For example, Nurse C has a single 12-month goal of developing a complete, three-hour patient education program for new diabetics to be given throughout the hospital stay. The program provides essential information on diet, activity, insulin, symptoms, and problems requiring further medical attention. It will include a summative evaluation form for assessing patient progress, a flow sheet for nurse use, guidelines for nurses administering the program, patient handouts, and a list of available audiovisual materials.

Individual standard setting can be made more appropriate when the manager introduces such factors as observation, past performance, incidents, and areas for growth, along with comments on area or hospital directions. When the manager and employee agree, the goal is written to include the goal statement, how it will be measured, deadlines, and steps required for successful completion. Generally, standards are written to reflect the quality of job completion that will be accepted as satisfactory performance.

About five goals should be developed for each employee involving regular work, problem solving, and innovation. Under regular work, some statement should relate to how the employee will improve the quality, effectiveness, output (productivity), and consistency of regular job duties. Problem solving requires the employee to accept responsibility for finding solutions to an existing personal or work area problem. Innovation requires the employee to think of a new approach to some aspect of work.

Both employees and managers should write down anecdotes to document progress toward goals. To keep programs in line with defined performance standards, the manager should coach and counsel the employee in a positive manner, emphasizing the individual's autonomy and accountability. All employee discussions and counseling sessions relating to individual progress should be documented.

Once all employees have gone through this process, the manager needs to organize individual goals into a meaningful pattern for the center or department and construct a calendar to ensure timely and continuing follow-up.[10]

USES FOR PERFORMANCE APPRAISALS

Performance appraisals are used to make decisions on compensation and personnel matters and to develop employees.

Exhibit 13–7 Key Terms in Writing and Evaluating Performance Standards

Job Duty: General statement about major job responsibilities.

Example: Writes nursing care plans.

Job Ideal: A job standard set so high that only a few can meet it. This is inappropriate for use as a job standard.

Example: Works for a year without making a medication error.

Performance Standard: A specific, realistic statement written in behavioral terms to detail quality or what, how, and when a job duty will be accomplished.

- A qualitative standard denotes exactly what is expected in substance.

Example: An accurate, complete physical biopsychosocial assessment, nursing history, and care plan with at least two expected outcomes will be written on each patient chart. (Qualitative)

- The time frame defines the time limits within which work will be accomplished.

Example: Adds "within 24 hours of hospital admission" to the first statement to denote the deadline. (Time)

- Quantity or expectation of workload is stipulated.

Example: The nurse will take an average of one minute to report on each patient's progress at the change of shift report. (What)

- The process to be followed is described.

Example: The care plan will be written according to the applicable policy and procedure. (How or Process)

Judgment Standard: Criteria are established to denote what means supervisors will use to assess performance standards.

- Critical incidents will be identified.

Example: A diary will be kept on each employee of unusual events or positive and negative exceptions to usual practice.

- Skills checklist will be developed.

Example: An audit form will be devised for use at specified intervals to measure a specific set of behaviors: Chart audit, bedside audit, sample work audit, productivity audit.

- Observation with specific examples will occur at preset intervals to determine whether the nurse complies with policies, procedures, and performance standards.

Example: Vital signs and initial admission assessment will be complete and charted within 30 minutes after the patient has arrived on the unit, 75 percent of the time. (Six observations in three months showed no delays.)

Example: Patients will receive prn medications within five minutes of their request, when the request is appropriate, the order is written, and the drugs are available on the unit, 60 percent of the time. (Two spot checks per month revealed that Nurse B administered 90 percent of the prn medications within five minutes.)

Compensation Decisions

A major use of performance appraisals traditionally has been their relationship to compensation policies. In the 1970s high inflation and low unemployment characterized nursing, and cost-of-living raises, often couched as merit increases, were given. The advent of cost containment, lower census, and needs for employee reductions have changed that practice.

In the 1980s, many hospitals were offering minimal or no cost-of-living increases. They often explained to employees that increases would mean that some jobs would need to be eliminated to balance the budget. Discretionary actions are further limited by state rate setters, so that fluctuations that vary with the market basket or defined budget must be offset in other areas of the budget. However, to encourage productivity, managers need to earmark some funds for use in providing merit raises to employees who do their part to work productively and meet their individual work goals.

Administrators, unsure of the volatile, competitive future, have opted to grant one-time bonuses to avoid setting precedents, such as that established when a specified percentage of increase is locked in. Union contracts are following the same pattern. Because of the expense of staff—the major cost of operating a hospital—some hospitals are constructing a two-tiered wage scale so that current employees receive different (higher) rates than new hires. This system is ill-advised, since it creates animosity between employees who receive different compensation for doing the same work. The two-tiered system should not be confused with the step system that provides salary increases for time in the job and for merit.

In some settings, administrators are linking the performance appraisal to monetary rewards on a pay-for-performance basis. When this is done, the performance appraisal method must be structured to reflect standards. For example, the method of weighting items on the performance appraisal and multiplying the total by the three levels of complying with standards lends itself to this reward-for-performance method.

Some personnel directors believe wage increases should be separated from the performance appraisal and discussed as a separate issue with each employee. This thinking arises because, even when excellent performance is obvious, the hospital may not be able to afford increases as a result of budgetary restrictions. When employees expect rewards, they can become very discouraged when improved performance does not result in increased compensation.

However, even when individuals are told that goal setting and accomplishments are important to the center, department, and hospital, they may not be motivated to produce extra effort if the system does not reward that effort. If individual contributions can be valued, it should be possible to provide varying percentages of funds to individuals based on their efforts in relation to everyone else's in a profit/cost center. Some hospitals have even encouraged better performance by giving employees 10 percent of documented savings resulting from the implementation of a specific idea. For example, two pharmacy employees saved a hospital more than $60,000 by analyzing and arranging the intravenous mixing schedule after, not before, physicians' orders were written each day. As a result of their documented efforts, they were given more than $6,000 to split.[11,12]

Personnel Decisions

When the performance appraisal is used to make promotions, layoffs, discharges, or other personnel decisions, it must be fair, objective, and defensible. Employees who disagree with their evaluation should have access to a review procedure. This step provides a systems safeguard that shows the employer's good faith and sincerity in having an objective rating system. Such a mechanism provides employees with a sense of equity while helping the nursing department find areas of bias before problems mushroom into legal actions, employee unrest, and possible union organizing. Managerial retaliation against employers who use this review process is unwise and shortsighted.

By studying performance appraisal results globally, the nursing department also can construct better selection criteria for hiring new employees. For example, if poor performance is the hallmark of students from a particular type of program or school, interviewers can strive to hire candidates with qualities that ensure a higher success rate and a more economical, briefer orientation.

Because interviews should be conducted with the job guidelines and performance appraisal in hand, items that are weighted unrealistically as a standard for performance can be changed on the basis of experience. Standards and expectations for performance must be emphasized from the hospital's initial hiring process so as to clarify and achieve desired staff behaviors, attitudes, and productivity levels.

In studying performance appraisals, managers also can determine if they are effective in encouraging individual performance that supports the achievement of center and nursing departmental objectives. When different behaviors are desirable, the method can be adjusted to reinforce priorities.

Periodic evaluations of the method are needed to be sure there is no discrimination against a protected class of employees. For example, rapid change in nursing sometimes means that older employees are outdated so their evaluations are not as good as those of younger workers. When this occurs, the need for training opportunities is evident.

Employers are functioning in good faith if all employees are given the same, documented chances to learn new techniques and methods through inservice programs, workshop offerings, local college courses, and managerial counseling, and if scheduling is arranged so that they can take advantage of these learning opportunities. Typically, much of this training is done at the employee's expense, since it is an individual responsibility to remain competent, current, and safe. However, some specific new programs, equipment, orientation or hospital methods are offered free as an employee benefit by the education department.[13]

PROCEDURAL MATTERS

Nursing centers and divisions need to structure the performance appraisal system to meet employee objectives for feedback, goal setting, direction, motivation, job satisfaction, and rewards, as well as employer objectives for motivating the work force to be productive, cost-effective, safe, and quality conscious, meanwhile documenting information for personnel decisions and providing material for human resources planning.

In conducting a thorough appraisal, managers should give employees advance notice so that they might prepare, allow privacy and sufficient time for the interview, and use interview techniques that facilitate the process. When performance is not adequate, the hospital disciplinary guidelines should be called into play.

Performance reviews must be kept in the main personnel file, available to others only on a need-to-know basis. Because a negative review can affect a person's future, outsiders and subsequent employers should be denied access to the file. In some states, employees have the right to see their performance appraisals.

While the review process should be positive, employees become discouraged if peers are not disciplined for behavior that is not in compliance with performance standards. The failure to establish an equitable practice in discipline can have an adverse effect on productivity for all of those persons who are striving to do their best.[14,15,16,17]

If this process seems overwhelming, a 1984 book can provide an unusual insight about how nurse managers can view their roles now and each decade of their working lives. The book, *Corporate Steeplechase*, is a collection of case studies and comparisons with which managers will find many points to identify.[18]

COMMON ASSESSMENT TRAPS

In conducting the appraisal, nursing executives will find the following list of common traps helpful:

1. Being too quick on the trigger. Sometimes time is needed to resolve a situation.
2. Personalizing issues inappropriately. This can cause defensive behavior that blocks judgment.

3. Lacking imagination and common sense. Usually the most logical approach is the one that works best.
4. Making false analogies. It is easy to jump the gun when data are insufficient.
5. Mismatching cause and effect. Sometimes the obvious answer is not the right one. Only thorough investigation proves the point.
6. Giving in to habit and prejudice. It is important to separate personal whims from business needs.
7. Begging the question. When too many things are shoved in the closet, they may crash down on the manager one day.
8. Being narrow minded. In most personnel situations, things are not black and white but actually gray compromises of both extremes.
9. Ignoring poor performance. Denying or overrating poor performers can result in legal problems later when inappropriate behavior has been tolerated over a long period.

SUMMARY

To motivate employees through the performance appraisal process, nurse managers need to follow some basic guidelines:

- Evaluate employees in light of what is really critical to the performance on the job. Asking them to perform beyond their job scope is unreasonable, and can result in the setting of ideals instead of realistic standards.
- Be certain that the performance appraisal is a true reflection of what nurses are doing. Inaccurate or biased reviews compound employee hostility and apathy.
- Include employees in setting attainable but challenging goals. Nurses are much more likely to succeed when they participate in the process of goal setting, evaluation, and goal modification.
- Allow sufficient time for the nurses to explore individual concerns, obstacles, and deficiencies in a problem-solving format.

From this process, training needs can be identified and appropriate programming can be incorporated into specific, individual goals. Moreover, it puts in place a system that can be used to award raises on the basis of merit.

When participating in this process, nursing managers must be cognizant of the fact that employees have a difficult time in striving for goals that do not result in positive outcomes. To avoid promising what the system cannot deliver or deviating from acceptable hospital practices, managers who use participatory goal setting by employees should remain current in institutional policies. This provides a better opportunity for linking tangible and intangible rewards to what managers and nurses define as being important. However, privacy of individual ratings and problems is a legal mandate and should be made available to other administrators in the hospital only on a need-to-know basis.

Generalized results of individual sessions can be included in group meetings for action by the entire team when similar needs or problems are identified. Such group efforts facilitate the process of team building and peer cooperation and support. This establishes a positive climate that encourages staff members to support the goals of the center, the department, and the hospital.

To keep employees motivated, productive, conscious of quality, and moving on a positive course, managers should reserve the right to initiate the performance appraisal process whenever the need arises. If behavior is inappropriate or unacceptable, further disciplinary action can be started. Formal reviews, where there are no special problem circumstances, generally are done on an annual basis.

NOTES

1. Cecilia Golightly, "MBO and Performance Appraisal." *The Journal of Nursing Administration* 9, no. 9 (September 1979): 11–19.

2. Tracy Breton, "Overweight Nursing Student Sues over Ouster," *The National Law Journal* 18 no. 8 (November 18, 1985): 8.

3. R.W. Beatty and C.E. Schneider, *Personnel Administration* (Reading, Mass.: Addison-Wesley Publishing Co., 1981).

4. Joan M. Ganong and Warren L. Ganong, *Nursing Management* (Rockville, Md.: Aspen Publishers, Inc., 1980).

5. T.A. DeCotiis, *Organizational Behavior and Human Performance* (New York: Academic Press, Inc., 1977).

6. *Employment Coordinator* (New York: Research Institute of America, 1985), ¶PM 14,051–831.

7. E.F. Gruenfeld, *Performance Appraisal: Peril and Promise* (Ithaca, N.Y.: Cornell University Press, 1981).

8. *Bouzianis v. U.S. Air Inc.*, No. 84–3798–K (D. Mass. filed September 30, 1985).

9. Val Olson, *White Collar Waste: Gain the Productivity Edge* (Englewood Cliffs, N.J.: Prentice-Hall, Inc., 1983).

10. T.C. Alewine, "Performance Appraisals and Performance Standards," *Personnel Journal* (March 1982): 210–213.

11. Daily Labor Report, Special Supplement: Impact on Employee Relations in the Health Care Industry. (Washington, D.C.: Bureau of National Affairs, 1985).

12. Arthur D. Rutkowski and Barbara Lang Rutkowski, "Bargaining Issues in Health Care," *Health Employment Law Update* 1, no. 6 (October 1985): 5.

13. Howard S. Rowland and Beatrice L. Rowland, *Nursing Administration Handbook* (Rockville, Md.: Aspen Publishers, Inc., 1980).

14. P.B. Crosby, *Quality Is Free* (New York: New American Library, 1979).

15. J.D. Council and R.J. Placy, "Performance Appraisal Is Not Enough," *The Journal of Nursing Administration* 10, no. 10 (October 1980).

16. C.A. Dailey and A.M. Madsen, *How to Evaluate People in Business* (New York: McGraw-Hill Book Co., 1983).

17. *Employment Coordinator*.

18. Srully Blotnick, *The Corporate Steeplechase: Predictable Crises in a Business Career* (New York: Facts on File, 1984).

ACTION CHECKLIST

1. Does the performance appraisal encourage employees to strive for improved performance in line with the unit, divisional, and hospital goals? Do employees view the method as being equitable and realistic?
2. Does the appraisal method include specific, measurable performance standards that are evaluated by the end result and a predetermined time?
3. Are the items in the performance appraisal weighted to show their significance to total performance?
4. Do managers keep specific incident records to document all aspects of employee performance? Do they use skills checklists to make detailed, direct observations of work behaviors?
5. Do staff members have input into the development, revision, and standards used in the form?
6. Does the system include some provision for allowing staff members and managers a way to set individual goals for performance? Is the success of achieving these goals tied into any type of reward system?
7. Have managers had specific educational programs on how to evaluate job-related critical behaviors so that untoward conduct or action can be corrected equitably?
8. Does the performance appraisal lend itself to the making of objective personnel decisions?
9. Are any group evaluations done to identify weak and strong staff members for purposes of establishing mentoring systems?
10. Are any group evaluations done on specific traits, such as documented methods of improving productivity, so that individual efforts can be identified and rewarded?
11. Are the performance appraisal methods reviewed regularly to be sure that they are not discriminatory?
11. Has a separate type of appraisal been constructed for different levels of nursing staff?

Chapter 14

Establishing Performance Priorities

Establishing performance priorities and productivity standards as a part of the nursing delivery and control system is a three-part process that includes (1) the development of strategy and organizational direction, (2) the definition of functional necessities, and (3) the delineation of performance standards in which comparisons and evaluation mechanisms are an integral part of the approach.

DEVELOPING STRATEGY AND DIRECTION

Hospitals' ability to thrive is contingent on the foresight of top-level leaders in linking the mission of the institution with strategies for profitability, improved productivity, marketing, growth, and sensitivity to staff and consumers. To do this, hospitals must develop a philosophy of care delivery that can be branded on all of its activity. Such a philosophical definition provides some direction to future growth and expenditures. The philosophy is a general, brief description of the value and belief system that underlies the operation.

Hospitals may narrow their global statement further by identifying a particular mission to which they assign priorities. Such a statement delineates institutional specialness.

For example, if research is the primary mission, patient selection and professional staff choices would be aligned with this objective. Marketing programs and budgetary expenditures would be geared toward scientific endeavors. If the personal touch or mercy is the objective, patients and staff should be able to sense many ways that care is both personalized and sensitive to individual needs.

Once the philosophy is accepted by all planners and the marketing department, it can be made more concrete when captured in a theme tying all parts of the corporation together in a form that everyone can relate to, such as: "I am a good Samaritan every day," "You can count on me," or "We treat you like family."

These themes imply an employee attitude and work style that should be visible. To these slogans, marketers should add a statement that emphasizes that niceties have an equal priority with cost containment, quality of services, and improved productivity.

Nursing Philosophy

Once the institutional direction is established, nursing can interrelate its philosophy with that of the entire organization. Some nurse leaders choose to select a specific theory of nursing to govern their actions while others adopt an eclectic model or combination of several theories. To avoid burial in the aging documents file, this philosophy should be pragmatic, clear, concise, realistic, and actually give direction to the way the nursing services division should practice. This document should then be reflected in every program instituted. It should provide guidance for all practicing nurses.

The "voice" of the document should be that of the entire staff, so that implementation rests squarely on each staff member. A philosophic statement written by administration for staff sets up the we-they problem and fails to place accountability for implementation on the shoulders of each nurse. Thus, the philosophy should be so identifiable that staff members and patients know what it is and how it has been translated into action as it affects them.

Key Points to Assess

Whatever the theory chosen, nursing leaders should be certain that it addresses the following points:

1. When was it written? By whom? How does it need to change, if at all?
2. What relationship does it have to the way that the department operates in practice and to the performance and productive standards to which each staff member performs and is accountable?
3. Does the document accurately reflect the division's current beliefs, values, constraints, and activities?
4. Does the document indicate a realistic future direction for nursing that integrates fiscal responsibility with goals and performance standards aligned with strategic plans?
5. How does this document explain the relationship between:

   - the client/family and nursing
   - the community/society and nursing
   - administration and nursing

- nursing department and individual staff practitioners
- education and practice
- nursing department and each profit/cost center
- institutional commitments and nursing

6. Does the theory coincide with a well-known model? Does the philosophy commit the department to specific values such as primary care or holistic care without walls?
7. What provisions does the philosophy make for conducting or applying nursing research?
8. Does the philosophy indicate a commitment to a management style?
9. How does the philosophy link the department to the hospital and the nursing profession in general?
10. Does the philosophy include collaboration, joint efforts, or cooperative pursuits with other hospitals, schools, or professional organizations? If the operation is part of a chain, does the nursing division's philosophy differ from or concur with that of the corporate owners?
11. Are human rights and basic commitments to employees and patients well articulated?
12. Are there more specific philosophies identified for specialty areas such as pediatrics, ambulatory care, psychiatry, rehabilitation, surgery, emergency services, etc.?
13. Does this philosophy truly communicate what the nursing department is about?

For many nurses, the last item—communicating what they are all about—is the most pivotal. If the belief system is hard to translate into words, it also is unclear in practice. Delivering on ideals for practice involves all staff members. If everyone is not clear or is uncommitted to the philosophy, the division will continue to present an undesirable image to the recipients of care. This dilutes nursing's effectiveness and its marketing position. When the philosophy is clarified, departmental goals can be delineated.

For example, quality can mean:

- providing patients with the best in care, tests, and services
- treating patients like family
- implementing quality control to be sure that patients get exactly the care that they need
- delivering the most current, safest care in the most effective manner possible.

Because quality means different things to different nurses, it is wise to ask staff members to explain their interpretation of the nursing philosophy, complete with a definition of different components such as quality, cost effectiveness, staffing standards, etc.

Nursing divisional goals can be categorized as continuing or permanent and as temporary. Continuing goals require constant attention, effort, and monitoring to remain as a central priority. Examples might recommend that the department:

- Advance the practice and productive capacities of clinical nursing by testing and applying the latest concepts in patient care delivery.
- Promote a work environment that fosters creativity, individual growth, and research in practice.
- Provide educational and supportive services to keep staff members current and motivated to provide cost-effective, quality care commensurate with departmental profit/cost center standards.
- Maintain a positive human relations program that supports excellence in attitude, work patterns, and contemporary personnel practices.
- Participate in interdepartmental collaboration and cooperation efforts to boost hospital productivity, reputation, and cost containment, as well as quality-of-care efforts.
- Enhance effectiveness, productivity, cost-containment efforts, and personalization of patient/family-centered service consistent with the quality of care.

Temporary goals would be those set annually to focus on deficient areas that need improvement to be in line with the permanent objectives. These objectives are established both by the central nursing office and by each profit/cost center. If they are to be reached, they must be congruent. For example, if the central departmental goal is to reduce staff on cardiac care by two aides while the profit/cost center goal is to increase staff by two aides, the two objectives are counterproductive.

Similarly, if the long-term goal is to keep staff current in specialty areas, while the annual goals and budget priorities allow little for continuing education and needs assessments, the opportunity for success is limited. The same principle holds true when the nursing departmental efforts are not synchronized carefully with institutional strategies and directions.

Temporary goals should be broken down into more specific objectives that have temporal deadlines and specific persons accountable for accomplishment. Otherwise, implementation and follow-up can be difficult.[1]

FUNCTIONAL NECESSITIES

The area of functional necessities is composed of the organizational structure, management directives, and plans.

Organizational Structure

The American Hospital Association reported that in 1984, hospitals made record profits of $2.5 billion on revenues of $128.5 billion. The highest were the for-profit hospitals, which accounted for less than 25 percent of the facilities but reported profits of $826 million. However, in this sea of plenty, nearly 20 percent of the nation's hospitals lost money, and will continue to do so because of patient mix and location in geographic areas where they have less opportunity for diversity.[2]

The profits did not go unnoticed by the debt-ridden government, which was operating with a concept of "cut and freeze." Thus, to continue to be profitable, or to improve conditions where the budget is sorely strained, hospitals must examine factors for more efficient operation. Moreover, staff members need to understand that the hospital is a business that is entitled to make profits, as some hospitals are doing. Such profits can be used to make necessary capital improvements, expand the business, add staff, or reward staff members for their efforts.

Efforts of the first generation of cuts were noticed most in reduced lengths of hospital stays and reductions of unneeded procedures, radiologic tests, and laboratory procedures. To optimize reimbursement, hospitals have become very good at coding patients properly and screening out those who should be treated in outpatient or day surgery settings. Networking among chains of hospitals or others in cooperative arrangements has resulted in more competitive bids on supplies and significant cost reductions (see Exhibit 14–1 for examples of shared service programs). Triaging in critical care units has resulted in savings as these highly staffed units have become utilized more appropriately. The most macroscopic efforts have involved improving staff productivity, policies, and some management practices as a means of containing costs.

The next generation of cost reductions, however, will be more challenging. Some of the most obvious changes have been made already but even more improvements will be necessary to remain competitive, be productive, and be effective in achieving desired outcomes. One of the major areas targeted for change is the organizational structure itself, since it can help or hinder performance priorities.

Reinventing the Corporation

The book *Re-Inventing the Corporation* posits a number of useful thoughts that need a great deal of refinement to fit into nursing, since the book's premise is that most corporations have widgets to produce and have control of the entire product cycle.[3] Conversely, hospital nursing does not control entry or discharge—only the process of integrating patients' responses and life styles with the medical problem of illness.

Exhibit 14–1 List of Shared Service Programs in One Area

Shared Service Programs

- MATERIAL MANAGEMENT SERVICE
  - -Pharmacy
  - -Dietary
  - -Laboratory
  - -General Purchasing

- BENEFITS/PERSONNEL SERVICES
  - -Retirement
  - -Life Planning
  - -Personal Financial Planning
  - -Insurance Programs
  - -Unemployment Compensation

- EDUCATION SERVICES
  - -Conferences, Seminars, Workshops
  - -Patient Education
  - -Professional Staff Education

- HEALTH VENTURES, INC. (Long-term care services)

- HOSPITAL FINANCE CORPORATION (Self-pay financing)

- CENTRAL HOSPITAL SERVICES, INC. (Bad debt collection)

- CANCER DATA SYSTEM (Tumor registry)

- ADDITIONAL SERVICES
  - -Ohio Department of Health/Hospital Medical Claims
    (Indigent auto accident follow-up service)
  - -Bureau of Workers' Compensation Shared Terminal Service
    (Telecommunications claims monitoring service)
  - -Coding Service (ICD-9-CM temporary coding service)
  - -Architectural Design and Engineering Service
  - -Shared Travel
  - -Shared Terminal Services (Telecommunication welfare eligibility service)
  - -Executive Recruitment
  - -Areawide Paging
  - -Telecommunications Consulting

1226 Huron Road • Playhouse Square • Cleveland, Ohio 44115 • (216) 696-6900

Source: Courtesy of The Center for Health Affairs, Greater Cleveland Hospital Association, Cleveland, Ohio, 1986.

The nursing division employs about half of the employees in a hospital and historically has experienced low morale because of job insecurity, rapid change, increased workloads, and demands for improved productivity. The new challenges and economic realities have made many nurse managers wonder how they can change to cope.

For many years managers have attended courses and seminars on humanism and responsiveness to employees. However, the traditional hierarchies in which they function daily have been slow to change in response to the new beliefs. The Tax Equity and Fiscal Responsibility Act of 1982 (TEFRA) (P.L. 97-248) shocked them into a value review geared toward getting more power in the system and surviving this era of cost containment. In interviewing nurses, managers find that they harbor many negative feelings and that they fail to identify with the hospital corporation as their business.

Effectiveness, efficiency, and improved productivity are not possible with dollars alone. These require the honest valuation of each employee as the most priceless corporate treasure. Managers must strive to make work a positive and professional experience aligned with each individual's life as a total entity. According to Naisbitt and Aburdene, the context for these changes already is shaping up as human resources are highly prioritized. A summary of their key points adapted to nursing includes:

- In the information society that the nation has entered, resources that can edge a hospital into success are the human qualities of information, knowledge, creativity, and know-how in the form of "TLC"—thinking, learning, and creating.

- As the desired strategic resource becomes outstanding nurse professionals, the competition for the best people will accelerate.

- Management layers will be collapsed and simplified because of computer technology and economic need, and new organizational charts will be established. Effective managers will be operating in closer proximity to patient care and will be more sensitive to needs of the staff. The entire system of management will be more flexible and responsive, and less fractured and complicated.

- Innovation and intrapreneurial endeavors will be encouraged to transform hospitals into healthy, profitable businesses. For example, could the ostomy or diabetes programs become a free-standing business within the institution?

- Vision and intuition in predicting future directions accurately will be a valuable managerial ability rewarded by more autonomy and resources.

- Education will need retooling to meet the needs of the hospital corporation for talent, timeliness, and change. Lifelong learning will continue to be the hallmark of this era, and will be made more convenient and available. Outmoded practices will be challenged and replaced by more relevant and continuous education. Educational goals will need to be realigned so that higher education can result in a management track or an expert clinician track.

- New patterns of lifelong female careers combined with family life styles will need to be valued and included in the plan of retaining experienced staff and improving the total skills of individual nurses. A holistic approach to nursing will replace the prior compartmentalized work and private life needs and patterns.

- Fitness, high-level wellness, and illness/problem preventive employee assistance programs will be highlighted and prioritized as cost-effective ways of keeping employees on the job and making them more productive.[4]

Getting inspired and building strong cohesiveness and team spirit while casting off the shackles of outmoded patterns are the new mandates. Practically speaking, this will occur a little differently in every hospital because of variations in organizational needs, structure, and personalities. The important point is to continue to use a problem-solving methodology to revise the organizational structure in nursing until it is effective and flexible enough to operate optimally.

Many nursing departments have progressed to the point of knowing that change is needed but of not knowing just how to begin. According to Bill Gore, founder of W.L. Gore and Associates, "Commitment, not authority, produces results."[5]

New Vistas

Professional nurses are increasing in hospitals because of their cost effectiveness, licensed practical nurses are being phased out, and nursing assistants are getting new job descriptions to make them more useful to nurses. Patient service is being provided through primary or modular care, depending on the intensity of patient needs and available resources. The bottom line of this change is that professionals want autonomy and do not need the close supervision that was the norm. Managers cannot afford the time and money needed to continue this practice, either. At times, the continuation of central control of these modular teams has meant that progress and initiative in staff nurses have been squelched.

Managers in reinvented corporations need to be educators and facilitators, not distant bosses. Nurses need to be included as participants in unit and hospital decisions and encouraged to self-manage. Resources spent on authoritarian supervision are wasted and counterproductive to contemporary goals. In decentralized operations that are functioning well, fewer managers are needed.

For example, at Baptist Hospital East in Louisville, Ky., cutbacks and the unavailability of a nursing educational coordinator caused the associate director of critical care to take on that role as well. While this organizational idea was meant to be temporary, it became permanent—with excellent results. Two instructors in education have autonomy as they pursue preset objectives and a secretary coordinates clerical functions, scheduling, and equipment needs. The critical care director has power in the system, something that many educational coordinators lack, and is in constant touch with nurse needs through her clinical managerial role. As a result, this operation is decentralized, effective, and cost efficient.

According to Cheryl Stout, the director, "We are very proud of our educational system, and we wonder why more departments are not operating this way."[6] Conversely, in a comparable hospital, the director of education in a centralized operation gives workshops outside the facility to justify her salary. In that case, the diversification plan is ill conceived and is more a justification of an archaic system than an enlightened approach to productivity.

Flatter structures and truly decentralized profit/cost centers reduce waste and simplify frustrating, protracted, complex communications. Too much time is spent in meetings, and managers are reluctant to decrease that time even though they express the desire to do so. In fact, meetings take unit managers away from their jobs too often and too long, causing frustration among staff members, who usually cannot find any purpose in so many sessions.

To reduce time in meetings, the cost of each agenda item should be allocated to a project or a profit/cost center. A part of the problem here is that meetings are a political, power-bartering process in which managers identify and maintain their corporate status despite the issues being discussed. With a more simplified hierarchy and with true autonomy passed to the profit/cost center, there should be a decreased need to meet as a means of gaining enough authority to move on with worthy projects.

Graduate school needs to be refocused to support the move toward decentralization by being dual tracked:

1. It needs to give managers the business skills needed to manage a cost/profit center.
2. It needs to provide excellent practitioners with advanced clinical and business skills to establish a cost-effective clinical practice.

Clinical ladders, shelved during the nurse glut, should be reexamined. Effective nursing departments must value the performance of excellent practitioners, who have the important job of representing nursing to the public and pioneering ways of delivering, monitoring, and documenting the highest quality of patient care in the safest, most personal way at the least cost.

Getting Started

The two steps identified by Naisbitt and Aburdene are vision and alignment.[7] First, executives (including nursing) must have the vision to see where they are going and how they can get there. Then they must get everyone in the department aligned and synchronized in the effort.

Getting nurses to own the vision of building a truly productive, motivated nursing department produces one of the highest forms of self-expression. To achieve greatness, individual goals must mesh with organizational goals, so that corporate aims reinforce nursing's professional purpose and mission in life. Getting people involved means that leaders cannot project a double message of encouraging autonomy while smothering initiative with an authoritarian approach.

Where management is collapsed and the corporate ladder is not a tall vertical one, energy can be rechanneled into smaller, productive work units that network well. These smaller, autonomous units can be characterized as flexible, speedy, and results oriented. To reinforce this value, monetary rewards, special privileges, and individual recognition must be a part of the system. It is time for nursing leaders to stop acting like they value things that are truly beyond the institution's resources.

For example, they could initiate a point system based on the job description and the current productivity goals for nurses who contribute significantly to the division. Some factors that might win them points would be: meeting performance appraisal personal goals, volunteering to float, working extra shifts, taking an added workload, getting positive consumer comments, developing a new form or method, presenting an inservice course or class, developing a way to achieve documented savings, or getting a new client for the hospital.

The points won could be used for gifts, trips, extra paid days off, bonus money, or whatever the hospital can create that would appeal to staff members. This list can change as the needs of the unit or division require new priorities.

A part of setting up a system to enhance the implementation of performance priorities is to understand the reality of the operation. How do things get done? If nurse leaders really want something done quickly, they must be skillful at circumventing the system. When they really need action, many managers use the "lattice work," or personal connections within the system, to network their way around the hierarchy. An example of this is the trend toward calling a needed change a "pilot project" so that typical committee sandbagging can be avoided.

Experience with quality circles taught that they keep managers too far from the point of action, and those on the firing line lack the power to accomplish what is needed. In revamping the organization, executives must see that those who set the objectives are the ones who will implement them. Like other industries, nursing needs to find a point system for matching individual contributions to specific system awards.

For example, Nurse D devised a patient education program that helped diabetics be better prepared in a shorter time. As a result patients were released two days sooner from the hospital and had 50 percent fewer problems in managing their disease. This program saved the hospital $750 a patient. The nurse should have received a percentage of the savings.[8]

The nursing organizational chart in the waning 1980s was out of step with the needs of nurses giving direct patient care. Jobs need to be redefined to decrease fractionalized functioning and red tape caused by dispersed power and authority. Managers should view their major roles as support, assistance in getting employees what they need to do their jobs, educational guidance, and people building.

In other words, managers need to go from "boss" to "facilitator." Instead of the organizational hierarchy's being a hindrance to progress, it must be a mechanism designed to augment desired performance priorities. For example, if a nurse is assigned to work on a videotaped presentation on ostomy care for nurses and patients, the supervisor should be sure that the nurse has the necessary resources and feedback to achieve that goal.[9]

Management Directives

The traditional management directives have been control, effectiveness, economy, and efficiency. Those functions remain in the revamped nursing department, although they need to change conceptually to be applicable.[10]

Control

Control is the most important aspect of setting objectives and realizing the desired result. Yet control has eluded many nurses. Nurse managers have not had the power commensurate with their responsibilities to deliver the set level of quality care in the most cost-effective manner. That means that the vice president and assistant vice presidents must continue to work harmoniously with the board, administration, and other departments to get the requisite power to operate.

The next level of executives needs to strive for this interdepartmental harmony in daily working relationships with others. That spirit has to be communicated to staff members as well. This activity is political, and is essential in assuring nursing the resources necessary to get the job done. However, those politics are beyond the scope of this text.[11]

Control also involves the measurement of outcomes related to objectives and resource consumption. Part of this is evident in monetary profits of the cost/profit center. However, there is a qualitative aspect evident in staff and consumer satisfaction levels and in quality assurance efforts that evaluate the relationship of work to standards. Decentralization will make the tracing of efforts to outcome more direct, since that measurement can be related more readily to those accountable at the point of patient care delivery. Moreover, the feedback mechanism designed to adjust system deficiencies will be flexible and effective in smaller work units.

Effectiveness

Managers have a number of mechanisms to measure effectiveness, including employee surveys, performance appraisals, patient "happiness" questionnaires, reviews by accreditors, patient classification systems, and quality assurance efforts designed to measure outcomes statistically. Measurements of effectiveness must relate to the long-term and short-term goals of the department and the philosophy and objectives established by individuals and profit/cost centers.

To be effective, the nursing center or department needs to set qualitative and quantitative standards against which outcomes can be evaluated. While such standards start in global terms, they must be made much more specific before effectiveness measurements provide enough direction for revising plans of action. The nursing centers will need to calculate the costs of all items in detail to know whether they are as effective as possible in light of resource expenditures.

For example, in Maine, nursing departments are required to provide itemized bills for services. However, breaking costs down much further than a general acuity range is not possible in most hospitals because there is such a paucity of research on what really is needed to accomplish a specific educational or patient care task.

Economy

In nursing, economy often means cutting costs. Sometimes that philosophy has been penny-wise and pound-foolish, as resources saved can result in greater expenditures for brush-fire management. Certainly, in allocating money for capital expenditures, nurse executives must envision what will be used most and how those expenditures will generate the most dollars.

For example, it is unwise to continue purchasing ever-disappearing nurse stethoscopes. Each nurse should own her own stethoscope. In buying for physicians, the equipment chosen should be what can be used by the greatest number or by those who show the greatest promise for increasing future revenues and admissions.

However, the greatest economy must be in human resources, since that is where the bulk of budgetary dollars in nursing are spent. Many nurses feel they are short-staffed. That is true in some instances. However, more often, a productivity audit shows that the real problem is that nurses have not formulated a clear standard of care and may be striving for idealistic, yet unstated, goals. That is a quick path to frustration. Many nurses have problems in setting priorities and in considering the benefit of the services they offer.

There is a difference between needed care and amenities. These need to be distinguished, so that all patients receive care commensurate with the philosophy of the department while staff members feel satisfied with the level of delivery. One of the most important roles of first-line managers will be to mentor staff members in setting and achieving realistic goals so that they feel more positive, while working smarter, as a result of learning the tricks of the trade that increase the quality of the productive effort while decreasing the time and/or resources expended.

Efficiency

Efficiency is a quantitative term that becomes meaningful only when it is used in a context in which qualitative aspects are considered. Being productive is more than being quick and doing things at minimal cost. It also involves achieving desired results. Without meeting important objectives of timeliness, effectiveness, and appropriateness, efficiency loses its meaning.

This term is getting particular attention as hospitals discharge patients with shorter stays. Many experts predict that lawsuits will abound if hospital documentation and patient education efforts are insufficient since discharged patients generally are much sicker than they used to be and can encounter more problems and complications after they leave.

Once nursing leaders have determined that their efforts are efficient, effective, and economical, they may proceed to the next step: reevaluating standards in light of a cost-benefit analysis to be certain they are providing services appropriately and economically in relation to their use of resources.[12]

Plans

Plans are all documented courses of action formulated to pursue and support strategy objectives. In making plan statements, it is important to focus on accountability, deadlines, control, and opportunity for reasonable success. The following list of criteria can help in assuring that a nursing department's plan of action is well formulated:

1. Is the plan specific and realistic in terms of available resources?
2. Has the plan been critiqued in light of area needs and available research so that it is relevant and worth the time to pursue?
3. Have alternative approaches been studied thoroughly, so that another option can be used as a contingency plan?
4. Is the plan positive, simple, and stated in relation to behavioral outcomes?
5. Are control feedback mechanisms elaborate enough to ensure desired results without being unnecessarily cumbersome?
6. Do those responsible have sufficient authority, clarification of plan roles, and adequate guidelines to be able to accomplish their tasks?
7. Are interim and terminal deadlines specified?

8. Are interim and terminal objectives clear enough to provide yardsticks of progress? Do those objectives mesh with institutional and departmental objectives?
9. Have adequate resources, time, and administrative support been provided to allow the plan to go forward?
10. Is there a budget for the plan?
11. Is an administrative liaison person working with the project to avoid duplication and promote systems communication between the program and the department?
12. What benefits/rewards do employees receive for making the plan succeed?
13. Have data collection systems been included to assess both qualitative and quantitative success of the plan?
14. Are the criteria used to determine the success of the plan specific, measurable, and predefined?

While plan objectives can be expressed qualitatively, they also should be presented in terms of dollars. However, planners are cautioned not to confuse the accounting system (which is concerned with history) with the plan. (which is a prospective process that utilizes accounting data as one type of measurement approach).

PERFORMANCE STANDARDS

All of nurse executives' efforts in establishing performance priorities come together when they set performance standards with specific outcomes in mind. To be useful, information on needs and compliance with standards must be timely and current.

For example, in a project on streamlining and improving cost-effective care for diabetics, the computer is needed to help in analyzing the numbers of cases treated, the lengths of stay, and the cost of treatment before and after the start of the new program. A follow-up system is essential for assessing the effectiveness in terms of patient/physician satisfaction and reduced needs for postdischarge care. If such data are not readily available, appropriate alterations in the program cannot be made in a timely manner. However, deciding what data to regard is critical to avoid excessive costs in evaluating extraneous information.

The internal control system also requires a reliable audit for assessing standardization of patient education and quality of staff efforts. Such an audit may take the form of a checklist to ensure compliance with the standards of patient care. If a deficit is found, the continual monitoring system makes it possible to provide the appropriate remedial intervention to the nurses involved.

Unusual situations or exceptions should be recorded and analyzed to determine their significance for revision of the program. For example, Mrs. S has filed a lawsuit alleging that she did not receive care to avert an insulin reaction when she returned home after a premature discharge. The issue raises important questions:

- Does this complaint have merit?
- Do chart documentation and care plan guidelines provide ample information to assess this problem?
- Can it be determined accurately what care she received?
- Should any changes be made to avoid this problem in the future; for instance, do nurses need an inservice program on legal aspects of care and documentation?

The keeping of statistics also allows nurse managers to compare the current approach with past efforts and with new methods identified in the literature and at other hospitals. In so doing, the managers can evaluate their intervention strategies by assessing their effectiveness, their cost, the rationale for continuing them in light of new trends, the ease of implementation, and their acceptance by staff and consumers. It becomes possible then to begin to align costs with specific interventions as a step in justifying what is important and in determining more exact costs for care. These calculations provide a baseline, using this program as a standard for comparing other pilot projects featuring new approaches to patient care.

Involving Staff Members

In establishing priorities, it is imperative to make standards of performance apply both to staff and to managers. Because participation by staff members is imperative to get grass-roots commitment to the standards and to minimize the need for direct, autocratic supervision, ground rules should be established. After a thorough investigation of nursing's current status as a profit/cost center or department, executives are ready to move forward in the setting of goals.

Ground rules could include the following:

- All goals, objectives, and plans will be written in a manner that allows final outcomes to be assessed.
- Goals must be written, approved by two-thirds of those who will do the work toward the goal, and made available to all staff members involved in their implementation.
- Individual nurses and managers will use performance appraisal sessions to establish individual, functional goals that blend with center or departmental goals.

- All goals will be analyzed to be certain that they support the strategic plan of the department and the hospital.

Long-term and short-term goals must be balanced. Where there are several goals, priorities must be set in advance of work efforts. Final goals are written only after items such as standards, resources, and schedules have been discussed thoroughly between staff members and management. Managers are involved in every step of the process of setting goals, objectives, and plans to be sure that each item is delineated clearly and developed logically, challenging, and cohesive, with broader institutional direction and accreditation/reimbursement mandates.

Participatory Planning

In carrying out the development of participatory planning, nursing executives should:

1. Work to be certain that all staff members identify with the philosophy and strategic goals, objectives, and plans to the extent that they feel their efforts are a significant contribution to center or departmental success.
2. Coach and counsel employees constantly to assist, monitor, and recognize the ways that they implement personal objectives.
3. Strive to connect each individual's goals and efforts with the entire center or departmental direction.
4. Work to standardize performance levels and systematize procedures so that individual performance can be assessed readily and communicated continually to each employee.
5. Provide adequate latitude for managers to be creative in directing, controlling, and assisting their portion of the hospital to relate to broader institutional objectives.
6. Strive to create a working climate in which individuals, teams, and managers are rewarded for getting results rather than for merely performing activities.

SUMMARY

Establishing performance priorities and productivity standards requires the hospital and the nursing division to clearly formulate their philosophical position, their goals, and their expectations of staff and to pragmatically communicate these to staff.

NOTES

1. Barbara Stevens, *The Nurse As Executive* (Wakefield, Mass.: Nursing Resources, Inc., 1980).
2. Leah Curtin, "Reinventing the Corporation," *Nursing Management* 14, no. 11 (November 1985): 10–12.
3. James Naisbitt and Patricia Aburdene, *Re-Inventing the Corporation* (New York: Warner Books, 1985).
4. Ibid.
5. Lucien Rhodes, "The Un-Manager," *Inc.* 14, no. 8 (August 1982).
6. Cheryl Stout, director, Baptist Hospital East, Louisville, Ky., Personal interview, 1986.
7. Naisbitt and Aburdene, *Re-Inventing*.
8. Allan Cohen and David Bradford, *Managing for Excellence* (New York: John Wiley & Sons, Inc., 1984).
9. G.H. Kaye and Joy Utenner, "Productivity: Managing for the Long Term," *Nursing Management* 16, no. 9 (September 1985): 12–15.
10. Peter F. Drucker, *Management: Tasks, Responsibilities, Practices* (New York: Harper & Row, Publishers, Inc., 1974).
11. P. Kalisch and B.J. Kalisch, *Politics of Nursing* (Philadelphia: J.B. Lippincott Co., 1982).
12. Robert Heller, *The Business of Business* (New York: Harcourt Brace Jovanovich, Publishers, Inc., 1981).
13. Richard Sloma, *How to Measure Managerial Performance* (New York: Macmillan Publishing Co., Inc., 1980).

ACTION CHECKLIST

To set performance priorities, nursing managers need to determine the current status of their center, department, and hospital. The following questions can be helpful in identifying critical areas:

1. Is management time spent primarily on prevention and strategic planning or on brush fire management?
2. Are managers guided by patients' needs and applicable new trends in clinical care, or are approaches outdated?
3. Can managers handle authority properly? That is, do they refrain from unjustly blaming others while providing staff members with enough authority to act on delegated responsibility?
4. Are managers respected by staff members for their knowledge and ability to apply it appropriately?
5. Are managers free to express views and set solutions for their areas, or is some type of power struggle preventing the implementation of what is proposed on paper?
6. Do managers and staff members agree on work priorities and know what their role is in improving the organization? Does the hospital reward people for their efforts and special contributions?
7. Are successors identified and trained to replace any managers who may leave the system?
8. Are mistakes a negative or positive experience? In other words, are errors allowed and utilized as a learning experience or are they regarded as untenable risks?
9. Is there real trust and openness in the organization, or does the "don't make waves" attitude prevail?
10. Has the hospital ever had a systematic analysis of its performance, both generally and specifically, to determine the institution's effectiveness from all perspectives?
11. Are the hospital philosophy and goals known by all employees? Do employees agree with the institutional direction and feel that they had input into establishing the guiding policies?
12. Are adequate budgetary resources allocated to achieve goals and plans that have been prioritized?
13. Do center and departmental goals interface effectively with overall institutional directions?
14. Do managers have adequate financial information to be able to write and budget their programs? Have they all had enough education to be able to understand and apply financial information, and track costs? Is there some type of reporting system that encourages cost effectiveness and quality in program implementation on a continuing basis?
15. Do all managers have input into the hospital budget?
16. Are problems and programs with a great effect on productivity and profitability given priority?
17. Do employees understand the performance standards that apply to them and to their managers? Do these standards really translate into everyday practice?
18. Is enough inservice education conducted to support the strategic planning process at the hospital?
19. How responsive is the hospital to the need to review, modify, delete, and/or add new services on a continuing basis?
20. Does the hospital enjoy good relations with the public, the patients, the staff, other health care disciplines and providers, and the medical community?
21. Do employees agree with the executives'/managers' opinions about how the center is functioning.[13]

Chapter 15

Developing a Comprehensive Human Resources Program

The key to gaining the competitive edge in productivity is in the enlightened, aggressive management of human resources by all nurse managers. The largest budgetary expenditure in hospitals is labor costs, yet many managers have failed to find the best way to motivate nurses and improve productivity without increasing frustration and stress in nurses. Problems in people management insidiously undermine efforts to improve productivity in a cost-effective manner.

Nearly any hospital has similar problems—complaints of understaffing, resentment of the rigidity and lack of effectiveness in some supervisors, intershift strife, peer conflicts, problems in floating, anger over physician-nurse relationships, difficulty in controlling absenteeism, stress related to job insecurity—and the list goes on. It is time to tackle these problems since their resolution is pivotal to improving productivity. Troubled employees do not work up to their capacity.

THE NEW MANAGEMENT AGE

Important changes begin with examining the role of the nurse managers, since they need to be proficient in what they do before they can ask their staff members to make changes. Managers used to accomplish their jobs by issuing orders, or even using their line power, to motivate nurses. However, there is now a generation of new thinking that makes this approach outdated and antithetical to productivity.

Nurse managers interested in reading more about the new age of management can look to such books as *Leadership and Empowerment* by Warren Bennis,[1] *Theory Z* by William Ouchi,[2] *The New Achievers* by Perry Pascarella,[3] *Corporate Cultures* by Terrance Deal and Allan Kennedy,[4] *Re-inventing the Corporation* by John Naisbitt and Patricia Aburdene,[5] and *The Change Masters* by Rosabeth Moss Kanter.[6]

In these books, nurse managers will find that employee participation has replaced intimidation and that human values are being emphasized over purely technical skills. Satisfied nurses who sense they are valued by the hospital feel more committed to improved productivity goals. Many nurses now remain in the work force for most of their working years. The strategies that worked when they worked for only a few years no longer are effective. People (specifically including nurses) refuse to tolerate unreasonable demands, inequities, and excessive stress for their entire careers.

Cooperating vs. Bossing

Management, instead of being synonymous with bossing, has become a role of serving, mentoring, coaching, and guiding employees while they grow and excel at doing their life's work, as opposed to merely punching the time clock. The focus is on a participatory style that emphasizes the desire to share power and a switch from controlling people to encouraging their creativity. These qualities underlie grass-roots efforts to encourage productivity and economical work patterns.

The new-age manager knows that the people actually doing the job are the best ones to make decisions about their work. Thus, there needs to be a flattening of the hierarchy to place decision making as close to the point of action as possible. Other industries are finding large middle management groups ineffective and are eliminating as many such layers as possible, with the net result that employees seem more satisfied with their jobs.

Some hospitals have followed this trend by not replacing some managers who leave. This has given more decision making power to professional nurses. They tend to adapt to needed change most readily and improve work output best when they contribute to the plan of action, since that process gives them a sense of ownership in its success.

Nursing is decentralizing rapidly so that specialty areas become organized into profit centers with adequate power to operate effectively and productively. However, many hospitals have a distance to go in augmenting staff nurse efforts rather than hindering them. Because many layers of managers and specialized nurses still stand between timely decisions and their implementation, further work is needed to reduce frustration in nurses who have good ideas that deserve quick implementation. Nursing executives should evaluate their organizations to determine whether they are top-heavy.

Because a promotion into management has been accompanied by increased status in most business settings, managers are readily visible by their status symbols. However, many companies are doing away with such status symbols since they seem to serve only to keep barriers between workers and managers. In nursing, status and rewards traditionally have been assigned to those who leave direct patient care to become managers or educators. If giving superior, cost-effective care is what the profession values, then status needs to be returned to the caregivers. However, problems in making nursing into a profession that is accepted and respected by others have resulted in continued emphasis on external status symbols that cause their holders to feel more acceptable. Infighting within the profession about who holds status also has aggravated the gaps among staff members, management, and educators. Such wasted emotional efforts dilute the productivity of the entire profession.

The Changing Role

The new management era represents a radical departure from former years. Because of the influence of Frederick Taylor, the father of scientific management, managers through the 1950s used a rational model to solve problems—the brains behind the brawn.[7] By the 1970s, they were heroes who set objectives, monitored performance, made sure that work was done, and put out brush fires when problems occurred. However, intense competition and changes in workers' values have made these approaches obsolete.

The order of the late 1980s is to give professional nurses what they want from the job in addition to a paycheck. That something is a sense of responsibility, autonomy, recognition, and opportunity for achieving the goals of quality patient care, improved productivity, and cost containment. The pride and satisfaction that ensues results in their creating more efficient ways to do the job as they work more harmoniously with peers and patients. That combination is vital to enhancing productivity, meeting the cost-reduction demands of third party payers, and making patients happy with their choice of hospital.

A big part of making staff nurses a part of the team is to share vital information with them. For example, when managers say that costs need to be cut to make a profit on abdominal hysterectomies, workers need to know what is meant. It means improving productivity by sharing the average cost per case, the cost for materials, and the profit margin, so they can help replace unneeded expenditures with better resource utilization. Hospitals have been slow to provide staff nurses with the information they need to become committed to improving productivity and containing costs. However, until such efforts become an automatic part of everything nurses do, many opportunities for reaching these goals through small steps will be lost.

Employees need formal and informal programs to give them the personal and professional skills to improve their lives and assist them in working smarter, not harder. Such programs can be directly job related or may be those that generally enhance the quality of life. Institutions are finding that committed, positive, healthy employees are the most important resources in ensuring success and improved productivity within the entire hospital.

While this realization makes sense, some managers still resist these new notions as threats to their traditional power and control. Nursing is losing time while its managers learn to change the ways they think. The success of this endeavor will be reflected directly in the productivity and profitability of the nursing division. Where management refuses to satisfy the needs of employees and help them understand their important role in the hospital business, unions may intervene. Such intervention not only increases hospitals' resource expenditures but also limits what management is free to do.

UNIONIZATION IN HEALTH CARE

Update on Health Care Efforts

Where workers do not feel valued and do not understand their roles in making the business more productive and profitable, they can turn to the union, which listens and recognizes them, at least throughout the organizing campaign. Several unions are targeting health workers in nationally coordinated organizing efforts because they know that industry leaders have not been able to adapt to the rapid changes inherent in the health care revolution in such a way that workers feel positive about their jobs and the quality of care that they deliver and feel rewarded for achieving desired productivity and cost containment goals.

For example, the AFL-CIO opened an office called Comprehensive Organizing Strategies and Tactics (COST) in the summer of 1986 to seek out these kinds of Achilles' heels in various organizations as a basis for nationally coordinated drives to organize target corporations. The first target was Blue Cross/Blue Shield, where five unions affiliated with the AFL-CIO have targeted the 28,000 nonunion employees eligible for union membership; some 9,000 others already are represented by a union.[8]

The prototype for this action was the success of the Service Employees International Union (SEIU) in organizing Beverly Enterprises Inc. By February 1984, the union had won 23 of 37 elections in the chain and by June 21, 1985, the number of facilities organized had climbed dramatically to 78.[9,10]

As of mid-1986, only 15 percent of the six million employees in health care were organized, in comparison with 17.5 percent of the nation's total labor force. However, Labor Department projections indicate that the health care field will have about three million additional jobs by 1995. The untapped potential in this vast pool of health care workers is attractive to unions as they continue to lose members in the traditional smokestack industries.

In the past, health care workers resisted union organizing, either because of their professional status or their fear of job losses in lesser skilled categories. However, the advent of governmental cost containment and similar programs by other third party payers resulted in layoffs by a number of institutions as hospitals suddenly pushed to be "businesslike."

Many nursing staffs felt that working harder only caused administration to make further staffing cuts and to continue to ignore their needs and concerns about delivering quality patient care. The resulting confusion about changes in hospitals and the subsequent angry feelings and low morale (and lower productivity) made nursing staffs vulnerable to unions.

It is this vicious cycle that hospitals must counter to ensure increased productivity and adequate employee recognition. Administrative recognition can involve a diverse program of creative awards when employees contain costs and work more productively. Ideas for rewarding employees could include recognition in the hospital newspaper, a week of free lunches for accomplishing something unusual, the right for outstanding ones to have first choice in the time schedule for the next month, "nurse of the week" buttons, specific verbal recognition for outstanding effort, or other means that staff members themselves may put forward. When hospitals lack recognition efforts, nurses can feel frustrated and unimportant.

Unions such as the National Union of Hospital and Health Care Employees, the American Federation of Teachers, the SEIU, the United Food and Commercial Workers Union, and others report a sharp increase in dialogue with health care workers.

Organizing Techniques

While diagnosis related groups (DRGs) can be blamed for some of this increase, the other major factor responsible is the growing sophistication in union organizing techniques. At Beverly, these included the use of a toll-free hotline, widespread leaflet distribution to targeted facilities, reports and shareholder resolutions claiming deficiencies in patient care, and the circulation of a newsletter to health care regulators identifying problems in the industry. Unions are beginning to rely on professional pollsters to ascertain worker concerns. Once those are known, specific organizing strategies can be designed to appeal to the employees.

Nurse managers should ask themselves: "When was the last time that we *really* listened to nurse questions and concerns?" Their first step in improving productivity is to get the commitment and trust of their employees by discussing problems and making the nurses a part of the solution.

The virtues of being organized by the International Brotherhood of Teamsters are espoused in a professionally produced videotape in which nurses at St. Luke's Hospital in Newburgh, N.Y., discuss the positive features of their contract. However, the tape conveniently omits the 38-day strike required to gain the contract.

Union activity has extended to include political activity to block health care organizations' financing efforts. For example, an issue of $15.5 million in industrial revenue bonds was unsuccessful because a coalition of labor and religious groups protested that Beverly spent less than the industry average on patient care.   The Beverly chain in rebuttal declared that these union efforts, plus propaganda and wide publicity, had distorted what the union had gained or failed to accomplish, especially in contract negotiations. Citing what it describes as its creative approach, the National Union of Hospital and Health Care Employees (NUHHCE), also known as "Old 1199," claims a 70 percent win rate in organizing elections.

Organizing drives now begin with low-key contacts in coffee shops and through meetings with interested persons until sufficient momentum develops. Unions continuously grade employees' sentiments so that organizing efforts can be focused more effectively. Workers then are coached in the typical comments and tactics they might expect from management consultants and attorneys. The head of steam is built quietly to avoid management awareness and efforts to squelch early efforts.

Union organizers read management and professional journals and conduct a variety of seminars and parties to accomplish their end. Their aim is to dispel the "gangster" stereotypes sometimes applied to unions. They also have attacked management consultants who work to thwart their efforts.[11]

However, nurse managers can effectively explain issues to staff and counter union efforts during an organizing campaign by showing the videotape "Working without Unions: The Healthcare Story." For more information write Health Employment Law Update, Box 15250, Evansville, Ind. 47716–0250.

In its 1986 convention, the AFL-CIO designated younger and more educated persons as desirable targets for unionization. To accomplish this goal, it established an "associate" membership category. These associate members would be drawn from those losing jobs from downsizing, leaving union jobs, and union supporters in unsuccessful organizing campaigns. While these associate members could not be fully represented by the union, they would get reductions in home, health, and auto insurance and a fee-free charge card.

The American Federation of Teachers gained 1,000 members in Texas over a two-month period with a similar effort in which participants joined a "Professional Educator's Group" for an annual fee of $50 for group insurance benefits, a Visa card, and magazine subscription discounts. This associate member approach is designed to give individuals favorable feelings about the union so they will want full membership.[12]

The Ohio Campaign

In Ohio, Old 1199 waged a 21-month campaign at a cost of $2 million to represent 9,000 state hospital employees. As a result of this election, the president of the AFL-CIO imposed a sanction on the NUHHCE because it was raiding a fellow AFL-CIO union—trying to represent persons already in the American Federation of State, County, and Municipal Employees (AFSCME). NUHHCE ignored the sanction and won its election, beating both AFSCME and the Ohio Nurses' Association.[13]

Physician Unionizing

On June 11, 1985, in a letter to 17,000 Massachusetts physicians, Dr. John T. Larossa, president of a union titled Physicians and Surgeons Association of Massachusetts (PSAM), cited the state as "the most repressive in the nation for physicians." Massachusetts was one of four states involved in a statewide special hospital cost-containment program. More than a year later, only a few hundred physicians had paid the $400 annual dues and joined the union, but similar efforts were occurring in a number of other states.[14] This union sought to assist members in regaining more control of their practice and restoring the traditional doctor-patient relationship.

Since cost-containment efforts have revolutionized health care through such measures as preadmission standards, concurrent reviews, outpatient surgical emphasis, health care agency constraints, and new provider options, doctors have lost ground in policy planning. Some feel that profits have taken precedence over quality care and that physicians sometimes are denied the right to define services and tests as being necessary. Larossa proposes to represent physicians as they work to identify issues related to their practice and cost containment with third party payers, governmental agencies, hospitals, health maintenance organizations (HMOs), and lobbyists.

In Connecticut, a union known as the Connecticut Federation of Physicians and Dentists (CFPD) began with 80 members paying $360 in annual dues. According to its president, the union was attempting to give physicians the power to deal with insurance companies and medical organizations through collective pressure.[15] An article in *American Medical News,* October 18, 1985, further underscores this issue, as it explains the action of the Health Care Financing Administration's Health Standards and Quality Bureau in linking physician Medicare payments with hospital Medicare payments. This policy states that physicians will be denied payment for services associated with a hospital stay that the Peer Review Organization later deems unnecessary. If physicians have been paid for such services, they will be required to reimburse Medicare after the fact.

In another example of increasing physician unionization, a strike highlighted current issues.[16] Spurred by a quality-of-care issue, physicians covered by a union contract that expired on March 1, 1986, engaged in a 24-day strike at Group Health Association (GHA), the largest HMO in Washington, D.C. The controversy was sparked when GHA told its 168 physicians that they would have to see more patients in less time. This proposal would mean that physicians would spend a guaranteed minimum of 20 to 35 hours per week, depending on their specialty, in

GHA office visits. Physicians in this instance viewed the increase in patient visits as encouraging assembly-line medicine and struck.

The vote to end the strike occurred when members of the Capital Alliance of Physicians (CAP) approved an agreement by a vote of 80 to 19. The resulting contract included provisions about tying the incentive system to productivity, increasing some salaries and benefits, and possibly disciplining physicians who did not live up to the prestrike agreement.

The contract underscored the fact that these physicians are employees like any other health care workers; their major concerns were with setting standards for performance and tying incentive rewards to meeting these standards.

How does this affect nurse productivity and cost containment in hospitals? Some experts believe that there has never been a better time for nurses to gain a strong collaborative relationship with physicians to maintain control of patient care. That can advance the drive to contain costs and improve productivity, while ensuring quality of patient care.

How? Since physician orders directly determine the nursing workload, cooperation can result in frugality in physicians' orders, with subsequent noticeable reductions in the nursing workload, so that important care and teaching may be better accomplished. Moreover, such collaboration can ensure nurses of getting the orders they need to do the best job.

For example, some physicians send in the same typed list of routine orders for each admitted patient, regardless of diagnosis. Some of these orders consume a great deal of nursing time without being truly essential to the patient's condition or care. These routine admission lists need to be replaced with orders tailored to the needs of each patient.[17]

Reduced Staffing Levels

Unions are capitalizing on the issue of reduced staff levels in hospitals. Unions are telling nurses that the quality of patient care is suffering from reduced staffing. Nurses nationally claim most of their problems are the result of inadequate staffing until discussion of specific situations reveals that problems in this health care revolution stem not from one but from a variety of causes.

For example, in one intensive care unit a nurse was crying after a particularly frustrating day in which she had not been able to provide quality patient care because of interruptions from assisting physicians with numerous unplanned diagnostic procedures. At the same time, two other nurses on the unit had enjoyed a long lunch, two coffee breaks, and a relatively easy day. The problem was not short staffing but instead the lack of commitment by staff members to assist each other when one nurse finished a task early. They did not subscribe to the notion that "no one is done until everyone is finished." By examining this problem, the staff members were better able to complete their work satisfactorily without increasing personnel. This issue, along with economics and job security, is a major emphasis of unions in luring nurses to become unionized.

In addition to tuning in to staff, fostering true problem solving, allowing implementation of creative ideas, and facilitating wise time and resource utilization, hospitals may want to consider broader approaches such as that used in Minneapolis when declining census and efforts to reduce staffing resulted in a major nurse crisis. Roger Columbo, vice president of human resources at United Hospitals there, used the following approaches to restore a harmonious working relationship.

United Hospitals have a voluntary early retirement program that allows employees whose years of service plus age total 80 to retire early with six months' severance pay and continued health coverage until age 62. This move alone saved the hospitals $900,000 in five years. Other suggestions included:

- Voluntary phased retirement: The option of easing into retirement by working fewer hours
- Alternate work scheduling: Incentives to allow employees to work fewer hours with scheduling adjustments for school or child rearing, while maintaining health insurance
- Staff reductions with retraining: Laid-off employees remain on the payroll, receive the equivalent of unemployment compensation insurance, and undergo retraining to enable them to return in a new job.

A combination of regular employee opinion surveys and cafeteria-style benefits aid employees in being more self-directed and having more voice in hospital decisions. Three employee-management committees are in place to tackle such problems as absenteeism, budget cuts, staff scheduling, and cross-training. These committees are regarded seriously, with top management people on each one. According to Columbo, if nurses achieve quality of working life and employment security, they can better achieve quality patient care, improved productivity, and efficiency in patient care delivery.[18]

BARGAINING ISSUES IN HEALTH CARE

To avoid the problems inherent in being organized by a union, some health care managers are reviewing contract negotiations at other hospitals to ascertain bargaining issues. They then can implement similar policies to better support employees and avoid the need for them to organize. In addition to implementing such policies, managers must keep employees informed of why changes are occurring and how the hospital is working to build a strong business that optimizes the welfare of each employee and acknowledges their importance to the total effort. Otherwise, they may look to outside organizers to achieve these goals.

The following list highlights some of the key issues that hospitals need to address to be in touch with employee needs and concerns:

Caseload Distribution

The hospital is considering the equity of the caseload distribution because categories other than the registered nurses are being affected by layoffs, resulting in increased housekeeping, clerical, and transport duties for R.N.s. A part of assessing the registered nurses' workload is to evaluate and modify the duties of assisting personnel to better provide patient care.

On many units, nursing assistants usually are finished when they complete the baths and meals while the R.N.s continue to work feverishly throughout the entire shift. What tasks can be given to these aides to ease the R.N. workload? Should their work hours be modified to better cover the peaks in personal care, meals, and various errands?

Moreover, while patient classification systems address the need for staffing based on illness and service needs, they may not always deal with individuals' differences in care even when similar procedures are performed. Sensitivity is required to modify staffing to cover the needs of special patients whose needs exceed the norm.

Staffing Levels and Acuity

Hospitals are attempting to inform institutional regulators about appropriate staffing levels related to the intensity of illness. Some professionals believe regulatory agencies have unrealistic notions as to staffing requirements. When these changes are made, surveys can be equated more realistically with patient care demands. Moreover, as staffing is linked to the acuity level rather than the numerical census, the distribution of staff members and the appropriate skill mix can be achieved.

Job Security and Seniority

Job security and seniority are commanding a priority in contract negotiations. Unions prefer hospitalwide cutbacks rather than area cutbacks related to the closing of certain units and services. Unions also are pushing hospitals to formulate layoff and recall policies by seniority. This demand is undesirable.

For example, in one hospital three medical units closed while critical care units functioned at peak capacity. In selecting staff for cutbacks, this hospital needed to retain critical care nurses while laying off and/or retraining general nurses.

When voluntary cutbacks achieve institutional goals, unions are asking employers to grant nurses the privilege to reduce hours on the basis of seniority. Many hospitals have weathered the rapid shifts in census by working with all-volunteer staffs on a flexible basis. The retention of this flexibility is important. Unions are also striving to establish formulas in which severance pay is calculated by including years of service.

Reasons for Layoffs

Some contracts include explicit language on reasons for layoffs. Unions want to limit them to situations in which the actual workload is decreased, rather than to all circumstances, including financial problems, in the institution.

In one case the strong language required United Medical Center in Newark to notify the New Jersey State Nurses' Association of layoff plans 20 days before the layoff, state the reasons, and submit the necessity, validity, procedure, and persons involved to arbitration. As a result the medical center did not implement its layoff plans. Management rights were hampered severely in this situation.

Unions also are attempting to specify language that limits increases in the workload for the remaining employees. Such contract language is undesirable. Hospitals are businesses and must retain the right to modify their work forces in relation to whatever problems arise—budgetary or reduced census. Such management flexibility is essential to hospitals' survival.

Layoffs and Subcontracting

Strong clauses are being written to prevent the employer from laying off bargaining unit members and giving their work to subcontractors or nonbargaining unit employees. This clause is of more concern to aides and licensed practical nurses than to R.N.s. Again, hospitals need to retain this right to meet their business needs in the most productive and cost-effective manner.

Continuation of Benefits

Another area of intense bargaining is over the continuation of benefits for employees during the first few months of their layoff. Paying for these benefits is more feasible if the hospital is a part of a large consortium of institutions that pools resources to get price breaks on shared services. However, specific new nonnegotiable requirements on health insurance plans extend to all employees as a result of the Consolidated Omnibus Budget Reconciliation Act of 1986 (COBRA) (PL 99-272).

Float Nurses

Still other attempts are centered on floating nurses from a regular work station to a unit in greater need when they have not had appropriate training. This issue must be confronted directly. Since shifting census will require floating, both the hospital and individual nurses must create a program in which their specific training needs are cited and met. Such a program needs to be implemented now, so that the problem of floating is defused.

For example, the head nurse on each unit can construct a list of the 25 drugs given most often. This list can be given to all potential floats so that they may study the drugs before actually administering them. The head nurse also can write a skills checklist that emphasizes specialty procedures the potential float nurse may use to identify and correct skill deficiencies.

Part-Timers and Split Shifts

Unions are trying to negotiate ways that cutbacks are managed. For example, they seek contract language giving them more control over such measures as the use of part-timers, split shifts, low-census days without pay, and reduced work hours. Allowing union control in this area would be devastating. It is the creative use and flexibility of staffing patterns that allows nursing divisions and units to meet personnel needs in the most cost-effective, productive manner.

Education and Inservice Training

Union bargaining agents have added continuing education and inservice education demands to aid employees in staying current with technological changes. They are trying to get hospitals to provide specific training so that union members can qualify for job openings. Continuing education needs and programs are a high priority with most staffs that many hospitals are working to meet. Union help is not needed.

Lump-Sum Bonuses

Because of the uncertainty of the future, unions are negotiating lump-sum bonuses for members that do not affect annual salary increases. Many hospitals are likely to follow this pattern of providing such bonuses in good years to employees since it does not lock in long-term wage increases. Moreover, when employees know that they will share profits, they are more motivated to work productively and to exert peer pressure on others to do the same.

In related efforts, unions are working aggressively to educate their negotiators about the health care revolution so they can bargain more knowledgeably. Hospitals are expected to try to save money by using more part-timers, by reducing benefits, and by lowering starting wages. However, there are problems with morale and discontinuity of communications and care that must be considered with these cost-cutting measures. When reducing benefits and using part-timers, hospitals must weigh short-term advantages against long-term costs.

For example, on one unit the presence of part-timers was welcome until their numbers grew excessively. At that point several full-time nurses were lost because they no longer could handle the stress of doing their job and continually guiding and supervising the work of part-timers who were not familiar with patient care routines and treatments.

Hospitals are trying to reduce employee benefits by shortening the length of the full-time work week, by using cafeteria-style benefits (a method of allowing employees to select individual packages of benefits within a defined dollar amount), and by increasing deductibles on health insurance, especially when employees elect to use another health care facility than their place of employment in nonemergency situations.

Union-free employers should work to establish equitable, timely personnel policies so their employees remain satisfied without seeking union representation. While employers may wish to avoid seniority priorities, it is wise to construct policies that are widely supported by employees. In establishing equitable layoff and recall policies, it is important to realize that this also can avoid age discrimination lawsuits.

Because unions are trying to limit layoffs to situations caused by declining census, employers will want to remain union free. A number of other problems can cause financial difficulty in a hospital that may necessitate a layoff. The problem of what happens to the remaining employees' workload is one that has to be resolved to the satisfaction of all.

For example, in one small rural hospital threatened by bankruptcy, the administrators took their case to the employees, who worked to change job patterns and resource consumption. The resulting improved productivity and lower costs saved the hospital.[19]

WAGE GUIDELINES

In the past, unions counted on their ability to win large wage increases as a means of luring new members. However, this advantage has all but been erased by court decisions in this decade.

The Washington State Nurses' Association (WSNA) sought an injunction against the Washington State Hospital Commission for its rate-setting practices on the grounds that such activities interfered with state and federally protected rights to bargain for wage increases. The U.S. District Court for Western Washington found the Commission "indirectly, but purposely controlled the amount by which salaries for registered nurses . . . could be increased" and that such practices were an infringement upon federal collective bargaining rights. The Court of Appeals for the Ninth Circuit in San Francisco reversed that decision, holding that the Commission's administration of the health care cost-containment law did not infringe upon WSNA bargaining rights. (*Washington State Nurses' Association v. Washington State Hospital Commission,* No. C83-533T (W.D. Wash. July 27, 1984), 773 F.2d 1044 (9th Cir. 1985))

The appellate court ruled that the activities of the Commission were similar to those cited in *Massachusetts Nurses Association v. Dukakis,* 726 F.2d 41 (1st Cir. 1984). It said the Commission is authorized to "set the 'types and classes of charges' for hospitals and to review hospitals' financial records in order to establish the maximum rates each hospital can charge patients. . . . Federal labor policy does not preempt a state statute which regulates hospital costs by imposing an overall limit on what hospitals can collect for patient care" when there is no interference with labor-management issues.

The Commission guidelines measure total salaries and wages as one cost category. When it "disapproves" a wage increase, the Commission cannot prevent the hospital from granting increases; its only control is what hospitals can receive from rates. Thus, increases in one area mean only that hospitals must find additional revenue from other sources or cut costs in another part of the budget. Thus, the Court found that "the Commission's policies and statements were aimed principally at encouraging the reduction of overall wages as well as other costs" that "did not prevent or significantly inhibit the exercise of collective bargaining rights protected by the (National Labor Relations Act) NLRA."

While the lack of money for salary increases has discouraged some union organizers, it also has frustrated nonunion hospitals that want to reward their staffs. In one community hospital, administrators squeezed by cost-containment mandates did not have money to reward productive employees for their efforts. To retain a quality staff, the board and staff took their case to the community by holding a holiday Festival of Trees benefit, a four-day extravaganza with decorated Christmas trees for sale, a holiday ball and auction, boutiques, and constant entertainment for the public who paid admission to view the events. Proceeds were used to reward productive employees, and the event is planned as an annual affair.

On a related issue, in trying to maintain a competitive financial position in collective bargaining, employers need to state their case carefully. Is demanding takebacks and concessions in collective bargaining negotiations equated with "pleading poverty," in which an employer must open its financial records to the union? In the National Labor Relations Board decision of *Washington Materials, Inc.,* 276 NLRB No. 40 (1985), six ready-mix concrete firms maintained, in bargaining with the Teamsters, that they needed takebacks to make them more competitive in the local industry. The NLRB concluded that the concrete companies had no obligation to provide the union with all of their financial records as they did not claim that they could not pay the existing wages but merely said they could not remain competitive at those rates. Therefore, the Board held that the concrete firms did not violate the NLRA by refusing the union's request for their financial records.

The NLRB said it "will not assume that an employer, who no longer wishes to pay wages and benefits it once agreed to, is unable to make such payments." The key here is to avoid saying, "We are unable to afford the union's proposals" or to claim an "inability to pay." Instead, hospitals should state that they want to attain a competitive position in the health care industry; on that basis, the union cannot examine their financial records. The wise execution of this approach can be the difference between survival and extinction in troubled unionized hospitals.

ESTABLISHING A CONTEMPORARY PROGRAM

Discussion of the role of the manager in the union-organizing campaign and outlining a definitive, progressive disciplinary system is beyond the scope of this book. However, managers should realize that equitable and consistent treatment of employees is the cornerstone of building a satisfied, productive staff.

Helpful publications on this issue include the book *Labor Relations in Hospitals*[20] and *Health Employment Law Update*,[21] a monthly newsletter specializing in the needs of hospitals. The book provides an in-depth discussion of labor relations in hospitals, while the newsletter keeps nurse managers abreast of the latest legal cases and trends.

HUMAN RESOURCES MANAGEMENT

Proactive human resources programs are constructed to maintain open communication with employees. A key element in these programs is their approach to handling complaints, absenteeism, and discipline. The objective is to avoid expensive legal action when employees feel wronged as that results in large legal expenses that effectively undo the myriad other cost-cutting measures throughout the hospital.

The Dichotomy: Big Business and Individuals

One of the most perplexing problems in hospitals is the need to manage a wide array of complex issues in the operation of the business while dealing more personally with each employee. While managers increasingly have been forced to contain costs, become more productive, meet changing third party demands, expand the business, and remain competitive, the number of meetings and time away from employees has increased. Simultaneously, employees fearful of job insecurity and demoralized by new demands in the health care system seem to react dramatically to every new rumor.

The resulting low morale causes supervisors to dread unit rounds, where they face confrontation and negative feelings. This vicious cycle represents the brush fire approach to management that must be replaced with a positive preventive method. The goal then becomes the personal handling of employees, with subsequent easing of tensions, so that the leaders are able to move forward with the job of managing the business and nurses are able to become participants in the plan to improve productivity and quality patient care in a cost-effective manner.

One valuable technique for accomplishing this goal is termed "Daily Talks." This consists of brief, daily football-like huddles between top executives and front-line managers in which key problems are brought up. At least once a week, front-line managers are given an issue to discuss with all employees. Once their input is received, managers tally the responses and provide feedback on the results. This participative style allows employees to feel involved in the business and provides them with the opportunity to voice concerns regularly to their managers about other issues. The key to this method is its regularity, which dispels problems and concerns when they first appear. However, the daily talks do not replace participative staff meetings, which require more time and detail.

Daily talks topics can include a change of equipment, ways to avoid overtime, suggestions for the cafeteria menu, and methods to hasten the patient admission process. In one facility, employees were reminded of the emphasis on cost containment, then were asked how vacations could be covered better without additional personnel. Suggestions were tallied and employee feedback was passed on up the line. The resulting vacation policy was well accepted because everyone had a voice in its creation.

For employees who are uncomfortable with expressing ideas, some hospitals have initiated additional feedback mechanisms. One, which should be done yearly, is an employee attitude survey. This gives staff members the opportunity to react to all events and people in the environment. Compilation of the results and comments can provide management with important information for establishing strategic plans for improving productivity and employees' quality of work life.

Another method is the hot line or suggestion box "communigram" in which participants can make comments at any time and remain anonymous if they so choose. The communigram program requires the hospital to place suggestion boxes in convenient places and to post a notice as to their use. This message should explain why the hospital is glad to receive staff members' suggestions, ideas, concerns, and complaints. It then asks employees to provide enough information on the communigram form so managers can understand the situation—a description of the idea or problem, a remedy, and a thought for preventing future problems or improving the current situation. Employees should be thanked for their effort. Employee input in the communigram also is a good source of ideas for daily talks.

In some hospitals, signed, documented ideas that prove beneficial to the business receive an award and recognition in the house organ. As noted earlier, managers should give some thought to rewarding employees with a set percentage of savings for specific plans that result in cost containment. Other hospitals form a committee charged with the responsibility of regularly reviewing and channeling communigram messages to the appropriate person for action. The results are reported back to staff through the house organ, in daily talks, or in unit/center meetings when extensive discussion is needed. Problems and ideas could be fed into a staff group for analysis and action, such as generating a plan for improved productivity.

In establishing a communications group composed of staff members and top management, hospitals are cautioned to be aware of the potential legal liability that can occur in unlawful employer domination or support of a union-like committee in violation of the National Labor Relations Act. Such violations could occur if the committee makes decisions on wages, hours, terms, and conditions of employment. If the committee is not empowered to make such decisions, the hospital has no concern about unlawful employer domination or support problems.[22]

Handling Complaints

In the health care environment of the late 1980s, it is imperative to solve minor complaints before they snowball into major problems and possible union organizing activity. One of employees' main complaints is the need to be heard and to see results when they make complaints or suggestions. They also need to be assured that their complaints will not result in retaliation against them.

What are complaints? A number of in-house surveys of staff members' opinions suggest that they are really employee attempts to seek information or open lines for two-way communication.[23] Workable grievance systems have three major objectives:

1. Getting to the message/feelings underlying the complaint. Managers must have their fingers on the pulse of the organization. If they know what is happening and who makes it happen, they are in a good position to interpret complaints in a realistic perspective.
2. Encouraging employee use of the system. For this to succeed, it must be made credible, responsive, and safe to users. Employees will not use a mechanism that causes them adverse outcomes.
3. Maintaining employee morale. Supervisors must learn the theory of the mouse for an elephant: Sometimes they have to give a mouse to get an elephant in return. Thus, when staff members have legitimate complaints,

supervisors strengthen their own positions and develop employee trust by acknowledging the problems and working to set things straight. They must not let little complaints mount over the weeks, months, and years until they blow the lid off the pressure cooker.

Most employers have formal grievance procedures but may need to improve their open-door policies. That way, they should be able to get beneath the surface to the real demands of personal and financial well-being, confidence in management, and the need for fair, equal treatment.

To make the open-door policy work, administration and managers must:

- Advertise it so that employees know it is available.
- Make time available for drop-in complainers or set a meeting within one day of a request for one.
- Get all the facts before acting.
- Keep the employee posted even when managers cannot act or decide not to comply with the request.
- Give all employees some kind of appropriate feedback about what was done on their complaints. If action is pending, or it is decided not to act on a suggestion, the employee must be told that rather than receiving no feedback.

Ten major points make the difference in how an open-door policy will work. Managers should:

1. Phrase responses in terms of the facts rather than blaming individuals.
2. Phrase responses to avoid emotionally charged words; avoid rubbing on sore points.
3. Admit mistakes; be big enough to say, "I goofed" if that is the fact.
4. Do not expect many initial complainers until the first pioneers test the waters.
5. Take all complaints seriously; even if a complaint seems trivial, it is important to the employee voicing the concern.
6. Do not make the employee justify the complaint; instead, demonstrate to the individual an interest in allowing the problem to be aired and in working toward its resolution.
7. Listen for the real or imagined problem; the actual complaint may not be what bothers the employee most—it may be how something was done, rather than what actually was done.
8. Apologize sincerely when it is appropriate.
9. Say so if it is not possible to solve a problem without more information or authority.

10. Remember that the one or two complaints that come in may be only the tip of the iceberg.[24]

Absenteeism Revisited

When employees become stressed or frustrated because they do not feel that management is tuned in to their needs, they tend to work less productively and take more time away from the job. Absenteeism must be controlled if a hospital is to achieve true productivity and cost containment. Sometimes that can mean that employees who have excessive absenteeism need to be counseled and, if the pattern does not improve, discharged. Staff members resent working hard to cover the job of an employee whose attendance is unreliable.

However, discharged workers may sue, alleging that they were wrongfully discharged. In one case, managers scored a victory in the battle to clear their work force of dead wood. In *Eblin v. Whirlpool Corporation,* 36 EDP 91 34, 978 (DC Ohio, 1985), a federal judge held that the discharge of a woman for excessive absenteeism did not constitute unlawful sex discrimination, even though the absenteeism related in part to pregnancy and maternity. The judge made some perceptive findings in favor of employers in stating:

> The evidence in this case leaves no doubt that the plaintiff was not a reliable employee. Her supervisor could not count on her to come to work every day and perform the tasks for which she was employed. The reasons for her nonattendance were immaterial. *Excuses do not keep an assembly line running.*
>
> This case is *unfortunately rather typical of what is found in too many actions charging employment discrimination. The plaintiffs fail to face the reality of their own lack of ability to do the work for which they were employed, or to conform to the employer's rules.* When, ultimately, the patience of the employer is exhausted and the plaintiff is discharged, it must be because of the employer's prejudice against the employee's race, sex, religion, nationality or some other personal character that has nothing to do with performance. (Emphasis added)

Controlling absenteeism is a continuing concern. Many hospitals have looked to the policies of other industries to find a solution. Pareto's principle applies here: 20 percent of the people take 80 percent of the absent time. This undermines morale. Thus, it is imperative that employers firmly and consistently handle this problem that results in an enormous number of nonproductive days annually.

Several suggestions seem noteworthy. Rewarding those with good attendance can be one solution, although system abusers may feel that they benefit more by taking all of their sick days than by receiving small rewards. Moreover, it usually is the faithful employees who get the rewards anyway, and some hospitals have noted an increase in the absenteeism rate when the program ends.

There is the "Rutkowski method," in which managers have extensive personal contact with employees, including a personal interview on the day they return from sick leave. Through this immediate follow-up, employee assistance or counseling can be initiated before the trend gets out of hand.

Many facilities are adopting a policy for premium times, such as Saturdays, so that employees missing their scheduled weekend day must sacrifice a like normally scheduled day off. Other hospitals are adopting a policy in which more than three absences over a six-month period—regardless of the reason or length of illness—starts the employee through the progressive discipline course. Still another policy is not to pay employees for sick time until they miss three consecutive days. General Motors has initiated a policy under which it reduces benefits for employees who exceed a certain percentage of paid sick days.

Since no one method has proved fully successful, nurse managers may decide to implement a general policy but to feature occasional incentive programs to remind employees about the importance of nonproductive days to the financial health of the hospital. Factual reports of what nonproductive days actually cost each employee can be an important part of manager/worker unit meetings to reinforce the judicious use of sick time.

Regardless of the approach taken, the hospital must carefully apply the same standard to all employees. Legal cases arising from uneven application of any policy involve the evaluation of past practices with others in relation to what is being, or was, done to the employee in question. Additional problems may arise if actual policy deviates from that written in the policy book.

Avoiding Wrongful Discharge

When nursing executives find it necessary to discharge an employee, it is important to do so in a manner that minimizes their legal liability. Losing a discharge case can be expensive and can offset a lot of hard work in other hospital programs to achieve cost containment and improved productivity. To reduce the likelihood of a lawsuit, managers should award all of the accrued vacation pay, benefits, and wages to the individual during the discharge process.

Other procedural matters are important since the manner in which discharges are handled affects the security and morale of remaining hospital employees. It is important to consider whether the discharge involves an employee's right that is protected by public policy. As noted earlier, the discharge process should be applied evenly to all employees for a sound business reason. In short, managers need:

- a legitimate business reason for discharge
- evidence that stated policies were followed
- consistency and objectivity in documentation of all steps taken, including preliminary verbal warnings
- reasonable handling of the situation—thorough investigation of all facts, tact with the employee, and discussion of the situation with other executives on a need-to-know basis
- assurance that the action is consistent with hospital policies and stated or implied promises. For example, if applicants are told "This will be your office," they might assume that they have the job.

To determine whether there is a legitimate business reason for the discharge, managers should ask themselves: "Would I feel comfortable stating my reason for discharge in an open hearing before a jury and/or a judge?" The checklist in Exhibit 15–1 is a guide to be sure that a discharge case has been considered in

Exhibit 15–1 Test on Firing an At-Will Employee

The checklist that follows may be used to determine whether the discharge of an at-will hospital employee would be lawful. It applies to the discharge of both nonunion and union employees. A key to the answers appears at the end of the checklist.

1. Will the employee be discharged for any of the following reasons?

   (a) race
   (b) religion
   (c) sex
   (d) age (over 40)

   (e) national origin
   (f) children or childbirth
   (g) pregnancy
   (h) handicap

2. Will the employee be discharged for acting in concert with other employees to:

   (a) organize collectively?
   (b) push for a raise or shorter hours?
   (c) ask for changes in other working conditions?
   (d) support another employee in his/her protesting?

3. Will the discharge violate any type of contract?

   (a) Does the hospital's employee handbook provide that warnings must be given before an employee may be discharged or that an employee may be discharged only "for cause"?
   (b) Does the hospital have written employee policies that promise "fair treatment"?
   (c) Is there a written, signed employment contract?

4. Will the discharge constitute a tort?

   (a) Has the hospital committed the tort of *outrage* by being abusive during the discharge through either high-handed interrogation methods or flagrant misrepresentations to the employee as to the reason for discharge?
   (b) Has the hospital been *negligent* by failing to follow its own policies, which failure resulted in the employee's discharge?

Exhibit 15–1 continued

5. Will the employee be discharged for any of the following acts or omissions?
   (a) refusing to do an illegal act
   (b) filing a Worker's Compensation claim
   (c) reporting violations of EEO, OSHA, or ERISA regulations
   (d) "whistle-blowing" on the hospital's possible violations of laws

6. Will the employee be discharged for refusing to do a job he or she considers unsafe (giving rise to a possible OSHA violation)?
   (a) Would doing the job *reasonably* place the employee in imminent danger?
   (b) Has the job been performed safely numerous times in the past? If so, why does the employee now consider it unsafe? Has there been an accident on the job shortly before the refusal, so that the employee has reason for concern?

7. Will the hospital deny a hearing (with witnesses present) to provide the employee an opportunity to admit or deny the reasons for discharge?

8. Has the hospital failed to give the employee an oral or written warning to correct the conduct?

9. Has the hospital let other employees get away with what the employee is to be discharged for?

10. Did the hospital promise the employee, at the time of hire or subsequently, that "the job will be yours for as long as you want it"? Was the employee promised an "annual salary"?

11. Will the employee be discharged for a physical condition (for example, high blood pressure, diabetes, or a back condition) in violation of a state statute prohibiting discrimination on the basis of handicap? Has the hospital tried to make reasonable accommodations for the employee to work at some other, less strenuous job?

12. Is there no written evidence (for example, prior reprimands) of the conduct leading to the employee's discharge?

13. Did the employee give up a job and/or home in another city to work at the hospital? Were promises made to induce the employee to do so?

14. Will the hospital call the discharge one motivated by a need for reduction in force when in fact the reason is unsatisfactory work performance?

15. If the hospital plans to hold an investigatory interview prior to the discharge, will the employee be denied a union or coworker representative, despite his or her request?

Key: Each of these questions states the facts of a state or federal case litigating an employer's right to discharge an at-will employee. In each case, the employer answered "yes"—and lost. Still, the answer to any particular question does not necessarily determine whether the discharge contemplated would be lawful. It is the *process* of asking and answering these questions—with the help of counsel—that can alert a hospital to potential liability and thereby help to avoid liability.—*Arthur D. Rutkowski, J.D., partner, Bowers, Harrison, Kent & Miller, Evansville, Ind. Copyright 1984 by Arthur D. Rutkowski. All rights reserved.*

relation to its legal ramifications. When nursing executives are uncertain of their position on a point, it is wise to obtain such knowledge before the discharge so that legal liability can be minimized.[25]

When managers are preparing internal memos and notes on employees likely to be involved in a wrongful discharge suit or a sex, race, or age discrimination suit, the following heading on the top of all memos is recommended:

PRIVILEGED AND CONFIDENTIAL: PREPARED UPON ADVICE OF COUNSEL IN ANTICIPATION OF LITIGATION

In a subsequent lawsuit, such memos provide some protection from discovery by the opposing party.

Because testifying properly in a deposition, hearing, or courtroom often is vital to the hospital's winning the case, Exhibit 15–2 provides some guidelines that can be helpful.

SUMMARY

The well-organized human resources program is viewed as being fair and consistent by employees and is organized to minimize legal costs. This defensive posture is necessary to contain costs in the competitive health care environment.

Exhibit 15–2 Guidelines for Testifying at an EEOC Investigation, Court, or Arbitration Hearing, or in a Deposition

The following list is assistive in the preparation of witnesses who are deposed or are testifying at a hearing in behalf of the employer.

1. Tell the truth at all times.

2. Do not *volunteer* any information. Answer each question and then *stop*. Even if opposing counsel just waits, silently, inviting you to continue, DON'T.

3. Do not answer a question until you understand it. If the question is unclear, ask the examining counsel to repeat it or phrase it in clearer language. You can have questions read back to you for further clarification.

4. If you do not know the answer to a question, say, *"I don't know."* Do not feel that just because a question is asked, you are expected to know the answer. Avoid guessing. The law requires only that you testify according to your best memory.

5. Think about each question before answering it. However, avoid long pauses, if possible. Do not supply information not requested by the question, even though *you* may think that it is relevant.

6. Give factual information in answer to a question only if you have first hand—*not hearsay*—knowledge of the facts. Don't base your answer on "hearsay" information; that is, something that someone else said to you.

Exhibit 15–2 continued

7. Do not try to memorize your answers. Give factual straightforward responses to questions.

8. Avoid arguing, hedging, and editorializing with opposing counsel. For example, do not tell the opposing counsel, "You are trying to trap me," or "I know why you asked me that question." Do not make statements about conclusions, opinions, or secondhand information, unless your attorney has instructed you to do so.

9. Do not try to *hide* any facts, such as previous incidents about which you are specifically asked, unless you are instructed by your attorney not to answer the question.

10. If an *objection* is made *by your counsel,* immediately stop speaking. If instructed not to answer further, follow directions.

11. Unless your attorney makes an objection, you must assume that you are bound to answer the question, if you know the answer.

12. Do not look for *traps*. If any trick questions come along, your attorney will help you out by objection or other means. In trying to second-guess questions, you create the appearance of calculation, hesitation, apprehension, or possible ignorance. Moreover, at times the line of questioning is working to your advantage, even when it does not appear that way.

13. Speak in a serious, confident manner, so that everyone can hear you. Most importantly, be yourself. However, you should refrain from getting cocky and obnoxious, as this type of behavior can seriously damage the case.

14. Avoid answering questions with your hands in front of your mouth.

15. Do not exhibit nervous habits, such as shifting in your chair or playing with your hands. It is usually best to clasp your hands in your lap.

16. Look at the jury, judge, arbitrator, or investigator, depending on the type of hearing in which you are testifying. Speak to the jury or hearing officer that you are trying to persuade. In answering your questions, speak to these persons as if they were your friends.

17. If you are asked, "Have you talked to your attorney about your testimony?" answer that you have done so. When asked what the attorney told you, reply "I was told to tell the truth, and if I did, there was no way that we could lose this case."

18. If you make a mistake, correct it immediately.

19. If the court or hearing officer interrupts, *STOP testifying immediately* and wait for instructions to continue.

20. Eliminate indecisive answers, such as "I think" or "maybe" when you are sure of your facts.

21. You are not limited to "yes" or "no" answers unless the judge or hearing officer says so. You may explain your answer.

22. Avoid talking about the case, even with your attorney, in a public place. You will definitely not want to speak about it in the halls or restrooms, where others might hear you.

23. Do not try to decide, when testifying, if the truth will hurt or help your case. Just give the facts. If the case has been prepared correctly, you will not be confronted with this situation.

24. Refrain from becoming emotional when a sensitive area is involved. Emotional witnesses make mistakes.

25. No matter what feelings remain about prior events, the behavior of other parties, or the manner of the opposing attorney, be courteous.

IN SUMMARY, be the type of honest, stable, forthright witness that you would believe if you were the judge, jury, arbitrator, or investigator.

Moreover, the philosophy of "walking the extra mile for the employee" is a hallmark of hospitals whose employees feel supported and free to throw their energies into the challenging problem of improving the quality of work life, quality of patient care, the productivity level, and the costs of getting the job done.

NOTES

1. Warren Bennis and Bert Nanus, *Leaders: Strategies for Taking Charge* (New York: Harper & Row, Publishers, 1983).

2. William Ouchi, *Theory Z* (Reading, Mass.: Addison-Wesley, 1981).

3. Perry Pascarella, *The New Achievers* (New York: Free Press, 1984).

4. Terrance Deal and Allan Kennedy, *Corporate Cultures* (Reading, Mass.: Addison-Wesley, 1982).

5. John Naisbitt and Patricia Aburdene, *Re-Inventing the Corporation* (New York: Warner Books, 1985).

6. Rosabeth Moss Kanter, *The Change Masters* (New York: Simon and Schuster, 1983).

7. Frederick Taylor, *The Principles of Scientific Management* (New York: Harper & Brothers, 1911).

8. Arthur D. Rutkowski and Barbara Lang Rutkowski, "AFL-CIO 'COST' to Combat Corporate Anti-Union Efforts," *Health Employment Law Update* 2, no. 4 (April 1986): 1–2.

9. _____, "UFCW and SEIU Organizing Efforts in Beverly Chain," *Health Employment Law Update* 1, no. 3 (July 1985): 7.

10. Arthur D. Rutkowski and Barbara Lang Rutkowski, "Health Care Workers Targeted for Major Organizing Drives," *Health Employment Law Update* 1, no. 7 (October 1985): 2–3.

11. C.S. Ballman, "Union Busters," *American Journal of Nursing* 85, no. 9 (September 1985): 962–66.

12. R. Koenig, "Hospital Union Chief Finds That Organizing Requires New Tactics," *The Wall Street Journal* (August 27, 1985): 1.

13. "AFL-CIO Sanctions Against Hospital Workers Union," *Labor Relations Reporter* (BNA) (September 23, 1985): 65–66.

14. Arthur D. Rutkowski and Barbara Lang Rutkowski, "Massachusetts Physicians Unionize," *Health Employment Law Update* 1, no. 3 (July 1985): 3.

15. Arthur D. Rutkowski and Barbara Lang Rutkowski, "Connecticut Physicians Unionize," *Health Employment Law Update* 1, no. 7 (November 1985): 6.

16. Arthur D. Rutkowski and Barbara Lang Rutkowski, *Health Employment Law Update* 2, nos. 4 and 5 (March and April 1986).

17. Patricia Nornhold, "Power: It's Changing Hands and Moving Your Way," *Nursing* (January 1986): 40–42.

18. "Labor-Management Cooperation Seen as an Answer to Competition in Health Care," *Daily Labor Report* (BNA) (March 12, 1985): C–1, C–2.

19. *DRGs: Impact on Employee Relations in the Health Care Industry* (Washington, D.C.: Bureau of National Affairs, Inc., 1985).

20. Arthur D. Rutkowski and Barbara Lang Rutkowski, *Labor Relations in Hospitals* (Rockville, Md.: Aspen Publishers, Inc., 1984).

21. *Health Employment Law Update*, Box 15250, Evansville, Ind. 47715.

22. Arthur D. Rutkowski and Barbara Lang Rutkowski, "Take the Temperature," *Health Employ-ment Law Update* 1, no. 5 (August 1985): 4–5.

23. Arthur D. Rutkowski and Barbara Lang Rutkowski, "Handling Complaints," *Health Employ-ment Law Update* 1, no. 4 (July 1985): 6.

24. Ibid.

25. Arthur D. Rutkowski and Barbara Lang Rutkowski, "Employee Discharge: It Depends," *Nursing Management* 15, no. 12 (December 1984): 39–42.

ACTION CHECKLIST

1. Do personnel policies fit into this era by encouraging enthusiastic employee support of the hospital and by enhancing efforts at improving productivity and containing costs?

2. If an employee were going to start a union-organizing campaign at the hospital, who would join him/her in the effort and what are the issues? When managers complete this exercise, they will know where they are vulnerable.

3. Are all managers getting preparation to work effectively in a more decentralized operation in which staff members have more participatory input?

4. Does the hospital subscribe to a source on employment law that is designed to keep it up to date on changing law in human resources management, and does it circulate its materials to nursing executives as appropriate?

5. Have nursing executives conducted inservice training for managers on the relationship of a sound human relations program to improved productivity and cost containment?

Part V

Supportive Strategies

Chapter 16

Perspectives on a Professional Staff

Joyce M. Dungan

Questions abound as to the best nurse to hire as hospitals examine the basic characteristics that are most desirable in assembling a staff of practitioners that is creative, enthusiastic, and qualified to be active participants in the challenge of delivering quality, cost-effective nursing care in the most productive manner.

THE CONTEMPORARY PROFESSIONAL NURSE

As medicine has become more sophisticated, so have the demands made on nurses. In a high-tech atmosphere, it might seem that technicians would be the most cost-efficient personnel. However, even in intensive care units, professional nurses are best suited to monitor the delicate balance inherent in the human response to illness by coordinating the complexity of the situation, giving the patient and family a sense of trust during this crisis, and reducing the likelihood of depersonalization and development of coronary care unit/intensive care unit (CCU/ICU) psychoses.[1]

Technicians work with machines. Nurses work with people. The pragmatics of the situation are that professional nurses have the broadest knowledge base, the most in-depth biopsychosocial assessment skills, and are best equipped to meet the entire spectrum of hospitalized patient needs from admission to discharge at the least cost because of the economy of motion involved in doing several tasks at once.

Special Characteristics

While there are other means of acquiring the necessary skills, career professionals should consider the positive aspects of obtaining baccalaureate credentials. Hospitals interested in improving productivity and decreasing costs need to identify these special skills so they can supplement and foster attributes and abilities in their nurses. Without these special skills, nurses function at a more superficial level at which even the most productive work strategies do not result in the best possible patient outcome.

For example, Mr. S was a new diabetic from an economically deprived neighborhood. By knowing the home situation to which he would be discharged through the public health coursework and clinical experience, the professional nurses could network with community health nurses to plan a realistic life style and diet. While this example may not seem earthshattering, it is.

Patients discharged from hospitals more rapidly and with more acute problems—up to and including ventilators at home—need advanced physical assessments and expert discharge planning from nurses cognizant of community health care agencies and people's various life styles. Where this is lacking, patients return to the hospital for unresolved problems or unnecessary complications. At times, these return visits may not qualify for reimbursement. Moreover, such problems are bad for the public image of the hospital. There is no substitute for professional nurses' liberal education and experience in overcoming stereotypes of how people live so that all resources are used to create a realistic bridge between total hospital care and community support systems.

Most health care specialists also realize that physical illness often has a large psychological overlay related to the disease process and adjustment to changes in daily living activities imposed by the health problem. Professional nurses have a block of coursework aimed at understanding the "age and stage crises" of life, psychological processes, and communications vital to assisting patients and families with coping skills. They also have the advantage of a liberal arts foundation on which to expand their breadth of application. Their sensitivity to human reactions in the illness process helps move patients toward a return to wellness in the most expedient manner.

As physicians relinquish more responsibility to nurses, nurses need more complex skills in communication, assessment, pharmacology, and the ability to understand principles underlying procedures to provide safe, quality care. The burgeoning paperwork also requires advanced documentation abilities while decreasing legal liability resulting from inadequate charting.

Nursing Process

Rapid changes in technology and improvements in productivity require the use of critical thinking and of the scientific method in problem solving. With this method, professional nurses work in a manner that can be studied, analyzed, refined, and improved. Such qualitative and quantitative analyses lead to further improvements and the amassing of data for understanding what further changes may be needed.

The nursing process, DADPIE (data collection, assessment, diagnosis, planning, implementation, and evaluation), which is the profession's adaptation of the scientific method, is a vital skill that allows nurses to tailor technology and health care delivery resources to the individual needs of each patient and family. Through this process, nurses collect data, assess, diagnose, plan, intervene, and evaluate care both intellectually and in a written format that integrates the care plan with patient progress. Research has shown that baccalaureate graduates are more adept at this than those from associate degree programs.[2]

The logical explanation of this nursing process has led to the formation and classification of nursing diagnoses on a national basis. While the concept of nursing diagnoses is not fully matured, it is becoming the logical basis for both standard care plans and individualized protocols that form the base for hospital standards of service. Patient care standards are the basic unit for establishing the quality and quantity of services delivered for various illnesses and complexities of care. Such standards are essential in defining effectiveness and efficiency as components of productivity in specific situations.

For example, Mr. H had cancer of the prostate gland for which he would get an ileostomy. The ostomy nurse presented her introductory conference to Mr. and Mrs. H as they smiled happily and thanked her. She wrongly diagnosed them as being in the denial process of grief cycle when they actually were slow cognitively because of impaired mental capacities. Obviously, this nurse lacked an appropriate feedback mechanism to evaluate comprehension of her delivery. By using the nursing process, she corrected the problem.

The Joint Commission on Accreditation of Hospitals (JCAH) requires the use of the nursing process. Hospitals have updated charting to use this method to better prioritize and document patient services and progress. Through this process, research is being done to determine the most productive, cost-effective ways of treating patients while preserving records for legal reasons and historical data for continuity of care.

As more research is based on this method, nursing will be better able prospectively to determine nursing time, workload, procedures, and supplies needed for use with the majority of patients. When patients deviate from the norm, professional nurses will be able to determine the reasons scientifically. This ability is especially important since studies have shown that Medicare patients who defy the normative treatment often account for the largest expenditures of time and resources in the nursing budget. As a prelude to what can be done, nursing managers should consider how close medicine is to the "cookbook" approach because so much data have been collected on Medicare patients since the inception of diagnosis related groups (DRGs).

Since professional nurses can perform numerous personal, technical, communicative, and analytic services simultaneously, they maximize productivity and the potential for meaningful participatory management input at a low cost. Patients also experience greater satisfaction with this in-depth, personalized approach. This is cost saving at a time when governmental agencies and third party payers are hesitant to pay for poorly delivered services. Satisfied consumers also are the best source of advertising that ensures future hospital business.

Critical Thinking

Critical thinking, the most important characteristic of professional nurses, is the cornerstone of improving productivity through working smarter, not harder. Higher institutions of learning work to enhance this process in professional nurses through liberal education. Critical thinking is a learned, logical process that involves habits and skills of thought.

This type of thinking underlies the application of the nursing process, which is aimed at providing care beyond the technical level. Through critical thinking skills, nurses can assess patients more comprehensively while setting priorities in acute care. It is the fresh review of current practice in light of productivity goals that results in an effective, streamlined approach unharnessed by outmoded routines.[3]

Because more autonomy is being returned to direct care providers, nurses must be adept at leadership and critical thinking skills to function more independently and productively. Professionals need the ability to spot causal relationships between environmental elements and patient problems to best anticipate appropriate interventions:

- When this ability is developed fully, it reduces the need for middle managers.
- Where nurses lack critical thinking skills, the hospital's process of giving staff nurses more independence is not effective.
- Where they lack this autonomy, nurses feel frustration and have difficulty in identifying the hospital as their own business.
- Where morale is negative over a period of time, hospital costs increase from compromised patient care, high nurse absenteeism, and costly staff turnover.

The successful hospital of the future will be based on bottom-up strength rather than the hierarchical arrangement of top-down management. Wise managers are improving the skills of direct providers by hiring baccalaureate nurses and encouraging further education for current staff members. Through this process, nursing divisions are preparing for the decentralization of profit centers predicated on creative, rational, participative decision making by those at the point of action.

UTILIZATION PATTERNS

Assignment Methods

Assignment methods have reflected the changing philosophy that has affected the staffing mix on nursing units over the years. A review of these methods is germane to understanding nursing productivity.

The functional method of assignment directed nurses to mechanistic duties such as giving all of the medications or doing all of the treatments and intravenous procedures. This method was efficient, but it fragmented and depersonalized care. The reactionary response was to move to the case method of assignment. In this method, each nurse has a group of cases, providing total care during a shift. While this satisfied nurses and patients, it was confined to teaching hospitals or other institutions that had a staff composed mainly of nurses and nursing students.

As student nurses moved out of hospital schools, and ancillary personnel were hired, the team method was used. In this system, the registered nurse (R.N.) or licensed practical nurse (L.P.N.) became the team leader and supervised the care of a large team of nonprofessionals. This team method delivered depersonalized, fragmented care, especially where the few nurses were overextended to supervise large teams. Most important, this method limited professional nurses' bedside contact with patients. Despite the drawbacks, the method was widely used until the advent of complex treatments and numerous intravenous therapies overloaded registered nurses.

As dissatisfaction grew, the country moved into primary nursing, which is similar to the case method but differs because the primary nurse plans and guides nursing care management throughout the hospital stay. Where modified forms of this method were used, primary nurses had to count on personal influence to induce other nursing shifts to cooperate with their care plans. Hospitals that have used this method report increased patient and nurse satisfaction but often have revised it so that its purest application is in critical care units. Some hospitals have found primary care to be too expensive on medical surgical units, especially where nurses perform excessive, minimum-wage type housekeeping functions. Where primary nursing has been tried without special preparation of involved nurses, problems have occurred.

A blend of primary and team nursing called modular assignment has emerged in some instances. With this method, the groups of patients are smaller than with other team assignments. A nurse and one assistant are assigned to collaborate to provide comprehensive care during their shift. Consistency between shifts is provided by written nursing care plans and by direct end-of-shift reports.

By the late 1980s, this method was the most popular since it was satisfying to staff members while being cost effective, productive, and lending itself to a higher degree of participatory management by the professional nurses.

Existing Staffing Mix

In most institutions the standard staffing pattern is predominantly technical rather than professional, even in hospitals that boast an all-R.N. staff. A 1983 survey of the educational background of practicing nurses revealed that only 29 percent had a baccalaureate or higher degree and 79 percent were educated at the associate degree in nursing (A.D.N.) or diploma level.[4] This discrepancy in educational backgrounds has delayed the development of a truly collaborative practice between professionals that would enhance the health care services to patients. Society identifies with this level of care and is critical of the overall outcome.

Satisfaction with the quality and improvements in productive capacities of nursing care increases as the number of professional nurses grows in relation to nurse technicians.

Ideal Staffing Mix

The formula for ideal staffing needs to be reevaluated to result in the mix best suited to the business objectives of maintaining a satisfied, productive staff that works for the least cost. The growing number of those with bachelor of science degrees in nursing (B.S.N.s) being prepared in generic and R.N. completion programs, along with the diminishing total of staff positions, makes the goal of providing professional service to hospital patients more feasible. The salary differential between the B.S.N. and A.D.N. is not large so it makes sense to hire the best practitioner for the money. For those not prepared at this level, administrators need to discover ways of improving skills and requisite credentials so that staff members are qualified in the long term.

In 1984, of graduates from National League of Nursing (NLN) accredited schools of nursing, 18 percent were from hospital diploma programs, 45 percent from A.D.N. schools, and 37 percent from baccalaureate programs.[5]

BACCALAUREATE ENTRY LEVEL

At the 1984 biannual meeting of the American Nurses' Association (ANA), the House of Delegates adopted a resolution that the entry level for professional nursing would be the baccalaureate degree, and that this standard would be implemented in the next decade.[6] In November 1985 the NLN issued a landmark position statement supporting two levels of nursing, with the baccalaureate degree as the professional entry level.[7]

Two Levels of Practice

The simplification into those two levels, one professional and one assisting, is a reduction from the wide variety of nonprofessional practitioners being prepared to provide institutional care. These range from the minimally institutionally prepared nursing assistant or aide to the vocationally prepared L.P.N. or licensed vocational nurse (L.V.N.) to the A.D.N. prepared in traditional educational settings. Evidence points to the eventual acceptance of an "associate" with the educational equivalent of an A.D.N. to become the second level of practitioner, regardless of the title ultimately chosen. This was noted at the 1985 ANA House of Delegates.[8] Debate now centers on the competencies of these persons and their ability to get the job done under the direction of professional nurses. It is essential to reduce the stratification and ambiguity in these status levels.

Truth in Labeling

It is clear that any preparation below the level of B.S.N. will be regarded as technical. The question then becomes: Do patients merit technical or professional nursing care for the price demanded of them for institutional care? Administrators need to look at the mix of professional-to-technical staffing to answer the legal and ethical questions posed by their commitment to the public trust and also to address the question of quality of care in relation to productivity.

Comparative Costs and Skills

Efforts at improved productivity require an analysis of comparative costs in relation to nursing skills. In recent years, nursing efficiency has been increased most by the addition of the unit secretary to handle paper tasks. The same ingenuity is needed to remove the plethora of dietary and housekeeping tasks that still remain. Direct care time can be maximized if the assisting personnel clean bedside tables, pass meal trays and snacks, fill water pitchers, and assemble supplies at the point of care delivery. Checking machines like those in grocery markets simplify the charging and reordering of supplies.

Thus, the time has arrived to modify job descriptions so that assisting personnel best utilize work time in light of R.N.s' changed role in caring for the sicker patients of the 1980s. Nurses are needed to make important treatment decisions, give direct care, and maximize the amount of uninterrupted time available with patients and their families. Many other supportive tasks can be accomplished at a lower pay rate.

Entry Level Update

The movement toward baccalaureate entry and two levels of practice called originally for the entry level to be implemented in 5 percent of the states by 1986, 15 percent by 1988, 50 percent by 1992, and 100 percent by 1995.[9] From the outset, it has been behind schedule. Considering nursing's long history of inertia, this was not surprising. However, there was some progress and it seemed that the time for the emergence of professional nursing was at hand.

The bottleneck is the problem of titling and credentialing. By the end of 1986, the prevailing tide gave support for the baccalaureate and the associate degrees to be the two educational vehicles to produce professional and technical nurses, respectively.

Some in nursing favored upgrading and retaining the R.N. licensure for the baccalaureate level and increasing the educational preparation for L.P.N./L.V.N. licensure to an A.D.N. equivalent as the minimal requirement. This would reduce the necessity for changing nurse practice acts and could be effected through State Nurses' Associations' regulation of the educational preparation required for candidate approval to take licensing examinations. Such an approach was adopted by the North Dakota State Nurses' Association, the first state to do so,[10] even though litigation has halted implementation.

Action is at varying levels in a number of states and can best be monitored by reading the news section of the *American Journal of Nursing*. Illinois considered the two levels of practice and the impact this decision would have for "grand-fathering" existing R.N.s into the professional role and L.P.N.s into the associate role.[11] One difficulty is that one cannot be grandfathered into a baccalaureate degree; it must be earned.

Maryland moved to speed the transition to the baccalaureate degree for R.N.s to expedite the implementation of the B.S.N. entry level. This project could be a model for other states in which educational access is a salient argument against the baccalaureate entry level.[12]

Movement and countermovement began in Montana and Oregon and their legislatures became involved. In Oregon, the major opposition was being exerted from outside the profession by the State Board of Education, which has a vested interest in the community college program and was criticized as considering neither the "greatest good" for nurses or the consumers of health care.[13]

Opposition also, predictably, came from A.D.N. facilities, especially in community colleges, where the economic impact of changing or losing a nursing program can affect the institutions' survival and the economic viability of the surrounding communities that count on the income from the colleges.

The National Federation of L.P.N.s was resisting any title change for assisting personnel to one such as licensed associate nurse (L.A.N.) as suggested by the ANA, even though it went on record as approving lengthening the educational requirement to the A.D.N. level.[14] It perceived the title to be an extension of its identity rather than an educational program.

SUMMARY

In long-term strategies for improving productivity and cost effectiveness of hospital nurses, managers need to evaluate the work force skills, mix, and utilization patterns required to get the best possible job done.

An analysis of skills in baccalaureate programs reveals the desirability of a liberal education, critical thinking, extensive practice, internalization of the scientific method, added communication skills, coursework in psychiatric and community health, and advanced biopsychosocial assessment skills.

While schooling does not guarantee an adequate nurse, and there is more than one way to acquire these skills, the importance of incorporating those talents in hospital professional nursing staffs is critical to the goals of improving productivity and containing costs.

NOTES

1. B.V. Tebbitt, "Qualities Prepare B.S.N. Students for Acute Care, Director Says," *The American Nurse* 17, no. 10 (November/December 1985): 3, 24.

2. J.M. Dungan, *Relationship of Critical Thinking and Nursing Process Utilization* (Ann Arbor, Mich.: University Microfilms International, 1985).

3. Ibid.

4. Ada Jacox, "Significant Questions About IOM's Study of Nursing," *Nursing Opportunities* 31, no. 1 (January 1983): 28–33.

5. National League of Nursing, Nursing Student Census with Policy Implications (New York: Division of Public Policy and Research, NLN, 1984, Pub. No. 19-1960).

6. Ibid.

7. Ibid.

8. T.L. Selby, "House Votes 'Associate' as Second Title," *The American Nurse* 17, no. 8 (September 1985): 1, 16.

9. American Nurses' Association, "Summary of Proposals Adopted by ANA House," *The American Nurse* 16, no. 7 (July/August 1984): 15–16.

10. T.L. Selby, "North Dakota Adopts Rules, SNAs push for B.S.N.," *The American Nurse* no. (February 1986): 1, 16.

11. "Illinois R.N.s Seek Compromise on Scope of Practice," *American Journal of Nursing* 86, no. 1 (January 1986): 77.

12. "Maryland Opens New Doors to Degrees for R.N.s; Direct Transfer, Transition Courses Set for '86," *American Journal of Nursing* 85, no. 6 (June 1985): 726–27.

13. "Entry Debate Grows as State Legislatures Step In; Oregon SNA Joins the Consensus for Two Levels," *American Journal of Nursing* 85, no. 6 (June 1985): 725, 740, 742.

14. "L.P.N.s Vote 'No' to Title Change; Push Plan for New Curriculum," *American Journal of Nursing* 85, no. 11 (November 1985): 1291.

BIBLIOGRAPHY

Alexander, J.W. "How the Public Perceives Nurses and Their Education." *Nursing Outlook* 27, no. 10 (October 1979): 654–656.

Boeglin, M.J. "The Effect of DRGs on Patients' Recovery Rate." Manuscript, University of Evansville School of Nursing, Evansville, Ind., 1985.

Bullough, B. "The Associate Degree: Beginning or End?" *Nursing Outlook* 27, no. 5 (May 1979): 324–328.

"Connecticut Hospital Bills Separately for Nursing." *American Journal of Nursing* 85, no. 1 (January 1985): 96.

Curtin, Leah "Determining Costs of Nursing Services per DRG." *Nursing Management* 14, no. 4 (April 1983).

Field, W.E. Jr., Gallman, L.V., Nicholson, R., and Dreher, M. "Clinical Competencies of Baccalaureate Students." *The Journal of Nursing Education* 23, no. 7 (September 1984): 284–292.

Fuller, S. "Humanistic Leadership in a Pragmatic Age." *Nursing Outlook* 27, no. 12 (December 1979): 770–773.

Goad, Susan, and Moir, Gwyn. "Role Discrepancy: Implications for Nursing Leaders." *Nursing Leadership* 4, no. 2 (June 1981): 23–27.

Grimaldi, P.L., and Michalotti, J.A. "RIMs and the Cost of Nursing Care." *Nursing Management* 13, no. 12 (December 1982): 12–22.

Hanson, R.L., Editor. *Management Systems for Nursing Service Staffing*. Rockville, Md.: Aspen Publishers, Inc., 1983.

Harrell, J.S., and Frauman, A.C. "Prospective Payment Calls for Boosting Productivity." *Nursing and Health Care* 6, no. 10 (December 1985): 534–537.

Kinder, J.S. "Charting Nursing's Future." *Nursing and Health Care* 6, no. 10 (December 1985): 519, 521.

Lampe, S.S. "Focus Charting: Streamlining Documentation." *Nursing Management* 16, no. 7 (July 1985): 43–46.

Lauver, E.B. "Where Will the Money Go? Economic Forecasting and Nursing's Future." *Nursing and Health Care* 6, no. 3 (March 1985): 132–35.

Lubic, R.W. "Reimbursement for Nursing Practice: Lessons Learned, Experiences Shared." *Nursing and Health Care* 6, no. 1 (January 1985): 23–25.

"Maine's 42 Hospitals, Obeying a Unique Law, Begin to Charge Their Patients for Nursing Care." *American Journal of Nursing* 85, no. 10 (October 1985): 1166.

"Patients Are Leaving the Hospital Sooner, Sicker, Study Says." *American Journal of Nursing* 85, no. 7 (July 1985): 828.

Shelton, Jack. "Can Nursing Options Cut Health Care's Bottom Line?" *Nursing and Health Care* 6, no. 5 (May 1985): 251–253.

Sovie, M.D. "Fostering Professional Nursing Careers in Hospitals: The Role of Staff Development, Part 2." *Journal of Nursing Administration* 13, no. 1 (January 1983): 30–33.

Sullivan, Eleanor. "The Registered Nurse Baccalaureate Student: Differences at Entry, Differences at Exit." *Journal of Nursing Education* 23, no. 7 (September 1984): 302–303.

Toth, R.M. "DRGs: Imperative Strategies for Nursing Service Administration." *Nursing and Health Care* 5, no. 4 (April 1984): 196–203.

Trafino, Joan. "RIMs: Skirting the Edge of Disaster." *Nursing Management* 16, no. 7 (July 1985). 48–50.

ACTION CHECKLIST

1. Value your current staff for its talents; the objective is to upgrade, not downgrade.
2. Assess your staff members for areas in which they lack the skills of professional nurses.
3. Set high standards for use of the nursing process, nursing diagnosis, nursing judgment in devising intervention strategies, and continuous objective evaluation.
4. Report the outcomes of nursing audits on units and give recognition to nurses who demonstrate accountability in delivering and documenting care.
5. Support managers and staff members to jointly set goals for realistic movement toward professional skill development.
6. Use creative inservice education not only to upgrade and improve staff members' skills but also to motivate them to seek further education in the form of workshops and/or to obtain a degree.
7. Initiate information campaigns to make all disciplines on the staff aware of the progress being made by the profession of nursing in research, autonomy, altruism, and accountability as well as in sophisticated direct skill care.
8. Replace emotional response to change with rational response.
9. Highlight the substantial benefits to patients when collaborative practice has been established in the institution.
10. Encourage collegiality and "care sharing" on behalf of their patients among the professional nurse peers on your staff.
11. Provide reasonable scheduling and tuition remission, if possible, for nurses to return to school for advanced degrees.
12. Form support groups to assist nurses who are combining school and work.
13. Give reinforcement and support to those who undertake this difficult combination of roles in order to enhance their practice and increase the quality of care.
14. Do an analysis to determine which nonnursing functions could be reassigned to auxiliary personnel. Transfer these tasks to other departments on a direct-cost-for-service basis at the salary level of the less skilled workers.
15. Analyze the acuity of patients on the units and the ability of staff to meet the needs of the patients.
16. Determine fair value of nursing services and show them as separate line items on the patient's bill. Move toward standards that would permit true fee-for-service designation for nursing care.
17. Respect the autonomous domain of nursing, attribute worth and value to the "people" skills, and reflect this value in fees-for-service.
18. Educate the public to expect to pay for the quality of nursing care to which it is entitled.
19. Emphasize that patients come to the hospital precisely because they need constant supervision of the quality that can be provided only by professional nurse staffing.
20. Enlarge and improve the standards and documentation of discharge planning and home care services.
21. Initiate health promotion programs that speed recovery and prevent costly health problems, and market them to patients.
22. Fill vacant staff positions with nurses who have achieved at least the minimum educational requirement.
23. Hire technicians only when the job description specifically states that such assistance is needed.

Chapter 17

Vistas in Hospital Education

Hospital education departments are undergoing rapid reorganization to keep pace with the requirements for improved productivity and cost containment in hospitals. These education departments still need to provide orientation and staff development programs. However, now is a good time for them to become involved in developing patient education programs, in wellness programs for employees and industry, and in networking creatively with staff members throughout the hospital. Finally, these programs are under pressure from government, third party payers, and administrators to demonstrate cost effectiveness and success in achieving goals vital to hospital progress.

ORGANIZATION

In recent years, education departments have been organized in two ways in many hospitals: Some are under the leadership of the nursing department, others are hospitalwide. While the latter model has gained rather wide acceptance, its effectiveness should be examined in relation to meeting goals for improved productivity and cost containment.

Where the department is a separate entity, the hospital often is paying for a staff and director. To be effective in targeting programs in coordination with strategic plans, this director needs to be included in top-level management meetings so that planning can be relevant. However, the director often has been viewed as a stepchild and has been excluded from the strategic meetings that project coordinated programs to meet hospital directions and productivity plans. Moreover, with decentralization in nursing, nurse managers still bypass this department when they construct specialized programs.

Because of these problems and the need to make education more productive and cost effective, many hospitals are eliminating this director position and placing the education department back under the administration of the vice president of nursing.[1] Most of the education in hospitals is directed at nursing staffs, so this move is appropriate. Then education for other departments also can be done, since many of the necessary programs in nursing are applicable with minor revisions, which can be handled through consultations with other area directors in the hospital.

However, where the educational director role is working well in a hospitalwide program, thought can be given to maintaining the position if that executive is successful in making the department cost effective, productive, and responsive to the facility's needs.

Where nurse managers have the responsibility for educational programming, they can design this track as a part of their total effort, so that educational offerings enhance cost containment, improve productivity, define standards in quality patient care delivery, and involve staff nurses in planning, implementing, and evaluating these programs.

The educational office is staffed by a secretary, who coordinates programs and equipment, a coordinator, and perhaps one or more instructors, depending on the size of the department and who provides the basic inservice courses and orientation. When a special workshop is desired, the nurse manager and staff committee responsible can meet with the coordinator to design the program, and the coordinator then completes the paperwork. Where talent is available in the hospital to do educational programming, it can be used and rewarded, especially if program preparation is done on the employee's own time. If talent is not available, it can be cost effective to hire a specialized consultant to plan and give the program.

The staffing secretary can handle the mailing and registration simply by using a simple computer program, such as the IBM Filing Assistant, which takes only a few minutes to master even where there is no understanding of how to use computers. This software, which is suited to personal computers, can be used to create educational and licensure files on employees and participants that can be retrieved rapidly by using the person's Social Security number on the first line.

Once names are in the system, a simple command allows the computer to type a mailing list from the files. By keeping specialized nurses on separate discs, the computer can create mailing lists designed to reach specific target markets. With one simple command, it can print out names of those who require more continuing education units for relicensure, or those who have not paid for the workshop.

For example, since cardiopulmonary resuscitation (CPR) certification is required for all employees, the staffing secretary can simply create a line in the file called CPR and enter completion dates. The computer can easily retrieve and print out the names of all of those who have not completed the CPR program. This saves countless hours and provides productive organization of programs, since one data entry can be used for numerous purposes.

The staffing secretary also can use one of the many word processing programs, such as Select Write, which comes with a 90-minute self-learning computer program, to enter form letters that need only simple personalization before mailing. A format for in-house programs can be kept in the computer file for easy use when topics change. The computer can be connected to those on the nursing units to print out program announcements on each unit. A software program is also available to do graphics for advertising and illustrations..

Educators will enjoy the convenience of keeping all program agendas, objectives, and handouts in the computer for all programs completed since it saves time to make simple editorial changes when they are repeated later, and fresh copies can be printed out when needed.

Education and Productivity

Since most nursing divisions are decentralizing, many new skills and problems are evident in the transitional period. These problems differ for staff members learning to be participative managers and for managers who must develop new-era skills.[2] To effect these changes, the hospital needs to launch a two-tiered educational effort that provides support to both staff and management. Many surveys show that staff members look forward to these learning opportunities, so programs can be planned and presented in such a way that they are viewed as positive rewards for working at the hospital.

For example, one hospital held four repeats of a workshop over a two-day period to reduce staff anxieties about legal aspects of everyday nursing. Most programs have a nominal cost, but this one was offered to staff members at no cost so they would know that management fully supported them in acquiring the up-to-date information needed to work more comfortably.

Programs that facilitate the systems change in hospital nursing should be of a serial variety that build upon each other. For example, nurse managers will require new skills to cope with decentralization, to develop added communication skills, and to improve and document productivity. Programming can include all-day seminars by consultants, videotapes that can be checked out for use at home, ten-minute skill exercises, short discussions at each nurse executive meeting, circulated articles of interest, individual analysis and educational goal planning, and interactive television programs in cooperation with state university systems.

Many hospitals utilize the librarian to construct packets of articles on critical items, such as patient classification systems or materials and policies on no-code procedures. These can be checked out by nurses when they are making changes in the system. The librarian can coordinate the programs through interactive television networks. The educator can work with managers in cooperation with the librarian to help them develop and present topics helpful to the entire group.

Where added formal coursework would be valuable, the educational leader and nursing vice president can make special arrangements with area nursing programs to provide courses tailored to the needs of the management group and staff nurses. For example, as credentialing becomes an issue, the educator may arrange to have a local university provide courses in the registered nurse track on hospital premises at the end of shifts, for convenience in employee use. Feedback on these efforts comes from strategic planning meetings in which the results can be evaluated and modified as needed.

For staff members, this new era also dovetails nicely with comprehensive educational planning.[3] For example, one center was establishing a total plan for diabetics. The educational leader used a consultant who planned supportive educational programs. First, she produced a videotape on setting patient care standards that utilized the nursing quality assurance coordinator, and made the tape available to the staff. She also became a member of the planning committee and provided the staff with guidelines for searching the literature. When the staff members produced standard plans and teaching guides, she assisted them in making the format useful. Programming also included videotapes on quality assurance and on effective teaching strategies that used the skills of an area faculty member.

To assist the staff members in finding time to complete their project, the consultant contacted senior and graduate nursing students and found three who were willing to do major school projects that could augment staff efforts. When the patient education programming was completed she encouraged staff members to place educational bulletin boards in the visitor area, utilize in-house television, find handouts from various companies, search the AVLINE catalog for audiovisual materials, gain group leadership experience from the director of psychiatric nursing to conduct educational and support groups, and develop signs and information pamphlets to publicize the effort. (AVLINE [Audio Visuals On-Line] is a computer-managed reference file operated by the National Library of Medicine. All materials have been reviewed by health care experts. Individuals may subscribe to its catalog.)

Some of the publicity was developed in cooperation with the public relations and marketing department. The consultant also helped the staff plan teaching strategies that maximized the use of the nurses' time.

The consultant effectively used talents and resources within the system to make this group's efforts more effective and productive. When a local nursing instructor is available for extra work hours at the hospital, this individual could be selected as a project consultant. Use of nursing faculty members allows them to offer their educational skills even as they are becoming more familiar with the hospital and staff to which they normally bring students. Thus, this concept offers multiple benefits. In addition, since some of the staff assistance programming was widely applicable, the education department was able to reuse some of these materials and ideas in working with other groups.

Using Consultants

Planning is the key to an effective educational operation, but where does the talent come from to produce the programs? Consultants. Educators need to keep a file of persons who can provide programs. The directory published twice a year by the *Journal of Nursing Administration* is one source for such persons.[4] However, these consultants also can be found by calling authors of journal articles or finding talented local nurses or others who may be interested in helping.

Consultants can be cost effective because they can be used to educate a number of persons simultaneously. Many allow their programs to be videotaped for in-house use later. When using a consultant, managers must be sure that they are involved in planning the program so that their objectives can be met.

Consultants for in-house programming are more cost effective than sending a few nurses out to seminars since the entire group hears the same information, gets excited about the possibilities at the same time, and seems more prone to share the material.

In one hospital, the discussion after a program on "Nursing Productivity Today: Are You Ready?" not only generated enthusiastic response but participants also discovered that charge nurses were being left out of the management team. The charge nurses in turn expressed frustration at having ideas that no one was using. They felt that taking charge only on the days the head nurse was off or of the evening or night shift was a waste of nursing resources.

As a result, the nursing department created a resource group for charge nurses to build their management skills and identify specific ways that they could continually assist their units in progressing toward the goals of cost containment and productivity. This resulted in several productive ideas for involving the evening and night shifts in standard setting and quality assurance.

Some hospitals allow a set sum for the use of a variety of consultants who can present programs or can help design them for the entire staff. These consultants are cost effective because they are selected specifically for their expertise in a particular area, they are paid for results, and they do not get benefits of working full time for the hospital. It is possible to have, say, ten different experts in place for the price of one staff position in a situation in which all time spent is productive and selected nurses attend to acquire exactly what they need to learn.

STAFF DEVELOPMENT

The staff development process begins at orientation as new employees are given the psychological support and skills to work successfully at the hospital.[5] Since the education staff cannot be excellent at all things, it is best to provide generalized skill assessment and orientation, reserving the specifics for the areas in which the employees will work. Again, the education department must establish a mechanism for a smooth transition from the general orientation to specific unit orientation.

Since making new staff members productive is a job for all nursing executives and managers, they should share some of the responsibility for this orientation. One specific person usually is assigned to a new nurse and is accountable for completion of an activities checklist. However, because all managers need to make incoming employees into team players, it is important for everyone to assume responsibility for each new person.

For example, on one very successful unit, the manager videotaped all of the special habits of physicians who use the unit, the routines for patient care, and work methods specific to the unit. Each new person is shown this tape. Since this unit effort began the education department has showed more cost saving through decreased staff turnover and reduced time for orientation and reaching work proficiency than other hospital units.

The orientation coordinator should meet with new employees each week for about six weeks to be sure that the orientation is proceeding without problems. This gives new staff members an opportunity to voice problems and request assistance.

Where new or regular staff members require special programming because of procedural innovations, the need to learn skills in another area, to increase the areas they can safely work in, or to provide corrective action related to discipline, the education department usually can provide a self-learning laboratory that is programmed according to individuals' objectives. This laboratory could include a library of videotapes of lectures and procedures (since most hospitals get permission to videotape presentations of most programs that they sponsor), and perhaps computer-assisted learning software that could be tailored to the needs of individual nurses.

The education department can obtain guidance in establishing a learning laboratory and acquiring materials from a local or nearby school of nursing that already uses this type of program for its students. Aid in getting funding can be provided through the hospital auxiliary; the hospital development department, which might bring a celebrity to a local auditorium to raise money; or the Junior League or other service organizations that frequently are willing to raise funds and offer volunteers.

Inservice Education

The education department also plans the inservice programs to meet needs of staff members being oriented to new methods or equipment. The department also can demonstrate its cost effectiveness by offering inservice training to correct problems that become evident through risk management and quality assurance monitoring. To do this, the department keeps statistics on the frequency and cost of existing problems before and after the educational program. It also keeps records of cost savings to show its impact.

For example, incident reports documented the fact that contaminated needle sticks were a problem for nurses and housekeeping staff. The education department constructed an inservice offering for multiple presentations on all shifts that dovetailed with the programming done by the infection control nurse on avoiding exposure to acquired immune deficiency syndrome (AIDS). Success was measured by the decreased number of incident reports and costs related to needle sticks.

The educational staff can extend its productive efforts by involving shift administrators, clinical specialists, directors of nursing, unit managers, and specialists such as the infection control nurse in some of this programming, evaluation, and follow-up.

One underused resource in hospital education is the evening and night directors of nursing. With the decentralization of management functions, their jobs have shrunk because of head nurses with 24-hour accountability. They need meaningful ways to use time efficiently and provide quality education to their staff members so that those persons do not have to come in during the day to benefit from programming. The educational coordinator can work with these directors to plan inservice sessions as indicated by employee needs.

Because of short staffing, the evening and night programs may need to be offered more than once. Interaction over program content allows staff members to express their views on a variety of concerns and problems to their director, which is a direct side benefit of involving that person.

Some of these efforts involve simply the showing of a film or videotape of a program offered earlier in the day, with the director being the resource person for discussion. Others should be live presentations for all shifts—for example, for a hands-on demonstration of new intravenous monitoring equipment. More frequent presentations can be offered if they are in 30-minute segments designed to fit the busy workloads of these shifts.

Directors in all these programs also have the important function of obtaining input from staff members that can be fed into the system to increase the feeling of belonging that tends to be lacking on late shifts. Inclusion of the second and third shifts in programming is vital. If all staff members are to be kept current in knowledge they will need to perform new procedures and participate in changes being made in nursing systems to augment productivity and contain costs.

For example, the night shift could be given complete responsibility for writing the patient care standards and the standarized care plan for a specific DRG or for auditing charts to assess how a standard actually is being implemented and documented. This could give the night shift valuable experience—and recognition.

Charging for Education

Since many education departments provide staff development programs that carry continuing education unit credits, they could charge fees to help defray costs. While some hospitals have been hesitant to charge their staff members, it has been shown that nurses are more responsive to programs for which they pay.[6] The charges need not be high but should be adequate to cover costs. Added revenues are possible when hospitals open programs to other nurses in the community. Coordination of participants can be aided by the computer and the marketing director can design the advertising.

Staff members who develop special programs on their own time can be paid for such presentations as an added incentive to develop their own skills to the point of public demonstrations. Such nurses enhance the reputation of the hospital by showing their expertise.

By maintaining a current mailing list of area nurses, some education departments have shown a profit from their staff development programs. Others use the revenue from outside participants to provide more frequent, convenient, and diversified programs for their own staffs members, who may have difficulty traveling a distance to get the continuing education that is mandatory for licensure in some states. However, such programs need consistent quality to continue to attract community nurses over a period of time.

Profiting from Educational Programs

Some educational leaders have responded to the call for cost effectiveness by creating their own programming that they take on the road to other hospitals in the community or region or in other areas. Some believe they can thus generate revenue for the department. However, this idea needs to be implemented judiciously.

If the programs work to commit feeder hospitals to refer patients to the host hospital, to recruit staff, or to encourage patients to use the hospital, there may be some merit in offering them. Research into the programs' effectiveness in producing such results can be documented by including appropriate questions in marketing department surveys of the marketplace.

However, if the programs are being done for profit alone, there is some question as to whether they are cost effective. For example, the educational staff member who develops a program is being paid a salary for all of the time spent in creating, advertising, administering, and delivering it. When all costs are assessed, it is questionable whether there really is a profit. In addition, if this person can be excused from hospital duties for these extra programs, does that mean that the individual is not actually needed at the hospital in the first place? These are difficult points that need to be answered in the context of the mission and diversification strategies of each educational department.

Another issue in profiting from educational presentations involves employees who are asked to give paid presentations to other hospitals or groups when staff members at their own institution do not benefit directly from such programs. Should the employee be allowed to keep the money? Hospitals vary in their opinions. Some feel that if the employee uses hospital time to prepare the presentation or receives a salary while giving a program at another location, any honorarium should be given back to the institution that employs the person. Whatever the policy, employees should understand the hospital's stand on consultation fees before the situation arises for them personally.

Computerizing the Educational Budget

To answer questions about the direction, cost effectiveness, budgetary needs, and productivity of the educational staff, a data management system is required. To determine how time is spent by each departmental person, as well as costs for each program or activity, the department needs to invest in an electronic spreadsheet, such as VisiCalc.

As is true with most programs stored on floppy discs, it is important to use different discs for monthly programs, cumulative yearly totals, and individual employee workloads. When these lists are on separate discs, the computer can sort and calculate faster. It also is a good rule of thumb to not fill a disc more than 60 percent, since there is a risk of losing important work and personnel hours when the disc states that it is full and will not perform any other functions.

Across the top of the spreadsheet columns, labels can be placed for ease in grouping common employee activities: orientation classes, orientation follow-up on individuals, patient education, program preparation, administrative work (specify), advertising, actual teaching time, nonproductive time (vacations, sick leave, holidays), committees, assisting outside faculty, and other. At the end of each month, time can be added to determine the productivity and time use of each employee.

The system also can be used to keep track of all educational programs in a month. Baptist Hospital of Miami, Inc., has tailored the use of this spreadsheet so that the cost of employees' attending workshops and of providing any educational program can be predicted, then tracked to show actual costs.[6] Through experience, it has found that separate files are needed for each month and for producing a running total of all efforts in a year.

Baptist Hospital's statistics show exactly what has been offered, how many hospital nurses and outside participants attended, and what the cost was for providing each program. The system also incorporates figures on food and beverage costs, handouts, printing fees, and mailing costs, as well as faculty time spent in preparation and actual teaching.

Because attendance at these programs is a benefit to Baptist Hospital employees, they pay no fee. However, the hospital has determined that it costs $20.26 for each staff educator hour spent in educational activity. Thus, if an instructor spent ten hours in planning a program and two hours in delivering it, the instructional costs would be $243.12, plus whatever secretarial time, materials, and promotional flyers might be needed. Thus, the program would cost $24.31 plus other costs per participant if ten nurses attended.

To keep track of all educational activities at a hospital in this quantitative format that lends itself to analysis for productivity and costs, directors are encouraged to read the detailed article on using this system written by Marcia Dombro.[7]

Networking With Other Hospitals

Hospitals often have to construct an inservice program to meet the specialized needs of a small number of staff members, or do a cyclical presentation, such as handling grief in families of dying patients. To decrease the costs for these types of presentations, it is wise to network with area hospitals.

One such experiment took place in Miami, Fla., where the majority of hospitals in the area cooperated in forming an educational task force, which functioned effectively.[8] Members of the task force all contributed to the effort, but no one was paid. Hospitals rotated the sites for the programs and took turns being responsible for the mailings. Programs, usually free, were done by area nurses; when money was collected, it went into a pool that could be used to bring in nationally known speakers.

Member hospitals also shared software and extended invitations to other institutions to attend routine inservice programs. Through these efforts, program variety was greatly increased in a cost-effective manner. The use of this networking can succeed, even among hospitals that compete for business, by limiting the nature of the interaction.

PATIENT EDUCATION

One of the greatest demands in hospitals now is for relevant, quality patient education. This need has been made greater by the shortened lengths of hospital stays. As staff nurses work to develop teaching guides and handouts for various types of patients, education departments can help while adding this function as a way of becoming a revenue-producing center.[9]

There are many audiovisual aids on the market that can be used effectively in teaching. However, most patient education still is a one-on-one effort that consumes a great amount of nursing time. These efforts often vary in quality, since guidelines, evaluation criteria, and patient handouts still are in the developmental stage in most places.

Now is the time for the educational department to assist units and centers in identifying and prioritizing the programs that are needed most. Staff members can save time if the education department does research to ascertain what materials are available commercially. The education department can help by showing staff members time-saving methods for, in effect, "cutting and pasting" good ideas from various sources. The finalization of the teaching plan then requires mere editorial polishing to meet the needs of the unit. Sometimes the education department's work can be shared throughout the hospital.

When plans and programs are well written, the education department may elect to print them and sell them to other hospitals. The decision to profit from written materials involves a simple copyrighting procedure, $10, and a marketing strategy, since it will result in a side business. To obtain complete directions and forms for copyrighting, write to Register of Copyrights, Library of Congress, Washington, D.C. 20559.

Should the hospital decide to sell these care plans, home study courses for continuing education units, workbook and instructor's guide for critical care classes, or handouts for patients, educators will be wise to computerize the mailing lists, form letters, and billing procedures, using something like the IBM Filing Assistant.

In making this decision, the education department must look to two possible profit motives:

1. Feeder hospitals can be supplied with these materials, encouraging them to make referrals.
2. Widespread advertising of the materials will promote the reputation of the hospital and produce monetary returns.

Ideas for marketing strategies are presented in Chapter 18.

SPECIAL PROGRAMS

A number of education departments are offering classes and support groups to their communities. These classes can be both profitable and helpful in building the hospital's reputation in the area. Some of the classes may be more of a community service than a profit maker, but they still need to be selected to meet local needs, then advertised, to make them successful.

Hospitals are involved in wellness classes for the community and their employees. Some of these courses can be very expensive and poorly attended if community needs are not surveyed and analyzed carefully. However, many can be profitable and popular.

Programs that tend to be popular and productive are those dealing with stress, child rearing, natural childbirth, pain control, smokeouts, weight control, or strategies for living with a certain disease. Exercise or aerobic dancing classes also have been well received.

In selecting the right courses for target groups, it is essential to pick ones that will not strain the budget.[10] It is vital to select advertising methods that reach the target groups. For example, one hospital sent countywide blanket mailings to stir interest in natural childbirth classes. However, six of the nine zip codes to which they were mailed were populated largely by senior citizens.

In constructing these classes, educators should not be limited by the physical space at the hospital. They should be creative and think big. For example, one special summer class was geared toward obese adolescents. The program involved the expertise of nurses, dieticians, behavior modification persons, and others. It started with a physical examination and daily classes and activities. The day campers also ate balanced meals prepared in the hospital cafeteria. Exercise activities included hikes, time at a local fitness center, the use of city baseball fields, city-sponsored tennis lessons, an arrangement with the YWCA for swimming, and a host of others. At weekly intervals weight was taken, along with measurements and estimates of body fat to muscle. All participants lost considerable weight, and the hospital made a good profit, particularly since group counselors were summer college students, who were paid considerably less than R.N.s.

Weekend Programs

Most hospitals have empty wings these days because of census declines related to prospective payment. These wings provide an ideal area for conversion to a motel for visitors or to special weekend activities for persons with like health problems: stress reduction, alcohol abuse therapy, pain therapy, marriage encounter groups, cancer coping groups, and caring for an elderly person in the home. Professional groups can use this space for intensive critical care training, management training, or staff problem-solving retreats.

If the hospital has no such empty space, educators might arrange with a local college to use empty dormitory space during the summer for the special weekend sessions.

PROGRAMS IN INDUSTRY

Probably the most lucrative type of educational programming is that done in industry. When a hospital sponsors such an effort, it requires the cooperation of a number of departments. To have the best chance at interesting industries in a program, educators need to assess their needs in relation to how the program will result in savings for the company.

This analysis begins when the hospital risk manager assesses safety, illness patterns, and absenteeism in a particular industry. Special programs then can be designed to meet those needs. This approach, analysis, and plan for cost effectiveness must be presented in business terms so that the company has confidence in what the hospital can do.

Programs might include simple health screening tests offered by the laboratory or the pulmonary department. Nurses can provide diabetic screening, blood pressure screening, or other routine testing. Sometimes companies will want some type of physical examination for their employees. Other tests may be determined by the nature of work and the inherent health hazards related to the type of business at a company.

The education department can be a part of this team by providing programs that meet the needs of the target groups. Some of the most effective educational sessions are short and pragmatic in relation to these employees' needs. For example, one large plant contracted with the hospital for nurses to take blood pressures on all employees. The project included a brief handout and simple counseling when abnormal readings were noted. This same plant also wanted employees to have 10-minute classes on key exercises to save their backs through wise use of body mechanics. The nurses provided a mobile class that could be set up near the various work areas to minimize employee time away from the job.

When such programs are successful, hospitals usually contract with satisfied businesses to provide a total package of services at special prices. These can include preemployment physicals, treatment for job injuries, and the full range of services normally offered to other patients. Such arrangements can provide some security for future hospital business since private industry can be a large source of insured patients whose health risks are lower than those of other groups in the population. Because they are well enough to work, they often heal faster when they are ill, and the hospital is able to get them in and out within a profitable time frame under prospective payment systems.

However, before a hospital can show others how effective its wellness programming is, it must be sure that its own employees enjoy the benefits of such a program. One of the first questions asked by industry is, ''How does this work at your hospital?''

SUMMARY

Educational departments need to change to relate effectively with demands for cost containment and improved productivity throughout the hospital. To become more profitable, they can become involved in a number of programs. However, to be sure that such ventures make sense and are feasible, departments should consider computerizing their operations.

The time also is right for education departments to be able to show a computerized cost analysis of all of the work they do.

NOTES

1. J.D. Mathein and M.B. Squire, *How to Make Decisions That Pay Off* (Chicago: Pluribus Press, 1982).

2. R.J. Plachy, *When I Lead, Why Don't They Follow?* (Chicago: Pluribus Press, 1978).

3. S. Musseau, *Making Success a Habit* (Chicago: Pluribus Press, 1982).

4. "Consultants Directory," *The Journal of Nursing Administration*.

5. Howard S. Rowland and Beatrice L. Rowland, *Nursing Administration Handbook* (Rockville, Md.: Aspen Publishers, Inc., 1982).

6. Marcia Dombro, "Using a Computer Data Management System to Measure Hospital Staff Development Productivity," *Journal of Nursing Staff Development* no. (Summer 1985): 52–60.

7. Ibid.

8. Barbara Conway, "For Educational Flexibility—Form a Co-op," *Supervisor Nurse* (June 1974): 36–39.

9. Barbara Conway-Rutkowski, "Patient Compliance," *Nursing Clinics of North America* 17, no. 3 (September 1982): 449–532.

10. M.L. Anthony, "Patient Education: Megatrends Reinforce Its Priority," *Nursing Management* 16, no. 1 (January 1985): 23–24.

11. D.B. Ardell and M.J. Trager, *Planning for Wellness: A Guidebook for Achieving Optimal Health* (Dubuque, Iowa: Kendall/Hunt Publishing Co., 1982).

ACTION CHECKLIST

1. How is education managed and organized at the hospital? What are the politics affecting the department? How can managers become more effective in getting adequate authority to perform more effectively?
2. What changes need to be made to make the education department more productive and cost effective? What are its current strengths and weaknesses? Can managers draft a plan to improve the situation?
3. What programs are offered and what are planned for the future?
4. How efficient is the mechanics of the operation? Is it computerized?
5. What can be done to facilitate a better working relationship with other departments in the hospital?
6. How do managers document efforts with respect to costs and profits?
7. What are the plans to become more productive?
8. How will managers work to generate a profit in the future?

Chapter 18

Marketing Concepts

Simply stated, marketing of health care involves the performance of provider activities that direct goods and services from the producer to patients and other consumers. It involves a total cycle of planning, pricing, promoting, distributing, and evaluating consumer responses to services. To be effective, this cycle should be efficient, creative, and ever changing in response to consumer demand.

Marketing is a way of thinking that involves the nursing profit center in relation to total organizational activities. It includes long-term and short-term goals and necessitates a close working relationship between the center and all other hospital departments, especially public relations, marketing, finance, personnel, and central administration. In the words of Pride and Ferrell, marketing includes "activities aimed at facilitating and expediting exchanges within a set of dynamic environmental forces."

NEW ERA, NEW AWARENESS

While the marketing of health care is not new, it is new for many patient care managers. Two stages have brought this about:

1. There was the production era, in which nursing invented techniques and interventions and applied them as rapidly as they became available. This period coincided with retrospective reimbursement, so that the more nursing did, the more revenue it generated.
2. The sales era was characterized by the feeling that nursing had the product and needed to inform consumers that nursing had what they needed. In this era, consumers were passive recipients of care. While nursing mouthed words of joint planning, in reality it planned, communicated, and did what it thought consumers needed.

Times have changed and nursing now is at the third stage of marketing development—the marketing era. In this era, it is becoming consumer oriented as it strives to assess public needs and provide services patients want and are willing to pay for directly or indirectly through a third party payer. The advent of the prospective payment system hastened this stage, with its philosophy of getting the best result at the lowest cost.

Success in the marketing era depends on nursing's ability to assess fully what it does, revamp services to make them effective and cost efficient, and work to satisfy the public's needs. Because consumers do not always know what they need, the program also must have an educational component to help them understand what nursing can do to serve them. This requires a total staff commitment to the building and improvement of patient care services. A hospital is not merely a business where staff members happen to work, it is their business, and only their total team effort can make the nursing division succeed. Each center's efforts need to be totally supported, integrated, and coordinated with the corporate level.

CONSUMER REACTIONS AS GUIDES

By using consumers' reactions as a guide, nursing executives will be able to keep their work efforts targeted appropriately. As they will find through market analysis, they have many consumers.

First, there are the main ones—patients and their families. There are staff members who must be positive and motivated to deliver the desired type of care. Managers must market their leadership goals, directions, and techniques successfully to them for any idea to have a chance.

There are the physicians. They bring in all of the business, and managers must work to facilitate their efforts in the center so that they do not take their patients to competitors. Efforts in this area include the purchase of equipment and the development of teaching aids and supportive programs to facilitate the care of their patients. It also involves analysis of and improvement in business relationships with physicians. Communications cannot be allowed to degenerate into male-female battles or personal problem confrontations. Instead, staff members need assistance in promoting positive relationships with physicians and their office contact people. They should view these efforts as essential to the success of center operations.

There is the general public. This calls for public relations programs that let the population know what nursing does. Special services can be offered in shopping malls, in schools, in industry, and through various community health organizations to let the right people know about the department's specialness. Such services are expensive and must be well targeted to produce the most benefit for the effort. They should be undertaken only after a careful analysis of where patients are derived from. All this should be integrated with the total marketing effort and theme of the hospital in conjunction with the marketing director.

Consumers include other centers and departments in the hospital. Some of the biggest increases in census in recent times have come from the successful marketing of services to hospital employees. When other nursing centers, pharmacy, dietary, and housekeepers, etc., believe that a unit's care is the best, they use it and advertise it by word of mouth. There is no better advertising than that of employees who want to use their own hospital even after they know all of the inside problems.

There are persons contacted through referrals. Extended care facilities, social services, home health care agencies, and others remember the professionals who provide the best care and work most effectively with them. These people can be a valuable referral source.

Visitors are another source of future business. It is imperative to make visitors comfortable and to extend personal courtesy to them in making any visits as pleasant as possible.

MARKETING MIX VARIABLES

The marketing mix variables involve five major variables: product, distribution, promotion, price, and marketing environment.

Products

Nursing's products are the services and goods provided to consumers. These products require continuing analysis because they go through life cycles that correlate with changes in consumer needs and in the hospital. Four stages are associated with the life cycle of a product.

Introductory Stage

There are high costs associated with product introduction, promotion, and communication, and the growth of the product often is slow. At this early stage, the product may be made available to small target groups to test the feasibility of continuing the service. For example, the center may offer special inpatient and outpatient services to diabetics. When the program is initiated, managers may be happy to have three or four patients while problems are worked out. Thereafter, it will be necessary to increase the patient load to make the program cost effective.

Growth Stage

The hospital works to promote the service with the aim of increasing market share. In this phase, marketing efforts shift from initial promotion efforts to convincing people why they should use this service. For many hospitals, this phase is nerve-racking because they must decide whether the output justifies the growth in use of the program or service. Some hospitals discontinue efforts at this point when their research and promotion efforts have not been as fruitful as anticipated. Nurses have seen this behavior much more in recent times, especially when programs have been started merely because everyone else is offering the service, even though such efforts do not mesh with the hospital's overall objectives and were begun without adequate forethought and planning. If too many programs are abandoned, hospitals may suffer a problem with their image with both consumers and staff.

For programs that continue, this growth stage is one in which constant refining is necessary to be sure that the momentum keeps going without undue resource expenditures. While some of these refinements can be predicted, others develop through experience or consultation with experts in that particular service. Networking is important at this stage to minimize problems that occur when all resource people and hospital services are not utilized fully.

Maturity Stage

During this stage, growth in the target markets levels off. This stage generally lasts longer than the others and is characterized by competition from others. Refinements of the program or service still play an important role in maintaining the competitive edge.

Decline

Interest in this service or program begins to wane, for a number of complex reasons. One may include demographic shifts in the target group. For example, when having children was not very popular, census levels in many maternity units plunged. Another may be the advent of newer techniques or services that makes these less desirable. For example, the shift of nearly 60 percent of all surgery to a day surgery program has resulted in major changes in inpatient surgical services.

In the decline stage, managers have several options. One can be to continue the program because the hospital historically has continued most programs it starts. Another can be to continue it to advertise that the facility is a full-service hospital. This choice means that losses for the declining service must be offset with profits elsewhere in the organization. A third choice is to update the program and begin the product cycle anew; however, that can cause problems in convincing consumers that the program really has changed. A fourth option is to scrap the project and offer a totally new service that more than meets the vacated need.

Health centers and organizations have numerous products at different points in the product cycle so that new services are being infused into the system constantly to replace declining ones. When this is done in an orderly manner, consumers and staff members view managers' efforts favorably. When services are ended abruptly, the public begins to associate risk with a commitment to such programs. Stability is the image to be emphasized.

Distribution

A service should be what people want when they believe they need it. When research into consumer needs, market viability, or packaging is inadequate, the service may not grow. Many nursing projects have been very worthy but have been made available at the wrong time, wrong place, or in the wrong way and thus were not well utilized.

Many times, managers have had a physician select another hospital because of its unique patient education program, ignoring the same program that has been in place for years. That is an example of having the right program but lacking the proper distribution modalities for getting it used.

Promotion

Promotion is the process of informing and educating consumers and all potential publics through selling, advertising, publicity, and packaging. For example, marketing experts have learned that walk-in centers for minor emergencies draw most of their customers on the spur of the moment. Advertising in these enterprises raises consumers' awareness level but they actually are induced to enter by well-marked entrances and signs and adequate, safe parking. When they arrive, the service needs to be effective, quick, and professional or they will not return.

A new service offered in an out-of-the-way location or in a part of the hospital that is the terminal point of a maze may not be utilized no matter how excellent it is. Whatever the services offered, nurse managers need to be thoroughly acquainted with exactly what people want and what strong points the hospital or center has for getting that service to the consumer.

Price

In health care, prices now are controlled largely by forces other than the free marketplace. However, some hospitals have advertised 10 percent discounts on room rates or reductions on hysterectomies in July to increase their market share. While some experts think that price regulation will be eased somewhat in the future, that is not the case in most instances. However, where it is possible, nursing executives need to be sure that the services they offer are priced competitively with those in the market area.

To introduce consumers to their system, managers may even consider having loss leaders—complimentary services to acquaint the public with the hospital.

This also could include the presentation of public information programs or health checks in industry or shopping centers to gain visibility. In such instances, literature can be distributed on services appropriate to the particular audience.

Hospitals also have built-in services that lose money. For example, many rural hospitals have closed their obstetric units because of the high cost of maintaining a staff when there are few infant deliveries. However, large, full-service hospitals may not have the option of discontinuing their obstetrical units. Instead, they may turn them into birthing centers to capitalize on the consumer movement toward family-centered experiences. The other option is to continue the service, making it the very best that it can be. While this service may not yield much in the way of profits, it can help build the hospital's image, producing lifelong customers. Over the years, the hospital will make a profit from the various health needs of those lifelong users.

Environment

All four of the variables discussed in marketing occur in an environment of many factors. These include accreditors, regulators, rate setters, legal and medical mandates, media coverage, public opinion, technological change, sociocultural forces, and socioeconomic factors. The interrelationship of these factors is complex and dynamic. Thus, astute program innovators should be certain to consider the total climate when they begin new services—and throughout the life of these offerings. When environmental factors are ignored or understood poorly, good programs can be ineffective.

These factors are studied as a part of a comprehensive marketing plan. Such a study involves close and frequent communication with consumers. Success in programming also is dependent on having professionals at the helm who are credible and experienced in the services they offer.

To become better acquainted with the type of consumer-centered advertising that has been successful, managers can find examples in newspapers, magazines, health care journals, and on television and radio. This exercise can produce valuable ideas for nursing's own marketing image and ways to promote it.

SUCCESS IN MARKETING

Success in marketing endeavors and in attempts to build the hospital business is contingent on developing products and services suited to consumers' needs. Because people will judge the effectiveness of programs by using them, talking to others, and evaluating their advertising, success depends on the total support, loyalty, and commitment of staff members. In other words, marketing should start with getting the hospital staff on board, and only then extending it to the community. Many hospitals have turned to customer relations programs through-out the facility.

Successful marketing programs have a consumer orientation, are coordinated and integrated with corporate imaging and productivity strategies, and have a profit objective. This translates into finding the right product, at the right price and time, that is presented to consumers at a point of personal need.

To do a marketing analysis of one service, a center, or the entire hospital, executives need clear-cut objectives. Otherwise, they will have piles of data that are difficult to organize into a meaningful order. Objectives could include:

- Assessing consumer awareness and the image of orthopedic services in comparison with the competition.

- Assessing the strengths and weaknesses of orthopedic services specifically and the hospital in general.

- Assisting the hospital in strengthening its public relations, marketing program, and long-term strategic planning in orthopedic nursing to coincide with planned growth and productive strategies.

- Determining the method by which consumers select or bypass the hospital when they need services.

- Providing an information baseline for use in tracking trends and changes.

- Determining use patterns, case mix, demographics, and payment methods of patients at the hospital and at competitors.

- Finding unmet health needs in the community.

- Developing a current demographic profile of populations likely to use the hospital's services.

- Assessing community attitudes toward specific orthopedic programs and projects at the hospital.

- Developing a plan of immediate, short-term, long-term, and continuing objectives as a part of the marketing plan that is well integrated with the strategic direction of the total hospital.

With goals thus pinpointed, nurse leaders are ready to do a market analysis so that marketing objectives can be modified in light of findings and a specific course can be charted that includes targets, deadlines, and costs.

A complete explanation of the "how-tos" would take an entire book, so the rest of this chapter outlines important steps in the marketing process. To make this sequence more meaningful, assessment of orthopedic services is used as an example.

Preliminary Steps

The marketing analysis is like a large research project. When nursing executives begin, they may find it cost effective to have the first survey done by professional marketing consultants to provide a prototype to follow, some valuable information about the hospital in general, and some experience in the process. If this is not feasible, managers can begin the process by reading a comprehensive marketing book such as Pride and Ferrell's *Marketing: Basic Concepts and Decisions* to understand the process and its terminology. Managers probably will discover that they already know a lot about marketing, although they have not labeled it as such.

The next step is to begin saving all of the junk mail or advertising received from major companies, since they usually research the market well and hire large advertising firms to do their publicity. What appeals to nursing leaders probably appeals to others. For the time being, they should simply keep collecting material because when they finish the marketing analysis and prepare to advertise, they will have many ideas and samples from which to construct their campaign. Managers may audit a marketing course or buy its textbooks, since the recommendation of the marketing professional who is the teacher is expert and this is a form of free consultation. Once this background is acquired, nursing executives are ready to embark on the marketing analysis.

Defining the Project

As noted earlier, the first step in marketing is consumer research. Much information is available already in the hospital's administrative files and library, the public library, the chamber of commerce, American Hospital Association *Monitrends,* Department of Health and Human Services, and the U.S. Census Report. In gathering information on orthopedic patients and services, managers should not forget to contact all of the voluntary agencies and rehabilitation groups that have statistics on the incidence of orthopedic problems in the hospital's service area.

For example, the crippled children's commission would have statistics on childhood problems, the school system and universities could detail athletic injuries, the health department may have statistics, and services for the elderly and state nursing home bureaus could help with research on orthopedic problems in the elderly. When compiled, these statistics will provide background information for the specific market assessment.

The entire project then should be outlined before proceeding further. Deadlines must be set for each step of this research process, along with identifying responsible persons and listing ways to assess success with each major step. The development of this outline takes time but is crucial in keeping the project on track. The major steps of the marketing plan are as follows:

1. **Research Purpose:** To increase the census of orthopedic patients in the hospital. (It is important to be specific about which types of patient numbers should increase and what percentage of gain in market share is sought; for example, fractures from nursing homes, athletic injuries, congenital problems, car accident victims.)
2. **Objectives:**

   - To identify the orthopedic physicians and analyze their practice in the service area.
   - To analyze the types of orthopedic problems that require hospital service and the specific referrals from other hospitals and community agencies in the service area.
   - To analyze financial, utilization, and reimbursement trends in orthopedic patients.
   - To discern strengths and weaknesses in the orthopedic services.
   - To learn what all the hospital's publics think about existing services.
   - To identify specific programs that are needed in nursing to enhance orthopedic services in the hospital.
   - To summarize the assessments about the orthopedic business.
   - To identify feasible growth and productivity strategies in orthopedics.
   - To design and implement the marketing plan.

   (Each of these objectives also needs to include every question that nursing managers want answered, a specific person who has responsibility for each objective, a deadline, and a measurable outcome for judging success or failure.)
3. **Research Budget Design:** To conduct a valid and reliable survey, adequate persons and money are necessary. Where the budget is inadequate, the target markets will not be evaluated fully, and more money will be spent in poorly targeted efforts that do not meet consumers' needs. To get some idea of what the project's budget should be, nurse leaders should finish the outline of the marketing plan, using this chapter guide. They then should contact several vendors to ascertain what they would charge to do the job. From these estimates, managers will know roughly what their budget should be and whether it would be more cost effective to have a vendor do this project. In general, a bare-bones budget for a consumer research project that encompasses all programs in the hospital would be $15,000, the maximum $250,000. Beyond whatever amount is chosen, further spending produces only diminishing returns. A good rule of thumb for the hospital marketing budget is about .5 percent of the total hospital budget. Based on this amount,

the orthopedic project is assessed on the basis of how important the research questions are to the hospital's viability. Moreover, first-time research costs more than will subsequent projects.

4. **Analysis: Who Does It, What Follows:** Managers must be specific as to who will analyze the results and what will happen next. Whoever has this responsibility must be comfortable with simple statistics and the computer, if possible, to conserve time and personnel. Before finishing the project, managers must be sure that every question has been raised and answered satisfactorily.

5. **Develop Plan of Action:** Based on the research, managers must decide which target groups to select in orthopedics and what they want the public to know about the hospital's (or center's) image and services.

6. **Implement the Plan:** How will the plan be implemented, specifically in terms of time frames and logistics?

7. **Evaluate Costs:** Nursing managers must determine the expense of resources and personnel, the direct and indirect results of the marketing effort, and suggestions for changes. They will want to revise annual objectives based on the progress, demographic changes, technological advances, changes in available health care services, and other factors having an impact on orthopedics.

ANALYZING MARKET POSITION

After the blueprint for the project is in place, the next step is to analyze the hospital's (center's) market position. This process begins with the marketing committee. First, it recommends to administration what the hospital and orthopedic unit mission should be and how it suggests that impression be conveyed to others. While this sounds simple, progress is difficult if the direction is not clear. To assist the committee with this process, nursing executives should:

1. Describe in one sentence the major focus/purpose of the hospital and the orthopedic unit.

2. Ascertain whether others in the institution agree by conducting a survey; also determine what all of the publics think by interviewing physicians, community leaders, referral sources, employees, and patients.

3. Define what makes the unit special; think about market position in relation to convenience, personal touch, specialization, research, religious affiliation, or special services offered; propose slogans such as "we care," "we are good Samaritans every day," or "we treat you like family."

4. Write the unit's mission statement; take plenty of time on this step because it is a summary of what the unit is about; it is also the basis for what it wants to

communicate to everyone, including employees; the logo, communications, graphics, advertising, patient communications, and annual report all will flow from this statement.

INTERVIEWS WITH KEY PEOPLE

Nursing executives should design a list of specific questions about the hospital and its orthopedic unit on services offered, employees' attitude, quality of care, reputation, services that are lacking, attitudes about competitors, ideas for growth, unmet health care needs, changes needed, strengths and weaknesses of the orthopedic service, and specifics on physicians. The board of directors, the medical board, and hospital administration should be asked to respond to these questions.

Managers need information on the relationships of staff nurses and physicians with outlying referral hospitals, nursing homes, and other physicians:

- How effective is the continuing education link with these referral sources?
- Do they think of this hospital first when they want orthopedic expertise?
- What programs could be started to raise the unit's visibility, such as preventive calcium for women or body mechanics courses for nursing homes and local industries?
- What is being done to link orthopedics with community projects?
- Is one of the physicians working as an athletic team doctor for a big high school or college?
- How do the news media's reports reflect on the programs; does the unit get the type of coverage it needs?
- How is the public being reached?
- Does the hospital provide courses to help families care for and prevent injuries to their elderly members?
- Is networking with the nursing homes in town and with the physicians responsible for geriatric medicine effective?
- What programs that involve shared services need to be expanded?

The next interviews involve key community leaders in the area, government, business community, and the Chamber of Commerce. These should be followed by interviews with the leaders of competing hospitals, referral hospitals, and health agencies, then a random community telephone survey to learn public opinion (see Exhibit 18–1). The final survey should seek the opinions of employees and patients.

Exhibit 18–1 Community Telephone Survey

1. Which hospital would you choose if you needed one?
2. How does your doctor affect your choice of hospitals?
3. Why would you choose/not choose each of the area hospitals?
4. What do people think of each hospital?
5. Which hospital is known for the best/worst care?
6. What do you like most/least about each hospital?
7. What hospital advertising are you familiar with?
8. Do you think that hospitals should advertise?
9. How would you rank X hospital on food, care, service, patient education, etc.?
10. What are area hospitals doing to provide a higher quality of care while decreasing costs?

In summarizing each question from interviews and surveys, managers may use the format in Exhibit 18–2 as an example.

When all of these surveys are compiled, nursing executives will have a good indication of how the entire public views the hospital and its orthopedic services.

Exhibit 18–2 Summary Questionnaire

Question: How good a job are the orthopedic doctors and nurses doing in teaching patients and families what they need to know to take care of themselves at home?

Doctor X	Feb.	Oct.	Change
Excellent	8%	11%	+3%
Good	52%	33%	−19%
Excellent or Good	60%	44%	−16%
Fair	24%	30%	+6%
Poor	15%	22%	+7%
Fair or Poor	39%	52%	+13%
No Answer	1%	3%	+2%

Summary: Dr. X apparently has developed some type of problem between February and October. This must be investigated and corrected. If that succeeds, an effort should be made to promote a more positive public image of his work with patients and families; if it fails, his hospital privileges should be examined by the Medical Committee. To determine whether this is an individual problem or one that is related to numerous physicians and nurses, this assessment of Doctor X should be compared with that of all others individually and collectively.

ANALYSIS OF THE SERVICE AREA

This step involves a retrospective analysis of patients served for the last year. To place this analysis in better perspective, nurse managers will need a large wall map of the city and outlying referral areas with ZIP codes identified. The post office or public library can provide a map that can be enlarged or one can be purchased at a map or book store. Colored pins are placed on the map to indicate the number of referrals from each ZIP code.

In this service area analysis, nursing leaders should:

- Break out all orthopedic patients served in the hospital over the past year and compare them with the numbers serviced by competitors. Are there ZIP codes from which the hospital gets more patients, or no patients? Why?

- Summarize the demographic data on patients from each ZIP code and discuss the factors involved in building the caseload from each ZIP code. Include factors that will prevent market erosion. For example, one hospital continued to blanket three ZIP codes with materials on detecting scoliosis in children; the effort was wasted because in those areas elderly residents had replaced children over the years.

- Show the percentage and types of orthopedic patients that the hospital and its competitors get from each ZIP code. Summarize reasons for weakness or strength in each of these areas.

- Use the American Hospital Association *Guide to the Health Care Field* (a public library reference that also should be in the administrative library) and *Monitrends* to analyze all area hospitals by size, type, beds, number of admissions, patient days, occupancy, and average length of stay. Decide whether to engage in shared services with any of these hospitals or to strengthen ties to a rural feeder hospital.

- Compare the origin of patients by diagnosis among the ZIP codes to determine where to advertise certain illnesses in relation to such demographics as age or socioeconomic factors.

- Compare patient population gains and losses over the last few years with the population shifts in the most recent census and in the general information obtained from the library and Chamber of Commerce. Is the hospital geared to meet the way the service area is changing? For example, has it plugged in the growth of elderly populations, young families, new industries, and change in school districts?

- Project population growth patterns in the service area. How is the hospital positioned for these community changes?

- Compare the services offered in the hospital with those in competing agencies.
- Analyze the community agencies in relation to the number of referrals received. What community agencies are not contributing to the hospital's business as they could?

This service area analysis provides a good idea about where the hospital's marketing strengths and weaknesses lie. When the demographic factors are included, the hospital can determine what potential lies in its service area for program growth and promotion.

UTILIZATION, FINANCES, REIMBURSEMENT

Having large numbers of patients does not necessarily increase productivity or cost effectiveness. Hospitals that are thriving seek not only increased numbers of patients but also a more viable case mix. If many patients present complex conditions and are elderly, there may be so many outlier cases that the hospital (unit) loses money. Moreover, if it is drawing from an economically deprived area, the hospital may have a full census of patients who are not insured and who are unable to pay their bills. Thus, in evaluating its market position, managers need to analyze the type of patients who are utilizing services so as to balance the case mix to expand profitability.

The following steps will assist nurse managers in learning about these trends:

1. Construct a chart that lists physicians by number and show the number of patients that each doctor admitted in a single DRG each of the past five years (see Table 18–1).
2. Repeat this procedure for all other DRGs that involve orthopedics.
3. Be sure to look at all factors for evaluating the number of patients that the hospital receives. For example, in one orthopedic study the emergency room noted by tallying ambulance calls on the radio that most trauma victims were taken to the competing hospital. In analyzing the reason, hospital administrators discovered that the paramedics often are the ones consulted about hospital choice by their patients. This hospital increased its market share by offering free educational courses to paramedics and by having periodic free parties to encourage them to refer more patients. This strategy increased the market share of trauma patients by 100 percent in the next year.
4. Use the same diagrammatic procedure to analyze patient days and average lengths of stay by DRG and by physician. At the bottom of each chart, summarize the reasons for the statistics, and make suggestions about what can be done to strengthen the marketing position.

Table 18–1 DRG 235—Fractures of the Femur

						% Change	
Physician	1982	1983	1984	1985	1986	1 Year	5 Years
1	5	7	16	0	0		
2	90	112	223	290	421		
Others	6	12	17	23	25		

Summary: This hospital has two major orthopedic physicians; the other 16 rarely admit orthopedic patients. Dr. # 1 had a stroke two years ago and no longer is admitting patients. Dr. # 2 has a growing practice, is 40 years old, and is very supportive of nursing programs. Dr. # 1 has hired a new orthopedic surgeon, and all efforts should be made to enhance his practice by supportive nursing strategies at the hospital.

As a final step, members should compare the financial factors from patient care in each DRG by physician and in comparison with competitors:

1. Make a table for a comparison between the hospital orthopedic services and that of competitors in relation to beds, patient discharges by payer, patient days by payer, length of stay by payer, and occupancy rate.
2. Compare operating cost with competitors in relation to salaries and benefits/employee/year for full-time equivalents (FTEs), FTEs per occupied bed, and salaries and benefits per occupied bed.
3. Compare revenues with the competition in relation to expenses and incomes for inpatient and outpatient services, per patient day, and per discharge.

Nursing executives then should summarize the gross operating margin for each competitor to determine areas that require improvement in productivity and cost containment.

Case-Mix Analysis

Nursing managers should list all of their orthopedic diagnoses, including the number of patients seen in each diagnosis, and compare their market share with that of the competition. They then should compare the disease severity, age, and other demographics, and analyze these patients in relation to their length of stay and the average cost of treating each type. This analysis identifies whether the hospital keeps the same type of patient for longer or shorter stays than competitors.

More charts will be needed to analyze each DRG in relation to age and pay source. The form in Exhibit 18–3 is suggested for making this type of comparison.

These data will show the relationship of age to utilization and reimbursement factors and identify payer sources for various patient groups. Once this information is known, marketing strategies can be adapted to alter the marketing mix as a part of the productivity and cost-containment efforts.

Physician Analysis

Since physicians are the ones who admit patients and most directly affect census, it is vital to analyze them. First, general information is collected about their age, specialty objectives, and certification. Then a specific analysis is done to find what percentage of admissions is attributed to each physician. Referral back to the ZIP code chart shows where each physician's primary hospital business is based.

Discussion with each physician alerts the hospital to new specialized procedures that the doctor plans to perform as a result of recent educational advances. Finally, an analysis of the strengths and weaknesses of each physician is compiled (see Exhibit 18–4).

From this, nursing executives can ascertain where to plan capital expenditures to encourage practice by a prized physician and where to limit programs in an area where physician coverage is not possible. A realistic 10-year appraisal can be made as to which practices are growing and which ones are dying, for purposes of long-term investments. Some hospitals even offer free office space to promising physicians whose businesses are growing.

By analyzing the personalities and general attitudes of these physicians, nurse executives are better able to prioritize realistic ways to build new programs and implement productivity programs that physicians will support.

Exhibit 18–3 DRG Analysis by Age and Pay Source

DRG 000

# of Cases

Average Age in DRG

Average Age of Sickest Patients

Average Age in the Longest Length of Hospital Stays

Payer Source for Largest Number of Cases

Payer Source for Sickest Patients

Exhibit 18–4 Sample Topics for Physician Interviews

---

1. What are this doctor's projected plans for admitting each type of patient to the hospital?
2. What are the physician's opinions on nursing care, location and unit environment, supportive services, patient satisfaction, availability of needed space and operating rooms when desired, hospital administration, hospital/unit strategic plans?
3. Where should growth occur in orthopedic services?
4. What does the physician like best/least about how the orthopedic department and nursing services operate at this hospital?

Summary:

RECOMMENDED GROWTH STRATEGIES

To produce this in-depth type of analysis, most nursing executives will need help in constructing valid and reliable questionnaires and interview formats and in developing ways to collect and analyze data. Because some interviews are sensitive, those questioned may be more prone to talk with an experienced marketing consultant than they would with an employee of the hospital. However, nursing executives and their staffs may have the talent to do some parts of this marketing analysis.

Once the results are tabulated, realistic immediate, short-term, long-term, and continuing priorities for orthopedics can be set. Some groups do this best by using four large flip charts so that goals in each area can be separated in the first stage and blended later. Examples of findings might indicate that nursing executives should:

Immediate

- Capitalize on similar goals between the nursing and medical staffs in expanding programs geared toward the elderly and toward young athletes.
- Reduce staffing and increase productivity until it is more in line with competing hospitals.
- Reevaluate capital investments in the inpatient unit of pediatric orthopedics because of the decline in congenital problems in the service area.
- Increase visibility with area nursing homes and the local college and work to establish services that they will use, since they constitute the biggest area of potential growth.
- Implement a shared services program with the hospital in Rural City since it has expressed an interest in these orthopedic services; its referrals could increase business by 10 percent.

Short Term

- Evaluate involvement in wellness center activities since it is showing marginal returns.
- Establish a stronger tie to XYZ Manufacturing since it has a high incidence of orthopedic problems among its employees.
- Continue the discharge planning program and home health referral program since it has the potential for being cost effective, with suggested changes.
- Develop an outpatient pain management program.

Long Term

- Become a preferred provider for at least 15 businesses, including . . . over the next year.
- Expand the public relations program by designing better patient discharge instructions, making home visits and after-discharge phone calls, and incorporating the logo and hospital mission into all efforts.

Continuing

- Form a supportive relationship with Dr. X to encourage referral of more patients to the hospital.
- Increase attention to utilization review, discharge planning, and quality monitoring of inpatient care to reduce the average length of stay in all orthopedic patients.

These examples would require elaboration and would be followed by a specific implementation plan with deadlines and responsible persons assigned. There also would be a summary of total strengths and weaknesses and of what the services are and what nursing executives want them to become.

SUMMARY

This chapter provides an overview of a marketing analysis with a detailed step-by-step procedure for conducting such a survey. While this process takes some background and practice, nursing executives can use all or part of these steps in marketing and advertising their programs.

BIBLIOGRAPHY

Block, L.F. *Marketing for Hospitals in Hard Times*. Chicago: Teach 'em, Inc., 1981.

Pride, W.M., and Ferrell, O.C. *Marketing: Basic Concepts and Decisions*. Boston: Houghton Mifflin Co., 1983.

Guiltinan, J.P., and Paul, G.W. *Readings in Marketing Strategies and Programs*. New York: McGraw-Hill Book Co., 1982.

Kernaghan, S.G. "Nontraditional Revenue." *Hospitals* (December 1, 1982): 75–81.

Kotler, P. *Marketing for Nonprofit Organizations*. Englewood Cliffs, N.J.: Prentice-Hall, Inc., 1982.

MacStravic, R.S. "Being Patients' Personal Hospital Is Survival Strategy in Hard Times." *Modern Healthcare* (July 1984): 182–87.

McMillan, N. *Marketing Your Hospital: A Strategy for Survival*. Chicago: American Hospital Association, 1981.

Peters, T.J., and Waterman, R.H. *In Search of Excellence*. New York: Warner Books, 1982.

Reynolds, J. "Product Manager Must Decide What Products to Market and How." *Modern Healthcare* (July 1984): 176, 178, 180, 187.

Sonenclar, R. "Investing in Health Care." *Financial World* (July 25–August 7, 1984): 12–21.

ACTION CHECKLIST

1. What formal marketing assessment has been done on the unit/center or hospital?
2. Has an analysis been made of the unit's services in relation to its consumers that is documented in business terms?
3. Does it have the necessary administrative support to conduct this marketing analysis?
4. How does it plan to advertise differently and implement the suggestions that arose from the survey?

Index